Shipley Capture Guide™

Larry Newman, PPF. APMP

Shipley Associates
532 North 900 West
Kaysville, UT 84037
888.772.WINS (9467)

www.shipleywins.com

Third Edition
2011

Third Edition Reprint
2014

ISBN: 978-0-9714244-8-7

This Capture Guide has three aims: 1) Help individuals position their organizations to capture competitive business opportunities more effectively, economically, and consistently; 2) Guide individuals in capture planning roles to understand and adapt best practices for opportunities in any market; and 3) Record capture management and planning best-practice guidelines.

The most effective organizations are 10 times more effective in winning competitive new business than industry averages, based on several industry benchmarking studies dating back to the late 1980s. Researchers have concluded that the most effective organizations follow defined framework processes based upon fundamental principles. Less effective organizations follow defined processes but lose sight of principles that help them adapt to individual opportunities. The least effective organizations lack consistent processes, or defined principles, and rely instead on valiant efforts of heroes following *ad hoc* processes.

Help individuals position their organizations to capture competitive business opportunities

Guidelines are based on fundamental principles revealed by business development research:

- Align capture activities with the customer's analysis and selection process.
- Influence the customer to prefer your organization and solution early, and maintain that preference through selection, award, and delivery.
- Base your strategy on the customer's perspective of reality.
- Align your actions and messages throughout the business development cycle.
- Use decision gate reviews of potential business opportunities for determining the best manner in which to proceed and color team reviews to improve quality of the product and outcome.

Follow these principles to win more business, more effectively, economically, and consistently.

Guide individuals in capture planning roles

The structure for the *Shipley Capture Guide* originated with the *Shipley Proposal Guide.* While many capture planning principles were included in the *Proposal Guide,* clients repeatedly requested more specific advice. As organizations placed more individuals into capture planning roles, these individuals needed to understand how to adapt best practices and tools to their individual markets and opportunities.

This *Capture Guide* is designed to be a quick reference for individuals assigned to be capture managers or to contribute to capture teams.

Record capture management and planning best-practice guidelines

At Shipley Associates, we have observed and recommended industry best practices in business development consulting, training, and process re-engineering since 1972. We endeavor to follow these guidelines in our consulting practice, teach them in our professional development practice, tailor them in our process practice, and share them in our series of *Guides*.

This *Capture Guide*, like the companion *Proposal Guide* and *Business Development Lifecycle Guide,* offers guidelines, not rules. Reality encompasses more variations than can be covered in a guide intended to be concise. When in doubt, consider the underlying principles.

What's New in the Third Edition

Our clients, consultants, and international licensees requested more specific guidance in multiple topic areas. The focus is extended from capturing national government systems contracts to capturing competitive business with regional governments, prime contractors, commercial businesses, and task orders under master ordering contracts.

This *Capture Guide* 3rd Edition is arranged in three sections:

- Introduction to Capture Planning
- Capture Planning Topics
- Model Documents

Introduction to Capture Planning addresses two frequent questions about capture management:

- What is capture planning?
- What are the benefits of capture planning?

Capture Planning Topics comprises 19 topics organized alphabetically for easy reference. Sections relevant to a newly assigned capture manager are included. PRICING-TO-WIN was extensively revised from the 2nd Edition. The name was changed to reflect the focus on the process rather than the result and to define industry-standard terms. The following topic sections are more relevant to capture management than proposal management and were moved from the *Proposal Guide*: Customer-Focused Capture Skills and Tactics, Performance- Based Acquisition, Persuasion, Presentation to Customers, Process, and Sales Letters. All topic sections and model documents were reviewed and slightly updated. Extensive cross-references to other *Capture Guide, Proposal Guide,* and *Business Development Lifecycle Guide* topics are found in the margins.

Model Documents includes capture plan templates, sales letters, executive summaries, and capture plan excerpts. These models show adaptations to selling environments, media, review processes, and specific opportunities. In particular, Document 1 is designed to help capture managers develop a capture template for their organization.

We hope individuals newly assigned to capture roles, their managers, and even experienced practitioners will find this 3rd Edition to be an even more valuable tool.

Acknowledgments

My thanks to the many people who generously gave advice, assistance, and support:

- The hundreds of clients from nearly 30 countries who taught me so much while I was trying to help and teach them.
- My fellow consultants who patiently reviewed multiple drafts and suggested improvements. I apologize for not being able to name all reviewers, but David Bol, Ted Heath, Robert Horne, Mike Humm, Nancy Kessler, David Wagner, Robert Winslow, and Amanda Reid-Young were key Capture Guide 3rd Edition reviewers..
- My partners at Shipley Associates who supported the preparation of the *Proposal Guide.*

Several other people must be both thanked and named:

- Dr. Larry Freeman, for the inspiration in the original *Shipley Style Guide* (now *Franklin Covey Style Guide*), for setting standards for clarity and economy of writing that I strive to meet.
- Sonya Bankhead, for graphics, page, document design, and production management of the integrated, three-*Guide* series. Kathy Rettenberger and Doug Brewer for their editing support on this or prior editions.
- Nancy Rosen, my wife, for understanding and encouragement while I worked on all editions.

About the author

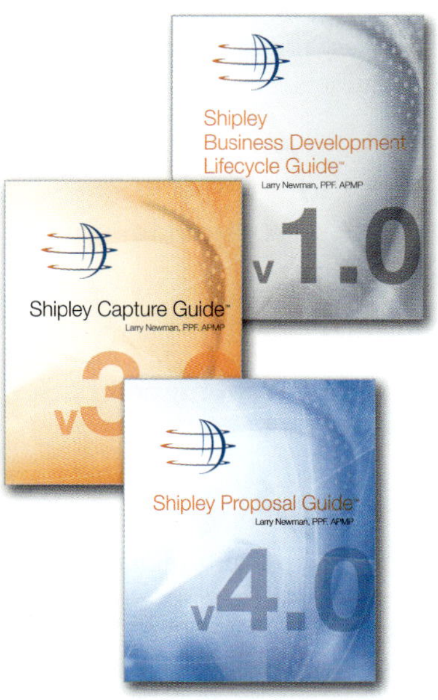

Larry Newman is Vice President and a founding partner of Shipley Associates. He joined Shipley Associates in 1986 as a consultant and training facilitator, helping clients win competitive business in 30 countries and varied selling environments.

Mr. Newman authored all three Shipley Associates *Guides*: *Proposal Guide, Capture Guide,* and *Business Development Lifecycle Guide.* The *Shipley Proposal Guide* was awarded the Society for Technical Communication's Award of Excellence in 2008. With approximately 50,000 copies in print since 1999, the *Shipley Proposal Guide* was selected as the basis for APMP proposal management professional certification. In 2010, he authored the *Shipley Capture Guide,* 2nd Edition. Like the *Proposal Guide,* several organizations have selected it as the basis for professional capture management certification.

He has developed and facilitated numerous Shipley Associates workshops in capture planning, proposal writing and management, executive summary writing, sales writing, and costing. He is an Association of Proposal Management Professionals (APMP) Fellow, is APMP accredited at the Professional level, and has presented at more than 20 professional association conferences. He also developed the *Proposal Guide* podcast series in 2008, downloadable on iTunes.

The Capture Planning Guidelines are designed to help business development professionals answer common questions about how to position their solutions and organizations to win competitive business more effectively, efficiently, and consistently.

Like the companion *Proposal Guide* and *Business Development Lifecycle Guide,* this *Capture Guide* is designed to be an easy-to-use reference. In the midst of repeated competitive pursuits, most business development professionals lack the time to read entire books that discuss capture planning from beginning to end. If you are seeking a process-oriented explanation to help you reengineer your business development activities, seek one of the many available process books. If you need immediate help winning important business opportunities, read on.

While capture planning originated within and is practiced predominantly by large organizations pursuing large, competitive, national government programs, the fundamental principles are adaptable to most market sectors and selling environments.

For new users of the *Capture Guide,* consider the following time-saving suggestions:

Read the INTRODUCTION TO CAPTURE PLANNING if you are unfamiliar with the concept or term. If you are looking for specific guidance, go directly to the topic sections:

- Use the alphabetical topic arrangement to find a specific topic. You might have to try several titles before you find the information you need. If you cannot find a topic, refer to the Index.
- After finding the relevant entry, review the short summary and the numbered guidelines in the shaded box at the beginning of the entry. Then turn to the guideline or guidelines that appear to answer your question.
- Read the guidelines and following text. Review the examples, where available. Because capture planning is more conceptual than preparing a proposal, the examples are predominantly tools rather than excerpts from capture documents. Many specific examples would only apply to one market or selling environment and, therefore, would be less useful to readers with diverse perspectives.

Review the notes, beginning with the word NOTE, and cross-referenced entries. Topics are cross-referenced within the *Capture Guide, Proposal Guide, and Business Development Lifecycle Guide.* Cross-references have this format: See ENGAGING PROPOSAL SUPPORT:

- If you are developing or adapting a capture plan template to be used in your organization, turn to **MODEL DOCUMENTS CAPTURE PLAN TEMPLATE.** Model 1 explains the presentation template, accompanied by adaptation suggestions by market and selling environment. Participants in Shipley's capture planning workshops will find this explanation helpful as they apply what they have learned to their opportunities and selling environments.

Different individuals, organizations, market sectors, and countries use similar and potentially confusing terms to mean different things. The following terms are used in this *Guide*:

- Bid request vs. Request for Proposal (RFP), Request for Tender (RFT), Request for Quote (RFQ), Invitation to Tender (ITT), or solicitation.
- Customer vs. prospective customer, prospect, prospective buyer, buyer, or client.

Contents Alphabetical Listing of Topics

Capture Planning is the process of identifying opportunities, assessing the environment, and implementing winning strategies to capture a specific business opportunity by influencing the customer to prefer your organization and solution. Consistently successful capture planning requires written, action-oriented capture plans and the discipline to implement, monitor, and adapt those plans to changing customer needs, internal issues, and competitive conditions.

What Is Capture Planning?

To understand capture planning, consider the **aim, potential outcomes, origin, context,** and **relationship with established selling methodologies.**

The **aim** of capture planning is to progress from an initial unknown position to a favored position as viewed by the customer. Initially, the customer is unknown by the seller and the seller is unknown by the customer. Your initial *unknown* seller's position is ignorance about customer needs, the customer's view of your organization, and your relative competitive position.

Capture planning consists of iterative activities designed to attain a favored position with the customer.

Because the customer's view is the only relevant view, the aim of the seller is to progress from *unknown*, to *known*, to *improved position*, and eventually *favored position* as shown in figure 1. Of course, relatively few initial positions are completely unknown, and achieving a favored position might not be possible.

To move from an *unknown* to a *known* position, research the market, interact with the customer, and analyze your findings. To move to an *improved* position, develop your strategy and tactics, implement, and validate them with the customer. Attain a *favored* position by repeating this iterative capture planning process.

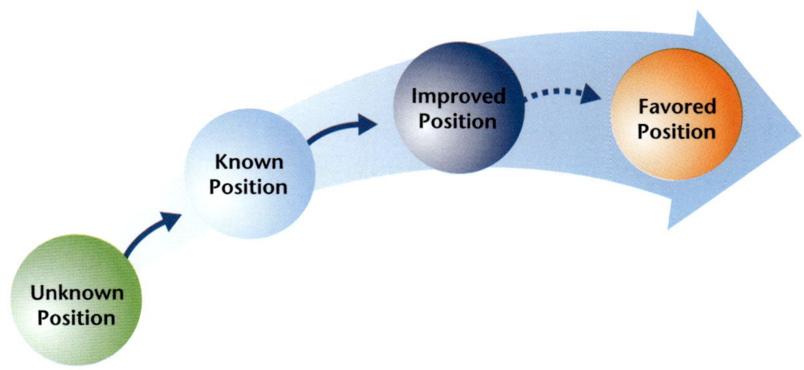

Figure 1. Capture Planning Progression. *The fundamental capture planning process is an iterative progression from an* unknown *to a* favored *position. The capture planning template is simply an orderly method to prompt research, analysis, strategy development, and tactical execution to achieve a favored position.*

Four **potential outcomes** are likely:

1. The customer opts to negotiate a contract without competition because:
   - Preparing solicitation documents, soliciting and evaluating proposals, then negotiating a contract are expensive and time consuming.
   - Implementing a solution promptly offers greater benefits than the potential cost savings from competitive bidding.
   - Finding a solution superior to yours is unlikely.
2. The customer prefers your organization and solution but opts to solicit proposals for one or more of the following reasons:
   - Purchasing regulations or guidelines mandate competitive bids.
   - Competitive bids often result in superior solutions.
   - Competitive bids often result in lower prices.
   - Competitive bids are less likely to be questioned by senior management or regulatory authorities.
   - Competitive bids give the customer additional knowledge and leverage in contract negotiations.
3. The customer opts for a fair and open competition. Customers typically insist every competition is fair and open, even if not. Determining whether a competition is truly fair and open (or can be influenced to become so) is a key element of decision gate reviews, competitive intelligence, and capture strategy development.
4. The customer prefers another organization's solution, and you are kept in the competition as leverage or *column fodder* to secure a better solution or price from the preferred vendor. You should usually not pursue or bid unless you have solid evidence that staying in the competition will lead to profitable, future business.

Intelligently adapt capture principles to your organization, selling environment, and the opportunity.

Capture planning originated in the 1980s as a phrase describing a recognized discipline. Capture planning became more recognized in the 1990s inside organizations primarily focused on large U.S. Department of Defense opportunities. However, the concept of influencing a customer prior to a procurement is as old as selling.

As the terminology of capture planning spread to organizations of various sizes serving a variety of markets in multiple countries, business development professionals noted that it was synonymous with complex sales cycles. Concurrently, a few commercial organizations pursuing large, complex opportunities were developing and practicing similar disciplines they called account or sales planning. Both are different ways of referring to the practice of engaging with a customer early in the business development process to improve win probability.

The usual **context** for capture planning is within organizations pursuing complex opportunities with some or all the following characteristics:

- High value or strategic significance (for either buyer or seller)
- Loosely understood requirements and solutions, at least in early phases
- Buying committees or teams, rather than a single purchasing agent
- Selling committees or teams comprising many skills and disciplines
- Long sales cycles (months or years)
- Significant communication prior to a solicitation between buying and selling teams, often including meetings and document exchanges
- Formally structured procurement environments

Talented individuals can win smaller and less competitive opportunities by themselves. Capture teams are required to win large, complex, highly competitive opportunities. The more your opportunity exhibits characteristics from the foregoing list, the more likely you are to benefit from applying the guidance in this *Capture Guide*. Skip the all-or-nothing approach by adapting capture principles to each opportunity that is worth winning. Intelligently adapt the principles based on opportunity size and complexity, time available, and importance of the opportunity to your organization.

See STRATEGY.

Some commercial organizations use the terms *account plan* and *capture plan* interchangeably. Classically, account plans are not opportunity-specific but intended to describe all potential opportunities for contracting services and products with a particular account or customer. The least sophisticated account plans merely allocate the selling organization's revenue objectives among accounts.

A capture plan, on the other hand, is a written, action-oriented plan analyzing and summarizing the situation and recording tasks and steps to influence a customer to prefer your organization's solution for a specific opportunity. While the length, complexity, and format vary, a written plan offers reviewable evidence of the quality of thinking of the planners and the soundness of the plan.

Capture planning is compatible with and supportive of major sales methodologies, despite minor differences in defined roles, titles, processes, and tools. Managers in many organizations opt to incorporate capture planning concepts into their sales methodologies or incorporate sales methodologies into their capture planning processes, depending on which are most mature.

Most popular sales methodologies comprise both strategic and tactical elements, a notion completely consistent with capture planning best practices.

Strategic elements focus on assessing your current position with the customer in the context of the competition and your desired or preferred position. In this context, capture planning and strategic sales methodologies are conceptually identical. Developing strategy requires extensive data gathering and analysis.

Strategic sales methodologies typically embrace a series of tools designed to support data gathering and analysis, much like capture tools. If you have an existing, embedded sales methodology, blend its best elements with capture planning principles, then follow a single, blended process.

Tactical elements comprise the actions that you will take to improve your position. Sales plans tend to loosely define actions, specifying only actions of the individual in the sales role. Capture plans define actions more precisely and broadly, specifying actions for an entire team.

In summary, capture planning can be thought of as a disciplined approach to influencing customers to favor your solution before actual procurement action begins and during the procurement *if permitted under procurement guidelines*. It relies heavily on research and analysis about the customer, the opportunity, and potential competitors. It involves working collaboratively with the customer to shape requirements and buying approaches in ways advantageous to your organization. Lastly, it helps harness diverse resources and skills from wherever they reside to help position your organization win.

What Are the Benefits of Capture Planning?

Doubling win rates, improving profitability, and predictably meeting revenue and profit forecasts are the most frequently reported benefits of capture planning. If you are not already practicing some form of capture planning, you likely will be after you learn of the quantitative, documented benefits reported by others.

Consider the potential benefits of capture planning from three perspectives:

- Theoretical justification
- Quantitative justification
- Applicability to your selling environment

The **theoretical justification** for implementing a capture planning discipline is linked to improving your ability and the ability of your organization to capture competitive business opportunities. Instituting a culture incorporating regular, structured capture planning processes can impart three major benefits:

- Increase top-line organic growth or total sales revenue in a competitive environment. Few organizations can grow total revenues by selling more of the same products and services to the same customers. They must expand beyond their core business to new markets with existing products or services, new products or services in existing markets, or new products or services in new markets as shown in figure 2.
- Reduce costs of capturing new revenue. Capture planning improves both efficiency and effectiveness of new business development, which translates to capturing more bids, larger bids, and perhaps more profitable bids at the same or reduced cost. Savings may convert directly to profit or fuel additional growth.
- Improve the predictability of quarterly and annual revenue and net profit. Capture planning puts organizations into closer contact with their markets and customers and gives management greater visibility over potential new contracts. Pursuit of only the most likely targets, but with better competitive intelligence and greater chance of success, reduces forecast uncertainty. Improving the quality of new business while lowering the costs of winning has a positive impact on profits.

Quantitative, documented, and verified benefits demonstrate that capture planning principles benefit organizations in most selling environments and markets.

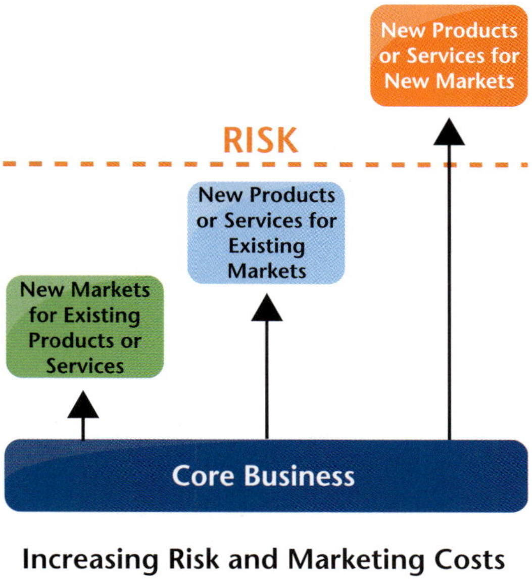

Figure 2. Avenues to Increase Revenue. *To meet revenue growth goals, most organizations must expand beyond core business areas. The least risky expansion is to offer proven products or services to new markets because you can predictably price and deliver. Offering new products and services to existing markets and familiar customers might seem less risky, but a stumble threatens current revenue. Taking new products and services to new markets requires solid strategic, business, and market planning and is beyond the normal scope of capture planning.*

The **quantitative justification** for introducing capture discipline into your organization must be that the benefits significantly outweigh costs. Make no mistake—implementing new systems, training personnel to use them, and then maintaining operational discipline require investment. Perhaps the best way to assess potential quantitative benefits is to consider the experiences of other organizations.

The quantitative results are summarized in figures 3 and 4. Across varied industries, countries, and selling environments, organizations reported remarkable results after incorporating capture planning into their structured business development processes. Results often exceeded their expectations and in relatively short time frames.

A common success factor in the organizations summarized in figures 3 and 4 was that one or more senior managers embraced and championed the changes. These managers knew that process mattered and capture practices were effective. Just focusing on improving proposal quality was no longer sufficient. Proposal quality does matter, but as competitive organizations improve their ability to submit quality proposals, front-end positioning, capture activity, and process discipline are more effective ways to improve win rates, business capture effectiveness, margins, and win predictability.

COMPANY DESCRIPTION	BEFORE	TIME FRAME	AFTER IMPLEMENTING CAPTURE PLANNING
IT services (federal, state, municipal)	• 1,200 proposals per year • Under 30% win rate • $440 million annual sales	9 months	• Less than 500 proposals submitted per year • Over 70% win rate • $1.05 billion annual sales
Engineering services	• $20 million annual sales	12 months	• Over $60 million annual sales
IT services	• $350 million annual sales	18 months	• $1 billion annual sales • Doubled capture ratio
IT services and logistics	• $1.2 billion annual sales	12 months	• $1.8 billion annual sales • Lowered costs by pursuing 40% less business
Defense contractor	• $1 billion annual sales	12 months	• $1.8 billion annual sales
Defense contractor	• 28% win rate • $223 cost per proposal page • 0.28 proposal pages per hour	24 months	• 89% win rate • $109 cost per proposal page • 0.65 proposal pages per hour
Telecom -$7 billion sales, 9000 employees	• 55% win rate • $49 million net profit	12 months	• Above 70% win rate • $64 million net profit
International business consulting	• 30% win rate	18 months	• 65% win rate • 50% annual sales increase • 50% fewer bids submitted
Legal services	• Under 30% win rate	24 months	• 70% + win rate

Figure 3. Before-and-After Metrics Show Benefits of Capture and Process Discipline. *If you doubt the benefits of a disciplined capture and business development process, review these before-and-after metrics reported by other organizations. Each organization collected and managed different metrics, but all reported improvements. (Companies shared their stories with the understanding that their identities would remain confidential.)*

COMPANY DESCRIPTION	DIVISION WITH AD HOC PROCESSES	TIME FRAME	DIVISION FOLLOWING STRUCTURED BUSINESS DEVELOPMENT PROCESS
Global telecom	• 51% win rate • 33% capture ratio (percent of total amount bid)	• 18 months	• 67% win rate • 80% capture ratio (percent of total amount bid)
Defense	• 65% re-compete win rate • 50% capture ratio (percent of total amount bid)	• 12 months	• 100% re-compete win rate • 67% capture ratio (percent of total amount bid)

Figure 4. Capture Metrics in the Same Organization. *In two instances, capture and business development process disciplines were implemented in only one of two similarly performing divisions within the same organization. The benefits of practicing capture and process discipline were clear within 12–18 months. (Companies shared their stories with the understanding that their identities would remain confidential.)*

It is important to note, however, that some organizations included in figures 3 and 4 were not able to sustain the improvements, usually because management focus shifted to other challenges, such as delivering the higher sales volume. Several organizations were acquired due to their outstanding top- and bottom-line growth. However, the new owners sometimes did not understand the reasons for this growth and eliminated capture planning and business development process improvements. By abandoning selective bidding, decision gate reviews, and early color team reviews, they precipitated a return to lower capture rates. Having experienced a better approach, many key business development professionals grew frustrated and left these organizations.

Capture planning and process best practices have proven effective in a range of organizations, not just large government contractors. While defense contractors were the first to embrace capture planning disciplines, best practices apply universally to large and small organizations, across market sectors, and in different selling environments.

Finally, consider the **applicability of capture planning to your selling environment** by assessing the characteristics of the opportunities you target.

The Capture Opportunity Evaluation Matrix depicted in figure 5 is an assessment tool, not a decision tool. Use and refine it to evaluate specific opportunities.

Refine the tool for your environment. Here are some potential refinement options:

- Add or delete characteristics. For example, if you consider the *strategic importance for competitor(s)* unimportant to you, delete it.
- Draft standards for the characteristics. For example, define what you consider *high value* and *low value*.
- Consider adding a *weight* to each characteristic. The importance of each factor is unlikely to be equal, so even a rough weighting will improve the tool. If so, multiply the weight by the rating before totaling the scores.
- Consider whether to use total scores to suggest levels of capture planning detail. For example, opportunities scoring below 30 (unweighted) in your market might not typically deserve the attention of detailed capture planning. Scores above 75 might require a full capture team, with everything else meriting scaled processes. Beware the trap of too many predefined categories; they can stifle thinking.

CAPTURE OPPORTUNITY EVALUATION MATRIX

CAPTURE PLANNING APPLICABILITY MATRIX FOR: (Insert opportunity name/type)							
#	*Characteristic: More Applicable*	*5*	*4*	*3*	*2*	*1*	*Characteristic: Less Applicable*
1	High value						Low value
2	Strategic for buyer						Not strategic for buyer
3	Strategic for us						Not strategic for us
4	Strategic for competitors						Not strategic for competitors
5	Loosely understood requirements and solutions (at least in early phases)						Well-understood and defined requirements and solutions
6	Buying committees						Single purchasing agent
7	Multi-disciplined selling teams						Single sales person
8	Long sales cycles (months or years)						Short sales cycle (days)
9	Significant communication prior to a solicitation between buying and selling teams, often including meetings and document exchanges						Minimal, impersonal communication between buyer and seller
10	Formally structured procurement environments						Unstructured buying process, process unlikely to be followed, dishonest, or illegal

Figure 5. Capture Planning Applicability Matrix. *Use this tool to evaluate whether a particular opportunity or type of opportunity tends to be in selling environments that would benefit from capture planning. Use it as an assessment tool, not a decision tool.*

BD-CMM (Business Development Capability Maturity Model®) is a basis and framework for process design and improvement. Increase your ability to effectively and efficiently win new business by emulating the model's characteristics and implementing its best practices.

Capability Maturity Model and CMM are registered in the U.S. Patent and Trademark Office by Carnegie Mellon University.

The BD-CMM documents common characteristics and best practices of the most successful business development organizations. Shipley Associates and the Association of Proposal Management Professionals (APMP) collaboratively developed BD-CMM patterned after the original Carnegie Mellon Software Engineering Institute (SEI) capability maturity models. The non-profit Business Development Institute International (BD-Institute) owns, promotes, and supports the model as an industry standard.

The model was validated as part of APMP Benchmark Study 2002, which measured key practices and performance across 62 diverse organizations. Practices embedded in the BD-CMM were directly related to enhanced performance and helped organizations meet the following goals:

1. Win more business at less cost.
2. Forecast and manage revenue accurately.
3. Improve working relationships with customers and colleagues.
4. Control and direct business development activities and costs.
5. Reduce delivery risk.
6. Reduce employee job stress and turnover.
7. Improve employee morale, work environment, and advancement opportunities.

When managers implement processes and procedures within the BD-CMM framework, their employees benefit directly by knowing exactly what management expects them to do, how management expects them to do it, and how employees' performances will be measured and rewarded. Figure 1 shows the BD-CMM with its maturity levels, key process categories (KPCs) and themes, and the individual key process areas (KPAs) that contain the key practices.

BD-CMM

1. Determine your organization's business development maturity baseline.
2. Set a capability maturity target for your organization.
3. Prepare and implement your improvement plan.
4. Maintain and extend your capability.

Key Process Categories	Customer	Focus	People	Capabilities
Themes	Increasing Customer Value	Improving Performance and Synergy	Building Competencies and Teams	Enhancing Systems and Processes
Levels	Key Process Areas (KPAs)			
5 Optimizing	• Innovation and Transformation			
4 Managed	• Relationship Management	• Enterprise Influence • Quantitative Process Managment	• High-Performance Teams	• Business Development System integration • Infrastructure Managment
3 Defined	• Solution Development	• Organizational Tactics • Quality Management	• Organizational Competencies Development	• Business Development Processes • Support Systems
2 Repeatable	• Responses Generation	• Business Development Administration • Quality Control	• Individual Skills Development	• Sales/Capture Procedures • Work Environment
1 Initial	• Ad hoc			

Figure 1. Integrated BD-CMM Framework. *BD-CMM describes organizations at various maturity levels. As organizations mature, they become more effective and efficient at winning business.*

1

While originally conceived in a large business, government contracting market, the BD-CMM is applicable to small, medium, and large enterprises; to business-to-business and government customers; to organizations in multiple countries; and to organizations competing for grants, services, and product sales.

Determine your organization's business development maturity baseline.

Business development executives should use the BD-CMM as a *yardstick* to identify best practices. Next, compare these best practices with current practices and list capability gaps and potential corrective actions. Figure 2 summarizes the characteristics of organizations at each of the BD-CMM levels.

You have two options to determine your organization's maturity level: self-assessment or independent appraisal.

Self-assessment is possible because the BD-CMM is descriptive, assuming that you have experienced people who can be dedicated exclusively (or nearly so) to the assessment. Self-assessment is more subjective but can be a valuable learning opportunity for the assessment team and your entire organization.

Independent appraisal is more objective, using BD-Institute certified appraisers. Certified appraisers use quantitative tools and gather objective evidence to maintain objectivity and credibility with executives. Most executives find clearly presented, objective observations persuasive and subsequently support and fund improvement initiatives.

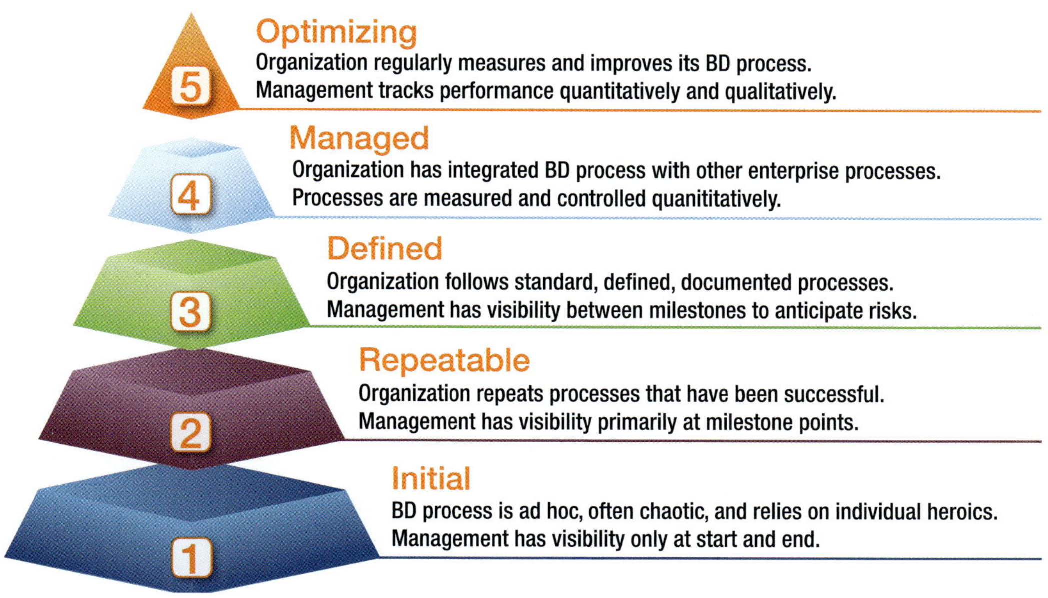

Figure 2. BD-CMM Maturity Levels. *Just as individuals' maturities are indicated by their behaviors, the relative maturities of organizations' BD processes are indicated by their business practices.*

2

Set a capability maturity target for your organization.

When targeting your maturity level, specifically consider financial benefits, people, business development goals, and the maturity and sophistication of your customers and competitors.

Analyze the financial benefits by looking at your current maturity level, business development costs, revenues, and profit. Then estimate the financial benefits at each maturity level, using your insight into market trends. In most cases, the financial benefits far exceed the costs. Investing in improving your organization's business development maturity can be your single, best investment.

Consider whether people in your organization will resist or fear change. A common reaction is, "Others need to change, but leave me alone." For example, if you define improved processes but fail to follow your new process, your organization will not increase its maturity level. Here are some change-management recommendations:

1. Stress the benefits to each contributor. Different contributors benefit differently.
2. Seek a senior management champion. Bottom-up change is rarely successful.
3. Develop a high-trust environment. Define your plan; stick to your plan; keep your word.

Also, consider what you are trying to accomplish through your business development efforts. Dovetail your maturity growth goals with your overall business objectives. For example, organizations with aggressive growth targets in highly competitive markets often need to improve the business development practices that will move them beyond their competitors' capabilities.

Note: While Model criteria require a Level 3 maturity level in all Key Process Areas (KPAs), some organizations target level 3 maturity in fewer KPAs.

In other situations, an organization may focus on improvement in selected KPCs, rather than an entire level. For example, if your markets are becoming increasingly commoditized, you might prioritize improvements in your systems and infrastructure over improvements in customer relationships.

Evaluate the maturity and sophistication of your customers, competitors, and external environment. For example, to consistently win complex procurements requires more sophisticated business development practices that equate to higher BD-CMM maturity levels.

3 Prepare and implement your improvement plan.

Prepare a thorough improvement plan and schedule that specify the start, interim milestones, and end for all tasks. Clearly define completion criteria and metrics to accurately measure progress.

A typical, spiral, BD-CMM process improvement project flow is shown in figure 3. The process is repeated for each maturity level. Follow these implementation guidelines:

1. Establish a business development process improvement group. This group should have a long-term charter to implement, manage, and continue to improve BD-CMM key practices.
2. Link performance metrics to BD-CMM goals by aligning project initiatives with KPAs.
3. Assign an experienced project manager with the authority to get the job done.
4. Allocate adequate resources, and define individual and process improvement team responsibilities.
5. Make *quick fixes* to consolidate support for more difficult tasks. Quick fixes are practices that are easily changed because few people are involved, relatively small changes where benefits immediately outweigh the cost, or where you have broad support for the change.
6. Communicate the benefits of improvements across the organization.
7. Validate improvements and confirm attainment of your target maturity level through an independent assessment.

The internal opportunity costs of BD-CMM improvements and the benefits of improvements prompt many organizations to seek outside help. Consider using BD-Institute approved providers if your personnel lack the time or skills to complete the following tasks:

- Prepare improvement plans and manage change
- Re-engineer business development processes and tools
- Train personnel to instill relevant skills and competencies
- Design, develop, and deploy improved systems and infrastructure
- Educate managers for next-generation BD-CMM innovations

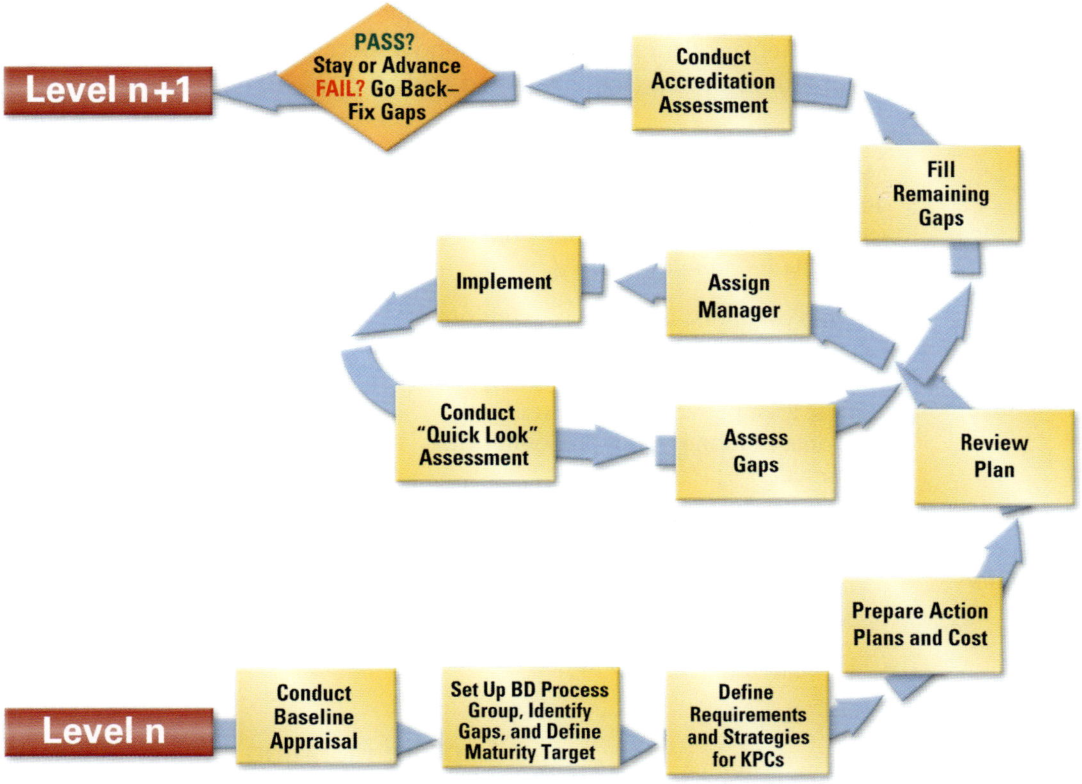

Figure 3. Idealized Improvement Plan. *Implementation plan should include these actions. Detail who owns each step, and tie each step to a schedule.*

4

Maintain and extend your capability.

What happens after you achieve your targeted maturity level? If you do not continue to grow and improve, you begin to decline. Fortunately, BD-CMM key process areas describe further process improvements at each level. The model is designed to help you determine ways to improve your capability and foster continuing improvement.

Here are some maintenance suggestions:

1. **Create and publish organizational best practices.** To achieve your new maturity level, implement key practices that represent industry standards. Transform these into best practices for your organization and business environment. Publish these best practices for easy reference by your entire organization.
2. **Adopt selected key practices** whether you decide to progress to the next maturity level or not. BD-CMM key practices of a higher maturity level would likely improve your business development effectiveness.
3. **Continue to adapt and improve your key practices** to maintain your current position and gain competitive advantage. The economy and your marketplace are not static. Anticipate, prepare, and be ready for change before it happens.

Capture Planning is the process of identifying opportunities, assessing the environment, and devising and implementing winning strategies oriented toward capturing a specific business opportunity. Consistently successful capture planning requires written, action-oriented capture plans.

Most sales and marketing veterans agree that 40 to 80 percent of the time, customers decide whom they would prefer to buy from before proposals are submitted.

The aim of capture planning is to position the customer to prefer your organization and your solution to the exclusion of competitors, or to at least prefer to do business with your organization prior to proposals being submitted.

See Bid Decisions *and* Process, ***Proposal Guide.***

The phrase *capture planning* originated in the 1980s in organizations that were primarily focused on large U.S. Department of Defense opportunities.

Concurrently, commercial organizations pursuing large, complex opportunities were developing detailed account or sales planning disciplines. Both were pursuing complex opportunities with the following characteristics:

- High value
- Buying committees (multiple people influencing the purchase decision)
- Long sales cycles (months or years)

Some commercial organizations use the terms capture plan and account plan interchangeably. However, many account plans are not opportunity specific and may merely allocate the organization's revenue objective among accounts.

See Model Documents *16 and 17,* ***Proposal Guide.***

Capture Planning

1. Implement a capture planning discipline to capture new business more efficiently.
2. Enhance capture planning effectiveness by aligning activities and capture plan elements.
3. Select a compatible medium (whether text, presentation, or web-based) to develop, review, share, and update capture plans in your organization.
4. Keep the process dynamic, flexible, interactive, and current.
5. Maintain a balance between planning and execution.
6. Complete the Integrated Customer Solution Worksheet and the Bidder Comparison Chart—even when time is short.
7. Gain and maintain senior management approval and support.
8. Commit the right people to the capture team.
9. Assign specific, measurable objectives, schedules, and completion dates to different department managers by name.
10. Establish regular decision gate reviews to determine whether to advance the opportunity to the next phase or end the pursuit.
11. Schedule color team reviews to improve the product—whether a capture plan, strategy, proposal, or underlying processes.
12. Use the capture plan to jump-start the proposal planning process.

A capture planning best practice is to prepare a written, action-oriented capture plan. While the length, complexity, and format may vary, a written plan offers reviewable evidence of the quality of thinking of the planners and soundness of the plan.

The primary audience for a capture plan is each person who will manage, approve, or execute the plan, the proposal, and the resulting contract.

A good capture plan will be realistic and specific, detailing the objective, action, responsible individual, timing, and frequency of review.

Organizations that use a formal capture planning discipline are helped in the following ways:

- More realistic understanding of each opportunity
- Improved bid decisions
- Improved solutions and capture strategies
- Greater consensus and information transfer among individuals pursuing each opportunity
- Saved time, reduced capture cost, and improved win rates

Capture planning is initiated following the pursuit decision process milestone and continues into program start-up.

1 Implement a capture planning discipline to capture new business more efficiently.

Capture planning offers benefits to everyone involved:

- **Executives** gain early and regular visibility over business development opportunities.
- **Sales and business development professionals** win more opportunities by efficiently specifying and managing capture activities.
- **Senior managers** increase sales revenue by efficiently deploying limited business development resources.
- **Participants** are motivated by knowing their efforts are productive.
- **Employees** stay employed.
- **Stockholders** make money.

Unlike the top-down, management-driven corporate planning process, capture planning is opportunity specific. Capture plans are driven bottom-up by the opportunity and the customer, as illustrated in figure 1.

To meet the organization's goals, sufficient specific business opportunities must be won. The discipline associated with best-in-class capture planning aligns organizational objectives and investment with high-win probability opportunities within approved strategic business objectives.

Capture planning nests efficiently within existing business development and planning processes, as illustrated in figure 2. Strategic business plans contain data about markets, trends, buying history, and competitors. Some organizations will prepare a strategic plan and a separate, annual business plan.

Account plans contain data about the customer's strategic direction, management, history, financial performance, issues, buying plans and patterns, competition, and suppliers. Strategic business plans and account plans are rich sources of data for the capture plan.

Much information in one plan can be reused in subsequent plans, such as proposal or closure plans. Business capture efficiency and effectiveness are improved when all employees have consistent information and communicate consistent messages to customers.

Business development professionals often question the emphasis on a written plan. Because a capture plan is the product of a collaborative effort, contrast the before-and-after states, summarized in figure 3.

Figure 1. Planning Hierarchy. *Capture planning is influenced top-down within the context of the overall corporate and sales planning process. However, it is driven bottom-up by the customer's opportunity-specific needs.*

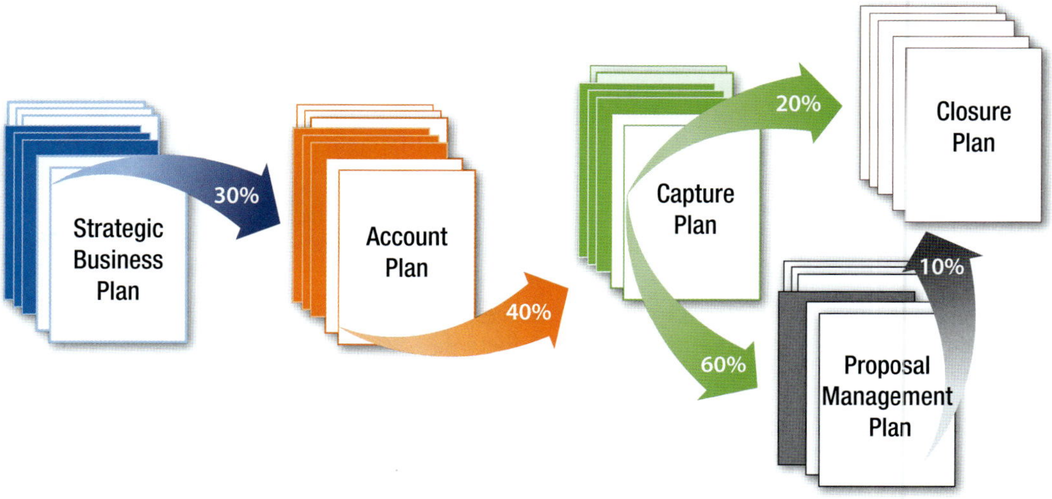

Figure 2. Capture Planning Improves Capture Efficiency. *Much of the data in each plan can be reused; it transfers or flows into the next plan. While the estimates vary, approximately 40 percent of the data from the account plan applies to the capture plan. Up to 80 percent of the capture plan data is reused in the proposal plan or closure plan.*

PRE-PLAN STATE	POST-PLAN STATE
Fuzzy concepts	Clear concepts
Information known individually	Information shared among entire team
Potential actions not aligned, assigned, or managed	Potential actions are aligned, efficiently allocated, assigned, and manageable
Willingness to take action is unknown	Willingness to take action is still unknown but likely increased

Figure 3. Benefits of Written Plans. *In the pre-plan state, each individual may have inconsistent information. When the plan is collaboratively written, individuals share information, every individual has more information, and potential actions can be agreed and aligned. Both states require the willingness to take action, or your efforts are wasted.*

2

Most capture plan templates structure the elements shown in figure 4 in four groups:

- External analysis
- Internal analysis
- Strategy development
- Execution and monitoring

See Model Document *1*.

Enhance capture planning effectiveness by aligning activities and capture plan elements.

In the overall context of moving from an unknown to a favored position with the customer, figure 4 shows the types of activities and the focus of those activities aligned with capture plan elements.

To move from an unknown to a known position with the customer, research, analyze, and validate your data with the customer. Validation is key because the only relevant view is the customer's view.

The next step is to develop and define your solution, strategy, cost, and price to win from a known position. The listed capture plan elements comprise tools and templates that help you develop and document your position.

Next, implement your action plans to influence the customer and improve your position. Change requires action.

Keep iterating to achieve and then maintain a favored position. With every action, factor newly gained information into your analysis. Fine-tune your solution, strategy, cost, and price to win. Update your action plans and implement.

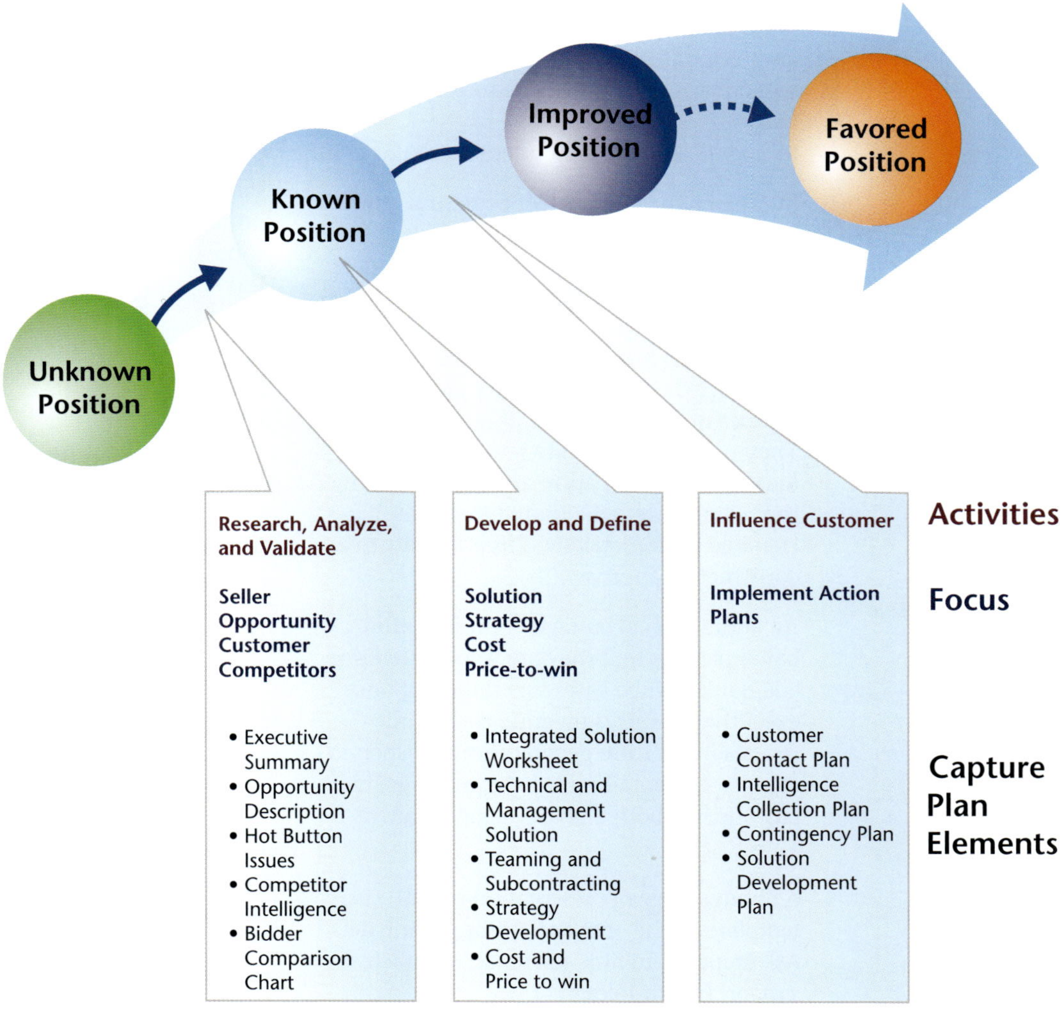

Figure 4. Aligning the Capture Planning Process to the Capture Plan. *In the over-arching capture planning process, you seek to move from positions of "unknown," to "known," and then to an "improved position." Elements of the capture plan are matched to this iterative process by phase. Specific content of your capture plans will vary depending on the opportunity, your organization, and the value of the opportunity to your organization.*

3

Select a compatible medium—whether text, presentation, or web-based—to develop, review, share, and update capture plans in your organization.

See Model Document 16, *Proposal Guide.*

Envision a capture plan as a framework, a series of folders or *buckets* where you assemble and organize data by topic. Ask capture team members to add, update, share, and purge data as relevant and permitted.

The original capture plan medium and structure was a **text-based** document that evolved from strategic plans, annual business plans, market plans, and account plans. Given a preferred table of contents, preparers knew what was expected, information could be adapted from prior plans, and the plan could be read before a gate review—which potentially shortened the information transfer portion of the review. Text-based plans are good vehicles to inform new capture and proposal contributors. However, text-based plans take more time to prepare, are harder to update, and often not kept current.

See Model Document 1.

Many organizations select **presentation-based** plans instead of text-based plans, primarily because they are easier to prepare, review, and update collaboratively. Some business development managers use the presentation format to collaboratively construct the first draft with a prospective capture manager.
They use the initial gate review to gain maximum participation and input, turning the review into a facilitated free-for-all. Handled diplomatically, this is an effective, constructive approach.

See Model Document 2 for a web browser-based example and Model Document 3 for a database example.

An additional advantage of presentation-based plans is that they are web-conference adaptable, which eases scheduling of busy executives, reduces meeting costs, and secures input from geographically dispersed experts. Presentation-based formats are easily customized, both a positive and negative aspect.

A disadvantage of presentation-based templates is the omission of supporting detail. Ask preparers to link, reference, or attach support files or folders.

Web browser-based collaboration tools are supplanting presentation-based plans as secure ways to collaboratively prepare and share capture information and documents. While many of these tools lack full drag-and-drop flexibility, they are an effective way to structure, collaboratively develop, share, and document current data in a single location. Keeping the latest data available to all authorized participants is far preferable to having multiple, outdated versions on laptops and desktops, where the capture manager and key participants cannot locate or identify the current version.

One of the best features of the web browser-based format is that senior managers can readily track progress, updates, and activity. The lack of updates suggests that nothing is happening.

Another advantage is immediate access for participants dispersed across multiple time zones. While conferencing might be inconvenient, web material is always available and can be updated while others sleep.

Many participants will have a collaboration tool installed as an organizational standard, but getting business development professionals to use browser-based tools takes some initial file structuring, training, and then management persistence to convince them to use it consistently. If not, participants will revert to old habits of keeping multiple, out-dated files on their laptops.

A disadvantage is that to maintain file security, each participant must be granted access to specific folders. The person controlling access must be readily available, or participants will become frustrated and not use the tool.

Database products with browser access offer advantages over web browser-based tools:

- Transparent and near automatic data reuse from plan to plan saves time and preserves data.
- Data security and control are improved.

For example, a customer requirement entered in the initial account plan could transfer to the capture plan, to the proposal plan, to section storyboards, and then to a section draft without re-keying. Verify that the data is still accurate before approving the transfer.

Database products might require additional software and training. While browser-based tools generally work well across operating systems and platforms, database products might not. Verify compatibility before selecting a tool.

4

Keep the process dynamic, flexible, interactive, and current.

Keep your capture planning process flexible to permit adjustments depending on the importance of the opportunity to your organization, the competitive situation, and the resources you can afford to commit. Avoid becoming a slave to your process. Adapt to the needs and acceptable norms of your organization.

Build the plan interactively to support a fast start with reasonable effort and to encourage regular updates. Capture plans are living documents that are repeatedly updated as you gain information. Information will change and become more specific as the opportunity matures. Figure 5 reflects a practical progression: populate, validate, update, and implement.

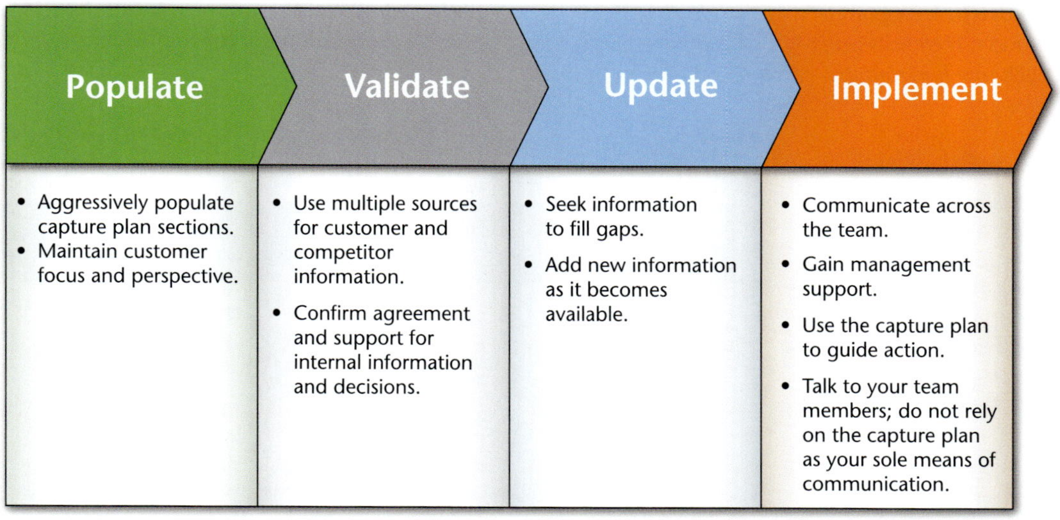

Figure 5. Iteratively Develop Your Capture Plan. *Keep capture plan current and correct by repeatedly updating the content. Populate: complete what you think you know; validate: check and confirm; update: add and correct data; and implement.*

5

Maintain a balance between planning and execution.

Changing perceptions requires action. Detailed plans without action are a waste of time because they fail to influence customers' perceptions.

Limit your plans to the resources available. If more resources are needed than your organization will commit to win, reconsider your pursuit decision.

Effective capture planning requires a balance between action and planning.

6

Complete the Integrated Solution Worksheet and the Bidder Comparison Chart—even when time is short.

See STRATEGY; *and* DISCRIMINATORS, ***Proposal Guide.***

The "gap" is the difference between the customer's requirement and your available solution.

The Integrated Solution Worksheet, shown in figure 6, is a powerful analysis tool that should be applied throughout the capture process. Early in the process, use it to focus collaboratively with your customer to define the issues and influence the requirements. If you discover an opportunity after requirements are defined, use it to define the underlying issues driving the customer's requirements.

Next, extend your analysis to outline your solution, outline your competitors' solutions, identify discriminators, and then develop your strategy and actions to better position your solution with the customer.

The Bidder Comparison Chart, shown in figure 7, is used to analyze the customer's current perception of how your solution compares to various competitors. Use it repeatedly throughout the capture process to measure the strength and effectiveness of your positioning.

ShipleyAssociates — Integrated Solution Worksheet

Enter Opportunity Name

Item No.	Customer Issues	Customer Requirements	Available Solution	Gap	Competitor Solution	Discriminators	Strategy	Action Required
1	System must be available.	8 hr. response time.	2 hr. response time	1 hr	3 hr. response time	Faster response but more expensive?	Emphasize no additional cost with cellular.	Show current response time. Show photo-service with cell phone.

Figure 6. Integrated Solution Worksheet. *Begin by filling down the* Customer Issues *column when you are early in the process. If the customer has already drafted requirements, fill-down the* Customer Requirements *column. Then complete each row horizontally, carefully relating each item.*

Additional uses and alternative approaches for the Integrated Solution Worksheet and Bidder Comparison Chart are discussed in **Executive Summary, Strategy,** and **Teaming.**

Customers have issues. Sellers have gaps. Essentially, gaps are sellers' issues.

ShipleyAssociates — Bidder Comparison Chart

Issues	Weight	Us		Competitor A		Competitor B		Competitor C		Competitor D		Competitor E	
		Points	Score	Points	Score	Points	Score	Points	Score	Points	Score	Points	Score
Specific Experience	10	8	80	7	70	5	50						
Low Price	10	3	30	5	50	8	80						
Familiarity with Manager Named	10	8	80	5	50	5	50						
Ability to Meet Schedule	10	8	80	7	70	5	50						
Totals			270		240		230						

Figure 7. Bidder Comparison Chart. *First list the customer's issues, then the relative importance of each issue as perceived by the customer in the* Weight *column. Then complete each row horizontally, indicating your estimate of the customer's perception of each competitor's ability to satisfy that issue. Scores can range from 0 to the total number in the* Weight *column.*

7 Gain and maintain senior management approval and support.

Top management must endorse and help communicate the plan to everyone managing and executing the plan, as well as those impacted by the reassignment of individuals to support the plan.

Management support must begin with the pursuit decision and continue through to the signed contract. If the opportunity remains worth winning, keep management sold by emphasizing the value to your organization. If contingent items change your assumptions, then revisit your pursuit or bid decision.

Recognize and avoid the bias towards *happy* information. Capture managers should feel free to reveal negative information to senior management. Similarly, senior management should never punish a capture manager for honestly revealing new information that might suggest a no-pursuit or no-bid decision.

8

See Capture Team Selection and Management.

Commit the right people to the capture team.

Organizations pursuing competitive business should assign their best people to capture teams. Organizations that assign only the people they can spare from other activities usually lose the sale. Figure 8 summarizes the focus of the capture, program, and proposal managers.

Capture manager is normally a role rather than a position. In most organizations, the sales or business development lead is assigned the capture manager role. However, in organizations focused on the largest opportunities, the capture manager role may be assigned to a person from program management, business development, or line management.

The capture manager role requires a person with customer and market knowledge, sales savvy, proposal experience, leadership skills, broad technical understanding, knowledge of the organization, and positive enthusiasm. The capture manager advocates the customer's position while focusing on winning the opportunity. The capture manager is concerned with the customer's budget, program cost, risk, competitive analysis, capture strategy, price to win, the customer's view of best value, and implementing the capture strategy.

Program manager is likely to be a position as well as a role. If the solution is design oriented, then a chief engineer, systems engineer, or solution architect might support or overrule the program manager. The program manager advocates for the selling organization, focusing on profit, the seller's risk, schedule, personnel, resources, assumptions, terms and conditions, and the shape of the delivery organization.

Proposal manager as a role, while not mutually exclusive to the capture manager role, requires different skills to integrate the concerns of the capture and program managers. The proposal manager focuses on **compliance, responsiveness, keeping the proposal strategy aligned with the capture strategy, proposal strategy implementation, and managing a team to produce a persuasive document within set deadlines.**

In addition to the triumvirate leadership, capture team members' skills must be suited to their assigned action, whether direct customer contact, internal development, or assisting the proposal team.

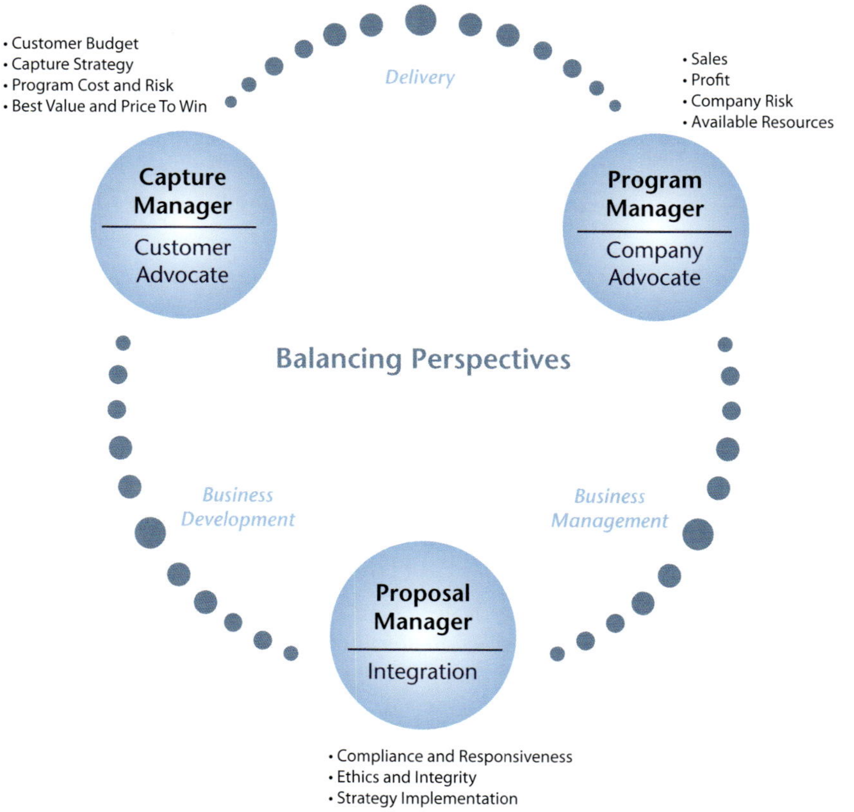

Figure 8. The Business Development Opportunity Triumvirate. *Win rates improve when the capture, program, and proposal manager triumvirate is balanced and integrated.*

9 Assign specific, measurable objectives, schedules, and completion dates to department managers by name.

Most capture team action assignments are part-time and for a limited duration. Only the managers of the assigned individuals can ensure task completion.

Many capture efforts fail because the individuals assigned to the task are expected to complete the task in their spare time.

Get serious about completing the task, eliminate the task, or no-bid due to lack of resources. The single biggest reason for losing competitive business is the failure to adequately influence the customer prior to proposal submittal.

The individuals assigned to the management roles listed in figure 9 manage the capture and proposal preparation action assignments.

The chart roughly depicts typical involvement by management role throughout the opportunity lifecycle.

Set and schedule specific measurable action objectives to simplify task management. Contrast poor and better objectives:

Poor

Discuss service call procedures with the customer.

Better

Demonstrate our on-line service call management system with Ms. Bell, Global's office manager, during the week ending May 15, 20XX.

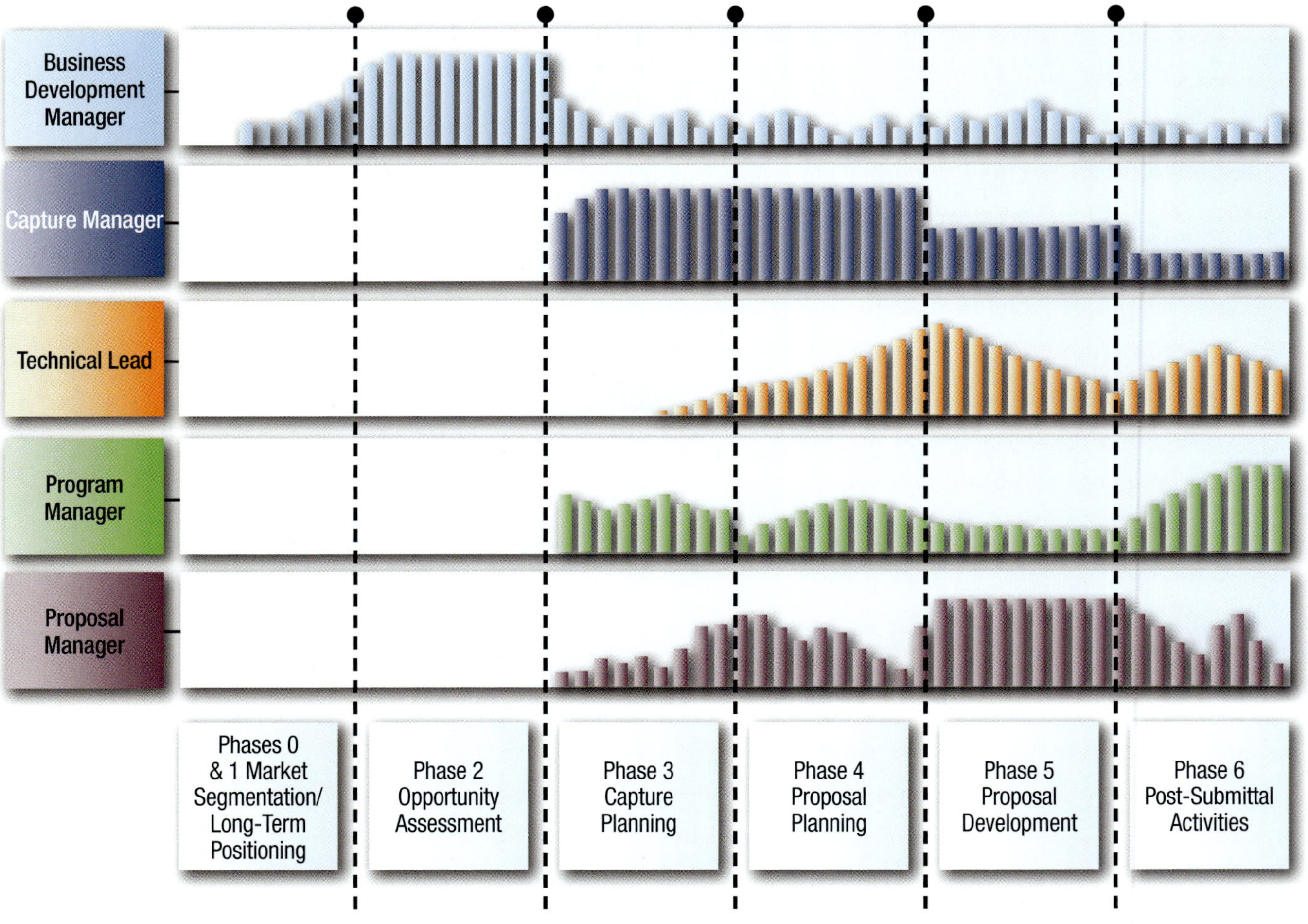

Figure 9. Capture Time Commitment by Role. *This notional representation shows how time commitments of individuals in different roles vary throughout the business development phases. A business development manager leads the process, then hands responsibility to a capture manager. The capture manager's involvement declines as the technical lead and proposal manager become more involved in proposal development. All but the proposal manager might have a spike in commitment after proposal submission in preparation for final contract negotiation and award.*

10 Establish regular decision gate reviews to determine whether to advance the opportunity to the next phase or end the pursuit.

See Decision Gate Reviews.

Decision gate reviews are milestones between business development process phases. Focus on four key questions:

1. Is the opportunity winnable?
2. Do the potential returns justify the expenditures?
3. Is the capture team prepared for the next phase?
4. What additional resources are required to win?

Decision gate reviews are the decision milestones between phases of the business development process, as shown in figure 10. Until you pass through a decision gate review, you remain in the same phase. For example, if senior management only reviews proposals before submittal, then you have a two-phase process.

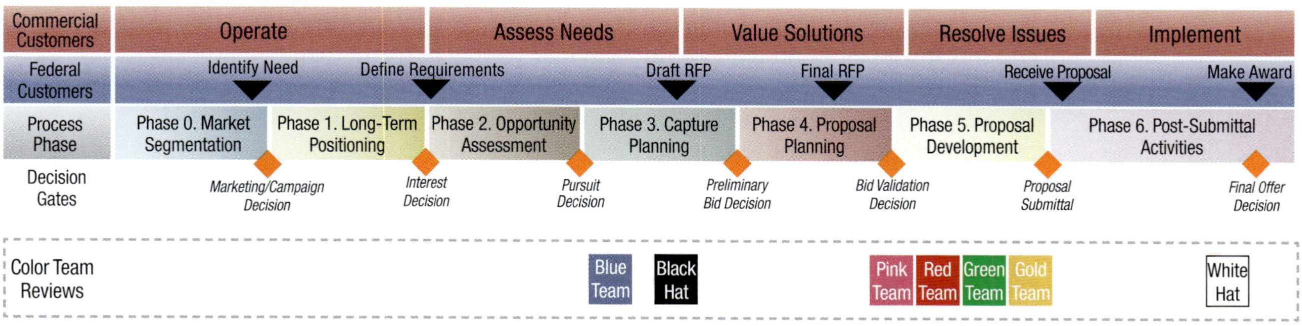

Figure 10. Relationship Among Selling Phase, Decision Gate Reviews, and Color Team Reviews. *Senior managers participate in decision gate reviews focusing on whether to advance, defer, or end the pursuit. The focus is on decisions. In contrast, color team reviews focus on improving the quality of the product, whether the capture plan, solution, competitive assessment, storyboards, draft, or final proposal.*

To keep reviews short and effective, focus on reviewing the actions taken, analyzing the results of those actions, and then adjusting future actions.

Base every decision gate review on the current capture plan. Keeping your capture plan updated eliminates the need to prepare for each review.

The most successful organizations eventually pursue less than 30 percent of their pipeline and achieve win rates of 70 percent or greater.

Establish organizational standards for each review. Set clear expectations by specifying review inputs and outputs linked to the value of the opportunity, selling environment, and strategic importance to your organization and the customer.

Progressively add content and detail as the opportunity matures and you advance through successive gates. Your initial interest decision gate review will likely be short, perhaps requiring less than 10 slides with information at a basic level, but successive bid and bid validation reviews might grow to 30–60 slides with increasing levels of detail, depending upon the opportunity, organization, and selling environment.

Recheck the underlying data, assumptions, and analysis only when objectives are not met or new data is uncovered. Reviewers that over-focus on the data and analysis usually under-focus on future actions. Changing a customer's perceptions requires action, not analysis.

Maintain a positive, constructive tone. Avoid penalizing contributors who raise unfavorable information that might lead to no-pursuit or no-bid decisions. Remember that the most successful organizations eventually pursue less than 30 percent of their pipeline and achieve win rates of 70 percent or greater. Seek good decisions while avoiding a bias towards go-forward decisions. Eliminating personal opinions, bias, and ego is difficult in most organizations.

Early warning signs leading to a no-bid decision are limited information, indecision about where to obtain needed information, and limited capture team or senior management commitment. Winning competitive business requires laser-focus on winnable opportunities.

Losing bids are the most costly bids. No-bid decisions free you to shift limited resources to winnable opportunities.

11 Schedule color team reviews to improve the product—whether a capture plan, strategy, proposal, or underlying processes.

See Color Team Reviews.

The essential quality-improvement principle is to review for the right things at the right time. Use color team reviews to solicit constructive recommendations for improvement.

Differentiate color team reviews and decision gate reviews. Focus color teams on quality improvement; focus decision gate reviews on whether to advance, defer, or end the pursuit.

Adapt the number and types of reviews to your organization, your business development process, selling environment, and the importance of the opportunity. While six different color reviews are shown in figure 10, most organizations conduct some variant of the following three reviews:

1. Competitors, competitive assessment, and probable discriminators (Black Hat review)
2. Proposal planned content and messages before writing (Pink Team review)
3. Proposal near-final content against the customer's needs, requirements, and evaluation criteria (Red Team review)

Both the number of reviews and color designations for reviews vary widely by organization.

Align the background of the reviewers to the color team review. Seek reviewers that offer varied perspectives on the customer, competitors, selling organization or team, and solution.

Seek comprehensive and constructive recommendations for improvement. Appoint an independent, experienced facilitator to manage the review team. Train inexperienced reviewers, and then establish clear instructions and standards before initiating the review.

Request consolidated recommendations from the review team. The capture triumvirate and executive sponsor then must decide which recommendations will be implemented, who will implement them, and debrief the team. Avoid direct color team debriefs, as unfiltered recommendations might have negative consequences.

12 Use the capture plan to jump-start the proposal planning process.

As shown earlier in figure 2, approximately 60 percent of the information needed to prepare the proposal management plan can be extracted from a current and complete capture plan.

Relying on the capture plan to quickly prepare the initial proposal management plan saves both time and maintains a consistent message. Without a capture plan, a newly assigned proposal manager starts from scratch, often with little help and under severe time constraints.

Capture plans and proposal plans have the common elements illustrated in figure 11. Information on the customer, requirements, and competitors transfers directly. The capture strategy needs to be extended or converted into a proposal strategy. Only the proposal outline, compliance checklist, proposal preparation schedule, and the writer's packages need to be created.

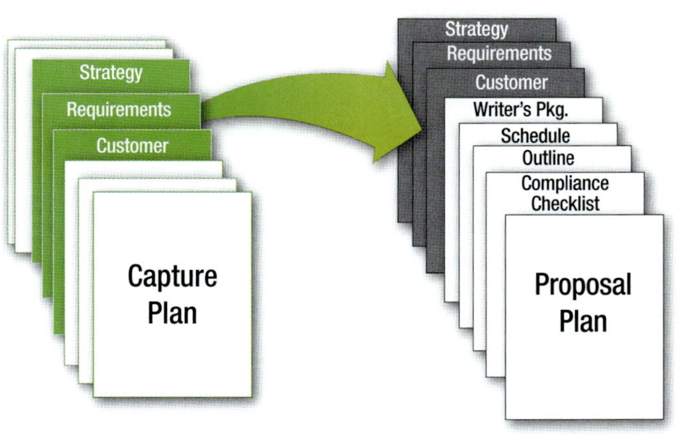

Figure 11. Capture Plans Evolve into Proposal Plans. *A current capture plan effectively front-loads the proposal plan. With approximately 60 percent of the information transferring from the capture plan, you only need to add proposal-specific material. Shortening the final proposal planning interval prior to kickoff leaves more time to develop a winning proposal.*

Capture Scheduling is essential to visualize, implement, and monitor progress of the capture plan. Unscheduled tasks are rarely completed.

Common scheduling principles apply to capture plans. Preparing a realistic schedule requires a clear understanding of each task, the situation, capability of assigned talent, and adequate support resources. Just developing the schedule clarifies your understanding of the task.

Adapt the complexity of the capture schedule to the market sector, value, and importance of the opportunity to your organization, time frame, and available resources. For example, a geographically distant and unfamiliar customer will require more time, expense, and visits to position than a proximate, prior customer.

See **Bid Decisions** *and* **Process, *Proposal Guide.***

Scheduling capture efforts is more difficult than scheduling proposals. Capture activities might be limited by customer procurement requirements and shifting end points. In addition, the earlier you discover the opportunity, the less you and your customer are likely to know about the procurement schedule.

With many government procurements, direct contact with individuals in the customer organization is restricted after the bid request is issued. If so, your ability to understand individuals' hot button issues, customer requirements, budgets, and anticipated cost information is severely restricted.

Customers routinely modify critical procurement milestones, meaning you cannot reliably schedule capture activities. You will not know when customer-centric capture activities must end. How many bid requests are issued as originally scheduled?

In contrast, while proposal submittal dates might extend, they still have a fixed end date. Hence, proposal schedules are built backwards from the due date. However, proposal and capture schedules are concurrent, as capture activity continues while the proposal is being prepared.

Assume a disciplined yet adaptive approach to scheduling capture events. Management and team members will test your discipline as you obtain new intelligence. Your challenge is to complete positioning activities in an uncertain, changing environment. If you defer action, your position with the customer often deteriorates or access is denied. If you push ahead, your actions might be second-guessed and premature.

Guided by your strategic vision, act and react as your knowledge of the customer, opportunity, competition, and potential solution evolves. Managing a capture schedule will never be as precise as managing a proposal.

Figure 1 summarizes some of the similarities and differences between capture and proposal schedules.

Capture Scheduling

1. Create, align, and adapt the capture schedule to the customer's actions, your organization's business development process, the resources available, and the selling environment.
2. Schedule capture activities as you would any other project, using the same scheduling tools.
3. Minimize sequential tasks; maximize parallel tasks.
4. Delegate intelligently.
5. Assign a person to each task with start and end dates.
6. Use gate reviews to complete action.
7. Considerately over-communicate.

DIFFERENCES	
Capture Schedules	***Proposal Schedules***
Longer and more variable time span from the pursuit decision through program initiation.	Shorter and less variable time span from the bid decision to proposal submittal and lessons-learned documentation.
Based on milestones, gate reviews, and customer activities.	Driven by proposal due date(s).
Uncertain dates driven by customer decisions and competitors' tactics.	Dates driven primarily by customer deliverable dates and internal resources and minimally by competitors' tactics.
Built after pursuit decision and extended through program initiation.	Build backwards from proposal due date.
Permitted customer-facing activities might be limited after bid request is issued.	Customer deliverable due dates do not limit internally focused proposal preparation tasks.
SIMILARITIES	
Requires a single manager to lead the effort and manage the schedule.	
Requires established budget to support approved tasks.	
Assigns a single person the responsibility to complete each task, with start and end dates.	
Arranged to minimize sequential tasks, and maximize parallel tasks.	
Requires senior leadership buy-in and participation in gate reviews.	

Figure 1. Differences and Similarities of Capture and Proposal Scheduling. *The timing and focus of the schedules differ, but many scheduling guidelines are common.*

1

Create, align, and adapt the capture schedule to the customer's actions, your organization's business development process, the resources available, and the selling environment.

Consider three questions:

- What phase-critical and time-sensitive activities must be completed immediately before circumstances change?
- What key activities must be completed to meet your management's expectations?
- What items must be presented at the next gate review?

Consider the following phase-critical and time-sensitive activities:

See Decision Gate Reviews.

- Access to the customer might be restricted after solicitation documents are released. If so, gathering intelligence early is vital to making an informed pursuit decision, developing your capture strategy, and positioning your solution as the preferred solution. Schedule customer intelligence gathering and solution positioning activity as early as possible, and continue until restricted.
- If your strategy requires teaming, you must identify the optimal partner and negotiate a teaming agreement before they team with a competitor. Schedule teaming discussions promptly after completing your competitive analysis and capture strategy.
- If your solution requires key personnel, identify and reserve or recruit them before they are committed to other activities, programs, or competitors.
- If new technology is required, use lead time to develop and verify that technology before promising it to the customer. Ideally, persuade the customer to specify your technology in the bid request.
- If past performance requirements are critical, identify appropriate experience and performance examples within your organization or via teaming partners. Ideally, preview this experience and performance with the customer, scheduling site visits or interviews, if possible.

With the next gate reviews identified, focus on scheduling the key activities required to prepare the mandatory inputs and meet management's expectations.

Once time-sensitive activities are identified, consider typical, key capture planning actions. Refer to figure 2 for general capture steps:

- Manage the Capture Process
- Build Relationships
- Gather and Analyze Data
- Develop and Implement Strategy
- Engage Proposal Support

Add, delete, or compress depending upon the time and resources available, customer's buying schedule, and selling environment. While key activities vary and dates might shift, include every gate and color team review on your capture planning schedule.

Figure 2 illustrates the key activities involved in effective capture planning.

	KEY ACTIVITY	ACTIVITY LEADER	START DATE	DUE DATE	COMMENTS
Manage the Capture Process	**Develop capture plan** ❑ Populate, validate, and update capture plan ❑ Hold review sessions to ensure team is moving forward				
	Determine key management actions ❑ Provide oversight for opportunity, key relationships, intelligence, strategy, and actions ❑ Establish capture/B&P budget ❑ Transition from capture to proposal planning				
Build Relationships	**Form and train capture team** ❑ Select capture manager ❑ Initiate a capture team (SMEs) ❑ Define specific roles and responsibilities ❑ Train capture team ❑ Hold kickoff meeting to initiate capture activities				
	Expand customer relationships ❑ Identify customer, program, and procurement organizations ❑ Define customer buying cycle ❑ Create a customer contact plan ❑ Collaborate on value propositions				
Gather and Analyze Data	**Perform program/opportunity assessment** ❑ Gather relevant opportunity/program data ❑ Analyze, validate, and update data ❑ Determine gaps and update findings as opportunity evolves				
	Perform customer assessment ❑ Gain clear understanding of customer requirements ❑ Identify/validate customer issues, wants, needs, and hot buttons ❑ Determine Source Selection Authority and key decision makers				
	Perform competitor assessment ❑ Determine key competitors ❑ Validate data from multiple sources ❑ Populate Bidder Comparison Chart ❑ Assess strengths and weaknesses from Bidder Comparison Chart ❑ Determine critical gaps and discriminators				
	Perform self (organization)-assessment ❑ Assess strengths and weaknesses from Bidder Comparison Chart ❑ Determine critical gaps and discriminators ❑ Create strategy statements to highlight key messages				

Table Continues .... ▶

	KEY ACTIVITY	ACTIVITY LEADER	START DATE	DUE DATE	COMMENTS
Develop and Implement Strategy	**Determine Price-to-Win (PTW) strategy** ❑ Gain understanding of customer budget and pricing history ❑ Learn what competitors are charging for similar work ❑ Create a should-cost analysis from customer perspective ❑ Align PTW strategy with customer, competitor, and should-cost findings				
	Develop win strategy ❑ Lay out key actions needed to win				
	Initiate teaming strategy ❑ Determine customer subcontracting requirements ❑ Build teaming strategy to complement your capabilities ❑ Initiate teaming discussions ❑ Formalize through executed teaming agreements				
	Develop high-level proposal solutions ❑ Lay out key points and issues for technical, management, past performance, and cost/price proposal volumes ❑ Document high-level solution on an Integrated Solution Worksheet				
	Initiate Black Hat activities and review ❑ Determine most threatening competitors ❑ Create capture strategies through the eyes of competition ❑ Incorporate key findings into capture plan				
	Determine program execution strategy ❑ Plan ahead to determine key actions necessary to begin work on Day One of contract award				
	Turn strategies into action plans ❑ Populate action plans with key strategies ❑ Manage specific tasks within each action plan				
Engage Proposal Support	**Identify proposal team** ❑ Select proposal manager ❑ Determine resource needs ❑ Integrate with capture team				
	Develop proposal management plan ❑ Transfer key capture data to proposal management plan ❑ Develop storyboards				
	Hold proposal strategy session ❑ Determine which actions may evolve into proposal messages ❑ Review strengths, weaknesses, discriminators, features, and benefits ❑ Turn strategy statements into win theme statements				
	Develop draft executive summary ❑ Populate executive summary with important key messages to drive proposal messages ❑ Share draft executive summary with proposal team				
	Collect high-level proposal collateral ❑ Gather potential documentation (i.e., past performance, resumes) ❑ Validate appropriateness of data for proposal use ❑ Manage data collection				

Figure 2. Potential Capture Activities. *Determine which activities are needed for each capture opportunity. Eliminate, condense, or expand as appropriate. Align these actions with gate review deliverables, then assign the activity leader, start date, and due date.*

See Capture Plan Models and Templates.

Capture plans are built over time. While the contents of a capture plan might look daunting, build and refine the content as you progress. Add increasing levels of detail over time, and keep the data current with frequent updates.

See Decision Gate Reviews.

Figure 3 illustrates capture plan elements and the expected level of detail needed for each gate review. The key interpretive points to follow are:

- Capture plan elements are aligned with the generic Shipley capture template.
- Capture plan elements, typically linked to one or more slides, are grouped under Internal Analysis, External Analysis, Strategy Development, and Execution and Monitoring.
- Pkg 1–Pkg 5 correspond to the packages of slides required for the five gate reviews.
- The expected level of slide detail is designated as C-Conceptual, D-Detailed, and U-Updated and linked to a specific review.

GATE REVIEW PROGRESS CHART

CAPTURE ELEMENTS	PKG 1	PKG 2	PKG 3	PKG 4	PKG 5
Gate Review	*Interest*	*Pursuit*	*Preliminary Bid*	*Bid Validation*	*Proposal Submittal*
Opportunity Overview					
Summary Chart	C	D	U	U	U
External Analysis					
Customer					
Background, Mission, and Roles	C	D	U	U	U
Program Organization	C	D	U	U	U
Key Decision Makers, Issues, and Hot Buttons		C	D	U	U
Buying Trends and History		C	D	U	U
Program Description					
Objectives and Requirements	C	D	U	U	U
Deliverables and Program Schedule		C	D	U	U
Terms and Funding Commitments		C	D	U	U
Contractor Role and Responsibilities		C	D	U	U
Procurement					
Evaluation Process and Weighting		C	D	U	U
Procurement Milestones Schedule		C	D	U	U
Competitive Analysis					
Competing Teams and Approaches	C	D	U	U	U
SWOT Analysis		C	D	U	U
Internal Analysis					
Strategic Assessment					
Strategic Intent	C	D	U	U	U
Program Fit with Plans	C	D	U	U	U
Strategic Market Outlook		C	D	U	U

Table Continues ▸

CAPTURE ELEMENTS	PKG 1	PKG 2	PKG 3	PKG 4	PKG 5
Strategy Development Plans					
Win Strategy					
Gap Analysis	C	D	U	U	U
Overall Win Strategy	C	D	U	U	U
Specific Action Plans and Status	C	D	U	U	U
Price-to-Win Analysis		C	D	U	U
Solution					
Business Solution	C	C	D	U	U
Technical Solution	C	C	D	U	U
Management Solution	C	C	D	U	U
Teaming Solution	C	C	D	U	U
Similar/Past Performance Baseline	C	C	D	U	U
Cost/Price Estimate		C	D	U	U
DTC, CAIV, and FPR Considerations		C	D	U	U
Gate Review	***Interest***	***Pursuit***	***Preliminary Bid***	***Bid Validation***	***Proposal Submittal***
Resources					
Capture Team	C	D	U	U	U
Pursuit Funding and Status	C	D	U	U	U
Capital Equipment and Facilities		C	D	U	U
Business Potential					
Short-Term Sales and Profits	C	C	D	U	U
Long-Term Sales and Profits	C	C	D	U	U
Cash-Flow and Return-On-Investment Projections			C	D	U
Risk Assessment					
Technical, Schedule, and Cost Risk Identification		C	D	U	U
Risk Mitigation Plan		C	D	U	U
Execution and Monitoring					
Pursuit Plans and Schedule					
Contacts and Customer Call Plans	C	D	U	U	U
Milestones and Action Items	C	D	U	U	U
Pursuit Schedule and Status	C	D	U	U	U
Issues and Recommendations	C	D	U	U	U

Legend: C-Conceptual Element, D-Detailed Element, U-Updated Element

Figure 3. Adapt Capture Plan Contents to the Gate Review. *Assuming a six-phase process, this conceptual chart shows the content and level of detail expected for each gate review. Content detail increases from conceptual, to detailed, to updated. Develop a similar chart for your organization's process phases and business development process. The review elements are aligned with the slides in the model capture plan template in the Capture Plan Models and Templates section of this Guide.*

Typically, you will identify key activities, add them to your schedule, but then lack sufficient resources to complete some activities. One option is to simply delete the activity and hope for the best, using the available resources as efficiently as possible. Alternatively, schedule the activity, but leave the task Unassigned to highlight the lack of resources to management.

Adapt your capture schedule to the selling environment. While much of this discussion has focused on sales cycles measured in months, a sales cycle measured in days requires a highly compressed and streamlined process.

For example, if you are responding to 5-day task order requests, your capture activity will focus on collaboratively developing task requirements with the customer or, at minimum, be the first to discover that a task order request will be issued.

Gate reviews will be short and few, but you should still address the key activities identified in this guideline. The text accompanying the **Model Capture Template** includes potential adaptations for different selling environments.

2 Schedule capture activities as you would any other project, using the same scheduling tools.

Simple timeline charts are adequate for smaller capture plans. Full critical path software tools are more appropriate for complex capture plans.

Because capture managers seldom manage direct reports, adapt your scheduling approach to your organization. If you use a common calendaring tool, enter *events* in your calendar and *invite* assignees to accept the event. Use web calendars, like those offered in SharePoint®, to coordinate your capture schedule.

One of the best ways to keep capture tasks on schedule is to publish the schedule prominently, and review it regularly. When assignees see their names on a late or incomplete task, it often prompts them to complete their tasks.

3 Minimize sequential tasks; maximize parallel tasks.

Clear task descriptions, quality standards, and start-and-end dates empower contributors to work in parallel with minimum conflict. If you hear contributors say they are waiting on someone else to finish his or her task before they start, you have sequential tasks and might be in trouble. When task owners are waiting for better information or for someone else to complete another task, they are often seeking an excuse to avoid action.

Capture managers frequently handle unnecessary sales tasks. It is important to mention, however, that the capture manager role should take precedence over personal direct-sales tasks.

4 Delegate intelligently.

Assign tasks to people with the expertise, time, willingness, and managerial support to complete the task. While the expertise and time suggestions are obvious, some individuals just refuse to accept capture tasks. For example, some people say: "I'm not in sales. I don't do that." Alternatively, identifying a supportive but less knowledgeable person might be a better choice.

Perhaps the greatest management challenge is identifying whether the manager of the person assigned to a task is feigning support. Capture tasks compete with previously scheduled tasks, which are often linked to revenue. Rather than refuse support, these managers set priorities for their direct reports, perhaps stating: "Support the capture plan, but first complete your assigned, billable work."

Best-in-class organizations support capture activities at all levels. If that is not the ethic in your organization, seek support from your senior management sponsor, present a persuasive justification to the manager of the person assigned to the task, or reassign it.

Simply eliminating the task from your schedule because you lack the resource sets a dangerous precedent. Consider leaving the task open and discussing it at the next gate review. If you lack critical information, why are you sure that you will win? Leaving the task open places accountability on the individuals who ignored your request for added resources.

5

Assign a person to each task with start and end dates.

People are rarely assigned full-time to a capture effort, including the capture manager. Establish realistic hours, schedule the task and subtasks, manage completion, and return them to their other responsibilities.

Assign one person primary responsibility, even if multiple people contribute. In some cases, that person might not be the primary content expert or the person with the largest role, just the person who will make sure the task is completed.

6

An incomplete capture plan and its qualitative general statements are early warning signs of no-bid decisions.

Use gate reviews to compel action.

Make gate review guidelines comprehensive and constructive.

The comprehensiveness of a review increases as the capture progresses. Because early reviews are shorter, develop summary charts that highlight exceptions. Consider a *stoplight* chart that rates tasks as *red*, *yellow*, or *green*.

Be constructive by praising the task owners and their managers for the *green* tasks. Be prepared to offer constructive options for the *red* and *yellow* tasks. The gate review might be your only opportunity to secure senior management support.

7

Considerately over-communicate.

When managing tasks assigned to indirect reports, maintain visibility and urgency through regular, repeated communication. Balance the medium, frequency, urgency, and tone.

Be considerate, as frequent messages or intrusive, inconvenient mediums irritate team members. Some of the most irritating time wasters are unnecessary late-night or weekend calls; over-addressing, hitting *reply all*, and blind copying on e-mails; and overly large, frequent, and long teleconferences.

Figure 4 summarizes the merits of increasingly varied team communication and schedule management options.

COMMUNICATION AND SCHEDULE MANAGEMENT OPTIONS	MERITS
Text message	Immediate, creates a sense of urgency, but reserve for relatively simple, informational messages. As texting increases, the messages are more easily forgotten.
E-mail	Works for everyone, but messages are often obscured by extensive e-mail traffic. E-mail does leave a trail, which improves accountability. Create a group list for standard messages. Limit the address list for other messages to individuals who need to take or approve the requested action. Make sure that messages to newly added people are not automatically diverted to their *junk* folder. Avoid *reply all* when the message could be more appropriately handled by replying only to the sender.
Phone call	Immediate, but leaves no trail. People forget details; written follow-up is often constructive.
Conference call	Set and communicate the agenda. Schedule when you can maximize participation. Set and observe time limits. Adapt the medium, from small-group, web-video to large-group teleconferences. New, low-cost, flexible options are introduced frequently. If not handled professionally, accountability can be a problem. (*See* Virtual Team Management, ***Proposal Guide***)
Live meeting	As the most expensive option, reserve meetings for the most important, sensitive, or confidential events. Given a limited capture budget, reduce the cost of live meetings by scheduling meetings concurrently with other events, locating a low-cost venue, or use an alternate medium.
SharePoint® Alerts	Set "alerts" when files are added or deleted. Notification is immediate, and prior files are archived. Customize to specific areas of interest. Folders require permission to view the content. Information is invisible to individuals who lack permission.

Figure 4. Capture Team Communication and Schedule Management Options. *Select a communication medium appropriate to the importance and urgency of your message and to individuals who must be involved.*

Capture Team Selection and Management are a matter of roles rather than positions. Capture teams range from a part-time person to a group of exclusively assigned individuals. Identify and commit individuals who have the skills, knowledge, availability, and interest to fulfill their assigned roles.

Capture managers are made, not born. Most organizations develop capture managers internally.

The composition of an ideal capture team varies by opportunity, depending upon customer issues and motivators, your competitive position with the customer, the technology, and individual experience with this customer. Larger, more complex opportunities usually require larger capture teams.

Assign capture team members with the right skills, knowledge, and availability. If you anticipate numerous meetings and reviews with a customer, then consider interpersonal and presentation skills. If you need to integrate or adapt new technology, consider technical knowledge.

While over-committed individuals are often the best qualified, realistically consider whether they have time within your schedule. If availability is the primary qualification, keep looking or revisit your pursuit decision.

Capture Team Selection and Management

1. Value capture management skills over technical and customer knowledge when selecting a capture manager.
2. Take a *triumvirate approach* to defining core capture team roles.
3. Identify an integrated capture team with the knowledge, skills, and experience needed to support the opportunity.
4. Persuade senior leadership to commit adequate resources.
5. Train the capture team.
6. Hold a kickoff meeting to jump-start the capture process.
7. Delegate capture work with clear expectations, schedules, target completion dates, and reporting.
8. Keep senior management informed and involved, and never surprise your management sponsor.
9. Evaluate capture success.

1 Value capture management skills over technical and customer knowledge when selecting a capture manager.

The strongest and most successful capture plans are based upon detailed, intimate knowledge and understanding of the customer. The only way to develop this skill is by interacting with the customer and not by web research, no matter how sophisticated.

International capture efforts need to be led by someone who is very familiar with (ideally, native to) the culture of the customer. If your organization intends to sell significant volume through international offices, consider individuals' capture capabilities by office. Enhance capture skills through training, coaching, and job aids.

Capture skills are paramount when selecting a capture manager, so distinguish skills and knowledge. A person with capture skills can develop technical and customer knowledge, or team with people who offer these assets. In many organizations, the person in the sales role is best equipped to fill the capture manager role. A person with deep technical and customer knowledge might never develop the needed interpersonal capture skills. Similarly, we might understand a sport and devote thousands of hours to practice, but few of us will become professional athletes.

While sales and capture professionals must both be persuasive, the ideal capture professional demonstrates the skills summarized in figure 1. Established sales professionals usually possess most of the skills listed, and they have a direct financial interest in winning the opportunity. Perhaps the greatest disadvantage is that individuals in sales roles often lack the authority to commit additional resources. If you can afford both a sales professional and capture manager, then select a capture manager with the authority to identify and commit additional resources.

Most capture efforts are lost due to poor capture intelligence.

In addition to direct-sales tasks, a capture manager manages the team's capture activities:

- Intelligence collection and analysis
- Strategy development and implementation
- Customer contact and positioning
- Teaming
- Establishing price to win
- Proposal initiation, planning, and review
- Solution development, testing, and communication
- Post-submittal negotiation and closure
- Program initiation, start-up, and extension

ESSENTIAL SKILLS	ACTIONS THAT DEMONSTRATE THE SKILL
Leadership	Builds a common vision with the internal capture team, customers, and teaming partners.
Facilitation	Initiates and encourages collaborative team discussions.
Strategy Development	Builds customer-focused strategies and tactics.
Motivation	Creates a winning environment.
Data analysis	Turns data into useful intelligence.
Management	Keeps the team focused on tasks, schedules, and standards.
Persuasion	Convinces senior management to commit sufficient skills and resources.

Figure 1. Essential Capture Manager Skills. *Technical knowledge is a plus, but not paramount. Assign capture managers who can demonstrate or develop these essential skills.*

2 Take a *triumvirate approach* to defining core capture team roles.

The three core capture roles of the capture process are the **capture manager, proposal manager**, and **program or project manager**. While all three roles might be filled by a single person, they are distinct roles with discrete responsibilities.

The **capture manager** is responsible for winning or losing. The capture manager directs customer contact before, during, and after the proposal is submitted, conforming to the customer's rules. The capture manager owns the capture strategy and aligns tactical actions with this strategy.

The **proposal manager** leads the proposal team and is responsible for proposal resources, planning, scheduling, development, and production of the proposal. The primary focus of proposal management is to produce a winning proposal document. The proposal manager owns the proposal strategy, derived from the capture strategy, and clearly implements that strategy in the proposal document or presentation.

The **program or project manager** develops a winning solution that is compliant and responsive and is acceptable to the selling organization. Generally, the program manager is responsible to the strategic business unit manager for profitability and risk management.

Refine the roles and responsibilities of the triumvirate for your organization, depending upon the size of your organization, market, value of the opportunity, and skills of the people assigned to each role. Figure 2 summarizes the potential responsibilities by role.

ROLE	KEY RESPONSIBILITIES
Capture Manager Customer knowledge, marketing savvy, proposal experience, technical insight, creative casting experience, leadership skills, enthusiasm, organization knowledge, project management ability.	• Manages opportunity from pursuit decision through program start-up. • Develops capture plan and capture strategy. • Gathers and updates intelligence on competitive positioning. • Develops and owns capture strategy throughout opportunity lifecycle. • Builds and sustains customer relationships. • Plans and manages customer interface. • Defines and manages capture budget. • Leads competitive analysis, price-to-win analysis, and establishes team cost targets. • Oversees transition of capture plan into the proposal management plan. Mentors proposal core team on win strategy and solution. • Develops the first draft of the proposal executive summary. • Instigates and schedules decision gate reviews. Supports color team reviews. Drives or contributes to gate reviews. • Briefs senior management at decision gate/milestone reviews.
Proposal Manager Proposal management expertise, strong corporate knowledge, writing skills, ability to manage and coach writers, ability to present information orally, research skills, management savvy, strong work ethic.	• Develops proposal strategy, proposal themes, and proposal discriminators that align with the capture strategy. • Completes the executive summary initially drafted by the capture manager. • Develops and implements the proposal management plan. • Focuses on producing a winning document or presentation.
Program Manager Program management expertise, technically capable and knowledgeable, fiscal accounting and management ability, schedule discipline, organization skills, customer relations expertise, written and oral communication skills, basic knowledge of contracting processes, negotiation skills.	• Participates in or guides solution development, including technical issues, trade-off analysis, and costing approach. • Positions organization and solution with customer in coordination with the capture manager. • Develops conceptual program team and management approach and resolves program issues. • Leads program planning: Defines delivery team organization, skills, and staffing levels, and timing; WBS; program schedule; preliminary teaming, subcontracting, and vendor selection. • Supports intelligence collection and analysis, strategy development, and implementation. • Validates capture/proposal solution for practical execution in managing the program.

Figure 2. Key Triumvirate Capture Roles and Responsibilities. *Adapt the potential roles and responsibilities to the nuances of your organization and opportunities. Summarize the responsibilities by role in an attachment to the capture plan or in business development process guide.*

3

Identify an integrated capture team with the knowledge, skills, and experience needed to support the opportunity.

Communicate when:

- In doubt
- You suspect a problem
- Things seem perfect
- No one is complaining

Communicate to maintain focus and commitment.

Working with your triumvirate and selected senior managers, identify the key resources needed to form an integrated core team of functional experts, such as those listed in figure 3.

Strive to build the best team possible from across your organization. Do not settle for individuals who happen to be available.

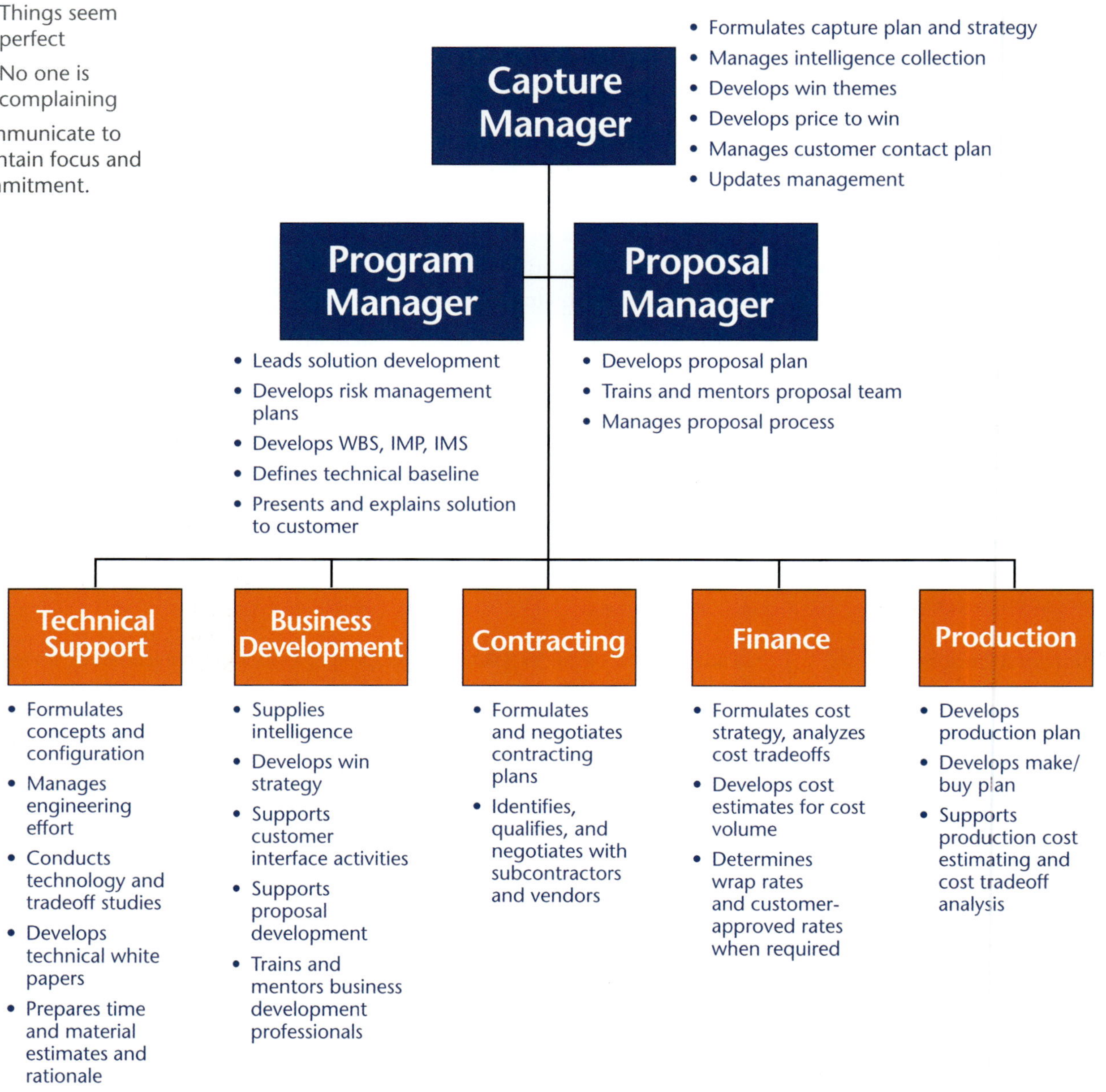

Figure 3. Involve Relevant Functional Departments. *Capture efforts are not a solo undertaking. Seek broad participation, incorporating functional departments whose expertise is needed to address evolving customer interests or concerns. While your organization might not look the same as the one illustrated, involve departments that support similar roles.*

4

The senior leadership sponsor *champions* the capture effort with the executive management team and mentors the capture manager. Link the champion with a counterpart in the customer organization.

Persuade senior leadership to commit adequate resources.

First, every capture manager needs a senior leadership sponsor. If one has not emerged naturally, seek and cultivate a sponsor. A capture team without a sponsor is usually wasting resources.

Next, identify the team and resources needed to capture the opportunity, and persuade senior leadership that your request is necessary, appropriate, and justifiable. Your objective is to position the customer to prefer your organization and solution. You need the personnel and resources to complete specific action and contact plan tasks. Justify the capture budget based on potential revenue, profitability, and the win probability.

Anticipate objections to team assignments and be poised to offer solutions. The best people often have prior commitments. Seek workarounds such as alternate schedules, parallel schedules, or advisory roles.

Place key individuals from subcontractor organizations into advisory roles for adding capture resources, reducing capture cost, and demonstrating to the customer that your subcontractors are as important and qualified as you claim.

Suggest other sources of funds. Identify synergies with other programs or capture activities.

5

See **Persuasion**, ***Proposal Guide***.

Differentiate generic and opportunity-specific capture training. Generic training familiarizes individuals with the purpose, principles, and concepts of capture planning. Opportunity–specific training focuses on the strategies and actions needed to win this opportunity. Team members who understand the concept can subsequently commit to their assigned role, task, and the need to integrate their efforts with the team.

See **Customer-Focused Capture Skills and Tactics**.

Trained, licensed MDs *practice* medicine. Similarly, trained capture professionals then *practice*, further developing their skills.

Train the capture team.

Train capture team members based on their roles and level of experience. Consider the role of senior management, capture team management, and capture team contributors. To be effective, members need to understand their roles and responsibilities and develop the skills to complete assigned tasks.

Opportunity-specific capture training fosters broad input, understanding of the opportunity, and acceptance of the capture strategy by team members. While the value of opportunity-specific training might be questioned, participants consistently conclude that
more progress was made in a few, highly focused days than was normally made in a few weeks. Minimize objections by linking opportunity-specific training and the formal capture kickoff.

Generic capture training focuses on developing different skill sets:

- Understanding the organization's process and individuals' roles within that process
- Developing interpersonal and collaborative skills in oral and written communication
- Using capture and proposal tools within a process framework
- Developing senior leadership's understanding of capture planning, their capture roles, and the impact of best practices on their organization

In a complex sale, interactions with the customer must be aligned. If not, customers doubt what you say. Training helps align participants' actions.

Involve your senior leadership sponsor in opportunity-specific training to signal the importance of this capture effort and foster continued member buy-in. If sponsors cannot attend the entire session, ask them to endorse the process, emphasize the importance of the opportunity, contribute to the strategy, and conduct an out-brief at the conclusion or immediately after the training.

If your senior managers cannot differentiate an effective capture plan from a poor capture plan, they need training. Having worked for the customer's organization is helpful but not sufficient to make them persuasive.

Training alone is insufficient to develop competent capture, program, and proposal managers. They also need coaching and experience.

Adapt how you train contributors based on their assigned roles and experience. Assess contributors' interpersonal communication and collaboration skills before asking them to interact with customers.

6

See Virtual Team Management, *Proposal Guide.*

Hold a kickoff meeting to jump-start the capture process.

Hold a capture kickoff meeting to demonstrate senior management support, empower the capture manager, and motivate the team to win the opportunity. While all kickoff meetings are motivational, informative, and directive, capture kickoff meetings tend to be more collaborative and smaller than proposal kickoff meetings.

When planning a capture kickoff, consider the following points:

- Invite key contributors, their immediate managers, and teaming partners if your teaming agreement is complete.
- Establish a competent, professional tone that inspires confidence in the capture manager and the entire triumvirate.
- Ask your senior management sponsor to open the kickoff meeting, validate the importance of the opportunity, and state what the win means to the participants and their managers. Managers of capture team members can be dismissed after capture activity priorities are discussed.
- Review and clarify roles, authority, and responsibilities
- Be realistic about problems and challenges. Be proactive in finding solutions, defining actions, and establishing responsibilities.
- Collaboratively solve problems. Encourage participants to raise issues and recommend solutions.
- Include vital contributors virtually if they cannot attend in person. Observe the additional ground rules for virtual meetings.

A basic capture kickoff agenda is shown in figure 4.

TIME	PERSON	TOPIC
5 minutes	Capture manager	Welcome and introduce participants.
5 minutes	Sponsor	Review importance, priorities.
10 minutes	Capture manager	Overview the opportunity.
5 minutes	Capture manager	Discuss process, roles of triumvirate and participants, expectations, rewards.
20 minutes	Capture manager	Review current capture plan.
20 minutes	Capture manager	Make task assignments and set the schedule; overview opportunity-specific information availability, access guidelines, and security arrangements.

Figure 4. Sample Capture Kickoff Agenda. *Incorporate these topics and approximate time allocations when developing your capture kickoff agenda. As the complexity of the opportunity increases, extend the time to overview the opportunity, review the capture plan, and discuss assignments.*

7

Delegate capture work with clear expectations, schedules, target completion dates, and reporting.

On major capture efforts, individual team members complete most tasks, not the capture manager. On smaller efforts, capture managers complete more of the tasks, and their role increasingly resembles the role of a sales or account manager.

For each assignment, define and clarify:

- Objective.
- Assigned individual(s).
- Deliverable, charge number, time allocation, and expected outcome.
- Expected detail.
- Key issues.
- Due date.
- Interim checkpoints/milestones.
- Linked tasks requiring coordination.
- Dependent tasks.

See Capture Scheduling.

Set completion dates for every task. Schedule gate reviews to communicate progress, seek management input, and gain management support. Schedule color team reviews, such as a Black Hat Review, to improve the quality of your capture efforts. Update task schedules as the opportunity progresses.

Synchronize capture efforts with the customer's buying process and schedule. Stay current on updates or changes to the customer's plans and schedules—good intelligence is vital. Decide how new information will be promptly and accurately shared within the capture team.

8 Keep senior management informed and involved, and never surprise your management sponsor.

Capture managers are an extension of management and are expected to keep management informed. Follow accepted protocol when addressing sensitive issues.

Discuss sensitive issues with your management sponsor. A surprised and embarrassed sponsor might cease support. Discuss if and how sensitive issues will be addressed in gate reviews or other meetings. Many issues are best handled in one-on-one discussions.

Consider the authority, accessibility, schedule constraints, and individual hot buttons of senior management. Identify and discuss tasks that will require hands-on management assistance.

Task senior managers to meet with customers and potential teaming partners. Seek management help to secure resources, compel indirect reports to complete tasks, and approve budgets.

9 Evaluate capture success.

The primary measure of capture success is the number and value of quality contracts won. Measuring interim success is more difficult.

Balance the effort to prepare a capture plan, and keep it current.

Define which elements will be reviewed at each gate review and the expected degree of completion of that element.

Color Team Reviews are business development milestones at which experts and managers work to improve opportunity pursuits.

See Decision Gates, Process.

Color team reviews, color teams, and *color reviews* all refer to the same type of event.

Color team members, color reviewers, and *review teams* all refer to people performing the color team review.

Color team can refer to the review itself or the group conducting it. Usually, context makes things clear.

Use color team reviews to enhance pursuit of leads in your opportunity funnel and effectiveness of your business development process. Conduct color team reviews to gain unbiased assessments of progress and constructive recommendations for improvement.

Differentiate color team reviews from decision gates. While decision gates determine whether to advance an opportunity to the next business development phase or end pursuit, color teams strengthen capture planning and proposal development efforts between gates.

Color team reviews are more tactical than strategic. Decision gates reflect executives' strategies, directions, goals, and priorities. In contrast, color teams help you move forward with the greatest chance of success.

Select reviewers with balanced customer, seller, management, technical, and cost perspectives. Align their backgrounds to the review. Select reviewers capable of offering constructive recommendations, independent of their seniority. Train reviewers if necessary. Do not assume they are qualified or knowledgeable based on their titles or seniority.

Make color team reviews constructive by defining and following a set process. Institutionalize key reviews for all opportunities. Add other reviews when they will benefit your organization.

Color Team Reviews

1. Define your organization's color team review points.
2. Follow a consistent process for each color team review.
3. Conduct a Blue Team to review capture planning and validate your win strategy.
4. Conduct a Black Hat Team to anticipate competitors' likely solutions and strategies and update your win strategy.
5. Conduct a Pink Team to verify compliance and execution of your win strategy.
6. Conduct a Red Team to predict how your proposal will be scored and make improvements to it.
7. Conduct a Green Team to review and approve pricing.
8. Conduct a Gold Team to confirm your proposal incorporates necessary changes from Red and Green Teams and is ready for the Proposal Submittal Decision.
9. Conduct a White Hat review to record lessons learned and make process improvements.
10. Select appropriate reviewers and methods for each color team review.

1

Define your organization's color team review points.

Most effective business development organizations are successful partly because they follow excellent and repeatable processes. While some organizations succeed in spite of or without defined processes, their probability of success could be increased by following known best practices.

Divide business development tasks into phases. Activities in any given phase reflect the maturity of the opportunity and customer actions. The number of phases might vary with the size of your business, organizational culture, and types of opportunities you pursue.

Schedule color team reviews suitable to the phases you establish. Figure 1 lists seven widely recognized reviews and their positions within Shipley's seven-phase model business development process. Several early phases have no reviews, either because individual opportunities have not been identified, or they are still being researched. Some later phases have several reviews, particularly Proposal Development.

No.	Phase	Color Team Reviews
0	Market Segmentation	
1	Long-Term Positioning	
2	Opportunity Assessment	
3	Capture Planning	**Blue Team:** *Reviews initial capture planning, focusing on development of win strategy* **Black Hat:** *Predicts competitors' solutions to support strategy development and infuse proposal with competitive focus*
4	Proposal Planning	
5	Proposal Development	**Pink Team:** *Reviews storyboards and mockups for compliance and execution of win strategy* **Red Team:** *Reviews proposal to predict scoring and improve effectiveness* **Green Team:** *Reviews pricing, consistency across volumes* **Gold Team:** *Reviews final proposal and price*
6	Post-Submittal Activities	**White Hat:** *Documents lessons learned to improve capture and proposal processes*

Figure 1. Each Review Has a Narrow Purpose. *Color teams' purposes are tied to the phases in which they occur. Blue Team and Black Hat help develop strategy during Capture Planning. Proposal Planning usually includes no color team reviews because the proposal is being planned to implement outcomes of those two early reviews. Pink, Red, Green, and Gold Teams occur in rapid sequence during Proposal Development and focus on creating a compliant, responsive, competitive sales document. White Hat reviews take place after proposals are submitted and help improve future efforts.*

See Process.

Explanations for color designations vary. One bit of proposal lore is that Black Hat originated with western movies in which the villain traditionally wore a black cowboy hat. Red Team may get its name from mark-ups in red ink on paper proposal copies. Some say Green Team refers to the color of money (though not in every country). If you hear a color associated with a team review, clarify what is to be reviewed.

As a minimum, systematically require reviews focused on three items:

- Competitors' probable offerings, to identify discriminators (Black Hat review).
- Proposal content and messages before drafting text (Pink Team).
- Proposal near-final content compared against the customer's needs and evaluation approach (Red Team).

Other reviews of your capture and proposal plans, solution, pricing, proposal documents, and lessons learned can be added when opportunities become larger, more complex, or simply play out over longer time spans. Some additional reviews will be new, with distinct purposes—but others will be second rounds of the same color teams as before.

Some companies use functional names instead of color identifiers to avoid confusion: strategy review instead of Blue Team or proposal design review rather than Pink Team. However, descriptive titles might not mean the same thing in different organizations.

Your goal for the review is more important than the name. Numerous additional reviews usually point to one of two situations:

- Customer personnel are delaying the procurement because they lack budget or agreement on what to buy.
- Your business development effort is not progressing as anticipated.

In either situation, consider ending the pursuit at a decision gate rather than holding more reviews.

A second Red Team usually signals the first went poorly, probably because a good Pink Team was not conducted before writing proposal text. Fewer, quality color teams are usually better than repeating color teams.

Finally, not including a named review in your process does not invalidate the goals for that review. For example, while pricing to win could be discussed at an early Green Team, the same activities and decisions might be encompassed by Blue Team or Black Hat reviews.

2

Follow a consistent process for each color team review.

Establish consistent standards for color team reviews. Insist that reviewers tell you how to improve, not what is wrong.

Make your reviews:

Comprehensive. Review all elements of any reviewed document using defined criteria. Consider all the facts, not just favorable ones.

Positive. Maintain a collaborative tone aimed at improving your chances, not demoralizing contributors.

Constructive. Require reviewers to recommend improvements and eliminate vague, negative comments.

Each color team review serves a different purpose, prompting a somewhat different form. Some emphasize review, discussion, improvement, or approval of capture or proposal team work. Others are hands-on working sessions that contribute directly to successful pursuit of the opportunity. Regardless of their nature, follow the general methodology outlined in figure 2.

PREPARE

- Plan and schedule in detail.
- Adjust dates to accommodate availability of key reviewers.
- Stick to published schedule.
- Identify members with requisite skills and authority for review.
- Limit involvement of capture or proposal team members to promote independence and avoid defensiveness.
- Train reviewers on purpose of review, tools to be used, and expected outcomes.
- Develop in-briefing with assignments, protocols, timing, documents to review, resources, and opportunity background.

CONDUCT

- Present in-briefing.
- Review individually, reading assigned documents, critiquing strengths and weaknesses, and recording findings and recommendations.
- Discuss as a group, categorizing and summarizing findings, consolidating recommendations, and agreeing on action items.
- Report results via review summary or debriefing for capture and proposal team members.

RESPOND

- Deliver debriefing to contributors.
- Collect, organize, and distribute products of review, including comment sheets, marked-up documents, scorecards, reports, and summaries.
- Support capture and proposal teams in responding to recommendations.
- Archive review materials for later reference.
- Execute and verify agreed action items.

Figure 2. Process for Color Team Reviews. *Take a consistent approach to all reviews. No matter the color of the review, follow the same process: prepare, conduct, and respond. At each step, follow the guidelines listed above.*

3

Conduct a Blue Team to review your capture plan and validate win strategy.

From Blue Team onwards, the capture team should follow the agreed win strategy unless evidence surfaces that it is not making you competitive.

The Blue Team review, often referred to as a win strategy review, is the first review of your evolving capture plan. Blue Team members are independent of the capture team and knowledgeable about the customer, your offerings and capabilities, and competitors' offerings and capabilities.

With inputs and outputs as shown in figure 3, the Blue Team's major objectives are to:

- Review your knowledge of the customer and the opportunity
- Review your potential technical and management solutions, verifying their compliance and responsiveness to customer needs
- Agree on strategic actions you can take to position your organization as the customer's preferred choice

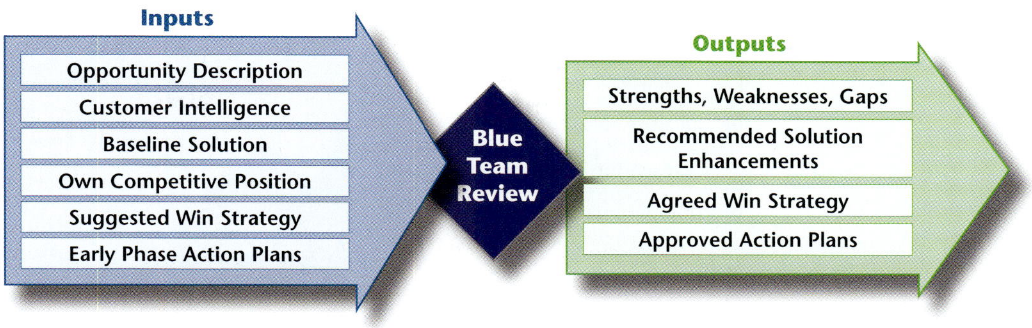

Figure 3. Blue Team Inputs and Outputs. *The Blue Team analyzes concepts represented by the initial capture plan. Members identify strengths, weaknesses, and gaps, and then recommend improvements. They affirm early capture team actions or recommend modifications. They do not allocate or withdraw resources; the capture manager and executive team will make those decisions at decision gates.*

Blue Team reviews often include both strategy development and approval. In large organizations, the capture team usually develops the win strategy. Blue Team then confirms or adjusts. In smaller organizations where roles overlap, Blue Team might be the working session where the winning approach is crafted. Without Blue Team approval, the capture team will be second-guessed on succeeding activity.

As pursuit cycles lengthen, multiple Blue Teams might be constructive. Where Blue Team #1 would look at a very preliminary capture plan and solution set, Blue Team #2 might assess a more complete plan, review a formal proposal management plan, and confirm a more advanced proposal strategy. Consider a second Blue Team if the Black Hat review prompts you to significantly modify your capture strategy or solution.

4 Conduct a Black Hat review to anticipate competitors' likely strategies and solutions and update your win strategy.

While ideal reviewers are independent of the capture team, embrace experts on your competitors wherever you find them.

Consider outside consultants as sources of knowledge about competitors.

The Black Hat review assesses relative positions of known competitors, including your own organization, providing a basis for improving your strategy and competitive posture. As shown in figure 4, the team predicts competitors' solutions and strategies so you can counter them during both Capture Planning and Proposal Development.

Schedule your Black Hat review about midway through Capture Planning. Feedback from the Black Hat review will help the capture team further refine their efforts, leading to the Preliminary Bid Decision.

The best Black Hats empanel separate groups, each knowledgeable about a different competitor and charged to create a capture plan for that competitor. This best practice approach is expensive and time consuming.

When separate groups are not feasible or affordable, have one team prepare mini-capture plans for two or three major competitors (or competitor types).

In the most affordable approach, have the capture team prepare the competitive analysis, construct or update a bidder comparison chart, and develop a win strategy based on relative strengths and weaknesses revealed. When honestly done, this method can yield excellent insights.

Black Hat reviews might be conducted multiple times in major competitions. Subsequent reviews are prompted by major changes in requirements, competition, or competitors' probable solutions.

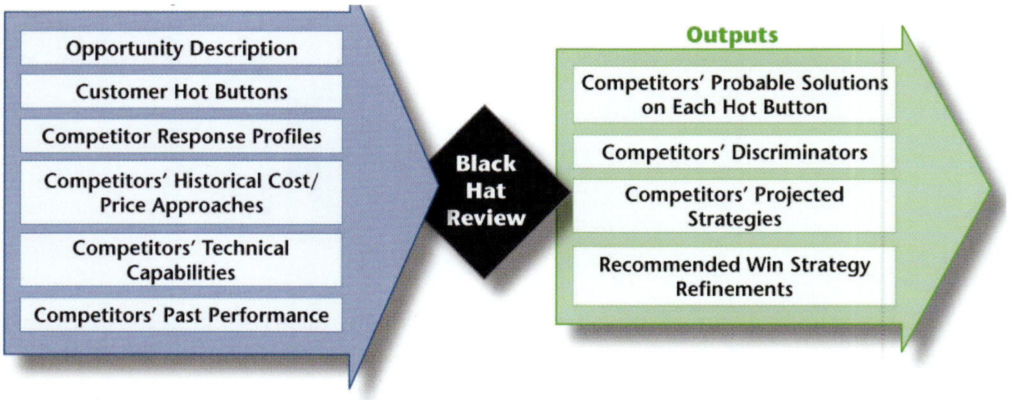

Figure 4. Black Hat Inputs and Outputs. *The Black Hat reviews a partial capture plan, which is somewhat more developed than the initial capture plan presented to the Blue Team. Depending on knowledge and sophistication of Black Hat reviewers, they either develop or critique the competitor analysis, construct or update a bidder comparison chart, and refine win strategy.*

5

Conduct a Pink Team to verify compliance and execution of your win strategy

The Pink Team reviews proposal storyboards, mockups, or writing plans before text is drafted. Top proposal practitioners consider Pink Team the most important review. More proposals fail because of poorly executed or nonexistent Pink Teams than any other cause.

Team members review inputs listed in figure 5 to verify compliance and responsiveness. They verify how well the proposal team is executing the approved win strategy and recommend necessary changes. This powerful influence over how the proposal will be completed dictates knowledgeable and empowered Pink Team members.

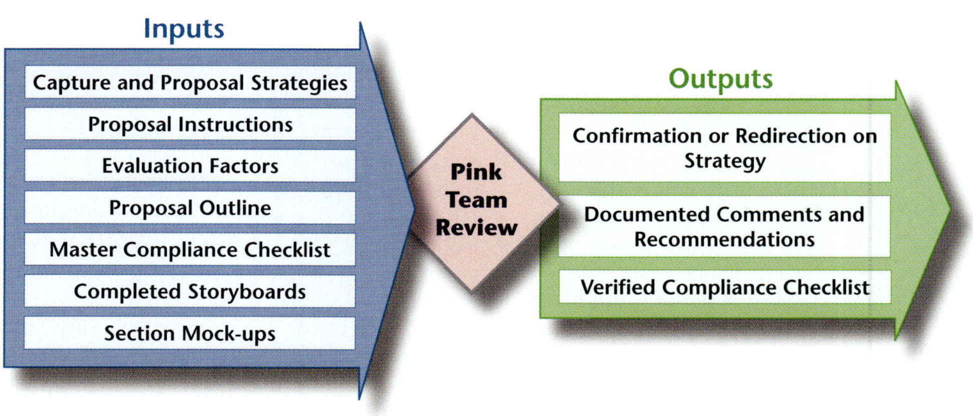

Figure 5. Pink Team Inputs and Outputs. *The Pink Team reviews the entire planned proposal—in the form of storyboards and mockups—against the customer's proposal instructions and evaluation factors. It verifies total compliance with requirements of the solicitation, responsiveness to unstated customer issues, and satisfactory expression of the approved capture and proposal strategies. It also reviews the effectiveness of theme statements, visuals, and action captions. Pink Team outputs should confirm or redirect strategy, document recommendations, and verify the compliance checklist.*

The Pink Team is usually scheduled approximately one-third of the way between the proposal kickoff meeting and submission. Consider two Pink Teams, especially if the customer issues a good draft solicitation. The first reviews early content planning. The second comes after the final solicitation and reviews updates and late changes in the customer's acquisition plans. You cannot verify compliance until the customer's final request is released.

The Pink Team should consolidate its findings and either brief the proposal team or furnish documented recommendations to the proposal manager for action. Present recommendations constructively to authors as suggestions for improvements rather than negative criticism of their work. Emphasize that early changes eliminate or reduce inconvenient, frantic, last-minute rewrites.

6

Conduct a Red Team to predict how your proposal will be scored and make improvements to it.

While much of this advice is aimed at proposal managers, your success as a capture manager often hinges on the effectiveness of your Red Team review. Stay involved before, during, and after the Red Team review. Help identify, recruit, brief, and debrief reviewers.

The Red Team review predicts how well your near-final proposal would be scored by the customer. It recommends improvements to customer focus, completeness, and clear communication of your solution and win strategy.

Avoid exploring new solutions, new themes, or major changes in direction. Strategy changes should have been directed by the Pink Team. Best practice is to arrange about one-third overlap between Pink and Red Team members to avoid conflicting suggestions.

Red Team members should be independent of the proposal team and offer different perspectives. Effective teams include experts on the customer; the customer's industry; competitors; your organization, technology, and approach; and on preparing and presenting winning proposals. To prevent Red Teams from degenerating into editing sessions, follow guidance in figure 6.

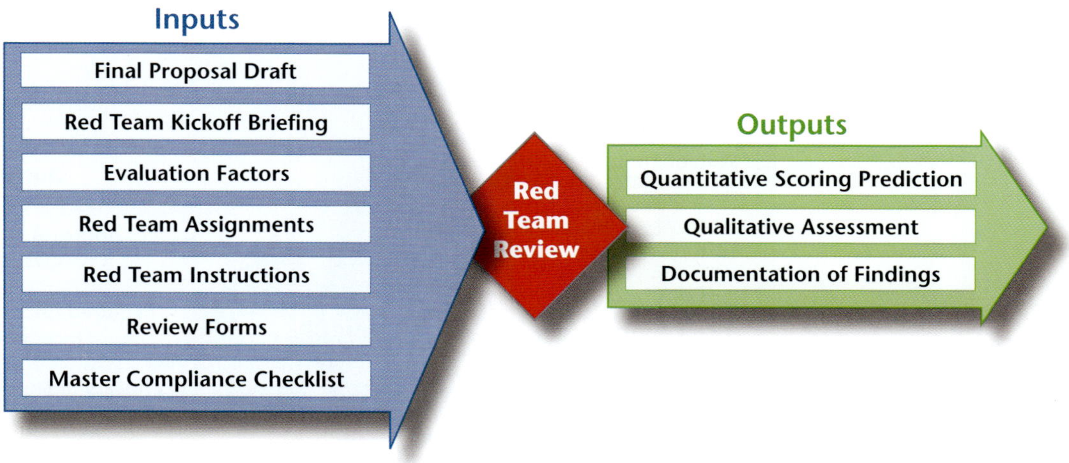

Figure 6. Red Team Inputs and Outputs. *The Red Team reviews the near-final proposal. Just as the customer's evaluation team will review your entire proposal, the Red Team must review every word, number, and visual. Thorough in-briefings are essential. Arm the Red Team with the customer's evaluation factors, detailed assignments, instructions, methods for recording review comments and results, and the master compliance checklist. Outputs include a quantitative scoring prediction, a qualitative assessment of the document, and complete back-up documentation.*

Schedule Red Team about two-thirds of the way through Proposal Development, early enough that when changes are made to one part of the proposal, coordinating adjustments can be made to others.

Include the price volume in your Red Team review. You may not have final numbers, but verify that required contents will have a place when available.

Ask reviewers to consolidate findings to minimize conflicting recommendations. Complicated reviews of larger proposals need to be controlled using a standard set of feedback tools. Train reviewers to use these tools.

7 Conduct a Green Team to review and approve pricing.

See Pricing to Win

The Green Team reviews near-final pricing. It compares your pricing against documentation of your technical, management, and other non-price solution elements to confirm everything is included in the estimate, helps prevent discrepancies, and maintains alignment with your price to win. It may also examine financial risk, cash flow projections, and return on investment.

Major objectives of the Green Team review are advance knowledge and approval of proposed pricing by relevant executives before the final Proposal Submittal Decision. Hasty, last-minute price cuts lead to frequent proposal errors. Exact estimating and approval procedures within your organization will dictate when it is scheduled.

Some organizations combine Green Team with Red Team, but in many cases, full pricing information takes longer to develop than the rest of the proposal, delaying review of the final price. In those cases, the Red Team can still review the price proposal narrative and graphics, subject to numerical updates. Other organizations prefer holding the Green Team first, allowing the Red Team to verify that changes caused by price modifications have been correctly folded into the proposal.

Because price influences competitiveness, Green Teams consider information from customer, capture team, and proposal team sources, as shown in figure 7. This information is often in spreadsheets, tables, bases of estimates, and raw calculations. Green Team members are seldom disposed toward detailed price volume review, focusing on the deal rather than the documents.

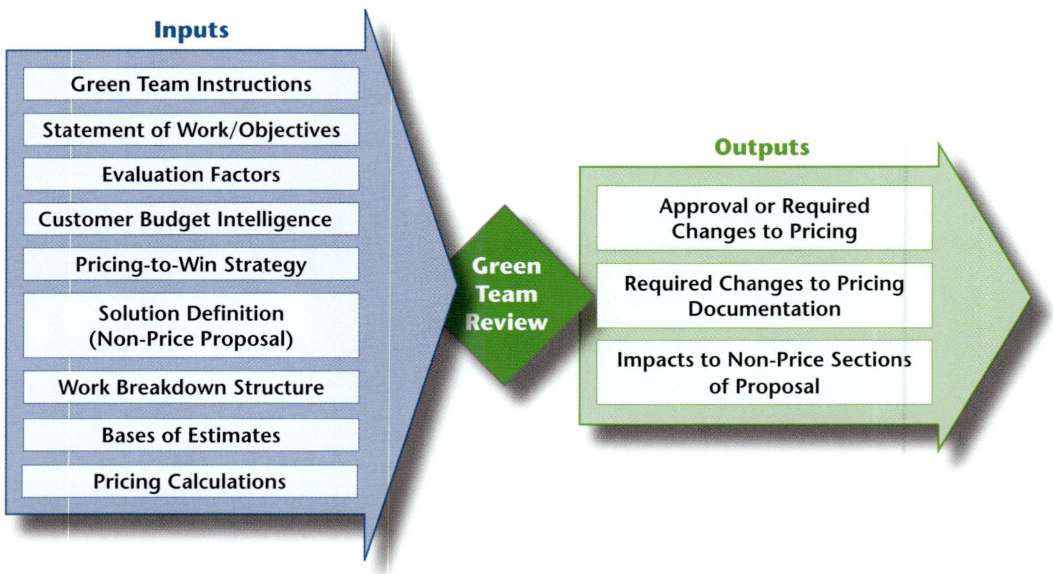

Figure 7. Green Team Inputs and Outputs. *Price both derives from and influences every other aspect of your proposal, so Green Teams use inputs from many sources. Outputs are fewer, including either approval or required changes to pricing and associated portions of the proposal.*

If multiple Green Teams are held, the first generally occurs during capture planning, and reviews your price to win—that targeted combination of capability and price thought to appeal to the customer's values. The second is the actual pricing review near the Red Team.

8 Conduct a Gold Team to confirm your proposal incorporates necessary changes from Red and Green Teams and is ready for the Proposal Submittal Decision.

The Gold Team reviews the final version of the proposal. It confirms improvements recommended by Red and Green Teams have been incorporated. It also verifies proposal document quality and conformance to organizational standards.

The Gold Team is not the time to modify your price, change your solution, or improve grammar. The Gold Team finds errors in the submission. In summary, Gold Team determines if the sales document is ready for the Proposal Submittal Decision—the final authorization to deliver it to the customer.

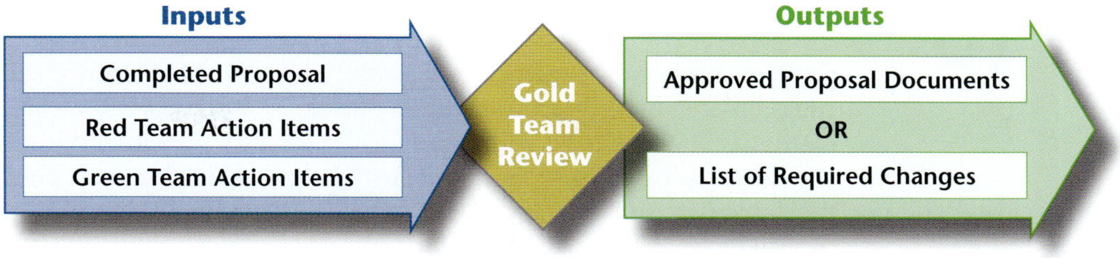

Figure 8. Gold Team Inputs and Outputs. *The Gold Team reviews the fully completed proposal, including all volumes, letters, electronic files, and other material requested by the customer. This version is checked against Red and Green Team recommendations. Two outputs are possible: approved proposal documents and files, ready for the Proposal Submittal Decision gate, or a list of required changes.*

9 Conduct a White Hat review to record lessons learned and make process improvements.

Your business development process should be owned by someone charged with constantly looking for ways to improve it. Include that person as a White Hat observer, but do not let them defend the process or you will receive less valuable feedback.

The White Hat review is a lessons-learned or after-action review conducted shortly after you submit your proposal. It helps improve your organization's business development operations. The White Hat's objectives are:

- Assess the effectiveness of your capture and proposal strategies
- Determine the quality of your competitive intelligence
- Critique your capture and proposal processes
- Evaluate management decisions

Unlike other reviews that focus on improving your chances of winning a specific opportunity, the White Hat focuses on improving your chances of winning future opportunities.

The first part of the review focuses on your internal successes, problems, and improvements. Conduct it while memories are fresh. The second part looks at the pursuit from the customer's perspective. Incorporate customer feedback about why you won or lost, if available. If not, delay the second part of the review until customer feedback is available, likely following the award decision.

Conclusions from both portions of the White Hat are documented and used to improve processes. Remember, lessons recorded are not lessons learned unless they motivate change.

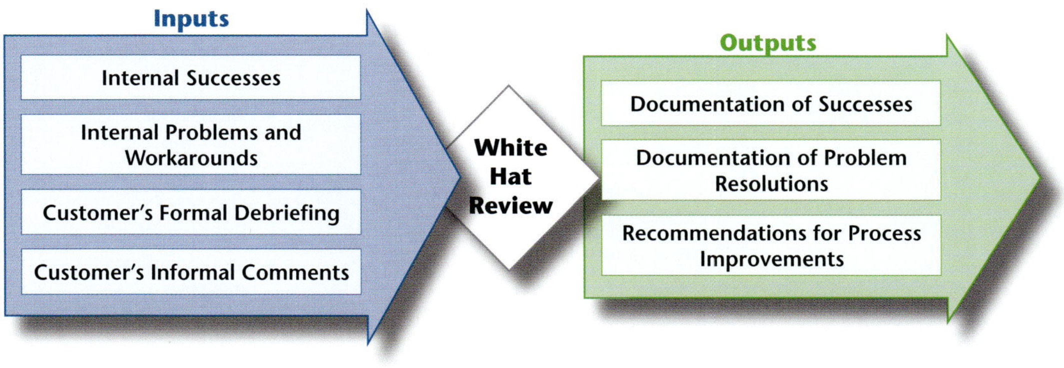

Figure 9. White Hat Inputs and Outputs. *Internal inputs on both successes and problems and their workarounds come from members of the capture and proposal teams after their efforts are complete. External feedback, both formal and informal, comes from customers. Document what worked well and what did not. Recommend steps and activities to continue and methods or approaches to change.*

10 Select appropriate reviewers and methods for each color team review.

Color team reviewers are managers, staff, subject matter experts, and sometimes outside consultants. Staff reviews with personnel who have the expertise to contribute to the particular team. Increase the breadth of each review by increasing the diversity of reviewers. Minimize reviewers who have been contributors. They seldom maintain clear perspectives. Once a review is complete, reviewers can often help implement recommendations.

If your organization values checks and balances, top executives should contribute primarily to decision gates, not color teams.

When executives become too invested in the work of a color team, they can lose objectivity for subsequent decision gates. And the color team recommendations are biased by executive input.

Figure 10 summarizes suggestions on planning and staffing color team reviews. Notice the emphasis on independent leaders of Blue Teams, Black Hats, Pink Teams, and Red Teams. However, Green Teams, Gold Teams, and White Hats should be led by personnel close to decisions and pursuit activities.

Align your methods or processes to the review as suggested in figure 10.

Review	Organizer	Candidate Team Members	Other Potential Attendees	Primary Documents	Methods to Consider
Blue Team	• Capture manager	• Independent Blue Team leader • Business development management • Operational management • Experts on customer • Product/service experts	• Capture manager • Capture team	• Pursuit Decision package • Initial capture plan	• Structured presentation • Individual review • Facilitated discussion • Brainstorming
Black Hat	• Capture manager	• Independent Black Hat leader • Business development management • Experts on competitors • Product/service experts	• Capture manager • Capture team	• Blue Team summary report • Partial capture plan • Black Hat summary report	• Competitor simulation by teams • Group discussion of key competitors or competitor types • Consultant analyses • Capture team analysis • Bidder comparison chart
Pink Team	• Proposal manager	• Independent, respected Pink Team leader • Line managers • Subcontractor executives • Business development managers • Subject matter experts	• Capture manager • Program manager	• Blue Team and Black Hat summary reports (or capture plan) • Request for Proposals • Compliance checklist and proposal outline • Storyboards and mockups	• Walking the wall • Sequential presentation • Virtual review of planning documents • Independent compliance verification

Review	Organizer	Candidate Team Members	Other Potential Attendees	Primary Documents	Methods to Consider
Red Team	• Proposal manager	• Red Team preparation leader • Independent Red Team leader • Executives • Teammate executives • Operations personnel • Subject matter experts • Customer experts • Pink Team members	• Capture manager • Red Team preparation task lead	• Final proposal draft • Customer's evaluation factors	• Mirror of customer's evaluation process • Detailed in-briefing • Vertical section reviews • Horizontal reviews of headings, theme statements, graphics and captions, and callouts • Independent compliance check • Gadfly review to check for consistency • Proposal team debriefing • Core team recovery to minimize personnel involved
Green Team	• Proposal manager	• Executive who must approve price • Operations Personnel • Pricing manager • Capture manager	• Proposal manager • Price volume manager	• Request for proposals • Capture plan • Complete solution definition, 4e, non-price proposal • Pricing documents and worksheets	• Pricing spreadsheet review • Cross-volume comparison • Closed-door meetings due to closely held information
Gold Team	• Proposal manager	• Proposal manager • Proposal volume managers (if assigned) • Capture manager • Pricing manager • Red Team leader (if available) or deputy • Green Team leader (if available)	• Publication and/or production manager • Proposal coordinator	• Completed proposal, with all letters, documents, electronic files, attachments, other required material • Red and Green Team action item lists	• Action item check-off • Horizontal spot checks • Delivery media evaluation
White Hat	• Capture manager • Proposal manager	• Proposal team • Capture team • Business development management	• Business development process custodian	• Internal survey results • Customer debriefing	• Well-documented team discussions • Customer debriefing analysis in context of business development lifecycle • Competitor success/ failure analysis • Standardized survey to compare effort to other pursuits • Direct, tailored questions about the pursuit

Figure 10. Appropriate Reviewers and Methods. *Adapt your choice of organizer, reviewers, documents, and methods or process to the opportunity, your organization, schedule, and strategic importance. The table summarizes a range of methods for quality reviews.*

Use vertical and horizontal reviews of customer-bound documents. Vertical reviews focus on a single topic or section. Horizontal reviews focus on the consistency, continuity, and quality of a single element across the entire proposal.

Costing requirements vary by market and are unique to every organization. In government markets with one customer and few sellers, sellers might be required to base their prices on a defined set of costing rules plus an allowable profit margin.

In open markets with many customers and sellers, cost is one of many factors used to set the price. In proposals to governments, costs often must be disclosed, profit margins must follow prescribed guidelines, assumptions and rationales are questioned, and the final price is usually negotiated.

Consider this paradox:

- Most sellers say customers in their market select the solution with the lowest price.
- Most customers say they seldom select the solution with the lowest price.

The reality is that most customers try to select the best value solution within their budget.

This Costing section focuses on developing the cost of your solution and then supporting and presenting that cost credibly to the customer. Determining the winning price (i.e., estimating the customer's tradeoff between capability and purchase price) is the focus of the Price-to-win topic section.

Costing

1. Differentiate cost, price, and value.
2. Develop should-costs or cost bogeys early.
3. Define a costing strategy that supports your sales strategy.
4. Base cost estimating rationale on the assumption that nothing is new; everything has been done before.
5. Prepare or tailor written estimating guidelines for each competition.
6. Minimize negotiated price decrements by using the most credible rationale.

1 Differentiate cost, price, and value.

Begin with common definitions:

- Cost is what it costs you to deliver the solution, not the cost to the customer.
- Price is what you charge for a product or service.
- Value is your customer's perception of what the product or service is worth.
- Added value is the difference between the customer's perception of the total value of the solution and what it costs them to fully implement the solution.

Value is both tangible and intangible. Tangible value is the quantified improvement in a customer's profit or a decreased loss. Intangible value is by definition not easily quantified and is often undervalued.

Even for government procurements, price is rarely the single factor that determines a buying decision. Other, less tangible factors influence the buying decision, contributing to the customer's perception of value. This is true, even for commodity items. When buying a gallon of fuel, a driver will value the relative safety, cleanliness, convenience, and courtesy of a service station to justify or rationalize a higher or lower fuel price.

2 Develop should-costs or cost bogeys early.

In early meetings with customers, try to understand the approximate cost of their needs and the potential budget to eliminate their problem. The earlier the process, the less precise the estimate. Note that most customers have some idea of what a reasonable estimate should be but are reluctant to disclose it.

Avoid giving your initial solution development and costing team a broad description of the customer's requirements without a cost bogey or target. Without a target, the first cost roll-up often reveals that the cost of your solution far exceeds the customer's budget.

When governments audit your costs, as is done in the U.S., should you disclose cost bogeys to the proposal team? Best practices vary. Depending on the local Defense Contract Audit Agency office, cost bogeys disclosed to team members may be considered cost and pricing data, and must be disclosed. For this reason, some proposal managers use cost bogeys to sanity-test estimates but do not disclose cost bogeys to the team.

Develop your should-cost using top-down and bottom-up approaches until they converge.

- Top-down costing begins with each customer's perception of value, the customer's budget, and comparisons with other similar projects, adjusted as appropriate. The overall target price is broken into target costs, bogeys, or should-cost estimates by task, service, and hardware.

  Establishing early should-cost estimates reduces the number of cost and design iterations. Accurate, top-down estimates assume similar methods, materials, and processes.

- Bottom-up costing is simply a cost roll-up of time and material estimates with appropriate overheads added. The inherent weakness of bottom-up costing is that estimators tend to incorporate safety factors at each cost level to avoid subsequent blame for cost overruns.

Seven alternative approaches to costing are summarized in figure 1, along with the advantages and disadvantages of each approach.

APPROACH	ADVANTAGES	DISADVANTAGES
Research: Collect information on customer budgets and program funding.	Rough target for bid price can be developed by deleting customer administrative costs from funding.	Does not consider competitive approaches; funding estimates are usually based on outdated historical data and poor understanding of technology.
Expert judgment: Consult with one or more experts.	Little or no historical data needed; good for new or unique projects.	Experts tend to be biased; knowledge level can be questionable.
Parametric models: Use design parameters and mathematical algorithms.	Fast and easy to use; useful early in program; objective, repeatable; often used by customer early in funding development.	Can be inaccurate if not properly calibrated and validated; expensive to maintain models; historical data used for calibration may not be valid for new project.
Analogy techniques: Compare with similar programs.	Based on actual experience.	Often, no truly similar program exists; not used alone; better used to check estimates.
Competitive analysis: Examine competitor history and technology to determine likely offering.	Provides understanding of strengths and weaknesses of competitors; can better target proposal at competition; investigates technology tradeoffs.	May not know teaming and vendor solutions; cannot be sure of pricing/profit decisions by competitor management; competitors may not share same understanding of program; historical data may not fit current opportunity.
Bottom-up techniques: Unit costs are totaled to determine cost and effort.	Provides a detailed basis for cost estimating; promotes individual accountability; useful mainly for cost tracking after award.	Time- and cost-intensive; sometimes results in double dipping on estimates and usually results in higher costs; historical data not always available to support estimates; may not capture costs of integration; focuses on individual requirements, not overall program.
Top-down techniques: Unit costs are based on customer budget and historical data.	Begins with customer budget information and results in customer-focused solution; helps enforce traceability between cost and technical; uses historical actuals.	Requires good information on customer and competition; requires significant amount of work and adherence to a pricing process; often is erroneously based on conjecture rather than supported with validated information.

Figure 1. Alternative Costing Approaches. *Organizations tend to select costing approaches based upon tradition, history, or convenience. If alternative approaches converge on a common cost, our confidence increases. Consider the customers' views; customers seriously question estimates based upon expert judgment.*

3

See STRATEGY.

See Service Proposals, Guideline 7.

Incumbents often have less latitude to suggest changes in how services are delivered. Customers wonder why the incumbent's cost-saving proposals have not already been implemented.

Define a costing strategy that supports your sales strategy.

A sales strategy that emphasizes leading-edge performance is inconsistent with a costing strategy that emphasizes selecting the lowest cost components, methods, suppliers, and subcontractors. Similarly, a sales strategy that emphasizes the efficiency and productivity of the seller is inconsistent with a high cost. When technical and cost teams are physically separate without an agreed costing strategy, the solution is usually technically superior and high-cost.

First, influence—or at least determine—whether the customer is seeking lowest total added value, maximum technical performance, market image, minimum acquisition cost, or total cost of ownership. Next, determine competitors' probable approaches. Finally, adopt a discriminating position aligned with the customer's needs.

Develop your solution based on what the customer values:

- Add low cost features that the customer values highly.
- Eliminate costly features that the customer does not value.

Try to persuade the customer to require a solution that is better matched to your capabilities than to your competitors'. The key is influencing the bid request early. Your aim is to establish requirements that are expensive for competitors to meet.

If you are late in the competition and trying to find a solution for a bid request influenced by a competitor, try to reengineer the customer's vision. Persuade the customer to value your discriminators more highly than competitors' discriminators. The success of this strategy hinges on whether the customer has the latitude to change the requirements or to select a noncompliant solution.

Do all you can to influence the requirements favorably. For example, when competing for a cost-driven services contract, brainstorm ways to reduce your cost by asking the following questions:

- How can we reduce management layers?
- Can we increase management's span of control?
- Where should we place people within grades?

4

Base cost estimating rationale on the assumption that nothing is new; everything has been done before.

Given this advice, a medical researcher asked, "How do I know what it will cost to cure cancer?" The reply, "That is not what you are proposing to do. That's the customer's goal. You are proposing to do a literature search, conduct certain tests, analyze the results, and then prepare draft and final reports."

Cost analysts in the government sector assume everything has been done before. Base your estimating rationale on the same assumption.

In any selling environment, few customers want to purchase serial #001. The risk of being the first is often too great. Base estimates on the most similar historic tasks. Break down the project until you can identify subtasks that are similar to subtasks from prior projects.

5

Prepare or tailor written estimating guidelines for each competition.

Unique, complex programs require new estimating guidelines for each competition. For services or products that are similar from bid to bid, consider whether your current guidelines warrant tailoring.

Estimating guidelines cover the following types of assumptions:

- Program schedule and milestones to determine when costs occur.
- Work Breakdown Structure (WBS) to indicate what work will be done by which cost centers.
- A make versus buy subcontracting determination.
- A Statement of Work (SOW) and WBS dictionary to define the services and products to be delivered.
- Relevant financial ground rules regarding escalation, facility capitalization, facilities and locations of work, direct labor and overhead rates, preapproved rates, etc.
- A deliverables list, including all hardware, services, and data.
- The level at which costs will be estimated, disclosed, and reported, if required.

Estimating ground rules should be written for the following reasons:

- Only written ground rules are auditable and defensible, both externally and internally.
- Estimators working in teams must be consistent.
- When costs must be disclosed, include the ground rules in the cost volume introduction to increase your credibility.
- Partners, vendors, and subcontractors need ground rules to give accurate and competitive estimates.
- Written ground rules reduce both schedule and cost risk.

6 Minimize negotiated price decrements by using the most credible rationale.

Government procurement officials typically require full disclosure of all task descriptions, cost estimates, and rationale. The soundness of the rationale determines their subsequent price negotiating position. A poor rationale leads to larger price decrements during negotiations.

U.S. government auditors rank estimating rationale in the following order, from most to least reliable:

1. Firm, negotiated, forward price agreement.
2. Actual historic cost with appropriate escalation.
3. Quotation from vendor (internal or external).
4. Engineering estimate.

Customer-Focused Capture Skills and Tactics

Customer-Focused Capture Skills and Tactics require an aligned team of individuals with the interface skills to listen actively, establish rapport, build trust, assess situations accurately, collaborate effectively, and communicate persuasively. Invest your time and attention helping customers meet their goals and objectives, and they are more likely to invest their time and money with you.

See Capture Planning.

The most overlooked aspect of capture planning is developing the ability of capture team members to interact persuasively with members of the buying team.

Selling and capture planning are similar disciplines. Selling is an ancient concept, but sales as a methodology began in the 1920s. Capture planning originated in the 1980s as a process to favorably position complex solutions.

Both disciplines emphasize engaging customers early in the business development process by establishing productive working relationships, thus improving win probability.

Selling methodologies, however, emphasize an individual selling to individuals or small groups, while capture planning emphasizes teams selling to teams.

Consider the following:

- Organizations selling to governments are more likely to embrace capture concepts and less likely to train capture participants to interact with customers. They often select people for marketing and capture roles because they previously worked for the customer or have broad service and product expertise, but they assume adequate interface skills.

  For example, a high-ranking government civilian employee is often hired by a large contractor because of customer *connections* rather than because of strong customer interface skills.

- Organizations in the B2B sector employ sales professionals and invest more heavily in their training and development than any other group of employees. Yet while management espouses team selling, sales professionals often limit fellow employees' contacts with their accounts because they doubt their colleagues' customer interface skills.

Three familiar quotes reinforce the importance of connecting with customers:

> *The aim of marketing is to know and understand the customer so well that the product or service fits him or her and sells itself.*
>
> —Peter Drucker

> *The fact is, everyone is in sales. Whatever area you work in, you do have clients and you do need to sell.*
>
> —Jay Abraham

> *This may seem simple, but you need to give customers what they want, not what you think they want. And, if you do this, people will keep coming back.*
>
> —John Ilhan

Few organizations offer services or products that sell themselves. Develop the interface skills of your capture team members so they discern what each customer wants, and jointly create the preferred solution. Then deliver the solution effectively so customers become repeat customers.

Customer-Focused Capture Skills and Tactics

1. Recognize how customers buy, and then exploit varied sales opportunities.
2. Help customers discover potential benefits.
3. Accord uniqueness to every individual and organization.
4. Never assume. Ask.
5. Actively listen during every customer interaction.
6. Establish rapport and build trust by becoming a trusted advisor.
7. Interact effectively with groups. Facilitate your meetings.
8. Anticipate and handle objections throughout the capture process.
9. Test your potential solution with the customer early and often.
10. Develop a logical business case for buying.
11. Seek agreement rather than close the sale.

1 Recognize how customers buy, and then exploit varied sales opportunities.

How private and public sector customers buy is affected internally by their vision, objectives, and immediate needs; externally by the economy, technology, laws, regulations, and customs; and by the personal issues, needs, and experiences of the individuals involved. In general, these principles apply:

1. Customers frequently buy from people who *know their stuff*. Customers will not waste their time or have patience with anyone who is less knowledgeable, less skilled. Often people are rushed, impatient, and demanding to tolerate an under-trained sales person.
2. Customers buy from people they trust. Schmoozing is likely to turn off rather than motivate the customer to buy, especially in a government environment. Schmoozers are viewed as time wasters and superficial people. Customers want to buy from those who will treat them right.
3. Customers want the best deal. That means value (perceived worth). Sellers who offer real value are most likely to win the contract, other things being equal. If you are perceived as rigid or stuffy, you will not make the sale unless you have a monopoly. Does your customer have to buy from you?
4. Capture team members who have the ability to listen and understand what customers want and need have the competitive edge. You must learn quickly what your customers need and how they buy.
5. Capture team members who know how to sell the way their customers prefer to buy have the competitive edge if they also have the products and services that customers need.
6. Capture team members who can demonstrate that they offer the best solution have the advantage.

Learning to interface with customers based on these principles will advance the relationship and the sale. Consider how many members of your capture team participate in these types of sales opportunities:

- **Industry days** are an excellent forum to meet potential decision makers, stakeholders, and influencers. Your attendance and participation are important; equally important is establishing credibility, rapport, and trust.
- **Bidders' conferences** are opportunities to gather competitor information and details about customer issues, requirements, evaluation criteria, and restrictions or limitations. Potential one-on-one connections, when allowed, are invaluable if you are prepared.
- **Trade shows** offer a showcase for personnel, services, and products. Decision makers and influencers are often more accessible than at their base location. Seize the opportunity to meet potential teaming partners, decision makers, program personnel, and competitors.
- **E-mail** is a frequently underestimated and overlooked opportunity to interact with customers. The frequency, tone, and content of your e-mail messages say a lot about you, your selling style, and your organization. Actively manage e-mail traffic and strategies to maintain consistent content and tone.
- **Telephone** conversations and conference calls advance the relationship. Leave detailed, concise, and relevant voice mail messages. Rambling, disorganized messages hurt the relationship.
- **Face-to-face meetings** require active listeners. Probe for information that is not publicly available. Proposing your solution before customer needs and issues are clearly identified and a business case can be established is unproductive at best and potentially arrogant and off-putting at worst.
- **Site visits** offer relatively unguarded opportunities for multiple one-on-one interactions among members of the buying and selling teams. Capture team members must understand their role, listen carefully, and stay on message.
- **Web 2.0** social media offer unguarded networking opportunities. Use, but use with caution. Assume that competitors will see your posts.

2 Help customers discover potential benefits.

You cannot fake sincerity or integrity. Being honest and up-front with your customer is your only option. Credibility is difficult to gain and easy to lose.

Plan, initiate, and maintain the focus of customer interactions on the customer. Help them discover, analyze, and quantify, if possible, the potential benefits to them and their organization. Discover the potential benefits the customer envisions before focusing on the benefits of your solution.

In complex sales with complex solutions, discover, explore, and analyze the breadth of customer issues and concerns. Undiscovered issues often turn into objections.

The stereotypical adversarial customer-seller relationship is outdated. Foster a relationship where you are collaborating to solve a customer problem. In most situations, your collaborative discussion will expose underlying issues and deepen your customer's and your own understanding of the potential benefits derived from reducing or eliminating the customer's problem.

Take the customer-focused capture challenge: *Can you attest that every person on your capture team accepts and practices a customer-focused capture approach? If not, what are you doing to make it so?*

3 Accord uniqueness to every individual and organization.

Think of every customer as a new friend you are trying to help. As with new friends, you cannot sound or appear to be overly familiar, or you will appear insincere.

Every customer has different issues and concerns that are important to that customer to achieve his or her objectives. Whether buying commodities, complex services, or products, each customer, organization, and situation is unique.

- **Commodities:** Commodities are assumed to be items with no perceived differences other than price. How many commodities meet this definition? For example, assume that you are purchasing flour in a market. Choices among just the wheat flours are whole, unbleached, bleached, all-purpose, bread, and pastry flour. Sources of the flours include store brand, national brand, specialty, and certified organic flours. Considering these options and as a unique buyer, do you select the same flour every time?
- **Complex services:** Your choices include: 1) buy exactly what you bought last time, 2) purchase internally, 3) delay, or 4) decide not to purchase anything. If you do purchase, additional variables include service levels, warranties, terms, mix of services, and delivery schedules.
- **Products:** Many organizations, such as car dealers, sell the same product. However the terms, conditions, warranties, services surrounding the sale, and post-sale support services are customized to address the unique issues of individual and organizational buyers.

If you agree that customers and their organizations are unique, why go into customer meetings with pre-set presentations? Prepare an agenda, but also expect to adapt your agenda to customer requests and actions.

4 Never assume. Ask.

By guessing rather than asking, you risk developing a solution that does not match customer needs or expectations.

Many customer issues and needs are not obvious based on publicly available information on websites, at bidders conferences, industry days, or trade shows. Capture team members must not assume they know and understand all of the issues, needs, or requirements. They have to ask.

As illustrated in figure 1, asking effective questions is much like measuring an iceberg—what shows above the waterline is a poor indicator of the real size or shape of the issue. Knowing what lies below the waterline is critical when selling in any market sector. Get below the metaphorical waterline with your customers by asking good questions.

The greatest enemy of communication is the illusion of it.

—Pierre Martineau

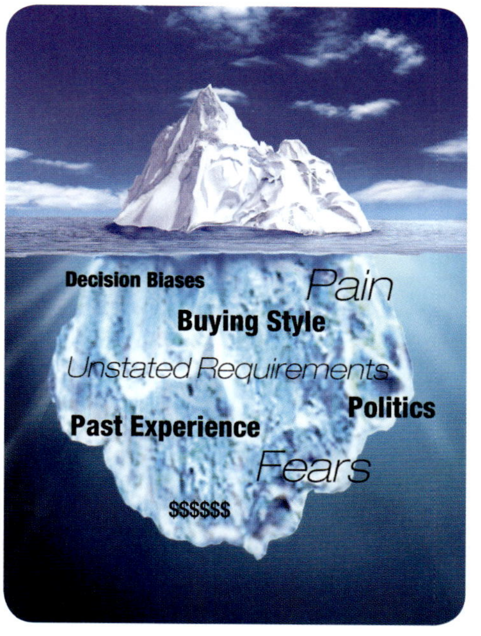

Figure 1. Probe to Discover Hidden Issues. *Like an iceberg where 90 percent of the ice is hidden below the waterline, many customer issues are hidden or poorly understood by both the buyer and seller. Ask, explore, and collaborate.*

Asking a customer to answer all of your questions in a single sitting is unlikely. Instead, ask questions by phone, e-mail, solicitation, and other means. Record questions and responses for future reference as you shape your capture plan and proposal. Memories are imperfect, and you will need to share responses among the capture team.

Gain perspective, and confirm the breadth of issues by asking different people similar questions. Customer issues evolve over time, so reconfirm issues without exasperating the customer.

Shape questions to discover and clarify issues, motivators, and hot buttons.

Validate issues and assess their impact:

- **Validate:** Is the problem, issue, or requirement real? Is it still a problem?
- **Assess impact:** How much is the problem or issue costing customers in lost time, inefficiency, or waste?

Observe three guidelines:

- Ask questions that help validate a need or requirement. Seek evidence that a need really exists. Identify motivators and issues.
- Explore the quantifiable impact of the problem, issue, or requirement. Identify who is being impacted and how.
- Listen actively by clarifying customer positions and concerns. Never assume. Ask.

Apply these three guidelines to your internal capture strategy sessions and planning activities. The more willing capture team members are to ask good questions, the better your plan, strategy, and solution.

5

Active listening engages you in addressing the customer's issues and needs. Active listeners accord uniqueness to the customer.

Actively listen during every customer interaction.

Capture team members who interface with the customer must apply sound active listening skills to establish rapport and trust.

The key to active listening is clarifying—asking the customer to clarify key requirements, issues, and needs as they arise. Clarifying is neutral. Your aim is to learn more about the customer, not to persuade the customer to change his or her position.

When talking to a customer, remember these points:

- Confirm your interpretation of what they have told you by asking, "What exactly does that mean? Why is that important to your organization?"
- Signal that you are listening by taking notes, nodding your head, and acknowledging what they are saying.

Judge a man by his questions, not his answers.

—Voltaire

- Make your clarification statements or questions conversational, not canned.
- Avoid the impulse to insert your opinion about a specific need, issue, or requirement.

Listen, seek clarification, and confirm the intent and content of what the customer is saying.

Customers do not like to be sold to, but everyone likes to buy. Help customers buy by actively listening. Customers want a business partner that listens, understands, and responds based on active listening and clarification. Guidelines for active listening are summarized in figure 2.

GUIDELINE	RATIONALE FOR BUILDING RELATIONSHIP
Clarify when you want your customer to feel understood.	If you want to build rapport, cooperation, and trust, clarify what is significant to your customer.
Clarify when you need to make sure that you understand.	If you do not clarify, you will not know for certain if your interpretation is right. You might be guessing or assuming.
Clarify what is appropriate; be selective and empathetic.	You cannot clarify every statement in your discussions. Consider what is appropriate and what is not. Focus on the key points or details, and exclude the extras.
Lead with clarifying phrases.	Clarification phrases signal your willingness to listen and confirm the message. "Help me understand...", "So, what you're saying is...", "You mean if you could implement this by March..."
Change the wording, not the content of the customer's statement.	If you vary the wording, you will sound more natural and not parrot your customer, which is annoying.
Converse; avoid canned phrases.	Clarification should sound as natural as conversation. Avoid clichés, jargon, or repeated clarifying phrases.
Keep it short and simple.	The average attention span is between 5–10 seconds. Keep it short.
Do not add your thoughts or opinions.	Clarification is neutral; no opinions or advice are allowed. Clarify before you refine.
Avoid questions when you should be clarifying.	Questions are fine for learning and discovery and building respect with your customer. They do not build understanding and should not be used as a substitute for clarifying. Put a question mark in your voice, not your content.
Clarify concerns; do not ignore or bypass them.	If you fail to build understanding on a customer concern or issue, you will have a terrible time resolving it. Customers do not forget important concerns. Clarifying concerns positions you to move the relationship forward.
Clarify answers to your questions.	Whenever you ask a question, clarify the response as a sign of respect. Without the clarifier, you might be perceived as being interrogative or probing.

Figure 2. Improve Your Active Listening Skills. *Apply active listening guidelines to your customer conversations to demonstrate that you are interested, want to understand, and are fully engaged.*

6 Establish rapport and build trust by becoming a trusted advisor.

When building rapport and trust as a capture team member, consider how you approach individuals in the customer organization, their working environment, and how you align multiple interactions with the same individuals.

The goal of capture team members is to become trusted advisors to individuals in the customer organization instead of a vendor. Establish and reinforce trust at every customer interface whether face-to-face, voice, electronic, or in writing.

Today's customers and customer team members exhibit these characteristics:

- **Demanding.** They expect more, expect it faster, and expect it better. Customers demand better products, services, sales skill, and knowledge.
- **Sophisticated.** They are more aware of products, costs, and ways to negotiate terms. Most know how to investigate you, your organization, your products and services, and competitors' products and services.

- **Skeptical.** They are skeptical and suspicious of sales people. They instantly recognize and detest hype, hard selling, and trick selling. Clichéd phrases, jargon, and generic language signal muddled thinking, minimal benefit, and potential arrogance. Their trust is hard to gain and easy to lose.
- **Conditional.** They are less loyal than ever before. They will buy from you if they believe you have the best value to offer. Each sale is new and *conditional*.
- **Cautious.** They are more hesitant and cautious. Many have been impacted by economic challenges and tough times.
- **Valuative.** They are more judgmental. They are more likely to test and debate the value they think they are receiving.
- **Open.** They are open to consider new vendors and other localities. This openness includes worldwide competition.
- **Pressured.** They feel pressured to make the right decisions, to be efficient, and to be productive. Stressed-out customers say they have less time to do more.

Because most capture team members interface with the customer in some manner, they must be aware of these environmental and customer issues to become a trusted advisor. Trust between a buyer and a seller takes time to establish. However, customers will lose trust in a vendor, supplier, or partner whenever they feel misled or misunderstood.

Consider the general and personal working environment of your customers. The general working environment encompasses the guidelines that govern their interactions with contractors. Customer working environments differ by market sector, organization, and situation.

How strict are the guidelines? Are they legally enforceable, policies, suggestions, or established to maintain correct appearance? In any case, avoid knowingly or unknowingly pressuring individuals into illegal or uncomfortable actions. Often they do not object. They just remember the negative feeling and will not be an advocate for your solution or organization.

Alignment might be one of the most overlooked concepts in selling, persuasion, and customer-focused capture. Trusted sellers keep their word. The same individual maintains the same position or story over time.

Rapport between individuals suggests a close, harmonious relationship. You develop trust by maintaining rapport over time, over multiple interactions. If the story keeps changing in unaccounted ways, trust is lost, even if rapport is maintained.

To maintain trust in a complex capture environment, both an individual's action and the actions of capture team members must be aligned over time. Are you confident that every member of your capture team offers the same story? Consider some of the reasons stories become misaligned. Capture team members:

- Forget what they said the last time.
- Say what they think the customer wants to hear.
- Want to stay positive and, therefore, deny, shade, or avoid bad news.
- Are caught by surprise and want to appear knowledgeable.
- Have no idea what others might have said to the same person.

While individuals struggle with alignment issues, you can see why sales professionals have anxiety attacks over unskilled, unplanned contacts between the customer and members of their own organization. Maintaining alignment might be the most important justification for preparing capture plans in a complex selling environment. The capture plan documents your messages. Then the capture manager focuses on keeping team members on message at every customer interface.

7

To be most effective in group presentations, persuade individuals one at a time.

Interact effectively with groups. Facilitate your meetings.

Prior guidelines focused on one-on-one interactions. But many capture events are group events, the nature of a complex sale. No one interacts with a group; you interact with individuals that comprise a group. Consider group dynamics and modify your approach. Guidelines and rationale for dealing with groups are summarized in figure 3.

GUIDELINE	RATIONALE FOR DEALING WITH GROUPS
Understand the roles and personalities of individuals within the group.	Someone may appear or profess to be the leader, to be managing the meeting. Direct much of the conversation to the leader, but also address the others. The other people often have a huge influence on the outcome.
Assess the personalities of individuals within the group.	Include everyone in the conversation. Observe body language. Practice active listening skills, and ask clarifying questions to expose hidden agendas.
Determine the group's decision-making process.	Begin by asking, and then clarify until you have agreement. Here are some common group structures and coping suggestions: • Strong leader and weak followers: Persuade the leader to champion your approach. • Strong leader and strong peers: Persuade everyone. One holdout can ruin the deal. • Weak leader and weak peers: Establish rapport with everyone individually, move slowly, and educate without arrogance. • Weak leader and strong peers: Address everyone's questions. The leader will seek consensus, and look to others to make decisions. • Information collector for an absent decision maker: Educate and rehearse immediate participants to convince the decision maker.
Control the meeting and agenda.	Establish immediate group roles, individual issues, and individuals' expectations for the meeting. Invite participants to briefly state their roles, issues, and objectives from a personal perspective.
Address each person's individual objectives during the meeting.	If you do not uncover each person's issues and then address them in the course of your presentation, you will be interrupted with questions from all angles and lose control of the meeting. As you address each issue, link it to the person who raised the issue, and then confirm that you have understood and addressed that issue. Unaddressed issues lead to subsequent objections.
Adapt to *ad hoc* groups with no leader.	Cross-functional teams, including many Integrated Product/Project Teams (IPTs), are often appointed to address an issue, but they lack an appointed leader. Ask: "Who is the leader?" If they say the decision will be made by the group, then ask: "What's your process?" You need to determine if the group does make the decision or if it will take the analysis and recommendation to an absent decision maker. If the committee decides, ask about the time frame, what they need to know, and how you can help. If they take a recommendation to an absent decision maker, you need to coach and prepare them to make the sale for you when you cannot be in the room. Offer to help by preparing slides or a single-page summary document. Make their job easier.
1. Respond to one question at a time. 2. Listen to the full questions carefully. 3. Focus on the questioner: • Face the questioner. • Lean forward or move toward him or her. • Establish eye contact. • Do not interrupt. • Listen for content (words) and intent (ultimate purpose). 4. If you do not know the answer, admit it. 5. Answer questions in the following steps: • Restate the question. • State a summary answer. • Support your answer. • Summarize or restate your summary answer. • Ask if the questioner is satisfied.	Following these guidelines helps you respond to the question asked, answer it logically and persuasively, and demonstrate respect for the questioner.
Do not restate negative questions. Agree with the questioner, if possible. Admit challenges, cite positive elements, and then bridge to two or three specific Very Important Points (VIPs). If you must deny an accusation, do so and then bridge to VIPs. Restrict negative, nonverbal language, such as touching your head or face or shifting your weight.	Following these guidelines demonstrates your willingness to acknowledge unfavorable information, and then turn the discussion to more positive aspects.

Figure 3. Observe Common Guidelines when Meeting with Groups. *Adapt your approach to group dynamics. Learn and practice a consistent process when responding to various types of questions. While presentations to groups are much more difficult to facilitate than one-on-one meetings, the rewards can be much greater.*

The person talking is the focus of the presentation. Sales materials do not sell anything. Visual aids should aid the presenter but must not be the focus of the presentation or a crutch for the presenter.

When presenting to groups, do not lose sight of the individuals in the group. Focus on meeting the individual agendas of everyone present and often the agendas of others represented by those individuals.

When faced with conflicting issues among group members, attempt to facilitate a constructive discussion. Avoid taking sides.

For example, one person is focused on a result, another person is worried about the cost, and another is worried about potential disruptions. Rather than taking sides, focus on identifying and clarifying stated issues and surfacing unstated issues. Address issues as a group only after all issues have been identified. If you side with one person, you often alienate one or more of the others in the group.

8 Anticipate and handle objections throughout the capture process.

Differentiate by how you sell as well as by what you sell.

Objections are a normal part of every sale. Anticipate objections, but do not treat objections like a ping-pong match where you supply a brilliant response to every objection. You are unlikely to convince the customer to buy no matter how rational your argument.

Customers will raise one objection after another if they are not completely comfortable with your solution and organization. Humans tend to decide emotionally and then justify a decision rationally. Seeking to overcome objections creates a rift and undermines trust.

Treat objections positively. Objections show the customer is still considering your solution, is not yet ready to buy, but is also not ready to end the process.

Differentiate objections and conditions. Objections are temporary reasons for not buying, often because the customer is skeptical or unclear about some aspect of your solution. Some objections stem from the human tendency to avoid making a commitment. You can work with objections.

Conditions are something that exists. You cannot control or influence conditions. Potential conditions include: no funding, someone else makes the decision, they are just gathering information for a future decision or to prepare a budget request, or senior management has decided to go in an entirely different direction at this time.

You cannot fight conditions. Accept the condition, perhaps acknowledge that you might have detected that condition earlier, and position yourself for when that condition changes. Keep communications open, network within the organization or industry, maintain your visibility, and continue to look for gaps in the services delivered internally or by existing vendors.

Interpret objections as requests, but not necessarily at face value. Objections as stated often conceal an underlying issue. Look beyond the words. Figure 4 summarizes some common objections, the underlying issue, and how you might treat the objection as a request.

OBJECTION	UNDERLYING CUSTOMER ISSUE	RESPONSE
Your price is too high.	Perceived benefits do not justify the cost.	Substantiate the value, supported by credible references.
We would like to think about it.	Afraid to make a bad decision or a decision that others could question.	Create comfort by citing a relevant success story. Articulate the opportunity cost of delay.
I would like to talk to my partner, management, or a trusted advisor.	Worried about owning and justifying the decision.	Seek ways to reduce the perceived risk.
I need to get additional quotes.	Unsure if you are meeting their needs. Concerned that they have not considered all alternatives or that the high benefits might permit you to earn inordinately high profit margins.	Emphasize your customized, targeted solution. Review or introduce your trade analysis. Some government buyers will require you to disclose your costs and margins.
We are all set with our current vendor.	They do not see your solution as sufficiently better to justify making the switch.	Review your discriminators. Offer to offset selected transition costs.
We had a poor experience with your organization or a similar organization.	They see minimal difference between your proposed solution and prior or familiar solutions.	Offer specific proof of performance linked to specific personnel proposed. Highlight lessons learned and improvements made compared to your solution or other solutions that they cited.

Figure 4. Handling Objections Is a Process. *Listen, acknowledge, and empathize. Ask questions in your conversations with customers to demonstrate that you are interested, want to understand, and are fully engaged.*

9

Everyone likes to buy. No one likes to be sold to.

Test your potential solution with the customer early and often.

Envision helping customers buy rather than selling to customers. Customers buy in a series of steps, and you are helping them advance step-by-step.

As you step through this process, test potential solutions to get feedback about what you will propose. Traditional sales methodologies call this a *trial close*. A trial close both tests your solution and prompts customers to develop the solution collaboratively. You determine if you are in sync with client expectations. A collaboratively developed solution is more difficult to reject.

Use discussions, white papers, site visits, presentations, documentation reviews, and other means to test your solution with the customer. Assess their readiness to purchase and the alignment of your solution to customer needs. Trial closes are especially important when pursuing a sole source, noncompetitive contract.

Test potential solutions using one of the following approaches.

Exploratory Approach

Ask customers what they want to do next. Help customers buy instead of trying to convince them to buy. For example:

- "Are you interested in learning more about...?"
- "What do you see as the next step?"

Clarification Approach

Confirm what you have heard or sensed from customer words or body language. For example:

- You seem to be ready to wrap this up.
- You seem to be saying that you want to meet our project manager and get the project moving.

Recommendation Approach

Suggest or advise your customer on next steps. Make a recommendation to measure the result, to quantify the improved outcome. For example:

- "I recommend that you give us the go-ahead so that we can get your project started before the end of the quarter."
- "Based on our discussion today, I think it's time for you to move to the next step, which is to execute an agreement and..."

A trial close cannot appear to be a gimmick, in any market sector. Use the trial close to gain approval to advance the sale, to confirm that you are moving in the right direction.

10

One thing we've discovered with certainty is that anything we do that makes the customer more successful inevitably results in a financial return for us.

—Jack Welch

Develop a logical business case for buying.

Most customers seek improved bottom-line results by improving their business approach and processes. As a capture team member with customer interface assignments, help customers establish a business case for your solution.

Sales and business development professionals are notorious for falling into the trap of showcasing features of their product or service. They thrive on talking about the speed of their technology, the accuracy of their weapon system, or their world-class people.

Customers typically have issues that are implicit or unstated. Customers explicitly state requirements that include the features they want. Benefits, the inverse of their issues, are the alleviation of their issues or pains. Customers will pay to alleviate these issues.

A logical business case might range from a series of statements that describe the benefits and features of your solution, to a fully developed value proposition based on collaboratively developed quantitative analysis. Consider both approaches.

Informal business case

Your capture objective is to position your services and products as the solution to this customer's needs, a means to alleviate issues. Specifically address each issue. Imagine these two linked scenarios.

Ineffective General Positioning Approach

Seller: *Here is our understanding of your requirements. You, need...(followed by a summary of the customers issues and requirements).*

Our solution comprises...(followed by a description of the solution).

The problem with this approach is that the link is general. Specific issues are not directly linked to features of your solution that deliver the benefits, so some features of your solution might appear to be extraneous. The customer is forced to accept or reject your entire solution. They feel trapped and manipulated.

Effective Issue-Specific Approach

Seller: *From what you have said, you are concerned about the cost, you want to avoid service interruptions, and you need to reduce customer inquiry response time. Correct?*

Customer: *Yes, that's right.*

Seller: *To minimize your cost, we will retain your current employee workstations, saving you $2200 per customer service representative. To avoid service interruptions, we plan to install the new server and software and run preliminary tests in advance. Then we can cut over during a 3-day weekend when you said that inquiries would be minimal. The live tests that we ran last week showed that CRM cut representatives' total response time by 28 percent.*

The model dialogue suggested is identical in content and structure to theme statements used in proposals. *See* THEME STATEMENTS, ***Proposal Guide***.

Note how each customer issue is directly linked to a feature of the solution. If you cannot link a feature to a customer issue, do not mention that feature. Customers buy benefits, not features. If they could get the benefit without the feature, they would.

Repeatedly cite a benefit when discussing a feature of your solution throughout the capture process, not just in your proposal. Benefit statements in discussions and correspondence repeatedly remind customers that you understand their needs and requirements.

Business case as a formal value proposition

Value propositions establish the quantified value basis for the business relationship. The best value propositions go beyond traditional theme statements by incorporating as many as possible of the following elements:

- Quantifies the anticipated business improvement.
- Specifies the timing of the benefits.
- Specifies the timing of the costs.
- States the payback period.
- Specifies how the results will be measured and tracked.

Executives, users, and technical buyers have different issues and values. Prepare a different value proposition for each type of buyer, and work them into your presentations, based upon the participants, and into your proposals and other customer-targeted documents. Model your written value propositions around the template shown in figure 4.

<Customer Name> will realize <quantified business improvement> by purchasing <our solution> for <total investment cost>.

Beginning <implementation date>, the improvement in <specific business process or function> will achieve an economic payback in <timeframe>.

We have agreed to document the delivered value by <results measurement and tracking approach>.

Figure 4. Use a Template to Develop Value Propositions. *The best value propositions are developed collaboratively with the customer and contain the elements listed. Value propositions sound stronger if the benefits are placed at the beginning.*

See VALUE PROPOSITIONS.

Value propositions, as shown, summarize the business case. Perhaps the greatest benefit of a value proposition is as a collaborative capture tool. You cannot build a value proposition without customer participation. Do not try. By collaboratively focusing on the quantified and unquantifiable benefits of potential, alternative solutions, the customer will come to understand the business case for selecting your solution. This business case is the heart of the capture plan and your capture strategy sessions. Unless the customer can articulate the business case within his or her organization, your solution is not credible and validated.

11

Seek agreement rather than close the sale.

Gaining agreement should not be a traumatic event for either party. You are helping customers buy something that they want and need; gaining agreement is the next logical step. You are not using tricks, exaggeration, or misrepresentation to close the sale.

Considering that most readers of this *Capture Guide* are not seasoned sales professionals and are uncomfortable with closing techniques, the following suggestions offer perspective and general guidance:

- **If you sense that the customer is reluctant to agree, step back.** Assess what is missing. Did you miss an issue? Was every issue addressed by an aspect of your solution? Are you dealing with the real decision maker? Is something distracting the customer, such that your timing is wrong? Perhaps you need to reschedule.
- **Be candid and direct.** Avoid crude, pressured closing statements, especially if they have not yet agreed to buy: "What color do you want?" "Would you like delivery on Monday or Wednesday?" "I need your answer today to guarantee your preferred consultant." If the timing of their decision affects the composition of your service or delivery schedule, say so, but do not make false or misleading statements.
- **Seek permission to close.** You do not want to scare the customer. Ask: *"Are we ready to move forward? Have we answered your concerns?* Your attitude should be that *"We are planning to do this..."* not, *"I think that you should..."* You are helping them buy, not closing a sale.
- **Wait for an affirmative answer.** If you do not hear something definite and presume agreement, customers feel manipulated. If the silence continues, identify the reason for the hesitation. Handle objections as previously suggested.
- **Outline next steps.** If the customer agrees, avoid asking them to immediately sign something. Instead, outline the next steps in the process. That might be a transition planning meeting. Link next steps to the transition plan in your proposal, which suggests that you plan to keep the commitments that you promised.

Gain agreement through collaboration, not tactics. Proceeding is the next, natural, logical step. Remember, you are looking for a successful outcome for both organizations and follow-on business.

Decision Gate Reviews are critical milestones in the business development process at which executives decide whether to advance an opportunity to the next phase or end the pursuit.

See **Process.**

Decision gate, decision milestone, and *gate review* are synonymous phrases, used interchangeably.

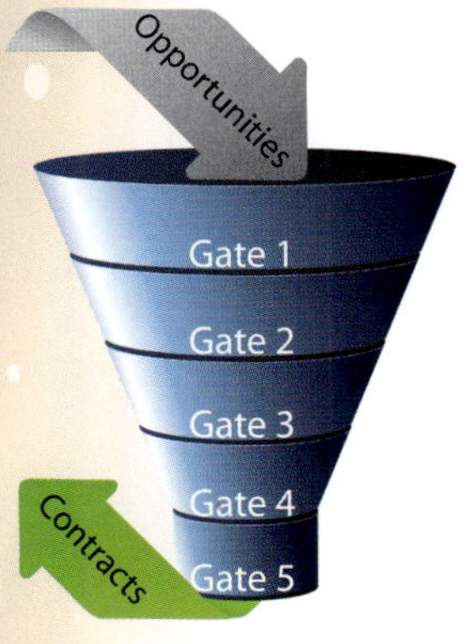

Figure 1. Opportunity Funnel. *Use decision gates to progressively limit pursuits to the most winnable opportunities that serve your organizational objectives.*

See **Color Team Reviews.**

Organizations that repeatedly win new business in complex markets typically approach business development tasks in phases. They win more business at lower cost by aligning their activities in each phase with customers' buying cycle activities. This alignment improves customer focus, promoting better solution development and greater competitor differentiation.

Business opportunities pass through a series of decision gates that control progression through the phases. At these gates, executives advance and allocate resources to opportunities the organization has the greatest chance of winning and that best match their organization's objectives. Typical objectives are to capture revenue, increase profit, enter new markets, or extend current market positions.

Executives end pursuit of and withdraw resources from less promising opportunities.

This winnowing creates an opportunity funnel as shown in figure 1. The opportunity funnel improves win rates because resources not spent on poor candidates can be redirected toward better opportunities. Organizations that eventually bid on less than 30 percent of their pipeline due to decisions at gates to end pursuits have historically achieved sustained win rates of 70 percent or higher in commercial and government markets.

Business development professionals often use decision gates poorly and fail to differentiate them from color team reviews. These critical milestones have starkly different objectives:

- Decision gates are to determine whether to advance business opportunities to the next phase.
- Color team reviews are to improve the pursuit of opportunities remaining in the funnel.

Decision Gate Reviews

1. Use decision gates to control progression through business development phases.
2. Include relevant roles and limit non-essential participants.
3. Hold decision gates at the right level.
4. Plan decision gates carefully.
5. Specify inputs and outputs for each decision gate.
6. Avoid over-focus on the technical solution.
7. Continue the decision gate until management reaches a firm, written decision.
8. Be prepared to end the pursuit.
9. Eliminate personal opinion, bias, and ego.
10. Consider using a facilitator if conflict is anticipated.
11. Record the decision, update the capture plan, archive information, and document lessons learned.

1 Use decision gates to control progression through business development phases.

Conserve resources and improve your win rate by using decision gates to control progression of opportunities through a series of business development phases aligned with your circumstances. Organizations normally establish from four to seven process phases, depending on these parameters:

- Company characteristics
- Size and complexity of customary opportunities
- Market nature, particularly speed at which opportunities develop
- Number and behavior of competitors
- Executive decision-making preferences
- Interest, willingness, and availability of senior management to participate in decision gates

Frame decision gates separating phases using one or more yes/no questions, as summarized in figure 2. The questions shown are posed for Shipley's model business development process; tailor them for your own process.

No.	Phase	Gate	Questions
0	Market Segmentation	Campaign/ Marketing	*Is the market niche congruent with goals in our strategic plan?*
1	Long-Term Positioning	Interest	*Does the opportunity merit expending resources to research and assess it?*
2	Opportunity Assessment	Pursuit	*Should we commit resources to developing a capture plan and influencing our customer to prefer our solution?*
3	Capture Planning	Preliminary Bid	*Have capture activities positioned us favorably enough with the customer to justify planning a proposal?*
4	Proposal Planning	Bid Validation	*Is the opportunity still worth pursuing and the proposal worth preparing, considering final details of the solicitation?*
5	Proposal Development	Proposal Submittal	*Should we submit our completed proposal? Is programmatic risk justified by the probable financial reward?*
6	Post-Submittal Activities	Final Offer	*After negotiations, is programmatic risk still justified by the financial reward considering terms of contract?*

Figure 2. Fundamental Decision Gate Questions. *Use questions like these to build your opportunity funnel. Note that Phase 0, leading to the Campaign/Marketing Decision, is not opportunity-specific. The Phase 6 Final Offer Decision is eliminated if a valid offer is accepted without modification. In between, your honest, fact-based assessments of opportunities, customers, and competitive positions help you efficiently allocate business development resources and improve win rates.*

Determining the number of phases and gates in your process is less important than defining, documenting, and following that process. Organizations that commit to a single, flexible, scalable business development process cite several benefits:

- Reduced business capture costs
- Increased productivity
- Better forecasting
- Improved management visibility and control

Ideally, seek one of only two outcomes at each decision gate:

- Advance the pursuit, obligating sufficient resources for successful pursuit
- End the pursuit, redirecting resources to other, more winnable opportunities

Sometimes, an executive defers a decision, but doing so usually means someone has not done their job well. Perhaps the executive did not define or convey criteria for advancement to business development staff, or the business development or capture teams did not collect the right information or present the right business case. Possibly, the decision gate was triggered by an unanticipated customer action, such as release of a solicitation, for which the organization was not prepared.

If the decision is deferred pending sufficient information, define what and when additional information is needed. Allowing poorly executed pursuits to drag on wastes resources and reduces your win probability.

Some organizations find their win rate on deferrals is higher than average because executives demanded better information and then made better-informed decisions. Ideally, executives use deferrals as teaching opportunities to improve subsequent pursuits.

Avoid being trapped by overly complex processes. Define categories according to opportunity characteristics, such as:

- Strategic importance
- New or existing customer
- Expected contract value
- Contract type
- Financial and programmatic risks
- Investment requirements
- Alignment with corporate authority levels

Specify required decision gates, participants, inputs, and outputs by category. If your organization has not already defined such categories, work with senior management to establish them.

Follow a process adjusted for each opportunity's category. For example, if a customer asks to double production, accept the order and skip capture planning. If you receive a large order for catalog items, forego a Preliminary Bid Decision gate; you have already advertised your willingness to sell at the catalog price.

2 Include relevant roles and limit non-essential participants.

Include personnel filling relevant roles at decision gates to reduce second-guessing, reconsideration of decisions, poor commitment, wasted resources, and poor win rates. Limit non-essential participants.

Roles are temporary functions only loosely related to positions or job titles. The person filling a role often varies by opportunity category or business development phase. For each business opportunity category, determine which roles are relevant and who within your organization will fill them. One person might fill multiple roles. Define responsibilities by role and hold individuals accountable for fulfilling them, whether they perform tasks themselves or delegate to others.

Assign the following generic roles, using role names acceptable within your organization. Adapt the principal responsibilities suggested in figure 3 to your needs.

Executive. The executive defines strategic directions and business criteria for the organization. He or she makes specific decisions to advance or end pursuits. Consider the decision gate as being held for this person, so the executive leads the group. The executive is obligated to formulate and disseminate expectations before decision gates. If the executive does not, everyone's time is wasted as opportunities are considered without supporting data, or opportunities are pursued that do not fit your strategic direction.

If you follow a consensus approach to decision making, separate influencers—the ones who whisper in the decision maker's ear—from the executive who pronounces consensus. Usually that is the person accountable to meet revenue, profit, and budget targets.

Many organizations assign executive authority based on their predefined opportunity categories. For example, a small contract to support an existing customer might be assigned to a department head. A large contract with a new customer might be assigned to a business unit vice president. And a major, strategic opportunity requiring corporate investment or exposing the organization to high risk might go to the president. Assign the executive role to a level sufficient to minimize superiors' second-guessing and micro-managing.

Operations. Operations personnel advise and support the executive, contributing critical information. They will eventually oversee and execute the contract. They manage personnel resources, direct manufacturing, schedule development and delivery of products and services, and have product or service expertise. Operations also includes functional support organizations, such as contracts and pricing. For complex organizations bidding on big jobs, numerous operational types might be included, but the mix changes as each pursuit progresses and issues shift.

Role	EXECUTIVE	OPERATIONS	BUSINESS DEVELOPMENT MANAGER	CAPTURE MANAGER	BUSINESS DEVELOPER
Primary Duties	• Define • Decide • Lead	• Advise • Support	• Assign • Monitor • Collaborate	• Engage • Inform • Execute	• Prospect

Figure 3. Primary Roles and Duties. *Generic business development roles are characterized by a set of primary duties. The executive role is relevant at all decision gates, though the person filling it may change. Business developer and business development manager roles are relevant at early gates when deciding whether to pursue opportunities. Capture manager, business development manager, and operations roles are relevant at gates following authorization to pursue an opportunity.*

A common issue arises when powerful individuals mistakenly believe they have decision-making authority at decision gates. If an operations person has the authority to make or veto a decision, he or she is actually filling the executive role.

Business Development Manager. The business development manager is responsible for starting, growing, and maintaining the revenue stream of a business segment. Generally, he or she allocates time and money across opportunities, assigning and monitoring capture and proposal professionals to maximize success. The business development manager also collaborates with capture and proposal staff to mentor and lend perspective.

Capture Manager. The capture manager leads the team that engages directly with the customer to determine needs and craft an acceptable solution. He or she develops and executes a capture plan, guides positioning activities to improve win probability, and oversees proposal strategy creation. The capture manager avoids surprises by regularly informing management of progress and strategic developments.

Business Developer. The business developer is the front-line representative of the company, presenting products, services, and capabilities in the market and identifying new bid opportunities. Business developers often are called account managers, sales executives, marketers, or sales directors, depending upon the market, organization, and industry.

While people executing business development tasks or contributing important knowledge might be included in decision gate meetings at your discretion, personnel designated to fill relevant roles listed in figure 3 must attend. Modify decision gate schedules, if necessary, to accommodate them.

If an opportunity is sufficiently mature to have teaming partners, consider whether members of those organizations need to participate as advisors, contributors, or executives.

Avoid filling the room with minimally connected managers or participants. Larger groups tend to be less constructive, with more time spent informing people instead of discussing the positives and negatives of continuing or ending the pursuit. Larger groups typically require more time to reach a decision, but the quality of the decision seldom improves as the group grows.

Limit presenters to individuals with significant capture roles, involvement with the opportunity, or specialized knowledge. Most presenters should attend only as agents of personnel filling primary roles. If you cannot identify someone's connection with an essential role, omit that person from the meeting.

3

Hold decision gates at the right level.

Strike a balance between remaining nimble in your market and ensuring that various levels of management have the knowledge to constructively direct and advise on new business pursuits. Make decisions too low in your organization, and critical oversight will be lacking. Make them too high, and top executives will be micromanaging day-to-day operations rather than focusing on strategic planning and growth.

Define who fills which roles at each decision gate for each opportunity category. For example, Interest Decisions are best made informally and low in the organization to encourage a wide opportunity funnel. A business developer could feasibly make the executive's decision on most leads with acceptable risk.

A business development manager might fill the executive role, even on large jobs, at a Pursuit Decision. But a business unit manager might be a better choice on the same opportunity when making a Preliminary Bid Decision because expenses will be rising and more parts of the organization and its supply chain will be involved. As potential contract size grows and critical customer relationships hang in the balance, a president's approval might be required at a Proposal Submittal Decision due to fiduciary responsibilities.

4

Plan decision gates carefully.

Decision gates are planned, structured events, not *ad hoc* gatherings.

Categorize the opportunity. When in doubt, categorize the lead as more valuable, more strategic, and riskier. Avoid jeopardizing progress or approval because things turn out to be more complex than expected.

Invite the right people for the category. Omit people if you cannot define their role. Set clear expectations and standards for all attendees. Attendees must understand the purpose of the meeting and their roles.

Schedule decision gates early to improve the attendance of key participants. If key participants are unable to attend in person, add them virtually using video or audio teleconferencing. If their time is limited, ask them to join for the summary discussion, wrap-up, and recommendations. To simplify scheduling and improve senior management turnout, some organizations set standing gate review dates and cover prepared opportunities in a single meeting, especially when simultaneously pursuing multiple opportunities.

Confirm prescribed inputs are complete and available. Prescribed inputs typically vary by opportunity category. Executives frequently set minimum information thresholds and presentation templates for gate meetings. For example, they might require signed teaming agreements before Bid Validation Decision gates but eliminate capture plans for task order proposals under master ordering agreements.

Avoid developing a culture where elaborate information packets substitute for the difficult and essential work of interacting with the customer and developing solid competitive intelligence. No decision gate package by itself is your objective. Your objective is to use gates to narrow your range of pursuits to the most winnable few.

Offer an honest recommendation on what decision is in the best interests of your company. Avoid the common trap of capture managers seeking approval for the next phase regardless of the pursuit's status. Sometimes your best approach is to convince management to redirect precious resources to more winnable opportunities.

5

Specify inputs and outputs for each decision gate.

Define mandatory and optional inputs and outputs for each decision gate by opportunity category. Adapt these by market, prospect, and strategic importance of the lead. When presenters' and participants' expectations are aligned, everyone can focus on making sound decisions rather than debating what information is missing or who is at fault.

For large, complex opportunities, most inputs come from your capture plan. Capture plans should evolve as opportunities progress,

See **Capture Planning** *and* **Model Documents 1-4.**

minimizing effort on early-stage pursuits that might not continue. Predetermine which capture plan elements will be required for each decision gate.

To illustrate this concept, figure 4 shows default recommendations for capture plan content at common decision gates in Shipley's standard process model. (Plan elements match the Shipley Capture Plan template.) An opportunity description is required at an Interest Decision; eight elements are suggested for a Pursuit Decision. As content is added for later gates, repeatedly update and enhance existing information.

Phase:	Long-Term Positioning	Opportunity Assessment	Capture Planning	Proposal Planning	Proposal Development	Post-Submittal
Decision Gate:	**Interest**	**Pursuit**	**Preliminary Bid**	**Bid Validation**	**Proposal Submittal**	**Final Offer**
Executive Summary		Basic	Detailed	Updated	Updated	Updated
External Analysis						
Opportunity Description	Basic	Detailed	Updated	Updated	Updated	Updated
Customer Profile		Basic	Detailed	Updated	Updated	Updated
Customer Issues and Hot Buttons		Basic	Detailed	Updated	Updated	Updated
Competitor Intelligence			Basic	Detailed	Updated	Updated
Our Competitive Position		Basic	Detailed	Updated	Updated	Updated
Bidder Comparison Chart			Basic	Detailed	Updated	Updated
Internal Analysis						
Our Estimate of Price to Win			Basic	Detailed	Updated	Updated
Our Technical/Management Solution		Basic	Detailed	Updated	Updated	Updated
Teaming and Subcontracting			Basic	Detailed	Updated	Updated
Strategy Development						
Leverage Our Strengths			Basic	Detailed	Updated	Updated
Mitigate Our Weaknesses			Basic	Detailed	Updated	Updated
Exploit Competitor Weaknesses			Basic	Detailed	Updated	Updated
Neutralize Competitor Strengths			Basic	Detailed	Updated	Updated
Action Plans						
Customer Contact Plan		Basic	Detailed	Updated	Updated	Updated
Intelligence Collection Plan		Basic	Detailed	Updated	Updated	Updated
Contingency Plan			Basic	Detailed	Updated	Updated
Solution Development Plan			Basic	Detailed	Updated	Updated
Customer Risk Management Plan			Basic	Detailed	Updated	Updated

Figure 4. Capture Plan Evolution. *Expecting full capture plans at early decision gates is foolish and wasteful. Align the level of information with the purpose of the gate and maturity of the pursuit. Basic information is preliminary and likely to change. Detailed information is more complete, but might evolve. Seek and add updated information throughout the business development lifecycle. Phase 0 (Market Segmentation) and the Marketing/Campaign Decision do not appear in the table because capture plans apply only to individual opportunities, not market sectors.*

For smaller, simpler pursuits, less comprehensive tools and inputs suffice. Your process may also require additional documentation at various decision gates:

See **Model Documents 5.**

- Opportunity assessments
- Competitive intelligence summaries
- Pricing-to-win analyses
- Solution descriptions
- Financial analyses
- Teaming agreements
- Color team review summaries

Decision gate outputs record the decisions made. To continually improve your capture process, consider including critiques of the capture team's work, instructions for future actions, or conditions attached to approvals in the opportunity file.

6

Avoid over-focus on the technical solution.

Conduct a comprehensive appraisal of your full offer before making a decision. Consider not only your technical solution, but also your management approach, price, quality assurance plan, transition plan, and the relevant experience and past performance by which you will bolster credibility with your customer. Senior managers often rise from technical backgrounds and are tempted to return to familiar territory.

Reduce reviewers' focus on the technical solution by adopting some or all of these approaches:

- Review and seek acceptance of the ground rules before beginning the meeting.
- Remind participants that they agreed to the ground rules.
- Suggest a separate review of the technical solution, identify who should participate, then set the time and place.
- Use a facilitator, per Guideline 10.
- If an executive refuses to continue without resolution of technical issues, you or that executive were ill-prepared for the decision gate. Reschedule when better information is available.

7

Continue the decision gate until management reaches a firm, written decision.

When a decision gate is scheduled, push to a definite conclusion—advance or end the pursuit. Defer as a last resort, recognizing that deferral usually means you or other participants were ill-prepared.

Before deciding to advance, realistically scope the people, activities, and funding needed to position your organization to win. Unfortunately, capture efforts are often underfunded, with good intentions but poor results. If you lack accurate capture cost data from previous pursuits, plan capture activities in detail, using the same approach you would for other services-based projects. Then track expenditures to improve future forecasts.

Do not defer a decision because the answer seems unclear. Lack of clarity is a no-bid indicator. Unfortunately, people recall the competition they won despite negative indicators and conveniently forget losses under similar circumstances. If you must defer, set a firm schedule for reconsideration. List events or intelligence on which a decision will depend. Then follow your agreed conditions.

Deferred decisions invariably have negative consequences:

- Subsequent activities are postponed, compressed, or eliminated.
- Executives remember capture managers as unprepared due to information gaps.
- Capture teams lose momentum when members delay completing assigned tasks because they sense management might end the pursuit.
- Managers returning to an unfinished review retain negative biases.

8

Be prepared to end the pursuit.

Ending a pursuit is often an excellent decision. If your organization lacks the resources, commitment, or capabilities to win, you are likely to lose to a hungrier, more resourceful, or more committed competitor. Redirect your time, energy, and resources to more winnable opportunities.

End the pursuit if the management team, the executive sponsor, or the capture manager is only moderately committed to winning. Believing you can win with half-hearted efforts is delusional. One highly successful company asks at every Pursuit Decision, "What are we prepared to sacrifice to win?" Strong indicators you should end a pursuit include vague decision-making information or a capture team that does not know if, how, where, or when better information can be obtained.

Submitting a poor proposal tarnishes your image with the customer. Customers assume your proposals accurately represent your capability. If they do not, do not submit them.

Before ending a pursuit, however, consider the availability of other opportunities, your market position, and the most productive alternative assignments for your business development team. Ask yourself whether business development skills or resources will be lost by not going forward. Sometimes, realities of the market dictate moving ahead under less-than-ideal conditions. Think about both positive and negative impacts before making your decision.

9 Eliminate personal opinion, bias, and ego.

Some participants approach decision gates as opportunities to display their expertise, knowledge, or political savvy. Others seek to impress management, settle old scores, bolster their egos, or embarrass other participants. Executives must not tolerate such counterproductive behavior.

Also avoid decisions based on conjecture. Examine estimates for reasonableness and coherence with facts; challenge unsupported assertions, including those from powerful individuals.

Establish a positive, collaborative tone. Remind presenters to focus on explaining and clarifying required information, not just reading from the capture plan or debating reviewers. Encourage individuals with alternative perspectives to voice their opinions; they can be invaluable resources at decision gates.

Avoid a culture in which decisions to end pursuit are viewed as failures and blamed on capture managers. Such shortsightedness dissuades business developers from considering innovative growth opportunities, discourages honesty, and focuses capture managers on short-term management approval rather than long-term corporate success.

10 Consider using a facilitator if conflict is anticipated.

Reviews should be crisp, professional, and productive. Minimize defensive behaviors, blaming, and nonproductive discussions. If you anticipate controversy, consider using a facilitator to help maintain a positive tone, keep participants focused on the competitive situation, and steer the group away from *ad hominem* attacks.

A skilled facilitator will have a number of methods to deal with the egoist, ranging from a courteous redirect to the meeting agenda to outright ejection from the meeting. If you anticipate such behavior, discuss it with a senior management participant and predetermine how you should deal with possible incidents.

Facilitators can reduce the possibility of participants taking personal offense by establishing the following ground rule:

> *"Please respect the professional role of each member of the team. As your facilitator, I will ask all of you to support your statements with evidence. I am not suggesting that your personal opinions lack merit, but others need to understand the basis for your position."*

Facilitators cannot simultaneously fill any of the decision gate roles. They should resist injecting personal opinions and limit themselves to the following activities:

- Introducing and stating the roles of the facilitator, executive decision maker, advisors, and presenters
- Emphasizing the objective for the decision gate as decision making rather than problem solving
- Explaining the decision options: advancing or ending the pursuit
- Stressing the negative aspects of deferral
- Presenting review guidelines
- Conducting the review according to a published agenda
- Bringing out conflicting opinion, while keeping things constructive
- Eliciting a decision from the executive, announcing it to the group, and having it signed off in a decision record

11 Record the decision, update the capture plan, archive information, and document lessons learned.

Promptly record and disseminate decisions. To support subsequent analysis of gate decisions and foster familiarity, develop a standard decision record for your organization. Include these key elements:

- Date
- Participants
- Decisions
- Recommendations
- Commitments
- Approved process deviations and extraordinary exceptions
- Lessons learned

Tailor the form to the complexity of the opportunity. A separate form for each decision gate is appropriate for complex opportunities or business development protocols. Simpler situations can be handled with a single form covering all gates.

Have the executive sign the decision record. Some organizations require every attendee to sign the form, but that practice undermines the perceived responsibility of the executive. Assessments after losses of large, important opportunities often show numerous signatures of lower-level managers, but none by the responsible executive. Good practice generally vests decision authority in a single individual, not a committee. Sign-offs by lower-tier participants are more relevant on input documents.

Add the decision gate record to your pursuit file. Note the decision and date on the capture plan title page.

Collect and record lessons learned after each decision gate. Waiting until the end of the pursuit leads to lessons lost. After the proposal is submitted or the contract is finalized, you will have forgotten numerous events and their causes, will have limited motivation, are likely to already have been reassigned to another task, and could be biased by your win or loss.

Engage the Program Manager immediately after the Pursuit Gate review. The program manager must have input on capture strategy and will help validate past performance, management, and technical solutions.

Best-in-class organizations appoint program managers early to ensure they are engaged and feel that they own every facet of the solution from start to finish, including the technical, management, past performance, price, and supporting plans such as quality assurance. Some business development professionals use the term *solution set* to broaden the focus beyond the technical solution.

Keep the responsibilities and goals of the capture triumvirate in mind:

- **Capture Manager:** Owns the opportunity and the customer—the goal is to win.
- **Proposal Manager:** Owns the proposal document—the goal is a quality, winning proposal.
- **Program Manager:** Owns the solution—the goal is a profitable, deliverable solution.

Successful, profitable, deliverable programs lead to satisfied customers and future opportunities. Every sales professional attests that poor products and poor performance are difficult and expensive to sell. Good products and services often resell themselves without re-competing, or at least ease contract extensions or renewals.

The initial program transition plan and execution strategy are conceived during capture planning and are documented in the capture plan. During proposal planning, the program manager individually or collaboratively extends relevant capture plan material into a program management plan. Larger programs require more collaboration. Figure 1 summarizes typical program manager tasks by business development phase.

Engaging Program Management

1. Appoint the program manager immediately after the Pursuit Gate review.
2. Develop the capture strategy collaboratively with the program manager.
3. Develop the Integrated Solution Worksheet.
4. Showcase and vet the program manager with the customer.
5. Delegate select tasks to the program manager.
6. Include the program manager in teaming discussions.
7. Ask the program manager to present the baseline solution at the proposal kickoff meeting.
8. Keep the entire solution aligned with your evolving strategy.
9. Assign the program manager to prepare the management volume and manage the preparation of other required plans.
10. Impose a solution freeze.
11. Assign the program manager to a significant role in orals, finals presentations, and negotiations as the face of the continuing customer-seller relationship.
12. Update your transition and internal management plans.
13. Formally transition program responsibility from the capture manager to the program manager.
14. Grow the contract during execution by identifying, positioning, proposing, and closing additional tasks.
15. Prepare and deliver the annual internal program review and prepare the mid-term program review pending contract re-competition.

CAPTURE PLANNING	PROPOSAL PLANNING	PROPOSAL PREPARATION	POST-SUBMITTAL ACTIVITIES
• Develop program management and execution approach. • Prepare the baseline program management solution. • Participate in teaming and subcontracting discussions. • Help define program management requirements. • Draft preliminary WBS/CWBS. • Contribute to make/buy and teaming discussions.	• Draft management approach, organization, and key personnel matrix for executive summary. • Complete the annotated outline and first draft of the program management plan. • Prepare preliminary WBS/CWBS. • Support proposal evaluation and negotiation activities. • Initiate and guide transition planning. • Prepare baseline solution.	• Present baseline solution at proposal kickoff. • Lead management volume and preparation of related plans required with the proposal. • Review alignment of management volume and plans with the technical, past performance, and cost sections. • Check Basis Of Estimates (BOEs) and task descriptions for adherence to cost targets. • Incorporate color team review recommendations. • Prepare and present management plan at orals.	• Support final proposal revisions. • Update transition and program management plans. • Support negotiations. • Present management plan at orals. • Coordinate availability of proposed program personnel, facilities, and systems. • Lead/attend customer debrief, win or lose. • Conduct delivery team kickoff meeting.

Figure 1. Program Manager's Capture Tasks by Phase. *The program manager is an integral part of successful capture efforts from the Pursuit Decision Gate through contract award and start-up. The program manager either leads or collaboratively supports listed tasks.*

1 Appoint the program manager immediately after the Pursuit Gate review.

Best-practice is to name the capture manager and permanent program manager as an output of an affirmative Pursuit Gate review. Ideally, the named program manager is immediately available to support the capture effort. For clarification, the named program manager is the individual who will manage the program upon award.

Customers regard the program manager as a key position, even when not stated in the bid request. Customers recount poor experiences when program managers are *parachuted in* post-award. Even worse, some newly appointed program managers criticize the proposed solution and make disruptive changes. Similarly, if suitable, proposed, and expected program managers are unavailable and changed post-award, customers see these as negative bait-and-switch tactics.

See RESUMES, RELEVANT EXPERIENCE/PAST PERFORMANCE, *Proposal Guide.*

Unfortunately, the named program manager might not be available for several reasons:

- Currently managing another program.
- Work overlaps with another assignment.
- Not yet employed by the organization.
- Size of opportunity or length of capture effort restricts immediate assignment.

When the named program manager is not available, seek an experienced if temporary replacement, rather than asking the capture manager to fill that role. The skills required for the capture and program manager differ.

The discriminating features of most proposed programs are the individuals assigned to key positions. One of the most important capture strategies is to position the customer to prefer or, at minimum, accept these key personnel. If another individual must assume the program manager role, persuade the customer that the named program manager is actively involved in solution development, is the ideal person for that position, and is personally committed to manage and deliver the program.

Carefully tailor the program manager's resume. Specifically address recent experience and performance on similar programs with this client and similar clients. Emphasize the program manager's role in risk management and reduction. Quantify the program manager's performance results, if available.

In technically complex systems programs, the program manager's role and responsibilities are often split:

- The responsible technical manager, solution architect, chief engineer, or chief systems engineer manages the design and development of the system to be delivered.
- The program manager manages the delivery of the system.

This division of responsibilities often reflects the seller's organizational split between technical design or engineering and program management.

Clearly and persuasively explain how technical solution development and program delivery management responsibilities are split to minimize customer-perceived risk. Avoid simply stating that design and delivery responsibilities will be shared. Such *trust-us* statements are seldom convincing.

2 Develop the capture strategy collaboratively with the program manager.

The initial draft capture plan requires extensive input from the program manager on the solution, potential risks, and incumbency issues.

The breadth of the program manager's role varies depending upon the products and services offered. A large, complex systems contract might require significant engineering design and configuration management input, while a services contract might be entirely within the expertise of the program manager.

See **Risk Management**, ***Proposal Guide.***

The program manager is best positioned to identify potential risks to the solution, schedule, and cost. The capture manager is best positioned to identify external risks relating to the customer and competition.

Incumbency is a major consideration, given the industry consensus that incumbents win 60 to 80 percent of re-competes. If you are the incumbent and the existing program manager is to continue, you have excellent but potentially biased insight regarding the customer's view of your performance. Corroborate this view with customer performance reports, surveys, and subsequent capture actions.

If you are not the incumbent, identify at least one powerful motivation for the customer to replace the incumbent. If you cannot identify a major performance shortfall, revisit your pursuit decision.

Incumbency relates closely to relevant experience and past performance. The most relevant experience and performance data in order are:

1. Performance on the current program.
2. Performance on other programs with this customer.
3. Performance on similar programs involving key individuals that will be named for this program.
4. Performance on similar programs.

The program manager should be in the best position to identify which programs are most relevant and obtain quantitative performance data.

3 Develop the Integrated Solution Worksheet.

The Integrated Solution Worksheet (ISW), figure 2, might be the most useful tool in the capture plan template. Complete the ISW, even if you omit other parts of the capture template.

While the capture manager owns the ISW, it must be completed collaboratively with the program manager and others with vital solution, customer, or competitor information.

The ISW is a collaborative tool, and the content repeatedly changes throughout the sales cycle.

The ISW helps you to prepare a customer-focused solution rather than the solution that you would prefer to convince the customer to buy. For example, if a feature of your solution does not relate to a customer issue, the customer does not need that feature and you are adding cost that could make your solution uncompetitive. If not, then you need to identify someone in the customer organization whom you might persuade to care about that issue.

ShipleyAssociates **Integrated Solution Worksheet**

Enter Opportunity Name Here

Item No.	Customer Issues	Customer Requirements	Available Solution	Gap	Competitor Solution	Discriminators	Strategy	Action Required
1	System must be available.	8 hr. response time.	2 hr. response time	1 hr	3 hr. response time	Faster response but more expensive?	Emphasize no additional cost with cellular.	Show current response time. Show photo-service with cell phone.

Figure 2. Integrated Solution Worksheet. *Begin by filling the* Issues *column when early in the process. If the customer has identified requirements, fill the* Requirements *column first. Then complete each row, relating each item in the row.*

See DISCRIMINATORS, *Proposal Guide.*

Discriminators might be positive or negative. Emphasize positive discriminators, and seek ways to eliminate, neutralize, or minimize negative discriminators.

The ISW helps you identify gaps in your available solution. You have to decide whether to close the gap, and if so, will you close it internally or externally via teaming or subcontracting?

Differences in your solution and competitors' solutions that link to customer issues are discriminators, the basis for your strategy, tactics, and sales messages.

If you identify deficiencies in the customer's requirements, decide if you will bring it to the customer's attention, and if so, how to do it constructively, without arrogance.

The overriding objective of your capture activity is to influence the customer to prefer your organization and solution. Repeatedly assess your position by updating the ISW before gate and color team reviews. Is your position improving? Have you met requirements, closed or narrowed the gaps, maintained your discriminators, and consistently highlighted your discriminators in your sales messages?

4 Showcase and vet the program manager with the customer.

Your management team is often your sole discriminator. The customer knows that the majority of the existing workforce will transition to the winner of the competition.

See CUSTOMER-FOCUSED CAPTURE SKILLS AND TACTICS.

See PRESENTATIONS TO CUSTOMERS.

The primary advantage of an incumbent is that the customer knows the program manager and key personnel. Even if the customer is less than thrilled with these individuals, the oft-heard phrase is: *The devil you know is better than the one you don't know.*

Introduce key program personnel early and repeatedly in the capture process by assigning them a prominent role in presentations to customers, bidders' conferences, site visits, and industry day events. Showcase their skills as knowledgeable, customer-focused communicators. Convince customer personnel that your key program personnel, starting with the program manager, are capable and compatible.

Prepare, rehearse, and coach program personnel to listen attentively, interact professionally, and present confidently. While the capture triumvirate must interact professionally with the customer, focus equally on preparing members of your capture and delivery team to do the same. Customers realize that the seller's senior managers and business development professionals will not be delivering a significant portion of the services after the contract is signed.

When presenting to customers, the capture manager should make introductions, clarify roles, review agendas, and direct questions to specific members of the presentation team. Key personnel should demonstrate ownership by discussing how they complete tasks, not how tasks are to be completed by some unnamed person.

Set objectives and define roles, actions, questions, and statements that you will make at bidders' conferences, site visits, and industry day events. Link each event to prior events, keep messages aligned, and do not unintentionally reveal confidential information to competitors.

As you develop rapport with individuals in the customer organization, seek feedback on the incumbent's and your key personnel. Identify who likes or dislikes them, assess the reason, and plan actions to reinforce or mitigate those perceptions. If the customer does not want a person, change the person, as the customer's opinion is the one that matters. Ask customers who they would like to see managing this contract, and then find a way to commit that person to the contract.

5 Delegate select tasks to the program manager.

If the program manager is to complete the program profitably while meeting the customer's expectations, they must own the solution. Ideally, they build the solution collaboratively with key individuals in the customer organization and solution experts in their own and teaming organizations.

Include your program manager in make/buy, teaming, and work share discussions especially on programs with significant service components. While make/buy decisions might appear obvious based on precedent, revisit them on every program.

Buy decisions prompt you to identify teaming partners, subcontractors, and vendors. Consider prior relationships, competitive situations, capabilities, pricing, the partner's reputation and history with the customer, work share, and risk sharing. Work share uncertainties can destroy a team and frighten customers. Customers want an integrated team, not a group of bickering, competing organizations.

Ask the program manager to lead or support the development of the following items:

- Solution
- Performance Work Statements
- Make/buy and work share plans
- Work Breakdown Structure
- Program plan
- Transition plan
- Program schedules
- Costing
- Price-to-win analysis

When delivering services, the program manager must understand the roles and requirements for every key position and the number of people required. Assign the program manager the following tasks:

When attempting to unseat an incumbent:

- Identify and assess the candidates working for the incumbent.
- Determine candidates' availability and cost.
- Prepare an incumbent employee recruiting plan.
- Determine which vacancies can be filled by internal candidates.
- Prepare to recruit remaining vacancies.

When you are the incumbent:

- Evaluate the customer's opinion of key individuals.
- Determine who will be retained, promoted, lateralled, or dismissed.
- Recruit replacements and new personnel.
- Secure recruits' commitments to accept positions, if offered.

If a new program:

- Identify and assess availability of internal candidates.
- Develop recruiting plan.
- Determine candidates' availability and cost.
- Secure recruits' commitments to accept positions, if offered.

A poorly defined WBS, program plan, and delivery schedule lead to pricing gaps and double pricing. Either both organizations assume the other organization owns and prices a task, or they both assume they own and price the same task. The result is higher risk and reduced margins in the former and uncompetitive pricing in the latter.

Confirm that your program manager understands how to manipulate labor rates and labor categories to prepare a competitive management and service delivery solution. Skill categories and titles matter. Offering an engineer when an analyst is sufficient leads to higher prices and lost bids. Similarly, customers often assume a *task manager* exclusively manages, but a *task lead* does productive work.

Leave most price-to-win analysis to specialists, but ask the program manager to help define assumptions, test rationale, and supply current data. Use price-to-win data and competitive analysis to improve or refine your assumptions, solution, and pricing approach.

6 Include the program manager in teaming discussions.

The program manager will manage the winning team, so include them in teaming partner selection and contracting. Discuss and conceptually define responsibilities, level of authority, reporting relationships, customer interface relationships, management systems, customer invoicing, and inter-company invoicing on the contract. In addition, determine each organization's role and financial responsibility in capture, proposal preparation, post-submittal, and mobilization activities.

Customers want to see a team that worked together successfully on prior, similar programs. Far too frequently, management decides to team, but the individuals involved can barely tolerate each other. Customers suspecting teaming incompatibilities turn elsewhere. Minimize internal dissention by predefining how subcontractors will be selected for anticipated tasks, overall workflow, and reporting relationships.

Separate work share and program management decisions. The organization with the best program management capability from the customer's perspective should manage the program. The organization with the largest work share might not be the best lead contractor.

Similarly, the organization with the best program management capability might select a program manager from one of the teaming partners, but make sure that the selected program manager is familiar with the lead contractor's management systems and procedures.

Include teaming partners in capture planning, positioning, and proposal preparation tasks. If you decide to position a team, then present as a team to the customer.

7 Ask the program manager to present the baseline solution at the proposal kickoff meeting.

As the owner of the solution, ask the program manager to demonstrate ownership and understanding by presenting the baseline solution at the proposal kickoff meeting. Clearly separate the roles of the capture triumvirate at proposal kickoff:

The **capture manager** summarizes the opportunity, customer needs, capture strategy and actions, current position, and competitive situation.

The **program manager** presents the solution; summarizes alternatives, trade-offs, and decisions made; introduces teaming partners and summarizes their roles; and discusses the approach to further refine the baseline solution. If the cost lead is not present, the program manager assumes this role until the cost lead is assigned.

The **proposal manager** discusses proposal tasks, assignments, processes, support resources, milestone and inchstone schedules, training, and quality standards. The proposal manager summarizes the proposal strategy, emphasizing alignment with the capture strategy.

8 Keep the entire solution aligned with your evolving strategy.

See PRICING TO WIN.

Capture and proposal contributors and activities tend to get *stove piped* as people focus on their own tasks and lose perspective. As the individual with the best overall understanding of the solution, assign the program manager to monitor the teams that are developing the entire solution: management approach, technical solution, past performance, and pricing. Instruct the program manager to keep the strategy and solution details aligned.

For example, technical contributors tend to focus on ways to enhance the technical capability of the solution. They like to stress meeting and exceeding requirements, which often leads to a higher cost. As the scope creeps upward, the risk increases and profit margins decline. Exceeding requirements is acceptable only if aligned with your capture strategy.

As part of your capture strategy, you decided where to position your solution in the capability-price trade space. Ask your program manager and proposal manager to help maintain this position by assuming the following tasks:

- Explain and justify your capability-price position to all contributors.
- Review your management, technical, and pricing position weekly with the leads from each group. Ask each lead to discuss solution refinements and changes.
- Review contributors' storyboards regularly. Program managers must not leave this task entirely to the proposal manager. At minimum, walk the walls weekly—and when change is rapid, daily. Post revised materials over the prior drafts (when physically posted), or insert version numbers in the file names (when posted on-line).
- When independent reviewers are supporting color team reviews, ask reviewers to personally check section and volume alignment.

9 Assign the intended program manager to prepare the management volume and manage the preparation of other required plans.

When organizations can assign a less expensive but readily available individual to prepare the management volume, they often do. Keeping an experienced program manager billable improves short-term revenue but often reduces long-term revenue.

Focus the management volume on how you will manage the proposed program. Customers detest a generic treatise on program management. The ideal management volume describes exactly how the named program manager will manage this team and deliver this program.

Customers increasingly require a number of management-related plans to be submitted with the proposal. Align these plans with the management volume, making it an integral part of your risk-management approach. The customer's justification is to better assess each bidder's capability and readiness to deliver. An underlying reason is to avoid paying for plans that are prepared pre-award. Mandated post-award plans are priced deliverables.

A recent proposal management workshop participant asked the following question:

We often submit our proposal, wait for the customer to make an award, and then we scramble to prepare our program plan in the short time between award and start-up. Would it be a good idea to begin preparing our program transition, start-up, implementation, and ongoing operational approach immediately after proposal submittal?

Transition plans are potential discriminators as well as essential to manage program risk and estimate transition costs. Like executive summaries, prepare transition plans when requested and when not requested. Unlike an executive summary, which is always submitted as part of the proposal, you might not submit an unsolicited transition plan because it could be written into the contract.

Do not propose at a level of detail beyond what is required in the bid request. When dealing with most governments, the greater the detail in your proposal, the greater the mandatory reporting detail. More detailed reporting increases your delivery costs. Negotiators will exploit that detail in negotiations. Plan in detail to hone your price and reduce risk, but avoid disclosing additional detail unless asked.

Plan transition activities from contract award through at least the first 90 days of the contract. Occasionally, transition implementation activities begin as soon as you are confident that you will win, both to reduce transition risk and to demonstrate your organization's commitment and willingness to invest in this opportunity.

Key aspects of the transition plan include your management approach; technical requirements; personnel; staff loading by area, schedule, teaming assignments and roles; work location; communication; reporting; and invoicing. Key personnel must be on-board during the transition.

Equally important, identify the customer's transition requirements. Customer transition support tasks are a weakness for non-incumbents. Ignoring this weakness is naïve.

While sometimes overlooked, incumbents have a potential transition disadvantage if supporting the capture and proposal tasks distracts from the ongoing contract. Incumbents must perform well on current tasks and immediately correct deficiencies, whether real or perceived.

As the incumbent, ghost competitors by showing the ease, low cost, and low risk of your transition. Continuity of service is usually the incumbent's major discriminator. Known people from the ongoing program offer minimal transition risk.

If you are not the incumbent, highlight your transition experience, early commitment, proven transition process, and transition specialists that support transition tasks. Plan how you will transition ongoing and new tasks.

Customers might not like the incumbent, but they still care about the future employment of individuals in the incumbent organization, especially if they work on-site. Address how these individuals will be transitioned onto your team.

10

Impose a solution freeze.

A favorite saying in the proposal world is: *At some point you have to shoot the engineers and write the proposal.* That is the design freeze. While originally related to product sales, the concept of a solution or design freeze applies equally to services.

No one can clearly describe something that changes daily. So if your solution keeps changing, inter-volume alignment is lost, and contributors are repeatedly required to re-work their drafts, time estimates, and material estimates. Contributors adapt by describing the solution in general, vague terms. Some people call this *generic specific language.*

As a result, evaluators reduce your evaluation score, and your contractual risk increases because you were not clear on exactly what you will and will not do when awarded the contract.

Determine who has the authority to freeze the solution, set the date, and make it happen. The program manager often has the authority to freeze the solution in a services bid, but the technical volume manager or chief engineer often has this authority in a complex, technical systems bid. Alternatively, a senior manager is the only individual with solution freeze authority.

In general, an early solution freeze leads to a superior proposal with an adequate solution. A late solution freeze often results in a losing proposal so poorly written that evaluators cannot understand your solution.

A late solution freeze stresses the pricing team, as the pricing must be adjusted every time that the solution changes. Remember, the cost of accidentally unpriced items falls to the bidder; the cost of over- or double-priced items can be deducted from payments on most government contracts.

11 Assign the program manager to a significant role in orals, finals presentations, and negotiations as the face of the continuing customer-seller relationship.

See **Oral Proposals**, *Proposal Guide.*

At the orals or finals briefing, customers see the capture manager as *the sales guy* and the program manager as the person they have to deal with during the contract. Much like a job interview, customers want to see how well the proposed program manager understands their needs, the proposed solution, the teaming partners, and how to work with their organization and in their environment. Customers want to know if the program manager can listen and then respond clearly, concisely, and courteously.

The program manager must appear to be in charge of the proposed team, have senior management's respect, and have the authority to make decisions. Customers observe how questions are answered, how teams interact, and if members of the selling team appear to value and respect teammates.

As a brief reminder, here are the roles on a typical orals or finals briefing team:

- The **capture manager** facilitates the presentation, sets expectations, seeks agreement from the customer, concisely introduces the team and their roles in the presentation, handles transitions, directs questions to individuals for answers, and closes the presentation.
- The **senior management representative** positions key personnel as best suited to their role, acknowledges their authority to make decisions, and offers to review performance with the customer at their request.
- The **program manager** introduces key personnel and teaming partners and reinforces why these individuals and partners were selected. The program manager speaks in the first-person about how he or she will manage the people, process, program, and interactions with the customer.
- **Teaming partners** discuss why they opted to join this team and work for the prime contractor.
- **Content experts** clearly discuss their topic in language appropriate to the audience and answer questions as directed.

People who lack the knowledge to answer a question admit it, and return the floor to the facilitator. Avoid correcting or adding to a prior answer unless asked to by the facilitator.

The program manager might not be the contract negotiator, but must understand, support, and accept concessions and changes. The program manager is in the best position to explain the consequences of changes to negotiators on both sides.

12 Update your transition and internal management plans.

As soon as you conclude that you are likely to win the contract, update your transition plan and internal program management plans.

No matter how detailed, plans are revised due to contract negotiations, personnel changes in the customer and delivery organizations, and changes in technology and business environment.

Internal management plans for a new contract are similar to the requirements to set up an entirely new business. For example, while you might have a common approach for program cost accounting, contracts are sufficiently different that just establishing accounts is a major task. Employee handbooks can often be adapted from prior contracts, but each one still must be reviewed and tailored.

As noted in Guidelines 5 and 9, incumbents have significant transition advantages. Making adjustments to existing plans is much easier than setting up new systems.

13 Formally transition program responsibility from the capture manager to the program manager.

Classically, the formal transition point is at contract signing when a prospective customer becomes a new or renewed customer. However, the transition timing varies depending upon the capabilities of the individuals, organizational demands on their time, and duration of post-submittal activities.

Capture managers are often asked to manage multiple opportunities, so the program manager might formally assume responsibility to manage on-going, post-submittal activities that largely focus on contracting details. When bidding as an incumbent, the program manager is already in place and is best positioned to handle post-submittal activity.

On new contracts, make the transition a formal event that includes key customer representatives. Ask a senior manager from your organization to attend to demonstrate the importance of the contract. Something always goes awry during transition, so the primary purpose of a formal transition is to clearly state who is responsible for the success of the contract. Discuss and identify individual *touch points* in the customer organization.

14 Grow the contract during execution by identifying, positioning, proposing, and closing additional tasks.

In addition to managing the quality delivery of contracted services, ask program managers to grow the contract by identifying, positioning, proposing, and closing additional tasks. Program managers report spending as much as 60 percent of their time proposing and closing added tasks.

The motivations of customers and contractors are varied and mixed. Customers add tasks because:

- Original budget was knowingly insufficient, and they are seeking or have secured additional funding.
- The budget has been reduced, forcing a scope change.
- Requirements as solicited were incorrect or incomplete.
- Improved technology or methods are now available, newly identified, feasible, or accepted.
- Objectives, issues, and requirements have changed.
- The in-place contracting vehicle is the easiest way to purchase.

Contractors seek to add tasks because:

- Someone in the customer organization requested a change.
- Contractor identifies additional needs that can be efficiently added to the contract.
- Contractor identifies tasks that are essential to meet customer requirements but were inadvertently omitted from the current contract.
- Additional tasks awarded without competition often improve profit margins.

Program managers are in a unique position with unfettered access to the customer organization. Customers increasingly view contractor personnel as fellow employees or as an extension of their work force. Hence, contractor personnel are viewed as collaborators, and these contractor recommendations are accepted as the constructive recommendations of experts.

Ask program managers to balance customers' interests with your organization's interests. The primary reason customers replace incumbents is poor performance, followed by excessive, costly change orders.

Here is a typical example:

> *An IT services outsourcing contract is awarded based on a proposed 25–30 percent cost reduction. Subsequent customer analysis reveals no cost savings and 20–30 percent cost increases in some areas. The contractor identified numerous additional available services, individuals in the customer organization ordered those services, and the contractor billed for the services per the contracted pricing schedule. The increased cost is due to increased demand for services, but the customer's overall objective was not met. In this example, the contractor failed to manage expectations, keep the customer informed, and emphasize the benefits derived from the added services. While the customer might have failed to monitor the contract and maintain focus on the overall objective, the customer feels abused at contract renewal.*

Program managers and their contracting team are in the ideal position to identify entirely new opportunities in the customer organization. However, they might fail to see or report these opportunities due to their focus on service delivery, remaining billable, and routine daily activities.

Ask program managers to devote a small portion of each internal program management meeting to discuss potential new business opportunities. In each meeting, remind employees to ask customers about their needs, review indicators of future or additional needs, and to report these needs to their program manager. Reward employees for their efforts, whether by recognition or remuneration.

Ask program managers to promptly refer new opportunities to business development. Customers object to program managers who appear to be focusing on new opportunities at the expense of the current program.

15 Prepare and deliver the annual internal program review and prepare the mid-term program review pending contract re-competition.

Regard the annual internal program review as your organization's check on the health of the contract. Customers expect senior management oversight, so approach internal program reviews as a customer update meeting. Summarize your performance, seek needed resources, recognize outstanding individual performance, and discuss added tasks. If a customer representative is present, review additional contract task opportunities and new opportunities in a separate meeting.

Schedule an internal, mid-term program review to summarize customer perceptions and recommend actions to position your organization to renew this contract. If the existing contract has renewal options, persuade the customer to extend the current contract as the best course of action.

If the customer cannot or will not extend the contract, then the mid-term internal contract review is the point where you initiate capture activity to renew the contract. Contract renewals are the single most efficient use of business development resources. No other opportunity offers a higher win probability at a lower risk and cost. If you have performance issues, correct them years—not months—before the contract expires.

Following the mid-term contract review, appoint a capture manager, prepare the capture plan, schedule the Blue Team review, and implement the capture plan.

Engaging Proposal support while continuing your capture activities is essential to ensuring capture and proposal strategies are aligned and implemented in the proposal.

Ideally, you should be able to win the order without submitting a competitive proposal. The reality is that few customers are permitted to award a contract—or want to award a contract—without soliciting competitive bids, even when they have a preferred vendor. Government regulations or corporate purchasing guidelines often require competitive proposals, usually from three or more bidders. Purchasing professionals believe competitive bids foster better solutions, lower prices, and better value. Seek a purchase order without competition, but you will probably have to submit a proposal.

If someone tells you that the capture phase ends when the proposal begins, they are uninformed. Capture activity continues in parallel with proposal planning, preparation, and review. Customers might limit contact with sellers, but the rules vary by country, market, selling environment, customer, and opportunity.

Capture management and proposal management require different skills, and few individuals have both skill sets. Most capture and sales professionals welcome professional proposal support. Capture managers and proposal managers can most effectively engage proposal support by following the guidelines in this section. If not, in the words of a veteran capture manager: *They will get the proposal that they deserve.*

Keep the responsibilities and goals of the capture triumvirate in mind:

- **Capture manager**: Owns the opportunity and the customer—the goal is to win.
- **Proposal manager**: Owns the proposal document—the goal is a quality, winning proposal.
- **Program manager**: Owns the solution—the goal is a profitable, deliverable solution.

The first engagement of the prospective proposal manager is after the Pursuit Decision Gate review as the capture manager begins to prepare a detailed capture plan. However, the heaviest involvement is after the Preliminary Bid Decision gate review through proposal submittal. Each of the guidelines comprises activities that engage some aspect of proposal support, whether managed or completed by the capture manager or the proposal manager.

Engaging Proposal Support

1. Seek proposal manager input when preparing the detailed proposal budget.
2. Extend the capture strategy into the proposal strategy and conduct Blue Team review.
3. Integrate the extended capture team in key pre-proposal activities.
4. Draft the executive summary.
5. Influence the selection of the best core proposal team members.
6. Support the proposal kickoff meeting.
7. Define and manage customer contacts.
8. Participate in but do not facilitate color team reviews.
9. Help analyze the final bid request and lead the Bid Validation Decision gate review.
10. Lead, guide, or contribute to post-bid submittal interactions with the customer.

1

Seek proposal manager input when preparing the detailed proposal budget.

The first task of a newly named capture manager is to prepare the capture plan. A key element is to estimate and secure a budget for proposal support activities. Seek input from proposal support to estimate the cost to prepare the proposal. Proposal professionals are the only people likely to have relevant cost metrics. When proposal managers prepare the budgets, they are more committed to completing proposals within those budgets.

Two primary proposal preparation cost elements are the cost to design the solution and the cost to prepare the documents. The cost to design the solution depends on whether the solution is new, a variant of a prior design, or essentially the same as a prior design.

The cost to prepare the proposal documents is directly related to the page count. The value of the contract is relevant but often less important; $500 million contracts have been awarded based on 35-page proposals.

See PRODUCTION, ***Proposal Guide.***

Formally solicited and evaluated proposals (as are typical with government systems purchases) are oftentimes more costly to prepare because everything must be written for the proposal. More generic bid requests (such as those prepared by industry consultants, local governments, or for smaller B2B buyers) tend to contain more boilerplate or general requirements. Consequently, boilerplate response materials are more easily adapted, which reduces the per-page proposal preparation cost.

Increasingly, bid requests specify the performance desired, leaving the specified approach to the ingenuity of the bidder. Responding to a short statement of objectives or a performance work statement can be quite difficult, lengthy, and expensive despite the relatively short bid request.

When asking a proposal manager to estimate proposal preparation cost, anticipate the following questions:

- How many volumes and copies of each volume, and what is the page count/ limit by volume?
- How similar is the solicitation to prior solicitations from this customer?
- Is your probable solution defined?
- How similar is the solution to prior solutions?
- How long is the preparation period?
- What and how many color reviews are planned?
- Do you anticipate draft and final solicitations? Extensions?
- Do you anticipate orals or a finals briefing after submittal?
- Is a demonstration required?
- What additional plans are required before, with, or after the proposal is due?
- Are cost and pricing data and estimating rationale required as part of the cost volume?
- What access and availability can we count on from content experts?
- Can I review your capture plan?
- Have you identified and can you supply relevant experience and past performance data?

Estimating proposal preparation cost is as much art as science, and the science is based upon realistic scoping and reliable metrics.

2

Extend the capture strategy into the proposal strategy.

See COLOR TEAM REVIEWS *and* STRATEGY.

Capture strategy is your plan to win a specific, definable opportunity. Strategy statements include strategic and tactical aspects. The strategic aspects define your position, and the tactical aspects define the actions that you will take to implement that strategy. Your capture strategy was reviewed as part of the Blue Team review.

Extending your capture strategy into the proposal strategy might be the single most important interaction that a capture manager has with the proposal manager. Align capture and proposal messages. Sellers lose credibility when capture and proposal messages conflict. Once your credibility is lost, customers doubt subsequent messages.

Extending capture strategy into proposal strategy is not as simple as transferring capture strategy statements from the capture plan to the proposal management plan. The strategy or positioning portion is the same, but the tactical implementation changes. The following brief example is extended in Strategy, Guideline 8.

Capture strategy example:

> What: (position).
>
> We will emphasize our ability to complete the design-build of a distribution center on time.
>
> By: (action).
>
> Taking the customer on a plant tour of the XYZ distribution center in Orlando, FL.

Proposal strategy example:

What: (position).

We will emphasize our ability to complete the design-build of a distribution center on time.

By: (action).

Including in our proposal photos of the XYZ distribution center in Orlando, FL.

Consider scheduling a second Blue Team review to improve the quality of your proposal strategy.

If so, the focus shifts:

Blue review 1	Focuses on capture strategy.
Blue review 2	Focuses on proposal strategy.

If you have a second Blue Team review, consider errors of omission and alignment as well as the correctness, comprehensiveness, and specificity of strategy statements.

3 Integrate the extended capture team in key pre-proposal activities.

See Proposal Management Plan, ***Proposal Guide.***

Integrate proposal support, program management, engineering, and key teaming partners in proposal planning, solution development, work share, WBS development, and price-to-win (PTW) activities.

Your primary focus as the capture manager is to win the contract. While proposal support, program management, engineering, and key teaming partners also want to win, they report to other managers with potentially conflicting objectives.

Successful teams are based upon trust, so successful team leaders focus on building and maintaining trust among team members.

Improve your capture success by integrating and aligning the activities of your extended capture team members. Review and clarify the roles, focus, relationships, responsibilities, and authorities of team members. If not, two outcomes are likely, both risky:

- The quality of the solution and proposal suffers.
- Technical and programmatic risk increases.

While the program manager owns the solution, anticipate conflicts between your technical design team, the people who will manage and execute the program, and teaming partners who are angling for maximum work share.

Team members make different assumptions, both explicit and implicit, which significantly impact cost and risk. Vaguely defined and poorly understood solutions and approaches will be described vaguely in the proposal, decreasing the persuasiveness and win probability of your proposal.

The proposal manager is responsible for preparing a compliant, responsive proposal that appears to be the product of an integrated team. Help the proposal manager define contributors' roles and gain the support of contributors' managers. The capture manager usually has greater influence than the proposal manager, so back your proposal manager.

Just as project managers prepare project plans, proposal managers prepare Proposal Management Plans (PMPs). Multiple elements of the PMP can be extracted, adapted, and amended from prior plans, as shown in figure 1.

Collaborate with the proposal manager on capture and proposal plan updates and encourage adapted reuse. Figure 2 lists PMP contents and potential material sources as defined by a large, U.S.-based systems integrator.

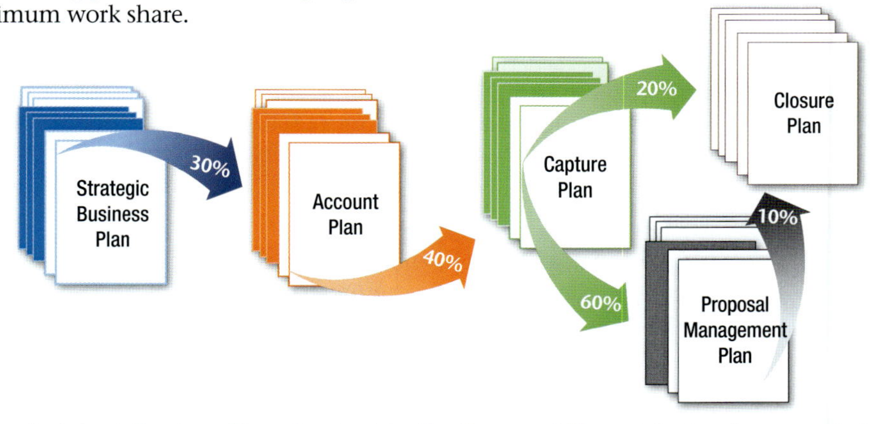

Figure 1. Adapt Capture Plan Content to the Proposal Plan. *Adapt and reuse material from prior plans. While estimates vary, approximately 40 percent of the data from the account plan applies to the capture plan. Up to 80 percent of the capture plan data is needed in the proposal and closure plans.*

SAMPLE PROPOSAL MANAGEMENT PLAN CONTENT

Origin: **C: Capture Plan**
N: New Material
B: Boilerplate (minor revision)

Section / Item	Origin
1.0 PROPOSAL PROJECT SUMMARY	
General Information	*N,C*
Project Focal Points	*N,C*
Project Scope and Deliverables	*N,C*
2.0 CUSTOMER PROFILE	
Intelligence in Customer Organization	*C*
Source Selection Process	*C*
Customer Needs, Issues, and Hot Buttons	*N,C*
Customer Perceptions of Our Organization	*C*
3.0 COMPETITIVE ANALYSIS	
Our Approach and Perceived Strengths/Weaknesses	*C*
Competitor Profiles and Strengths/Weaknesses	*C*
Bidder Comparison Chart	*N,C*
4.0 PROPOSAL STRATEGIES AND THEMES	
Overall Proposal Strategies and Themes	*N,C*
Technical Proposal Strategies and Themes	*N,C*
Management Proposal Strategies and Themes	*N,C*
Logistics Proposal Strategies and Themes	*N,C*
Cost Proposal Strategies and Themes	*N,C*
Past Performance Strategies and Themes	*N,C*
5.0 STAFFING, ROLES, AND RESPONSIBILITIES	
Proposal Management Team	*N*
Proposal Writers	*N*
Proposal Review Teams	*N*
Personnel Expertise Matrix	*N*
Team Responsibilities	*B,N*
Coordination Responsibilities	*B*
6.0 PROPOSAL OPERATIONS	
Proposal War Room	*B*
Method of Operation	*B*
Storyboards	*B*
Key Activities	*N,B*
Appendix 1: Proposal Development Schedule	*N*
Appendix 2: Proposal Outline, Cross Reference of RFP Requirements, and Writing Assignments	*N*
Attachment 1. Writers' Information	*N*
Attachment 2. Preliminary Executive Summary	*N,C*

Figure 2. Sample Contents for Proposal Plan. *Reusing material saves time and improves consistency, as long as each item is reviewed and adapted before insertion. In this example, a major U.S.-based systems integrator identified potential sources of proposal plan material.*

4

The executive summary should be the first and last item written for a proposal.

Draft the executive summary.

Develop the proposal executive summary over time, adding and correcting the content as your understanding of the customer, customer requirements, bid request, competitors, your strategy, and your solution evolve. Begin by preparing a mockup, leaving open spaces or gaps where missing information can be inserted when available. Draft text and add graphics in subsequent iterations.

The capture manager is the primary owner of the executive summary but seldom the only writer. The capture manager should prepare the initial mockup and present it at the Preliminary Bid gate review. Include, at minimum, these items:

- Customer's vision
- Hot button issues (citing sources or owners)
- High-level solution requirements
- Primary proposal theme(s)

See Executive Summary, ***Proposal Guide.***

At this point, the capture manager often lacks the following mandatory recommended executive summary information:

- Technical solution
- Program management structure and team members
- High-level deliverables schedule
- Teaming relationships
- Substantiating experience and performance references

Distribute your draft executive summary at the proposal kickoff meeting.

If so, leave places for graphics and text notes to remind you to insert this information in subsequent drafts. These gaps also remind management to make or approve these decisions regarding these items.

Schedule the Preliminary Bid Decision gate review only if you can present an executive summary mockup containing this information

Avoid these common executive summary mistakes:

See Presentations to Customers on how to align the executive summary and a customer presentation.

- Preparing the first draft by adapting an executive summary from a prior submittal.
  These drafts are never quite right, they are seldom sufficiently customer focused, and you will resist making subsequent changes.
- Preparing the executive summary last, just prior to the Red Team review. You lose the opportunity to guide proposal contributors and vet the executive summary with your management and potentially the customer.

A quality executive summary mockup offers proof that you understand the customer, have a
credible capture strategy, and that management
should support your request to commit business development resources to continue capture activities and engage proposal support.

After the Preliminary Bid gate review, ask the Blue Team to critique the draft executive summary in its current form, whether a mockup or initial draft. Realizing the importance, many capture managers prepare the first draft of the executive summary. Others delegate first draft writing to the proposal manager, especially if they have strong writing skills and have written executive summaries. Either way, the capture manager retains primary responsibility and ownership.

Use executive summary drafts to brief internal management, obtain buy-in, and refine your proposal strategy. Senior managers will review a draft executive summary when they would not bother to review a capture plan.

Use the executive summary to brief your extended capture team, including the proposal team, program management, engineering, and key teaming partners and their management.

Distribute and review the draft executive summary at the proposal kickoff meeting. When proposal developers understand your primary messages, they can align their drafts. Equally important, having and sharing a draft executive summary at proposal kickoff convince contributors that they will be competently managed and their contributions will lead to a win.

Preview executive summary information and drafts with trusted *coaches* in the customer's organization or former customer employees if legal, permitted, or practical. Alternatively, screen key points in customer presentations.

Drafting a customer-focused, concise, comprehensive, and persuasive executive summary is difficult. For guidance, refer to the Executive Summary topic section, attend training, and request independent reviews from customers and outside consultants. Often senior managers are too invested to constructively critique executive summaries produced within their own organization.

5 Influence the selection of the best core proposal team members.

Help the proposal and program manager identify and secure the best talent for key roles. Your goal should be:

- Make the right people available; don't try to make the available people right.

The right people are invariably overbooked and assigned to ongoing tasks. Capture managers often prefer to avoid getting too deeply involved in proposal preparation. While you might be confident that the customer prefers your solution and organization, they are usually bound by what is in your proposal.

Program managers might try to distance the capture manager from their solution. A capture manager advocating the customer's position naturally conflicts with the program manager who will be tasked to deliver the solution on schedule and in a profitable manner. Counter this bias by involving key members of the solution design team in capture planning activities. Solution designers who interact with the customer craft a more customer-focused, realistic, and responsive solution.

Discuss the selection of these key proposal team members with your proposal manager:

Technical volume leader: Select a technical manager in the program area who is technically knowledgeable and can locate expertise on technical sub-areas. Ideally, volume leaders can communicate vertically and laterally, are respected by management and peers, and can resolve technical issues on multiple levels. The ideal technical volume lead can draft technical sections if needed, but most importantly, can coach technical contributors.

Management volume leader: The ideal management volume lead is the person who will manage the program. If the designated program manager is not the management volume lead, ask the assigned person to write as if he or she will be the program manager.

Focus on key individuals' responsibilities, authorities, specific work processes, and working relationship with the contracting organization. The management volume lead typically must prepare or manage the preparation of a series of plans: quality assurance, configuration management, risks assessment, transition, subcontracting, and small and minority business.

Avoid preparing a generic treatise on program management or boilerplating the management volume. Neither approach persuades the customer that you are prepared to manage the program.

Cost volume leader: Select a person with solid costing experience who can construct a compliant, traceable, clearly organized document that convinces the customer that your costs are reasonable and realistic. Ask the cost volume lead to collaborate with the program manager and key teaming partners to define work shares, the work breakdown structure (WBS), the Contractor Statement of Work (CSOW), cost assumptions, and estimating guidelines. The cost volume lead should assist the price-to-win specialist and collaborate with fellow volume leads to ensure the solution they cost and price is identical to the solution proposed in other volumes.

Lead proposal writers: Support the proposal manager's efforts to obtain lead writers who have been successful on major proposals. Ideally, lead writers do not have to be trained, closely supervised, coddled, or micro-managed. Ask lead writers to mentor less experienced writers. If the only writers available are inexperienced, secure funding to train the writing team. Just-in-time, opportunity-specific training typically saves far more writing time than the time required for the training. Even when writers are experienced, make sure the proposal manager schedules brief, focused training sessions to review writing standards and reinforce best practices.

6 Support the proposal kickoff meeting.

While the proposal manager plans and conducts proposal kickoff meetings, the capture manager briefs the proposal team on the customer, opportunity, and competition. Proposal contributors commit their best efforts when they believe this particular management team is prepared and committed to win.

Overview the capture strategy, including actions planned, actions completed, customer feedback, teaming partners, potential subcontractors and vendors, and probable competitors. Stress the alignment between capture and proposal strategy, and endorse the proposal strategy, which will be briefed by the proposal manager.

Whether alone or in concert with the program manager, the capture manager reviews teaming considerations, qualifications, and teaming partners' roles and introduces key participants from the teaming partners.

Include teaming partners in the proposal kickoff. If confidentiality or disclosure considerations prevent including teaming partners, note why teaming partners are absent, and conduct a separate kickoff with teaming partners. Include key proposal personnel in the teaming partner kickoff, whether in person or virtual.

7

Define and manage customer contacts.

Note: Capable proposal managers often handle questions about the bid request and post-submittal clarifications. As capture manager, delegate these activities if you are confident they will be handled competently.

A primary characteristic of a high-value, complex sale is teams of people selling to multiple people in the customer organization. As the seller's face to the customer, the capture manager should define, schedule, and manage customer contacts, including bidders' conferences, site visits, and questions regarding solicitation documents.

Engaging proposal support might prompt an increase in people on the selling team, leading to multiple, uncontrolled direct contacts with the customer. Every contact should be managed so that the outcome advances rather than impedes the sale.

Early capture activities are easier to manage because the capture manager often plans, attends, facilitates, or arranges these activities. However, bidder conferences and site visits introduce new individuals who might know relatively little about the customer and the opportunity. The usual meeting guidelines apply:

- Name the event leader.
- Plan the event.
- Define each participant's role.
- Establish common expectations, objectives, and ground rules with your team prior to the event and with the customer prior to or at the event.
- Prepare and rehearse, if appropriate.
- Follow the facilitator's lead during the event.
- Conclude events by reviewing and confirming next steps.
- Debrief the team immediately after the event, summarize results, inform others as needed, and assign follow-up actions.

Every proposal team will have questions about requirements, conflicts, and omissions in solicitation documents. While the proposal manager, legal, or contracts representative might collect, review, and refine these questions, the capture manager should be aware of each question and strategize with the proposal team regarding if, how, and who will pose questions. Apply the same approach to additional customer questions.

8

Participate in but do not facilitate color team reviews.

See Color Team Reviews.

The capture manager participates in color team reviews but is too involved in the effort to impartially facilitate color team reviews. Identify an experienced and respected facilitator from inside or outside the organization.

Typical capture manager contributions include the following tasks:

- Brief reviewers on key aspects of the opportunity.
- Remain available to respond to reviewer questions during the review.
- Attend the review debrief, asking clarification questions that help you define constructive follow-up actions.
- Thank reviewers for their contributions.

9

Help analyze the final bid request and lead the Bid Validation Decision gate review.

When bid requests change, the capture manager is best positioned to interpret the customer's motivations, issues, and justification for the change. Wise strategists understand and address the underlying issue. Naive strategists simply accept the change.

As part of the capture triumvirate, review the final bid request and identify *show stoppers* or contingencies. Were any of these contingencies pre-identified in your capture plan? Is the opportunity still congruent with your organization's strategic direction and objectives? If not, revisit your bid decision. Walking away from a bid this late is difficult but better than winning a contract that you cannot afford to complete.

Do other bid request changes affect your strategy, solution, or pricing approach? If so, discuss and define adjustments, request acceptance at the Bid Validation Decision review, and implement adjustments post review.

10 Lead, guide, or contribute to post-bid submittal interactions with the customer.

The capture manager's post-submittal role varies greatly by organization. Some organizations reassign the capture manager after proposal submittal, delegating the follow-up questions, clarifications, and final bid price to the program manager and proposal manager. Others shift the lead to the program manager, but retain the capture manager to facilitate short list or orals presentations.

If the capture manager will have the primary ongoing relationship with the customer, keep he or she involved. In the Business to Business (B2B) sector, this might be the account manager. If the program manager will have the ongoing relationship, shift the capture manager to another pursuit.

The capture manager's charge is to win the contract, and you have not won until you sign the contract. In most instances, the capture manager supports but does not lead the following post-submittal activities:

- **Questions and clarifications** follow most proposal submittals and are typically coordinated by the proposal manager. Regard questions as a positive event; customers usually ask questions because you remain in contention. Strategize each response and respond with the same discipline and courtesy as in the proposal. Hand deliver your response, if permitted, to gain direct personal access to the customer.
- **Graybeard visits** are an opportunity to impress senior members of the customer's evaluation team. While the proposal or program manager might plan these visits, the capture manager should usually facilitate graybeard and site visits. Graybeard and site visits are positive signs that you remain in contention.
- **Contract negotiations** are often led by the seller's contract specialists, supported by the program manager. As capture manager, brief the lead negotiator regarding key customer participants and customer hot button issues.
- **Proposal debriefs** are usually requested, scheduled, and facilitated by the capture manager or proposal manager. Request a debrief, win or lose, and keep it constructive. Assign a note-taker. The capture manager should focus on listening, recognizing non-verbal signals, and asking constructive follow-up questions. Leave proposal document questions to the proposal manager, if he or she attends the debrief.
- **Protests** are best handled by contracts or legal representatives. Capture managers expecting to pursue additional opportunities with the same customer need to create some distance to maintain a positive or at least neutral relationship with the customer.
- **Program start-up** is often seen by customers as the official handover from the capture manager to the program manager. Introduce or re-introduce key program management personnel, clarify their roles, and reinforce their qualifications. As the long-time face of your organization with the customer, explicitly state your role, if any, in this program and future programs.

If your organization reassigns the capture manager after proposal submittal, then the program manager is already the primary customer contact. Ideally, the program manager has been active in the capture process and is well known by the customer. If not, the capture manager should introduce the program manager before moving to a new assignment.

A capture manager might maintain an ongoing role when pursuing:

- Task orders under a master ordering contract
- Change orders on a major contract
- Added tasks when supporting a prime contractor

Depending upon the market and selling environment, the capture manager might be identical to an account manager with an ongoing oversight role for all contracted services with the same customer. Alternatively, the program manager on a major program assumes a capture role regarding change proposals and added tasks.

Executive Summaries are often the most important pages in a proposal. They set the tone for individual evaluators and are often the only pages read by the decision makers. A draft should be developed during the capture process.

See Engaging Proposal Support.

A draft executive summary should be developed early during the capture planning phase. It provides a roadmap for the rest of the capture plan.

The capture manager should prepare the first draft of the executive summary and present it at the Preliminary Bid Decision gate review. Convince reviewers that you deserve their support by presenting evidence that your view of the customer's hot button issues, vision, and expected solution is correct.

Readers of your executive summary must clearly understand your solution and its unique benefits and be able to justify recommending your solution over competing solutions.

Effective executive summaries meet the following criteria:

- Connect your solution to the customer's business vision.
- Identify the customer's needs and make ownership of those needs explicit.
- Connect your solution directly to the customer's needs.
- Offer clear proof of your claims.
- Show how you offer greater value than the competition.
- Be brief, but comprehensive, by eliminating confusing technical details that are better explained in the body of the proposal.
- Indicate the next step, usually by previewing how your proposal is organized.

Executive summaries are also powerful internal tools:

- Help refine your bidding strategy.
- Become a vehicle to gain senior management endorsement.
- Communicate your strategy in-house to all contributors.
- Drive proposal development.
- Become a model for the complete proposal.

At the Pursuit Decision gate review, the person who briefs management should know and describe the customer's hot button issues, organizational vision, and desired solution. This Pursuit Decision gate briefer is not yet the capture manager because the capture manager is assigned at or immediately after this review.

Evolve the content, form, and detail in the executive summary until the proposal is submitted. The capture manager's first draft usually lacks the following mandatory executive summary information:

- Technical solution
- Program management structure and team members
- High-level deliverables schedule
- Teaming relationships
- Substantiating experience and performance examples/references

After the Preliminary Bid Decision gate review, ask the Blue Team review to critique the draft executive summary. Many capture managers delegate completion of the executive summary to the proposal manager; other capture managers opt to complete the first draft themselves.

Assign the person with the best perspective, writing skills, and availability to complete the executive summary.

At the Bid Validation Decision gate review, present a draft, four-boxed executive summary, which could be expanded into the full executive summary by the proposal team.

Executive Summaries

1. Always include an executive summary.
2. Maintain customer focus throughout.
3. Build on your existing sales process and strategy.
4. Organize the content to be clear and persuasive.
5. Expand the Executive Summary Organizer into a single- or multiple-page draft.
6. Develop your executive summary based on proven best-in-class practices.
7. Follow sound writing guidelines.
8. Follow a defined process when preparing on short notice.

1

See **Organization, *Proposal Guide.***

Three model executive summaries are included in **Model Documents 6, 7, & 8** in the ***Proposal Guide.***

Always include an executive summary.

If the customer asks for an executive summary, submit one. If not, do so anyway.

Call it whatever the customer calls it. Common alternatives are management summary and management overview.

Independent of what the customer calls it, understand the difference between a summary and an introduction. A summary summarizes the essential content of your proposal. An introduction indicates how your proposal is organized. Other terms for introduction are preview, roadmap, and informal table of contents.

To include an executive summary when the proposal outline is strictly defined in the bid request, you have several compliant alternatives. One is to include a separately bound executive summary. Another is to place a copy in every volume submitted, either in a pocket in the front or in the binder.

Note that in page-limited proposals, the executive summary is considered part of your technical proposal and is included in the page count.

2

See **Customer-Focused Capture Skills and Tactics.**

Maintain customer focus throughout.

Check every executive summary against the following criteria:

- States the customer's vision.
- Connects the vision to the immediate purchase.
- Cites the customer's hot buttons in order of importance or the order listed in their bid request.
- Makes the customer's ownership of the hot buttons explicit.
- Addresses each hot button in the order introduced.
- Names the customer more than the seller.
- Names the customer before the seller in the document, paragraphs, and sentences.
- Cites benefits before features.

3

See **Capture Planning** *and* **Proposal Management Plan** *in the* ***Proposal Guide.***

Build on your existing sales process and strategy.

To maintain a consistent message with your customers and to save time, exploit your existing internal information sources as much as possible.

Many organizations have embraced a strategic and/or tactical sales process. Exploit it to develop your executive summary rather than starting over. With a little effort, you can map the information from existing sales tools into your executive summary.

When business development people are asked to draft the executive summary, too many still pull the last one they prepared, do a *Search and Replace* for customer and product names, add one or two sentences, and submit. They continue to tailor their last executive summary for subsequent opportunities until the executive summary completely unravels.

Most of the information needed to prepare the executive summary is contained in the capture plan and proposal management plan. The three key templates summarized in figures 1, 2, and 3 are recommended to help assemble and organize the information needed for an executive summary.

Using the information in the three templates shown as sources, prepare the Consolidated Solution Matrix shown in figure 4 with the same hot buttons/issues consolidated from the three templates.

You now have the information needed to begin drafting your executive summary.

ShipleyAssociates **Integrated Solution Worksheet**

Enter Opportunity Name Here

Item No.	Customer Issues	Customer Requirements	Available Solution	Gap	Competitor Solution	Discriminators	Strategy	Action Required
1	System must be available.	8 hr. response time.	2 hr. response time	1 hr	3 hr. response time	Faster response but more expensive?	Emphasize no additional cost with cellular.	Show current response time. Show photo-service with cell phone.

Figure 1. Integrated Solution Worksheet. *The primary focus of this template is to arrive at a competitive solution that is aligned with the customer's issues and requirements. The strategic messages communicated in sales calls must also be communicated in the executive summary.*

For additional uses of the Integrated Solution Worksheet and Bidder Comparison Chart, *see* CAPTURE PLANNING, STRATEGY, and TEAMING.

ISSUES	WEIGHT	US (SCORE)	COMPANY A	COMPANY B
Specific Experience	30	25	20	15
Low Price	20	5	10	15
Familiarity with Manager Named	20	15	10	10
Ability to Meet Schedule	30	25	21	15
TOTAL SCORE	100	70	61	55

Figure 2. Bidder Comparison Chart. *The primary focus of this template is to discern how the customer organization perceives your team's solution versus your competitors' as it relates to the customer's issues. In this example, specific experience is seen by the customer as strength.*

STRATEGY STATEMENT WORKSHEET

- We will emphasize our strengths delivering 2-hr. response
  by including summaries of our actual service response in the customer's area.
- We will mitigate our weaknesses in: ______
  by: ______
- We will highlight our competitors' weaknesses in: ______
  by: ______
- We will downplay our competitors' strengths in: ______
  by: ______

Figure 3. Proposal Strategy Statements. *The primary focus of proposal strategy statements is to identify ways you can implement or convey your strategy in a written executive summary and proposal.*

To use all features of form, enable macros. See Word Help for instructions.
For context-specific help in most fields, press F1 (Windows) or Command + / (Mac OS).
If there are more than 4 hot buttons, use additional worksheets and renumber hot buttons.

ShipleyAssociates

Executive Summary
Planning Worksheet

Plan Around the Hot Buttons

Hot Buttons			
#1	#2	#3	#4
Improve system availability			
Solution			
2-hr. response			
Benefits or Value Propositions			
Greater availability			
Discriminators			
No additional cost			
Proof, Experience, and Past Performance			
List area clients & equipment Quote XYZ record			
Key Visual(s)			
Performance table			

Copyright 2012 Shipley Associates 1

Figure 4. Executive Summary Planning Worksheet. *Complete the worksheet by extracting information from previous templates, or simply start with this one. First, list customer hot buttons in priority order across the first row. Next, across the second row, list aspects of your solution under the hot buttons they most closely address. If a feature doesn't fit a hot button, consider leaving it out. Third, under each hot button, list benefits your solution provides, discriminators, and proofs. Note visuals that illustrate any of those points.*

4

Organize the content to be clear and persuasive.

See **Model Documents** *6, 7, and 8 in the* ***Proposal Guide*** *for examples of executive summaries in the four-box organizational style.*

Transfer the content that you developed and summarized in the Planning Worksheet into the Executive Summary Organizer, shown in figure 5.

The Organizer is based on fundamental principles for creating persuasive documents using what is called four-box organization.

Four-box organization is nearly always more customer focused than the narrative or mirror approach. The mirror approach is a mini-version of your proposal, most often used when the proposal is formally solicited and the structure is rigidly defined in the bid request.

The draft executive summary becomes a *working document* for the capture team as strategies and solutions evolve during the capture process. Teams should regularly review the draft to update and refresh content and win strategies.

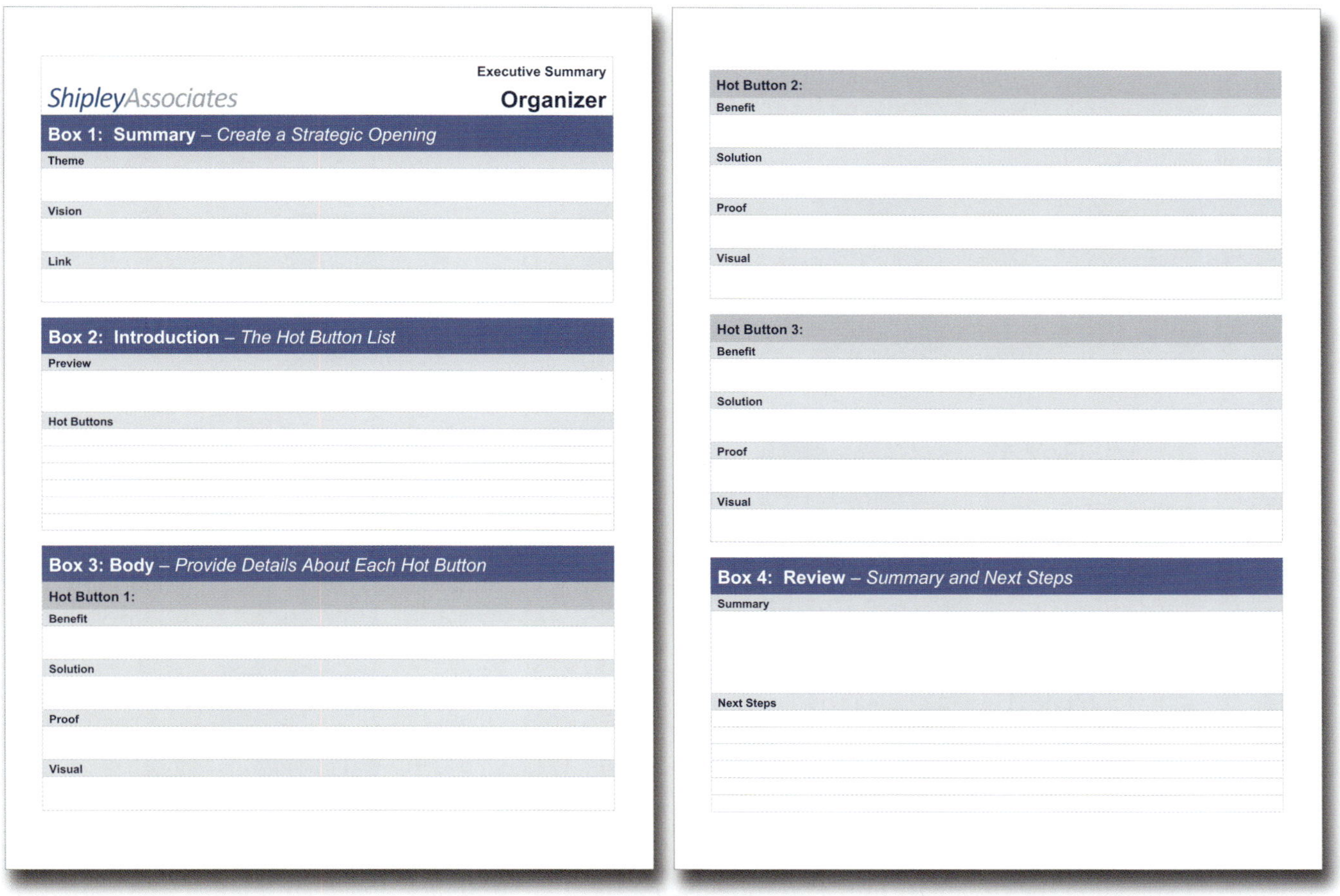
ShipleyAssociates
Executive Summary
Organizer

Box 1: Summary – *Create a Strategic Opening*
Theme
Vision
Link

Box 2: Introduction – *The Hot Button List*
Preview
Hot Buttons

Box 3: Body – *Provide Details About Each Hot Button*
Hot Button 1:
Benefit
Solution
Proof
Visual

Hot Button 2:
Benefit
Solution
Proof
Visual

Hot Button 3:
Benefit
Solution
Proof
Visual

Box 4: Review – *Summary and Next Steps*
Summary
Next Steps

CONTENT

Box 1–SUMMARY: Begin with a theme statement. Recognize the customer's vision, challenges, and objectives. Link the vision to this purchase.

Box 2–INTRODUCTION: Preview content of the proposal. Establish and prioritize customer's needs or desired outcome. List hot buttons and make the customer's ownership of them explicit. Introduce your basic solution.

Box 3–BODY: Using hot buttons as subtitles, address each one in the announced order from Box 2 with benefits and details of your solution. Provide proofs, including relevant experience. Include visuals whenever possible.

Box 4–REVIEW: State why the customer should select you. Summarize your unique contribution to your customer's success. Reiterate discriminators. Include cost if allowed by your customer. Indicate next steps, both in proposal evaluation (by summarizing order of material presented) and in the sales process (such as answering questions, meeting for negotiations, etc.).

Figure 5. Using a Four-Box Executive Summary Organizer. *Rearrange material planned with the Planning Worksheet into a persuasive order with the Executive Summary Organizer. The template assures a high degree of customer focus and helps produce an executive summary intuitively appealing to the customer. When proposal instructions are restrictive, an executive summary organized this way may be the only place you can tell a coherent story.*

5

See Value Propositions.

Expand the Executive Summary Organizer into a single- or multiple-page draft.

The Organizer helps you identify key selling points within a customer-focused, clear framework. Expand the framework into a first draft:

- Develop the visuals.
  - Draft action captions for the visuals.
  - Draft text directing evaluators to the graphics.
  - Draft text describing your solutions.
  - Draft text describing your experience and proof of performance.
  - Summarize your costs/pricing if permitted by purchasing rules.
  - Draft text summarizing how your proposal is organized.

Figure 6 illustrates how the Organizer is expanded into a multiple-page executive summary. Allocate pages in the executive summary according to the relative importance of the topic to the customer, tempered somewhat by the relative competitive strength of this feature or aspect of your offer. Determining the total length of your executive summary is discussed in Guideline 6.

If you develop value propositions as an integral part of your sales approach, summarize them in your executive summary. Present your summary value proposition in Box 1. Introduce individual value propositions in Box 2. Discuss each value proposition against your solution in Box 3. Summarize in Box 4.

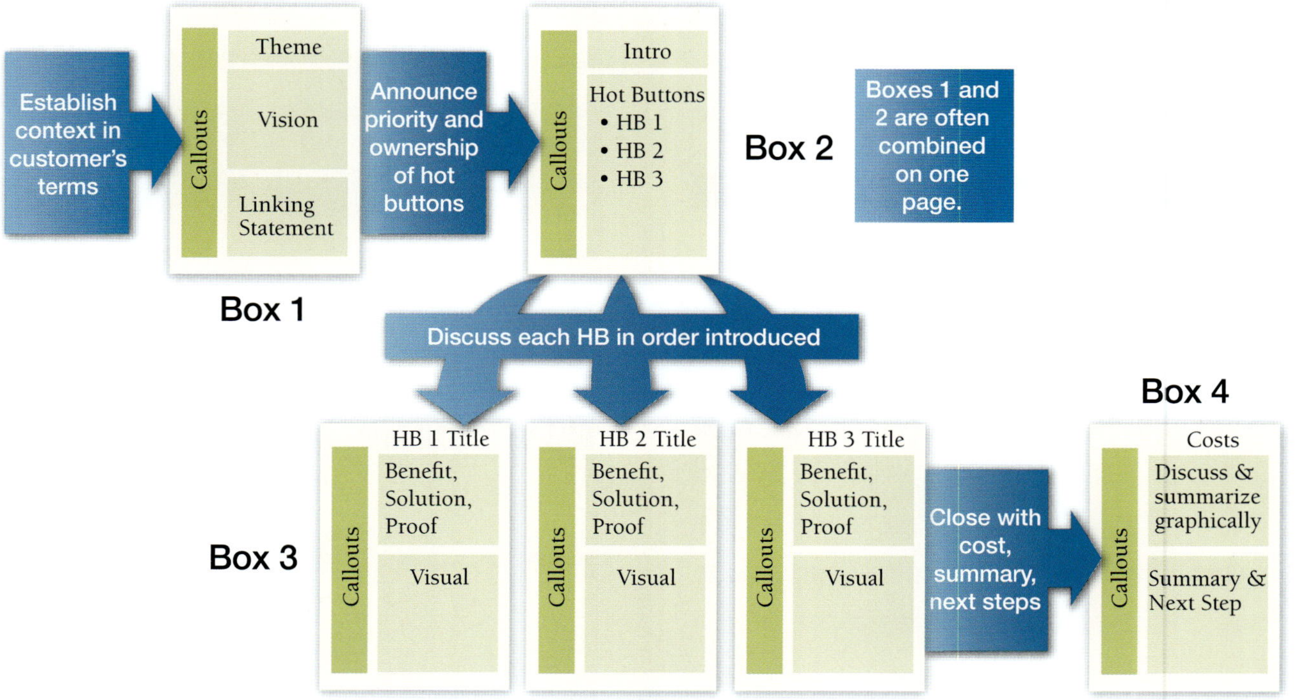

Figure 6. Expanding the Organizer into a Multiple-Page Executive Summary. *A four-box structure helps you quickly write highly effective, customer-focused executive summaries. Box 1 includes the vision and links it to the current acquisition activity, automatically requiring the customer to be named first. Box 2 announces the content of the executive summary by listing prioritized hot buttons and making their ownership explicit, encouraging the customer to be named more often. Box 3 addresses the hot buttons in order, describing your solution and benefits it produces, with customer-relevant proofs, making sure to list benefits before features. Box 4 summarizes and suggests next steps. In this example, Boxes 1 and 2 occupy separate pages, but they can frequently be covered in a single page.*

6

See **Presentations to Customers.**

Develop your executive summary based on proven best-in-class practices.

The following guidelines are based on years of consulting and observation of best practices in organizations with a proven ability to cost-effectively win business.

- Sales should complete the first draft of the executive summary prior to the proposal kickoff meeting.
- The proposal manager or sales support should review the draft, add detail on the solution, and complete it early enough to permit review by sales and management.
- Review your draft executive summary with your customer-coach if possible.
- Limit the total length to 5 to 10 percent of the page length of your proposal, tempered by how much you think this particular customer's managers will read.
- Make it more visual than the rest of the proposal.
- Use your executive summary as the basis for your finals briefing. Update it if needed and distribute copies to the prospect at the end.
- Maintain your customer focus from start to finish.

7

See **Relevant Experience/ Past Performance,** ***Proposal Guide.***

Follow sound writing guidelines.

Follow these writing guidelines to write consistent, effective executive summaries. As a manager, use it as a review checklist.

- Except in small proposals (under 20 pages), write the executive summary as a stand-alone document.
- Write executive summaries for upper-level, nontechnical decision makers.
- Make the executive summary brief but comprehensive.
- Include visuals throughout the executive summary.
- Do not assume that readers of the executive summary have been privy to information given during earlier sales calls.
- Organize the executive summary using a customer-focused framework.
- Clearly state what you are offering and how it benefits the customer.
- Offer clear proof of your claims.
- Tie major discriminators prominently and explicitly to a prospect issue.

8

Follow a defined process when preparing on short notice.

Use this abbreviated procedure when you are out of time or called on to draft an executive summary on short notice.

1. Define the customer's hot buttons, for Box 2. (Two to five hot buttons.)
2. Allocate all major requirements, high-level aspects of your solution, and your discriminators to at least one hot button for Box 3. If you have help, assign the drafting of one or more of the hot button portions of Box 3 after completing this step.
3. Draft a paragraph connecting the customer's vision, the customer's immediate need, and the most unique aspect of your solution for Box 1.
4. Summarize the price, your solution, *why you*, and indicate the next step for Box 4.
5. Review the content as a team, then edit carefully. Be especially careful if you have multiple contributors.
6. Spend the rest of the time available polishing. Resist changing your solution.

If you have the opportunity to present your proposal to the customer, use your executive summary as the basis for the presentation. Prepare the slides using your graphics and text, presented in the same order, and leave a copy of the executive summary with your customer as a written summary of your presentation.

Performance-Based Acquisition (PBA) is a contracting approach structured around the results to be achieved rather than the work tasks or process steps to be performed. Services market leaders embrace PBA as an attractive alternative to commoditizing their services.

In 2006, the FAR was amended, changing the terms Performance-Based Services Acquisition (PBSA) and Performance-Based Contracting (PBC) to Performance-Based Acquisition (PBA), reflecting that PBA contracting is not limited to services. Many official government agency websites continue to use PBSA and PBC. PBA is used in this ***Proposal Guide*** except when quoting a website or document that uses PBSA or PBC.

See DECISION GATE REVIEWS *and* PROCESS.

Traditional requirements-based contracts rely on a Statement of Work (SOW) to convey specific tasks the contractor must complete. In performance-based contracts, the SOW is replaced with a Statement of Objectives (SOO) describing a desired outcome, performance, or accomplishment.

The Federal Acquisition Regulations (FAR) defines a SOO as "a Government-prepared document incorporated into a solicitation that states the overall performance objectives." The SOO forms the basis for a Performance Work Statement (PWS). PWS is defined as "a statement of work for performance-based acquisitions that describes the required results in clear, specific, and objective terms with measurable outcomes."

Over time, customers tend to regard services purchased under traditional contracts as commodities. Commoditized services often erode sellers' margins and cut customers' costs, but not every customer benefits. Cell phone service, long distance calling, and broadband services are potential examples.

PBAs link customer objectives and performance goals. The customer pays for the level of performance delivered, freeing the contractor to determine the best delivery approach. PBAs are intended to motivate contractors to develop innovative approaches, increase efficiency, reduce costs, and improve customer satisfaction.

PBA contracting processes used by governments and industry vary and continue to evolve. These guidelines link U.S. Federal Government defined PBA contracting steps to the six business-development process phases described in the PROCESS section of this *Capture Guide*. While the business development process phases are identical, the tactical approach is tailored to PBA contracts.

Performance-based contracts have these characteristics:

- Requirements are described as results, not methods, stating what is done rather than how it is done.
- Performance is measured against standards.
- Contracts include remedies (penalties) for sub-par performance and possible bonuses for above-standard performance.

PBA offers the following benefits:

- Increased likelihood of meeting mission needs
- Improved solutions that focus on results, not process
- Reduced performance risk
- Reduced specification writing and process description pre-work
- Increased innovation and cost effectiveness
- Reduced protests
- Reduced surveillance
- Improved documentation of results

—Condensed from Seven Steps to Performance-Based Services Acquisition, website. http://www.arnet.gov/Library/OFPP/BestPractices/pbsc/home.html

Performance-Based Acquisition

1. Identify and analyze potential market sectors that are receptive to performance-based services.
2. Understand how each market segment acquires services.
3. Develop the process and infrastructure required to win PBAs.
4. Position your organization with key customers.
5. Identify leads early, and only pursue opportunities that meet your predefined pursuit criteria.
6. Collaborate with customers to shape the acquisition process and influence requirements.
7. Pass down-select milestones as the preferred vendor.
8. Learn to prepare Performance Work Statements and Performance Assessment Plans.
9. Emphasize past performance to support future claims.
10. Capitalize on oral presentation opportunities.
11. Exploit incumbency to improve performance, earn bonuses, extend the contract period, add tasks, and position for the eventual re-compete.

Performance-based contracting has been used in non-government sectors for more than 25 years. Over the last decade, the U.S. Government has encouraged performance-based contracting methods and set contracting targets as reflected in the following excerpts from the Office of Federal Procurement Policy (OFPP):

> *It is the policy of the Federal Government that (1) agencies use performance-based contracting methods to the maximum extent practicable when acquiring services, and (2) agencies carefully select acquisition and contract administration strategies, methods, and techniques that best accommodate the requirements.*
>
> *—OFPP Policy Letter 91-2, Services Contracting*

> *Agencies should apply PBSA methods on 40 percent of eligible service actions over $25,000, to include contracts, task orders, modifications, and options, awarded in fiscal year (FY) 2005, as measured in dollars. OFPP, in consultation with the Chief Acquisition Officers Council, will re-evaluate the target achievement levels for future years based on agencies' FY 2005 performance.*
>
> *—OFPP Policy Letter, September 7, 2004*

Most government agencies subsequently published implementation and operational guidelines and posted them on their web sites.

1 Identify and analyze potential market sectors that are receptive to performance-based services.

Use PBAs to gain a competitive advantage.

Performance-based contracting evolved from balanced scorecard and Information Technology (IT) Outsourcing Service Level Agreements (SLAs). Many outsourcing contracts include performance-based provisions for telecommunications, IT, healthcare, benefits management, facilities and equipment support, and human resources services.

While the private sector originated PBAs, national, regional, and local governments pressured to improve or maintain services without raising taxes are increasingly incorporating performance clauses in services contracts.

Many buyers and sellers poorly understand PBA contracting. Sellers who understand PBA contracting have a distinct competitive advantage. Sellers must contend with procurement officials' reluctance to make the following significant culture changes:

- Collaborate with contractors before contracting instead of maintaining arms-length relationships.
- Allow contractors to perform rather than closely directing solutions and monitoring compliance.
- Focus on long-term customer/contractor teaming rather than evaluating and awarding a definitive contract. PBA contracts are evolving, lifecycle processes rather than discrete events.

Identify, analyze, and target market sectors that might be receptive to and benefit from a performance-based approach. PBAs are potentially higher risk but more profitable than traditional time-and-materials contracts. Commoditized markets are potentially more profitable for sellers under a performance-based approach.

2 Understand how each market segment acquires services.

At the time of printing, this website continues to use the PBSA acronym.

Only the U.S. Government recommended approach is described in this *Capture Guide* because Business to Business (B2B) and commercial approaches can vary markedly by competition. Subsequent guidelines discuss what to do at each contracting step to improve your win probability.

Buyers conduct PBA competitions in a variety of ways as they develop and refine bidding approaches. PBA competitions might incorporate workshops, multi-step down-selects, and oral presentations or proposals. Many buyers follow processes defined by evolving laws and regulations, others hire consultants to conduct competitions, and some buyers have no process and are open to contractor recommendations.

PBA best practice is to establish an integrated solutions/project team to plan the acquisition, make the selection, and then negotiate and manage the contract. The integrated solutions team is a classic Integrated Project Team (IPT). Multi-disciplined IPT members should represent all stakeholders. Members with clearly defined, distinct roles share a common objective: to improve the organization's performance.

The U.S. Government supported an interagency partnership that defined the seven-step PBA process summarized in figures 1 and 2. Figure 1 summarizes the steps as depicted on the http://www.arnet.gov website. Figure 2 summarizes key elements of each step.

https://www.acquisition.gov/comp/seven_steps/home.html

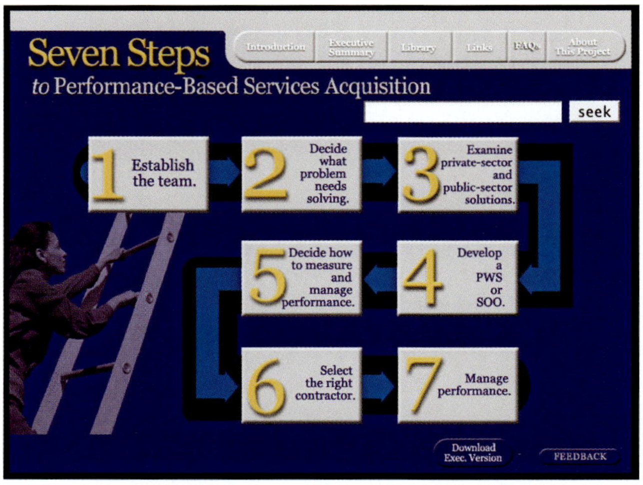

Figure 1. U.S. Government Interagency Partnering Recommended PBA Contracting Steps. *If you want to win U.S. Government PBAs, you must thoroughly understand the preferred approach. Recommend elements of this approach to interested customers.*

#	STEP	TASKS, FEATURES, AND BEST PRACTICES
1	Establish an integrated solutions/ project team	• Gain senior management support and multi-disciplinary expertise • Define roles, responsibilities, rules of conduct • Establish incentives linking goals and team members' performance
2	Describe the problem	• Link the acquisition, mission, and performance objectives • Define desired results and what constitutes success • Determine current, baseline level of performance
3	Examine private- and public-sector solutions	• Research market as a team • Identify public- and private-sector counterparts • Talk to private-sector companies; meet one-on-one • Identify existing contracts and document your market research
4	Develop Performance Work Statement (PWS) or Statement of Objectives (SOO)	**FOR PWS:** • Describe required results or outcomes, performance standards, and acceptable quality levels (AQL) • Document in Performance Requirements Summary: (1) desired outcomes; (2) required service; (3) performance standard; (4) AQL; (5) monitoring method; (6) incentives/disincentives • Write Performance Work Statement • Leave solution, including labor mix, to contractors **FOR SOO:** • Include purpose, scope or mission, duration, location, background, performance objectives/required results, and constraints, but no set format • Maintain high-level performance-objective focus and perspective • Performance incentives must correspond to performance standards • Requires less market research, offers maximum flexibility, but diverse solutions are harder to evaluate
5	Decide how to measure and manage performance	• Equally important as developing PWS or SOO • Ask contractor to propose metrics and performance measurement plan • Limit performance measures and associated measurement cost • Include provisions to change metrics and measures • Consider various incentives: contract type, profit level, extensions, bonus payments, awards, share-in-savings • Rely more on management by relationship than management by contract
6	Select the right contractor	• Use down selection to reduce buyer and contractor contracting cost • Use oral presentations by *managers/doers* to evaluate contractors' work teams to substitute for or augment written information • Emphasize relevant, current, and accurate past performance data
7	Manage performance	• Retain acquisition team to manage performance • Adjust IPT roles and responsibilities • Add contractor to the IPT in a formal kickoff meeting • Regularly review and document performance in Contract Performance Improvement Working Group

Figure 2. U.S. Government PBA Tasks, Features, and Best Practices. *The key elements by step are condensed from the "Seven Steps to Performance-Based Acquisition" publication. The government must prepare a SOO; the PWS is optional. Offerors use the SOO to develop the PWS when the PWS is not issued by the Government. The PWS usually becomes part of the contract; the SOO does not. (This process continues to evolve, so the elements are representative and not definitive.)*

3 Develop the process and infrastructure required to win PBAs.

To win PBAs, you need ready access to the following items:

- In-depth knowledge of the customer's performance requirements, mission, and issues
- Clear, concise descriptions of your proven processes
- Experienced, available, key personnel
- Relevant, quantitative, proof-of-performance

You must be able to rapidly link all of these elements during each collaborative opportunity and then summarize them in a persuasive oral/written proposal.

An effective PBA-focused business development process must:

- Emphasize early collaboration and positioning. You cannot be successful by simply responding to bid requests.
- Identify performance metrics that discriminate your solution.
- Incorporate milestone reviews: Which reviews will you require? Who participates? What are the ready-to-proceed criteria as well as go/no-go criteria?
- Develop a searchable database to support customer-IPT requests for oral and written proposals. Your database must include three elements: process descriptions, key personnel resumes, and quantitative proof-of-performance.
- Develop conceptual, graphic, process descriptions that can be modified quickly and positioned with action captions. Detailed, written process descriptions are less effective and are time-consuming to tailor.
- Develop a resume database that is searchable by customer issue, customer, market sector, key position responsibilities, and quantitative performance measures. Reverse-chronological position descriptions are relatively less useful.
- Develop a performance database that is searchable by customer issue, performance improvement, and key personnel as well as by customer and market sector.
- Assign a person to keep your database current as a primary duty, not a secondary duty. Databases that are to be maintained in a person's spare time invariably are not maintained. While this might appear to be an optional expense, it is a vital PBA process requirement.

4 Position your organization with key customers.

Performance incentives are objective, subjective, or both. Objective incentives are tied to defined, quantified, measurable performance requirements. Subjective incentives are not measurable or are subject to change beyond the contractor's control.

Performance remedies are mandatory in U.S. Government contracts; performance incentives are optional. Remedies are procedures to address substandard performance and may include penalties.

Position your organization throughout the seven-step PBA contracting steps described in figure 2. Contractors' potential positioning options are listed for each of the seven steps.

Step 1: Establish an integrated solutions/project team.

- Understand the customer's mission, goals, and PBA process.
- Note the potential performance improvement impact on their mission and goals when customer organizations are unfamiliar with PBAs.
- Help customers learn about PBAs. Add missing expertise; direct them to other successful IPTs. For more knowledgeable customers, contribute to the IPT.

Step 2: Describe the problem.

- Offer mission and performance analysis assistance.
- Offer white papers.
- Document baseline performance, especially if your organization is supporting this or similar customers.

Step 3: Examine private- and public-sector solutions.

- Assist with market analysis.
- Suggest relevant examples and key performance criteria; arrange meetings among the IPT, your organization, and potential teaming partners.
- Document the market analysis, if permitted.
- Cultivate the customer's trust and credibility.

Step 4: Develop Performance Work Statement (PWS) or Statement of Operational Objectives (SOO).

- Position the PBA as a combination SOO and PWS, or only a SOO, depending upon your organization's strengths and weaknesses. If you fear a competitor has an innovative solution that you cannot match, advocate a SOO and PWS.
- Submit a PWS white paper containing potential draft statements to influence the PWS.
- Emphasize the high risk of unproven approaches.
- Position a SOO as most advantageous to both organizations if you have a unique, innovative approach. A SOO reduces the customer's market research and PWS writing burden. In addition, a restrictive PWS might restrict your innovative solution.

Step 5: Decide how to measure and manage performance.

- Develop your PWS collaboratively with the IPT, if allowed. Alternatively, review potential work statements with IPT members you trust with confidential or company-proprietary information.
- Focus on performance incentives as well as penalties.
- Seek win-win approaches. Build trust between the IPT and your organization.

Step 6: Select the right contractor.

- Embrace every opportunity to put your delivery team in front of the customer's IPT. Train and rehearse them to present professionally and persuasively.
- Limit your senior managers and sales professionals to directing the play and rehearsing the players.
- Build the buyer-contractor relationship, which is as important as the PWS. The PWS is often modified throughout the contract.

Step 7: Manage Performance.

- Assume a major role in the Contract Performance Improvement Working Group.
- Advocate win-win provisions. Propose changes that add value for the customer and expand the contract.
- Document your performance, especially performance improvements and tasks completed at no charge.
- Position your organization for contract extensions. Strategically invest to avoid an expensive re-compete where you could lose margins or lose the entire contract.

5 Identify leads early, and only pursue opportunities that meet your predefined pursuit criteria.

See Decision Gate Reviews.

Organizations that discover leads first have common characteristics:

- They know the customer well, often through existing or prior contracts.
- They have helped the customer identify and/or define the issues, potential value, and requirements.

PBA pop-ups are exceedingly rare because customers should begin by forming an integrated solutions/project team. Most pop-up or surprise PBA opportunities have been extensively positioned by competitors and should be no-bid.

Pre-define your pursuit criteria to identify probable losers, make prompt bid decisions, and concentrate your resources on the best opportunities. Over time, improved pursuit and bid/no-bid criteria prompt sales and capture professionals to focus on the best opportunities well before pursuit decisions.

No single checklist works for every organization or market. Defining your pursuit criteria is a key part of defining your business development process. Figure 3 lists some potential pursuit criteria for PBA-focused leads.

	POTENTIAL PBA PURSUIT CRITERIA
✔	How has this customer purchased services, on a time-and-materials or performance basis?
✔	How well does this customer understand PBAs? Do we have time to educate this customer and/or opportunities to collaborate?
✔	Which acquisition basis favors us: time and materials, PWS, or SOO? Which approach favors which competitors?
✔	Have we influenced either the acquisition approach or the performance requirements? Have our competitors influenced the approach or requirements? If so, how?
✔	Do we have relevant performance history? Can we get it in time?
✔	Have they established a budget? Is it approved? Is the budget by category (capital vs. operational by period)?
✔	Do we have qualified personnel? If not, can we hire or commit them in time to be credible?
✔	What is the up side of pursuit? Are there opportunities to grow the contract, extend the contract, and negotiate incentives commensurate with potential penalties?
✔	What are the risks of pursuit? What could go wrong?
✔	Has the customer established an acquisition IPT? Do we know the members? Can we collaborate with the IPT? Will the IPT remain in some form to manage the contract?
✔	Are conversations with the customer directed toward the mission, goals, and desired performance, or toward cost-price-commodity issues?

Figure 3. PBA Pursuit Criteria. *Consider adding one or more of these criteria when defining your organization's pursuit and bid criteria.*

6 Collaborate with customers to shape the acquisition process and influence requirements.

PBA customers fall into three groups:

1. **Commodity customers:** Have a cost-price-commodity focus while saying this is a PBA.
2. **Inexperienced customers:** Embrace PBA conceptually but are unsure how to proceed.
3. **Experienced customers:** Contemplate whether to prepare a SOO and PWS or only a SOO.

Commodity customers are poor customers unless you are the low-price, commodity leader or you have time to move them into group 2.

Inexperienced customers are excellent if they are willing to collaborate. Seek opportunities to collaboratively define the acquisition approach benefits for both organizations. If you fear a competitor's innovative approach, seek a SOO and PWS. If you have an innovative approach, advocate a SOO that is open to your approach.

Help experienced customers draft the SOO and PWS. If they resist collaboration, submit a white paper containing a draft SOO and PWS that they can customize. If customers intend to prepare only a SOO, immediately outline your response. Do this collaboratively with selected, trusted individuals in the customer's organization while avoiding any violations of the customer's purchasing guidelines.

Perhaps the most important service you can offer is to identify PWS or SOO elements that specify *how things are to be done* rather than specifying measurable performance levels. Convert these *how* elements to performance-level elements, or get them eliminated.

Even if you fail to influence the acquisition process or performance requirement, your collaboration will enhance your understanding of the customer's needs and your relationship with the customer. Customers ultimately down-select solutions and then select compatible organizations to implement them. Customers seldom select unknown organizations, even if they offer a seemingly superior solution.

7 Pass down-select milestones as the preferred vendor.

The PBA process encourages down-select milestones to reduce the acquisition expense for buyers and sellers. Your goal should be to pass these down-select milestones as the preferred vendor rather than to just make the initial cut.

Preferred vendors follow many of these recommendations:

- Consistently focus on what is best for the customer.
- Support each assertion with at least one performance example. *Trust me* is insufficient.
- Collaborate openly, honestly, and enthusiastically.
- Complete all bid tasks as requested and on time. Being difficult to work with during the down-select suggests that you will be difficult to work with under contract.
- Make it easy for the customer to select your solution and organization. When presenting and discussing alternatives, link your recommendations to the customer's performance objectives. Avoid forcing the customer to make decisions with insufficient information.
- Place key delivery team members in close contact with customer influencers and decision makers whenever possible. Train and coach key delivery team members until they are competent, professional, and comfortable in these situations.

See Customer Focus, *Proposal Guide.*

8

Learn to prepare Performance Work Statements and Performance Assessment Plans.

The FAR defines four PBA documents:

1. Performance Work Statement
2. Quality Assurance Surveillance Plan
3. Statement of Objectives
4. Statement of Work

Figure 4 lists potential contractor Performance Work Statement elements. These elements will vary according to the type of work, agency, and preferences of the acquisition IPT. Figure 5 shows the alignment between typical government PWS elements and contractor response elements, when applicable.

Figure 6 shows the alignment between the typical government SOO elements and contractor response elements. Note that the Management Plan has no corresponding government element. When dealing with a SOO unaccompanied by a PWS, adapt this approach. You will have to prepare many of the elements typically found in the customer's PWS.

Modifications to the FAR broaden the scope of PBAs and increase agencies' flexibility when preparing PBA contracts and task orders.

TYPICAL PWS ELEMENTS
• Introduction • Scope of work • Requirements *(Text version of Performance Requirements Summary [PRS] Matrix)* • Define magnitude, quality, and scope of each outcome • Specify method of assessing contractor performance • Specify completion standards for each requirement • Supply historical data on previous contracts or work by in-house personnel • Data requirements • Attachments, appendices, exhibits • Schedule and performance period • Task orders

Figure 4. Typical PWS Elements. *PWS elements vary widely by organization, government, government agency, and immediate need. Most PWSs evolve over time.*

GOVERNMENT PERFORMANCE WORK STATEMENT (PWS)	CONTRACTOR RESPONSE ELEMENTS
(No government equivalent)	Management Plan
PWS (includes Performance Requirements Summary)	Statement of Work (SOW) including Work Breakdown Structure (WBS)
Performance Assessment Plan (PAP) (Includes Quality Assurance Surveillance Plan (QASP)/Metrics/ Acceptable Quality Level (AQL))	Quality Control Plan (QCP)/Quality Assurance Plan (QAP)
Incentives/Remedies	Addressed in Management Plan
Past Performance Requirement	Past Performance References

Figure 5. Alignment of PWS Elements and Contractor's Response. *While this is the typical structure and alignment, both are likely to vary along with the acronyms.*

GOVERNMENT STATEMENT OF OBJECTIVES (SOO) *[No Defined Format]*	CONTRACTOR RESPONSE ELEMENTS
(No government equivalent)	Management Plan
SOO	SOW (includes WBS)
PAP (may include Metrics/AQL)	QCP/QASP (if not provided, includes Metrics/AQL)
Incentives/Remedies (optional)	Incentives/Remedies (required)
Past Performance Requirement	Past Performance References

Figure 6. Alignment of SOO Elements and Contractor's Response. *The prescribed SOO structure is more flexible and variable than a PWS.*

While figures 5 and 6 show the alignment between PWS, SOO elements, and the contractor's response, figure 7 illustrates how the individual PWS, proposal preparation instructions, and proposal evaluation criteria are linked.

PERFORMANCE WORK STATEMENT (PWS)	PROPOSAL INSTRUCTION	EVALUATION CRITERION
Provide taxi service so that pick-up time is within 5 minutes of the request, 95 percent of the time	Describe how taxi service will be provided in accordance with the requirement	Evaluate offeror's approach for best value, considering technical merit, cost, and relevant past performance

Figure 7. Link the PWS, Proposal Instructions, and Evaluation Criteria. *If the customer issues only a SOO, the contractor will have to draft the PWS, linking proposal instructions and evaluation criteria to individual Performance Work Statement elements. This example illustrates how the three elements are linked for a simple service. Develop similar linkages for each Performance Work Statement element.*

The identical PWS acronym can be confusing. A Performance Work Summary includes multiple Performance Work Statements. Customers' bid requests often call the Performance Work Summary a Performance Work Statement and call the elements Performance Work Statements.

The PWS is typically communicated in the bid request in both text and/or matrix form. If the bid request has only a SOO, the contractor must draft a PWS. In your PWS, integrate desired outcomes, performance objectives, market analysis, and acceptable quality level (AQL) to prepare a series of Performance Work Statements, as illustrated in figure 8.

The heart of a PBA proposal is a completed PWS. Begin with the information furnished in the bid request, and then complete the remainder of the matrix. Relate every element of your proposal to the relevant portion of your completed PWS. Each column is discussed in the order listed.

- The **PWS Title** is a major category of the PWS. Typical major elements are Management Plan, Systems Engineering, Task Order Management, or major task areas. Adopt the customer's order and naming conventions.
- The **PWS #** is the number or code used by the customer in the bid request PWS. Adopt the customer's numbering convention. Extend their decimal numbering system, when offered a choice. Ideally, this number matches your WBS and SOW numbering system.
- The **Performance Objective** is the result to be accomplished. The bid request states the work desired; your proposal states what you propose to accomplish.
- The **Performance Standard** is the targeted level of performance or accomplishment. The performance standard is usually stated in a SOO/PWS bid request but is less likely to be included in a SOO-only bid request. If unstated, then define the standard. Typical performance standards are:
  - Response times, delivery times, timeliness: Meeting deadlines or due dates
  - Error rates: Number of errors or mistakes allowed
  - Accuracy rates: Usually stated in percentages
  - Milestone completion rates: Percentage completed by specified dates
  - Cost control: Staying within estimated costs or budget; often applied to cost-reimbursement contracts
- The **Metric** is what is being measured. The metric is usually stated in days, dollars, or numbers.
- The **Acceptable Quality Level** (AQL) is lowest acceptable performance before remedies are called for. The AQL specifies how much deviation from the performance standard is allowed. If no AQL is stated, no deviation is allowed.
- The **Method of Performance Assessment** is the method used to monitor or measure the work being performed. Sometimes the customer or their agent prepares quality assurance evaluation reports. Sometimes the contractor develops and completes reports, surveys, or audits.
- The **Remedies/Incentives** defines corrections for substandard performance or rewards for above-standard performance. Remedies are required; incentives are not. Often this column references the award fee plan to avoid restating the remedy/incentive.
- **The References Column** can be used in two ways. The most common use is to refer to relevant portions of the bid request. In some cases, this is redundant with the PWS Title column. However, when working with a SOO, the PWS Title might be more detailed than the SOO, so this lets you reference individual SOO items. The second use is to reference specific past performance examples and key personnel resumes. This is an excellent way to directly link your approach and experience while substantiating your claims.

PWS TITLE							
PWS #	*Performance Objective*	*Performance Standard*	*Metric*	*Acceptable Quality Level (AQL)*	*Method Of Performance Assessment*	*Remedies/ Incentives*	*References*
3.1	*Contractor* will develop a transition plan	Develop and implement a transition plan within 60 days of contract award	Date of completion of transition plan tasks	On time completion of all tasks. No acceptable deviations.	Monthly Quality Assurance Report by COTR. Weekly review in Contract Performance Improvement Working Group.	Award Fee Plan	SOO Section 3.1
5.2	*Contractor name* will operate a customer service center	**Emergencies**: Completed w/in 30 min. during working hrs., w/ in 60 min. all other times. **Urgent**: completed w/in 5 days **Routine**: completed w/in 30 days	Time caller accepts fix	**Emergency**: 100% **Urgent**: 98.5% **Routine**: 95%	Contractor metrics. Quarterly review of records; Annual random inspection or audit by customer or third party	**Positive:** When performance exceeds standard, pay 10% of monthly payment into pool. At end of 12 months, pay contractor amount accrued in pool. **Negative:** When performance is below standard, 10% of monthly payment will be withheld or deducted from the pool. Pay net accrual every 12 months.	Past Performance *Reference 3*; Key resume for *Customer Service Center Manager*

Figure 8. Sample Performance Work Statement. *Develop a Performance Work Statement similar to the one shown before drafting text for your proposal. When you do, your proposal will be easier to evaluate, tasks will be easier to understand, and you will slash proposal text. Both example tasks are for illustration and not necessarily consecutive or in the same proposal. Customers usually make the selected contractor's PWS part of the contract.*

9

When you lack identical performance, note your performance on similar subtasks.

See Guideline 4, Relevant Experience/ Past Performance, ***Proposal Guide.***

Emphasize past performance to support future claims.

Past performance is the only credible support for future performance claims. Consider not bidding if an incumbent has performed well, and you have no experience or poor performance.

When you lack identical performance, note your performance on similar subtasks.

Use the most credible sources of performance data available. Sources of performance data are listed in order of credibility to customers:

- Your performance for this customer.
- Your performance with similar, familiar customers they trust.
- Performance data from independent sources.
- Performance data that you supply (credibility improves when verified).
- Performance data about your organization leaked by competitors (credibility improves when verified).

Support performance claims throughout your oral and written presentations. Discussing performance in a specified Past Performance section is necessary but not sufficient. The most effective performance claim support is directly linked to the claim in short, relevant, success stories.

10

See Oral Proposals, ***Proposal Guide,*** and Presentations to Customers.

Capitalize on oral presentation opportunities.

Customers use oral presentations to assess key personnel, much like a job interview. Customers assess how key personnel interact with their own team members and individuals in the customer's organization. How your message is delivered is often more important than the content of your message.

Oral presentations, both informal and formal, cut acquisition costs for customer and sellers.

Customers' acquisition guidelines encourage industry day meetings and one-on-one meetings with sellers.

Use each meeting and presentation to develop a rapport with the customer. A selling truism is: *people buy emotionally from their friends, and then justify their decision rationally.*

11 Exploit incumbency to improve performance, earn bonuses, extend the contract period, add tasks, and position for the eventual re-compete.

The most cost-effective way to maintain and grow revenues and increase profitability is to exploit incumbency. The U.S. Government recommends converting the acquisition IPT into a *Contract Performance Improvement Working Group*. The group's focus is to measure contract performance and then to identify and negotiate contract improvements.

The Contract Performance Improvement Working Group uses the assessment methods listed in figure 9.

Anticipate and embrace changes as a win-win opportunity for both organizations. Customers are more receptive to your propositions and less receptive to those of your competitors when you are meeting or exceeding their performance objectives.

Do everything possible to earn performance bonuses while emphasizing the customer's gains. Otherwise, some customers fixate only on the size of your bonus. As you redefine performance requirements during the contract, balance the penalty risk and performance bonus.

The most economical way to win new business is through noncompetitive contract extensions. Incumbents win over 60 percent of re-competes, but extensions are 100 percent winners if acceptably profitable. Customers reluctant to accept performance-bonus contract clauses often accept automatic contract extensions linked to performance.

PBAs are flexible. Identify opportunities to add tasks that help the customer meet their objectives. Make changes easy:

- Collaboratively define the performance improvement, measurement approach, relationship to the existing contract, and cost with the Contract Performance Improvement Working Group.
- Draft a task Performance Work Statement.
- Review the draft statement with the Contract Performance Improvement Working Group, incorporate suggestions, and submit to the purchasing/ contracting lead.
- Note added tasks in the next Contract Performance Improvement Working Group meeting, and monitor performance as agreed.

ASSESSMENT METHOD	DESCRIPTION	ASSESSMENT METHOD CONSIDERATIONS *(For All Methods)*
Random Sampling	Statistically based method that assumes acceptable performance based on percentage of assessment; most appropriate for frequently recurring tasks.	• What is the most effective way to assess the contractor's performance against performance standards? • How critical is this task to this requirement and the overall mission? • Is performance assessment worth the government's time and effort? • Are the assessment period and frequency proportional to task importance? • Are enough assessors (quality assurance evaluators) available to complete the planned degree of evaluation? • Do proposed evaluation methods represent common commercial practice for this service?
Periodic Sampling	Similar to random sampling, but at specific intervals.	
Trend Analysis	Build baseline from data collected through performance assessments blended with contractor-managed metrics.	
Customer Feedback	Anecdotal evidence—supplemental to other forms of evaluation and assessment. The subjective nature of customer feedback makes it risky to use as a primary source of assessment.	
Third-party Audits	Conducted by an organization that is independent from both the Government and contractor.	

Figure 9. Performance Assessment Methods. *The U.S. Government recommends using one of the above assessment methods to evaluate contractor performance.*

Persuasion is fundamental to selling. Sellers use written and oral appeals to persuade customers to accept their ideas, services, and products.

Aristotle defined a rhetorician as "someone who can see what might be persuasive." Aristotle's rhetorician sounds like the ideal person to prepare and present oral and written proposals. However, Aristotle also said that although rhetoricians know how to be persuasive, they are not able to convince everybody.

Like a rhetorician, few sales and proposal professionals are 100 percent successful. However, applying the principles of rhetoric can make you a more persuasive writer and speaker.

The basis for persuasion is rhetoric defined as "the art of writing or speaking effectively." In his treatise, *Rhetoric,* Aristotle stated that persuasive writing and speaking are based on three types of appeals:

1. *Ethos* is appeal based on the reputation and character of the speaker. In written and oral proposals, reputation extends beyond the speaker to the sales team, the speaker's organization, and other sources of information about the seller. In written and oral proposals, the seller should trust the sales team and the organization that the team represents based upon prior events, the behavior of the team at the event, and the team's oral and written messages.
2. *Logos* is appeal based on reason or logic. Scholarly documents are often logos driven. In written and oral proposals, the seller's message should be reasonable and logical.
3. *Pathos* is appeal based on emotion, specifically, the emotional state of the customer. Advertisements are often pathos driven. In written and oral proposals, the seller should acknowledge, and meet or address the customer's emotional needs.

For simplicity and clarity, the terms *reputation, reason*, and *emotion* are used instead of *ethos, logos*, and *pathos*.

Persuasion is more ambitious than exposition. Exposition is to simply explain or inform. Persuaders seek a specific response: to have another party accept their ideas or agree to a specific activity, such as buying their service or product.

Business development, proposal preparation, and sales methodologies are replete with lore, a "body of knowledge held by a particular group." This *Capture Guide* largely comprises business development lore, but several specific guidelines are directly supported by defensible scientific research. *Guide* guidelines stem from years of practice, trial-and-error, and professional assessments of best practice across hundreds of organizations.

Persuasion is the common denominator found in most selling and business development lore. Sellers who understand the elements of persuasion can more effectively apply the lore of business development and proposal preparation. These sellers are in a better position to assess what will be persuasive in specific written and oral proposals.

Each seller's goal is to persuade a customer to decide either to purchase the seller's solution or to agree to take the next step in the sales process. Hence, research on how people make decisions is highly relevant. Both contextual

Persuasion

1. Assess the customer's vision, motivators, and hot button issues.
2. Determine your next realistically achievable objective.
3. Collaborate with the customer throughout the sales process to gain information, develop rapport, validate assumptions, and assess progress.
4. Maintain credibility.
5. Use classic communication techniques to present persuasive selling points.
6. Align your persuasive techniques to the specific needs of individuals in the buying process and their preferred communication styles.

and psychological constraints affect buyers' decision making. While decision-making theory is fluid and research is ongoing, some reliable key points are:

- **A human's ability to make a purely logical decision is limited.**

  Complex circumstances, limited time, imperfect data, and an inadequate ability to analyze the data form a decision-maker's state of *bounded rationality*.
- **Humans knowingly make unreasonable decisions.**
- **Every decision involves reason and emotion.**

  Research with brain-damaged patients shows that when logic is cut off from emotion, patients could not make decisions. PET (positron emission tomography) and fMRI (functional magnetic resonance imaging) scans show that all decisions involve a complex interplay between the emotional and logical centers of the human brain.

  Individuals in controlled experiments and real life situations will ignore their economic best interest (reason) and make decisions for emotional reasons (anger, revenge, immediate gratification, irrational fear, risk avoiding, or risk seeking). Essentially, the emotional sector of the brain overrides the reasoning sector.

Which type of appeal is most effective? Aristotle said reputation was the most effective appeal, based upon trust in the credibility of the speaker. Advertisers rely heavily on appeals to the emotions of the customer, but use credible speakers to deliver the message. Most sellers make *reasonable* arguments, even though their arguments might not withstand the scrutiny of the customer or a logician.

Reputation, reason, and emotion are all essential persuasive elements in crafting complex sales arguments. Like a three-legged stool that is unstable with a single leg removed, you are far less likely to make the sale if you omit any element.

All techniques recommended in this *Capture Guide* are rhetorical devices originating in Aristotle's three types of appeals. The guidelines in this section integrate the research on what is persuasive with the lore of selling and proposals. Fortunately, if you are an experienced proposal writer, you have probably been using many of these techniques. Ideally, you will become a rhetorician skilled at blending reputation, reason, and emotion in an integrated appeal that might be more persuasive.

1

Assess the customer's vision, motivators, and hot button issues.

Most motivators are directly linked to reason. However, the individuals identifying motivators are often influenced by their personal emotional needs.

Similarly, organizational motivators drive organizations; personal motivators drive individuals who make or influence purchasing decisions.

See Features, Advantages, and Benefits, *Proposal Guide, and* Strategy.

Start with the premise that people seek benefits based on two factors:

- *Perception:* whether it is good or bad
- *Possession*: whether we have it or not

Buyers seek one of four types of benefits derived from perception or possession as illustrated in figure 1, and sellers promise benefits in exchange for money or power. Sellers must link their solution to the customer's needs.

Effective sellers begin by analyzing customer needs and by determining their organizational *vision*, *motivators*, and *hot button issues*.

Vision refers to the customer's organizational image of what the future will or could be like. Sellers that clearly demonstrate how their solutions will help customers achieve their vision usually win the sale. Note how this vision statement powerfully appeals to reason and emotion:

> **Imagine:** doctors operating on a patient can point a RxT laser at live tissue, analyze the reflected light with a spectroscope and PC, and immediately determine if the tissue is malignant or benign. Further imagine that this scenario can be made real within 16 months if you fund our program.

Issues are the customer's concerns—the worry items that keep the customer's managers awake at night. To address issues effectively, determine the source. Is this an issue because the customer does not trust you or your organization, because the customer cannot see a logical reason to purchase or cannot see how to justify the purchase, or because the customer has an emotional need?

The customer's issues typically become motivators:

- Improve profits
- Increase sales
- Reduce costs
- Improve safety
- Reduce risk
- Improve quality
- Increase productivity

All motivators are issues, but not all issues are motivators. In complex sales, most motivators usually stem from reason and are logical.

Hot button issues are a consolidated subset of issues and motivators. Typical hot button issues are owned and repeatedly cited by several people in the customer organization. Because hot button issues often relate to reputation, reason, and emotion, address them by incorporating all three types of appeals.

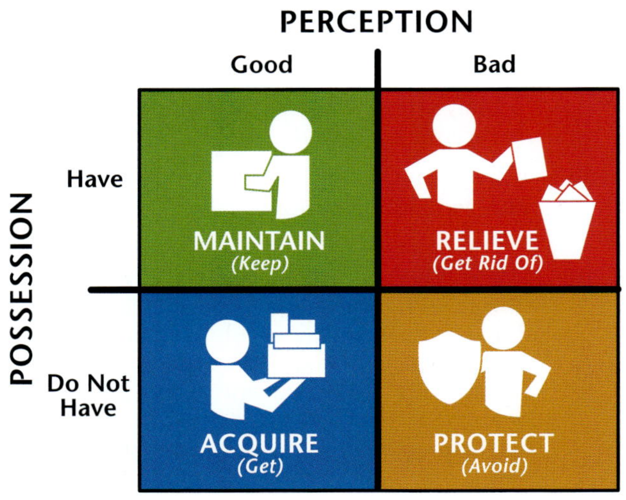

Figure 1. Buyers Seek Four Types of Benefits. *Buyers' motivations rely on their perceptions of good, bad, and possession. The four possible combinations are: 1) Maintain: Keep the good; 2) Acquire: Get the good; 3) Relieve: Get rid of the bad; 4) Protect: Avoid the bad.*

2 Determine your next realistically achievable objective.

Customers become customers via a consistent, cyclical process:

- *Operating* in their normal environment. In normal environments, things age, wear, and decay; customers' needs evolve.
- *Assessing need.* Customers perceive a need or opportunity to improve and then determine if they really have a problem/ opportunity.
- *Valuing solutions.* Determining which, if any, solution offers the best value.
- *Resolving remaining issues* with the solution that offers the best value.
- *Purchasing.*
- *Implementing the solution.*

Persuasion can be applied at every phase.

To advance the sale, determine where customers are in the process. Find answers to their questions, and then state your next realistically achievable objective. *Exactly what would you like this customer to agree to do next?*

Before attempting to persuade customers to take action, test your readiness by asking three things:

1. Where are they going? *(Vision, objective, or goal)*
2. What is their next realistically achievable step towards that goal? *(Advance complex sales in a series of steps.)*
3. Why is it in their best interest to agree to take the next step? *(Motivators, hot button issues)*

Advance at the customer's pace; pushing the pace in a complex sale alienates the customer. Perhaps the only tactic sellers can effectively use to increase the pace is to note the opportunity cost as the customer delays implementing improvements.

Determine what credible combination of reason and emotion will address customers' underlying issues. If you misjudge customers' issues at this point in their purchase-decision process or cannot adequately answer their questions, you risk not advancing, delaying the purchase, or losing the sale.

Examples of not seeking to advance the sale and advancing too fast:

Not seeking to advance the sale

Thank you for agreeing to meet with me today. Should you have any questions in the future, please do not hesitate to call.

Advancing too fast

Thank you for agreeing to meet with me today. We offer the best environmental remediation services available in North America. Can I have your purchase order today so that we can reserve a place in our June work schedule?

See Sales Letters.

This visual representation of the sales cycle follows the same business development process defined in **Process**, rules 2 and 3.

State sales objectives clearly so they will be easy to assess. If sales objectives are vague, no one can tell when or if they are met.

Examples of next realistically achievable objectives:

- Agree to tour a site where your system is operating, preferably Wednesday, December 4, at 10 AM.
- Agree to collect and share their engine design specifications and productions costs, sending them to U.S. via courier by 4 PM, September 30.
- Agree to meet Thursday, 8 AM, to review and approve final drawings and specifications.
- Agree to consider a change order, adding construction management services to our ongoing design contract.

Vague sales objective

I plan to meet with the customer to better understand their future needs.

This objective leaves many details unattended. When is the meeting? How many meetings will it take and who will attend? What understanding is sufficient? Where is this going?

The generic sales cycle illustrated in figure 2 illustrates sales phases (linked arrows) and tactical steps (boxes) a seller might take to advance a sale. Whether a meeting, phone call, or document, the objective for each tactical step is to incrementally advance the sale.

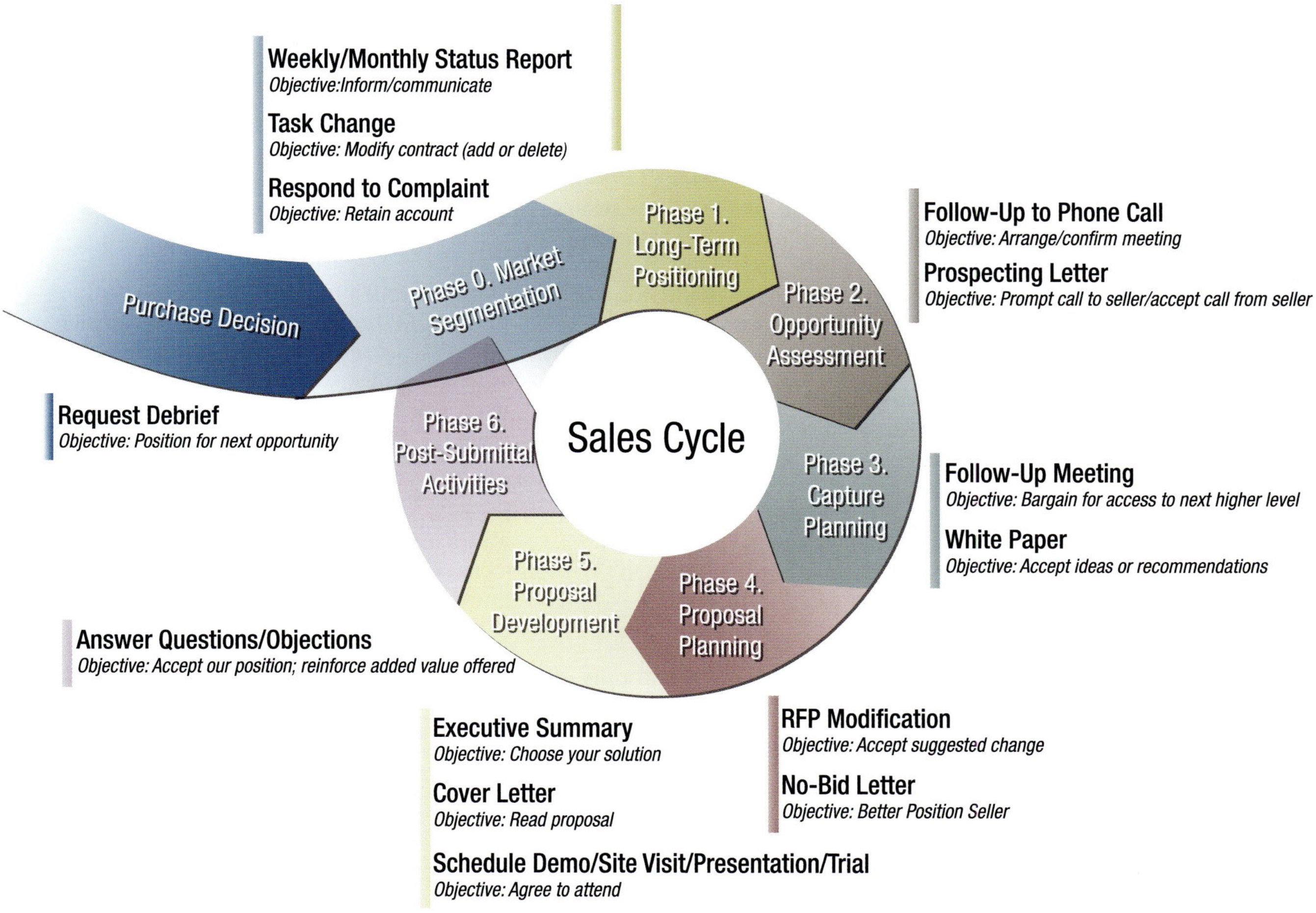

Figure 2. Sales Cycle, Tactical Steps, and Sales Objectives. *Each tactical step has a specific, measurable, are realistically achievable sales objective.*

3

Collaborate with the customer throughout the sales process to gain information, develop rapport, validate assumptions, and assess progress.

See Strategy.

Collaboration is persuasive because it integrates appeals based on reason, emotion, and reputation. While most collaborative discussions are based on reason, both parties disclose emotional needs. Customers willingly share information in a collaborative situation. Collaboration builds trust and credibility; ongoing collaboration nurtures this emotional bond. Ultimately, customers prefer purchasing from people they like.

Complex sales involve buying and selling teams, extended buying cycles, and multiple meetings. In complex sales, few customers know exactly what they want at the onset.

As the sale advances, customers' implicit needs become explicit, and sellers can directly address these explicit needs.

Needs, issues, facts, and assumptions evolve. Collaborative sellers repeatedly validate assumptions (reason and emotional needs) while building their reputation.

Use your collaborative relationship to validate your solution before finalizing your proposal. Solutions that have been validated by the customer win more frequently.

4

Maintain credibility.

Customers readily accept negative seller admissions as truth. Use this to your advantage by admitting a weakness that you can mitigate. Your subsequent assertions will be more credible.

See Oral Proposals, *Proposal Guide*; and Presentations to Customers.

Sales professionals are rightfully adamant about maintaining their personal credibility with customers. The sales professional's credibility extends to the sales team, the seller's organization, and other sources of information about the seller. Maintain credibility by adhering to established ethical standards, introducing appropriate authority figures, substantiating claims, and staying on message.

Customers must trust what you say and recommend. In addition, many customer organizations have mandatory ethical standards. For example, the U.S. Government requires sellers from publicly traded organizations to maintain ethical standards established in the Sarbanes-Oxley Act, requiring audited compliance to compete for U.S. Federal contracts.

Sellers present themselves as either authority figures or friends. Authority figures are experts, endorsers, users, developers, managers, or owners of the product or service. Friends are people the customer likes, identifies with, or wants to emulate. Sales professionals usually present themselves as friends, and then introduce authority figures to answer questions, discuss solution details, and substantiate claims.

When introducing authority figures to substantiate your claims, consider their credibility with the customer and what this customer knows or believes they know about your organization. Customers rate the credibility of sources in this order:

1. What they know/believe
2. What similar, trusted customers say
3. What independent sources say
4. What you say
5. What competitors say

Improve your credibility and persuasiveness by increasing the percentage of substantiation from the first three sources. Too many sellers rely on the fourth-level source, themselves.

Messages from all sources must be aligned throughout the sales cycle. Political campaign strategists repeatedly counsel, *stay on message*. Misaligned, inconsistent messages reduce credibility. Once lost, credibility is difficult to regain.

If customers doubt your credibility, they assess the nonverbal conversation elements, as summarized in figure 3. Skeptical customers focus on how you talk and what you do, noticing your body language and actions or behaviors.

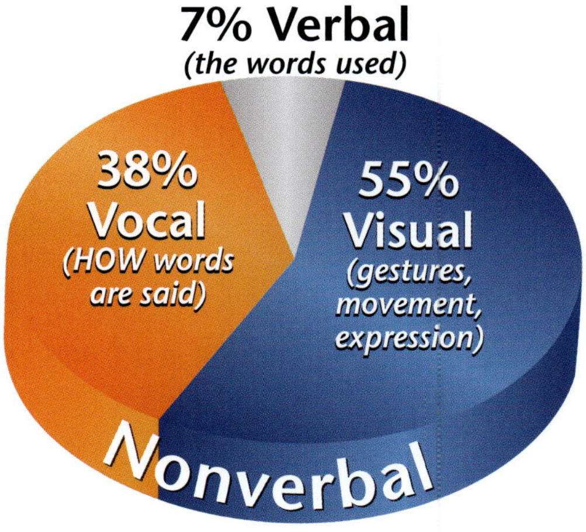

Figure 3. Importance of Nonverbal Communication. *Research by Dr. Albert Mehrabian at UCLA demonstrated that as much as 93 percent of the emotional content of a message is conveyed by visual and vocal cues.*

5

Use classic communication techniques to present persuasive selling points.

Repetition integrates credibility, reason, and emotion. Trusted sellers keep their word and present a logical, consistent message. Treating buyers consistently satisfies their emotional needs for improved efficiency and reduced stress.

Use consistent terminology. Using synonyms to make your proposal more varied and interesting usually confuses your customer.

Composition incorporates emotion-, reason-, and reputation-based appeals. Emotion is often the most powerful element.

*See the following **Proposal Guide** topic sections:* ACTIVE AND PASSIVE, CLICHES, CUSTOMER FOCUS, FALSE SUBJECTS, GOBBLEDYGOOK, JARGON, ORGANIZATION, PAGE AND DOCUMENT DESIGN, REDUNDANT WORDS, *and* STYLE AND TONE.

Persuasive sellers communicate their key selling points using these key techniques:

- Repetition
- Association
- Composition
- Selection
- Redirection
- Ghosting

Repetition is an easy, simple, and efficient persuasive technique. The more times we consistently see, hear, and experience something, the more we remember it. Repeated statements, experiences, and actions prompt us to identify with the statement or action unless we have already accepted a conflicting position.

Humans embrace repeated behaviors (habits) because they meet a near-universal emotional need for reduced stress and improved efficiency. A decision that is repeated is really a decision that does not need to be made. Repetitive decisions save time and reduce stress. Note how people tend to sit in the same seat in a classroom, select the same item at a restaurant, and buy the same product. Once a decision about an item or circumstance is made, it is easier to repeat it than risk a new decision.

Here are some of the ways we use repetition in business development:

- Make similar statements throughout the sales cycle.
- Make identical statements in sales presentations and the subsequent proposal.
- Summarize at all levels of a proposal.
- Echo common themes in each proposal volume.
- Carry similar statements through headings, theme statements, action captions, and body text.
- Repeat key body text in margin callouts.
- Repeat introductions in subsequent subheadings.

In a presentation or proposal, restate points from a subtly different perspective.

Your customer is interested in a low-cost solution. You repeatedly emphasize how cost influenced your solution design.

Technical section: *To minimize the cost, we selected commercial off-the-shelf components whenever available.*

Management section: *Our relatively flat organization and increased span of control per key position are specifically designed to reduce overhead burden.*

Task management section: *A team leader, who is a working member of the team, manages each task order. To minimize management cost, we only appoint full-time project managers when teams exceed 12 people.*

Deliberate, word-for-word repetition can be reassuring or insulting depending upon how it is done. The following example is reassuring:

You must answer identical questions repeated in two places in the bid request. Answer the question fully the first time it is asked. When the question is repeated, state whether you have repeated or cross-referenced your answer:

Repeat

This question was also asked in Section 3.2. We have repeated our answer here for your convenience.

Cross reference

This question was also asked in Section 3.2. We have summarized our answer here. For the full answer, please turn to Section 3.2.

Association, the second persuasive technique, is linking your strengths to something positive that customers already like or want, or to something negative that customers want to eliminate or avoid. Successful association relies upon prior Guidelines 1 and 3. Assess what customers desire or want to avoid, and reassess through collaboration with the customer.

Association is primarily an emotion- and reason-based appeal. Similar, positive associations are comforting and supportive. Knowing that others have achieved similar positive outcomes is also logically appealing.

Associations are direct or indirect. Direct associations link customer requirements to outcomes in theme statements, informative headings, section summaries, tables, body text, slides, and assertions in presentations. Most of these associations directly and explicitly link customer issues and requirements to features of your solution.

Association fails when customers fail to see the link. These customers are thinking: *Sounds good, but I do not see why I need the other approaches.* Or, *Sounds pretty much like all the other approaches.*

Indirect associations are subtle suggestions tailored for a specific customer. Sellers use pictures, graphics, metaphoric language, allusions, backgrounds, and contexts, as illustrated in figure 4.

Word choice also has a subtle, persuasive impact. Choose words and phrases familiar to the customer.

Selling IT services to an engineer

> I've analyzed your IT systems and think you should consider re-engineering your network. My calculations show that delays have increased 23.6 percent. After you review my calculations, I'm sure you'll agree.

Selling IT services to a banker

> I've analyzed your IT systems and think that we can make your network as secure as your vault. I've estimated the revenue enhancements and cost savings, noting that the complete change is revenue-neutral within 2 years.

- Sellers are increasingly using audio and video components in sales presentations and embedding links in sales documents to similar online presentations.
- Many sellers prepare quantified value propositions, and most proposals attempt to quantify the value of their solution versus the existing approach or alternative solutions. Many proposals describe the results from trade studies.
- Both time and space are important elements in sales presentations. Persuasive sellers consider length, timing, transitions, room structure, visual aids, and positioning of sellers versus the customers as a few examples.
- While *scratch and sniff* proposals might not have been used in business, publishers insert perfume cards in magazines and catalogs, and new car scent is sold in aerosol cans.

Many of the sections in the Shipley *Proposal Guide* relate to elements of composition. Figure 5 links Shipley *Proposal Guide* topics and summarizes one or two key points.

Sellers instinctively downplay their weaknesses, and potentially mitigate competitors' strengths, through selection, redirection, and ghosting. Clear, persuasive communicators always place the most important points to the customer first in a document or presentation. Position infers importance.

Composition, the third persuasive technique, is the manner in which parts of speech and writing are combined to form the message. Composition includes the following elements:

- Verbal (the choice of words)
- Nonverbal
- Visual elements (color, shape, and size)
- Aural elements (music, sounds)
- Mathematics (quantities, relationships)
- Time
- Space
- Smell

Composition incorporates appeals based upon reputation, reason, and emotion. For example, consider your home-buying experiences. Did you consider reputation of the community, neighborhood, realtor, builder, and owner? Did you reason why a certain home was a better value than the alternatives? Did a home or apartment have curb appeal, feel good, smell good, and evoke strong memories and emotions? These are all examples of being influenced by elements of composition.

Sellers routinely apply elements of composition to oral and written proposals. In many competitions, your first priority is to gain the evaluators' attention and retain it long enough to convince them you offer the best solution. Consider these varied examples illustrating how various elements of composition have been used in proposals:

- Sellers commonly use words, terms, phrases, and acronyms that their customers use.
- In oral proposals, sellers rehearse extensively to prevent nonverbal elements from conflicting with verbal elements.
- In a competition to sell telecommunications services to PetSmart®, one competitor created a strong, positive stir by submitting their proposal in the customer's branded pet carrier emblazoned with "Caution! Live proposal. Handle with care."
- In a U.K. competition, one bidder increased the graphical content of their executive summary to nearly 80 percent because the decision maker was dyslexic.

Selection, the fourth persuasive technique, is forced on us by the linear nature of communication. Selection forces two decisions on a seller:

- Whether to include or omit a point
- Where to position or order a point

Customers often limit the time that they will spend with sellers, the page length of proposals, and the time for sales and oral proposal presentations. In the limited time and space available, what will you say? Your decision to say one thing forces you to omit saying something else or saying it later. Hence, all communication is limited and arguably slanted or biased to include or exclude items.

Selling IT services to an architect

> I've analyzed your IT systems and see some need to change the structure of your network. I've sketched a few ideas that will give you a better foundation to sharpen your firm's network design. As you review the blueprint, . . .

The seller mirrors language that customers use routinely in their work. Subtle but effective.

TYPE OF INDIRECT ASSOCIATION	EXAMPLE(S)
Metaphoric language	To enable pilots to perform at their best throughout long, grueling missions, our ergonomically designed, adaptable seats can be pilot-tuned to simulate their favorite lounger.
Allusion	While no one can promise zero risk, your retirement nest egg is invested in U.S. Treasury notes that are as secure as Fort Knox.
Background	Throughout 6 weeks of collaborative exchanges, your senior managers have emphasized that the ideal solution must be 100-percent compatible with the Easy-Link™ software that we installed in 2002. Easy Link II™ is backwards compatible.
Context	With the end of the Cold War and increasing threats from rogue states, the Royal Navy is increasingly concerned about protecting the fleet in brown water. Nearly 80 percent of our I.R.&D. investment since 2000 has focused on countering this threat.

Figure 4. Using Indirect Associations to Persuade. *Subtly persuade customers by indirectly associating features of your solution to the benefits sought by the customer.*

PROPOSAL GUIDE TOPIC	USE IN PROPOSALS
Active vs. Passive Verbs	Passive verbs obscure actor; suggests lack of ownership or responsibility for the result. Correct choice depends on your strategy.
Abbreviations	Acceptable when known; confusing and potentially arrogant when unknown.
Clichés	Noticeable use suggests lack of thought and perhaps outdated knowledge.
Choosing Correct Words	Incorrect choice suggests broader incompetence, poor quality.
Customer Focus	Naming customers before sellers, placing benefits before features, naming customers more often than sellers, etc., increase customer focus. Suggests seller understands customer's needs.
False Subjects	Less clear, forces busy customers to reread, obscures key points.
Gobbledygook	Obscures meaning; suggests seller is difficult to work with.
Jargon	Must balance between suggesting seller is knowledgeable (insider) vs. arrogant and difficult to understand; impact is customer dependant.
Organization	Organize according to readers' interests, summarize at all levels, announce and follow your organization. Suggests seller is competent, clear, deliberate, and thoughtful.
Redundant Words	Acceptable for occasional emphasis, otherwise, cumbersome. Overuse suggests seller is vain, a braggart, inefficient, or exaggerating.
Style and Tone	Style choices are a subset of composition; tone is the impact on the customer, whether or not it is persuasive.

Figure 5. Composition Is a Key Persuasive Element. *Successful, persuasive oral and written communication reflects excellent composition and the recommendations in this Capture Guide.*

Most decisions to include or omit information are not harmful or deceptive. For example, the late development of a new product would probably not affect your ability to support an unrelated, existing product. Your recent decision to hire 15 software engineers to develop a new application would probably not affect your ability to deliver outsourcing services.

Selection can involve ethical considerations. Unethical selection can be a deliberate, calculated, strategy of silence, usually to downplay weaknesses. Unethical sellers deliberately conceal by selection, but the separation between ethical and unethical is narrow.

Consider the difference between proof and support for sales assertions:

> This customer is concerned about completing the project on schedule. You must promise to complete it on time as a bid requirement. A proof statement, assuming a similar probability of on-time completion, would be:
>
> ---
>
> We completed 8 of 10 similar distribution centers on time, as listed in figure 1.

A support statement, offering evidence that on-time completion is possible, would be:

> Global Computers needed to complete a similar distribution center in the same, 6-month period. After a brief oral proposal process, they selected Shipley Constructors. We completed the distribution center 2 weeks ahead of schedule and were cited as Global's Star Vendor for 20XX.

Your reputation is destroyed when customers discover a deliberate omission.

Unethical sellers that deliberately use omission tactics generally follow a four-step pattern:

1. Omit the information
2. Deny if discovered, saying:

   There is nothing wrong with it. (Deny it is bad.)

   We did not cause this. (Deny responsibility.)

   We did not mean it. (Deny intent.)
3. Minimize the harm, saying: *It won't matter . . . only a few people were involved . . . that seldom happens . . .it could have been much worse.*
4. Divert attention, saying: *You were extremely lucky that xxx didn't happen . . . this gives us the opportunity to . . . I was more concerned about . . . Did you hear what happened to . . .*

Would this statement be unethical if the Global distribution center was the only project Shipley Constructors completed on time?

Taking quotes out of context is a form of selection. At what point is a quote about your organization's excellent performance no longer relevant? Is it relevant 6 weeks, 6 months, or 6 years after the customer said it? If that same customer is now displeased with your organization due to another event, is the original quote still true because it was true when they said it? Must you disclose the unconnected event? How would your immediate customer react if they contacted this reference?

Half-truths are statements that deliberately omit facts or information necessary for a full description or account. Half-truths are unethical and might be illegal, depending largely on the speaker's intent. For example, many statements in ads are true, but incomplete. Are these ads unethical if the omission is deliberate?

To limit deliberate half-truths and lies, governments enact disclosure laws, requiring sellers to disclose certain information, or certify that they comply with other legal requirements. For example, the U.S. government requires sellers to disclose full cost and pricing data and reserves the right to subsequently adjust payments if insufficient data was disclosed. Deliberate omission of relevant cost and pricing data is fraud, a criminal offense.

Here are some questions to ask to help you determine if a selection decision is unethical:

- What are the potential consequences of the omission?
- Would discovery reflect unfavorably on how customers view you or your organization?
- Would discovery affect their decision on this purchase?
- Would publishing this omission in the newspaper embarrass you or your organization?

The order of presentation is an important selection element of persuasion. Readers predominantly associate order with importance. The first item presented is most important, and following items are presented in decreasing order of importance. If you intentionally adopt a different convention, explain your decision to avoid misleading the customer.

Key proposal guidelines relating to order are summarized below:

- Order points in decreasing order of importance from this customer's perspective. For example, cite benefits before features.
- When items are of equal importance, say so.
- Announce your order, and then stick with it unless redirected by the customer.
- When reusing material, reorder your points for this customer. Omit nonrelevant points.
- When compelled to discuss bad news, open with a positive point.
- Begin presentations with an attention-getting statement you can support in your presentation.
- In presentations, consider using your most powerful point for a memorable close if you are sure the audience will be present and attentive throughout.

Redirection, the fifth persuasive technique, is the tactic of shifting attention to other points. Customers usually want a range of features. A common ethical redirection is to counter a weakness in one area with an offsetting strength in another area.

For example, a customer requested a search and rescue helicopter that could meet the following requirements:

- 250-mile search range
- 2-hour loiter time over the search area
- Winch 15 survivors from the water
- Maintain 1-hour reserve fuel capacity

The positive response follows:

> Our aircraft can maintain all required search parameters and successfully winch 8 survivors from the water. However, if the search range is reduced from 250 to 225 miles, we can maintain all other search parameters AND successfully winch 15 survivors from the water.

Another common and ethical redirection is to offset a performance shortfall (weakness) with lower cost (strength), or vice versa. Here is an example in proposal text:

> Our firm, fixed-price construction cost is $10,000 greater than the target cost in your bid request. However, our fast-track construction approach enables you to move in 2 months ahead of schedule, saving $10,000 in rent at $5000 per month.

Humor and collaboration can be ethical redirection tactics. We all use humor to defuse tense situations, relax people, and build rapport. Skilled sellers occasionally use humor in sales presentations once they have established an acceptable relationship. Upon entering potentially contentious negotiations, a seller stated: *Don't you just hate this part?*, thus defusing some of the tension and perhaps personal animosity.

Collaboratively involving customers in determining the solution to a problem diverts attention from: *What is wrong?*, to: *What do we agree will make it right?* Customer service representatives are routinely taught to use questions like *What would you like me to do to fix this problem?* They are using collaboration to redirect the customer from unproductive venting to productive problem solving.

Sellers routinely redirect customers' focus from price to value by collaboratively developing a quantified value proposition. Once customers quantify the added value of the improved solution and the opportunity cost of delays, the outright price or price differential versus the alternatives becomes less important.

Unethical redirection tactics usually intensify unrelated or trivial side issues. Traditional names for these redirection tactics are *bait-and-switch, hairsplitting, red herring, busy work, legal harassment, loophole,* and *cosmetic difference.* Attacking the messenger is a second unethical redirection tactic, where the credibility of the messenger is questioned.

A third redirection tactic is to rename the problem. *Taxes* become *revenue enhancers*; *deficits* become *revenue shortfalls*, *power failure* becomes *current interruption*, *problems* become *challenges*, and *change orders* become *opportunities for further enhancements*. The term *spin* is a redirection tactic, where the speaker or writer attempts to create a favorable (or unfavorable) impression. Exactly when ethical spin becomes unethical is a difficult judgment that rests on the user's intent and the impact on the customer.

Ghosting, the sixth persuasive technique, is calling attention to unnamed competitors' weaknesses by highlighting the importance of, or differences between, alternative approaches or solutions. Whether emphasizing your strengths or highlighting competitors' weaknesses, the following ghosting tactic is the same:

Emphasizing a seller's strength (excellent safety record)

With our lost-time-accident rate less than one-half the Montana state average, construction can continue on schedule.

Highlighting a competitor's weakness (poor safety record)

Our safety record is better than any other Montana contractor. With our lost-time-accident rate less than one-half the second-place contractor, construction can continue on schedule.

Ghosting and trade-off analysis are similar. Trade-off analysis is simply discussing your analysis of alternative approaches and then noting why one alternative was selected and the others were rejected. The most sophisticated trade-off analyses bound the alternatives, noting the conditions where the preferred alternative changes. When one of the rejected alternatives is the same as a competitor's approach, you have ghosted or cast doubt on that competitor's approach.

The following example illustrates how ghosting was used ethically to win a recompete:

The incumbent operator of a medical laboratory for a large, government agency was seeking a third, 5-year contract. Competitors' complaints about favoritism towards the incumbent prompted the contracting officer to limit proposals to 100 pages to neutralize the incumbent's advantage. The incumbent's strategy was to convince the customer that managing this complex laboratory was too risky to shift to a new operator. Their tactical approach was to use detailed graphics to depict all processes. Such detailed information caused the customer to see the risk of allowing a new vendor to take over its complex operations. The incumbent retained the contract.

6 Align your persuasive techniques to the specific needs of individuals in the buying process and their preferred communication styles.

Complex buying decisions are made by buying committees. The individuals on buying committees assume the five, classic decision-making roles as described in figure 6. Individuals in each role have typical needs or issues in their decision-making role, also listed in figure 6.

Sellers that are aligned with their customers are meeting the individual business and emotional needs of each person on the buying committee. Not only do sellers supply customers with the business information that they need when they need it, but sellers also recognize and address customers' emotional needs. Staying aligned becomes more challenging when you consider that the needs of individuals on the buying committee change over the buying cycle.

Individuals have different preferences in how they take in information. Educators classify learning styles as visual, auditory, and tactile/kinesthetic.

Visual learners learn through seeing. Visual learners need to see the teacher's body language and facial expression. They often think in pictures, learn best from visuals, and take detailed notes to absorb the information.

Auditory learners learn through listening. They prefer lectures, discussions, talking things through, and listening to what others have to say. Auditory learners interpret the nuances of nonverbal speech, such as tone, pitch, and speed. Written information is less accessible until it is heard.

Tactile/kinesthetic learners, a much smaller segment, learn by moving, doing, and touching. They are hands-on people. They often find it hard to sit still for long periods and may become distracted by their need for activity and exploration.

Most adults develop the ability to take in visual, auditory, and tactile/kinesthetic information, but we retain preferences. We all can cite colleagues who tend to be visual, auditory, or tactile/kinesthetic. While well beyond the purpose of this *Capture Guide*, sellers that adapt their style of communication to meet the needs of specific customers will be more persuasive. Most sellers sense when they click with customers but might not recognize why they clicked.

While useful to recognize customers' preferred communication style, the usefulness and reliability of adapting your communication style are limited in complex sales. For example:

- Few sellers can accurately and reliably "read" a customer's preferred communication style. Most adults have learned instinctive adaptations but have difficulty consciously adapting their communication styles.
- Most sales presentations and documents are prepared for a buying committee. Even when documents are prepared for one individual, these documents might be forwarded to others in the buying organization for comment or approval.

Hence, follow the persuasive communications guidelines suggested throughout this *Capture Guide*. Integrate visual, verbal, and tactile/kinesthetic elements in reasonable, credible, and emotion-based appeals.

ROLE	DESCRIPTION OF ROLE	COMMON NEEDS
Recommender	Gathers data, prepares specifications and bid request, manages the evaluation process, prepares oral/written recommendation. Builds buy-in towards a consensus decision. U.S. Federal example: Source Selection Evaluation Board Chair or end user.	Enough data but not too much; quantitative justification for what might be an emotional decision; timely responses to meet procurement deadlines.
Approver	Has power to veto the recommendation, whether formal or informal. Veto can prompt a modification of the request or escalation to the "Decider." Often technical, legal, contracts, finance, or a consultant. Could be approver due to personal relationship with decider or user. U.S. Federal example: Contracting Officer (CO), CO Technical Representative (COTR), or other purchasing official.	Enough data to satisfy "technical" information needs. Credible reputation with fellow specialists. Bidder must demonstrate understanding of the specialists' disciplines and meet specialist requirements and regulations
Influencer	Asked for their opinion because they are involved in implementation. Strong influence but no veto power. U.S. Federal example: CO Technical Representative (COTR), or Small/Minority/Disadvantaged business representative.	Bidder must acknowledge importance of this person's role and opinion. Spurned influencers may work to undermine offending sellers.
Decider	Final authority; accountable for the decision; power to commit organization. Some organizations require a consensus. U.S. Federal example: Source Selection Authority.	Solution must be compatible with organizational vision, decision rules, direction, and other initiatives. Evidence of commitment and risk sharing. Acceptable, manageable risk. Accessible, responsible counterpart identified in selling organization.
Implementer	Implements, executes, uses, or operates solution. Could also be the recommender.	Requires past-performance data. Reviews reputation of seller with colleagues; specific measurable milestones; transition plan; training plan; credibility, reputation, and experience of key individuals committed by seller.

Figure 6. Buying-Decision Roles. *When determining what might be persuasive to individuals on the buying committee, consider their roles in the buying decision. Each role might include multiple individuals, and some individuals might have multiple roles.*

Presentations to Customers are intimately related to written proposals. Both are planned and structured to advance the sale. Any disconnect or conflict between what you say and what you submit in writing creates dissonance and confusion, reducing your credibility.

See PERSUASION.

Customer presentations usually have one of the following primary objectives:

1. To persuade
2. To convey information

A secondary objective is to solicit feedback and new information.

Effective persuasion relies on 1) Reputation and credibility of the speaker, 2) Logic of what is said, and 3) Emotional needs or state of the customer. All three elements are essential.

Presentations to Customers

1. Maintain consistency throughout the sales process.
2. Keep a balance between content and delivery.
3. Identify the next realistically achievable sales objective.
4. Analyze your audience and present logically according to their priorities and needs.
5. Consider the parameters and environment.
6. Include evidence to support your points.
7. Use effective slides to support your message.
8. Deliver with confidence.
9. Establish the ground rules, then follow them.

1 Maintain consistency throughout the sales process.

See CUSTOMER FOCUS, *Proposal Guide*.

Complex sales involve multiple sellers and presentations. Unexplained changes in your message cause dissonance, doubt, and objections.

By organizing all of your presentations and documents in the same customer-focused manner, you will save time, be more consistent, and be more successful in achieving your objectives.

2 Keep a balance between content and delivery.

When you plan a presentation to a customer, spend equal time developing your content and practicing your delivery.

Writers use graphics, color, lists, fonts, white space, and style for emphasis. Presenters rely on gestures, voice dynamics, eye contact, posture, movement, and facial expressions.

These nonverbal messages can either reinforce or contradict the verbal message.

When verbal and nonverbal messages conflict, the listener tends to trust the nonverbal elements to determine the meaning.

3 Identify the next realistically achievable sales objective.

Begin by answering two questions:

1. What is your objective?
2. What would you like the customer to agree to do next?

The answer to the first is usually broad, to persuade the customer to buy your idea, product, or service.

The answer to the second is far more focused, to agree to change a specification, for example, or to commit to attend a product demonstration.

Open your presentation by stating your objective:

> Today I will demonstrate how outsourcing network support can save $240,000 annually and free your managers to focus on Global's core activities.

Stating the next step at the beginning might be premature.

4 Analyze your audience and present logically according to their priorities and needs.

To present effectively, you must understand your customers' priorities and needs. When presenting, state your understanding of their needs and ask for confirmation.

> In your (bid, phone request, initial meeting) you asked us to address the following issues:
>
> *(List the issues.)*
>
> Have we gotten them correct? If so, with your agreement, we will address each one in order.

If you are too early in the sales process to have a basis to state their issues, then either ask them or cite your understanding and the basis for your understanding.

> We agreed to meet today to discuss how we might help you establish bottling facilities in South America. Our experience with other organizations developing manufacturing facilities in South America suggests that most are concerned about the following issues:
>
> *(List the issues.)*
>
> How would yours be similar or different?

See Executive Summary *and* Organization, ***Proposal Guide.***

Presentations organized around the seller's key points are rarely persuasive and successful.

Organize in order of importance to the customer, unless directed otherwise by the customer. Presentations can be logically organized by order of importance, time, cause and effect, or spatially.

Prepare an early draft executive summary and use it as the basis for customer presentations to maintain a consistent sales message, save time, and be customer focused.

The similar organization of customer presentations and the executive summary is shown in figure 1. Note two differences:

1. Presentations require more emphatic summaries and transitions among main points.
2. Graphics will have to be adjusted for the medium.

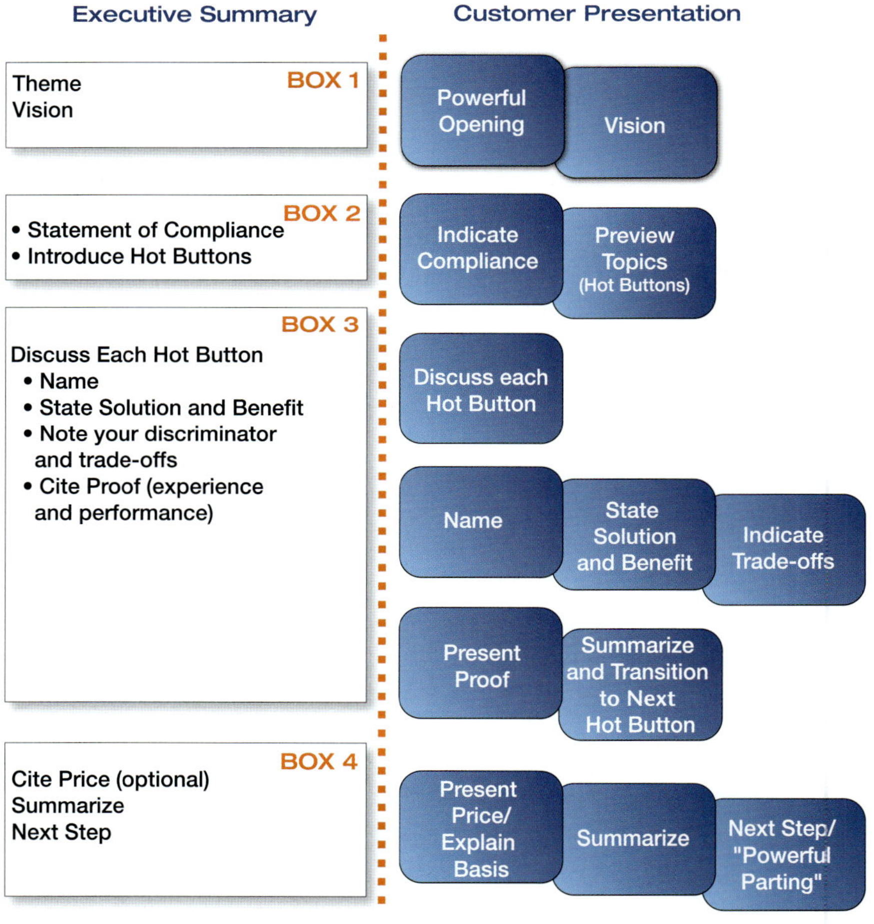

Figure 1. Use the Same Organization for Your Customer Presentation and Executive Summary. *Note how the Four-Box organization directly maps to slides in a presentation or sections in an executive summary. If you organize your customer presentations as shown, you will save time preparing the executive summary and maintain a consistent message. If your executive summary is prepared first, simply add slides as needed, following sound slide preparation guidelines.*

5

Consider the parameters and environment.

The *location* will determine the physical distance to your customers and often the presentation aids that you can use.

The *time* available will affect the depth of content.

The *number* in the audience will affect the visual medium selected and the design of your graphics.

The *occasion* will affect the expectations, motivation, enthusiasm, and level of expertise of the audience.

6

Emphasize visual evidence rather than textual evidence, if possible.

Include evidence to support your points.

Develop adequate support for each main point. Remember evidence of support is not necessarily proof in a scientific sense. Support includes definitions, evaluation criteria, explanations, experience, proof of performance, and testimonials.

Definitions establish a common basis of understanding, and *evaluation criteria* establish a basis for judgment or comparison.

Explanations are nearly always necessary, but match them to the expertise of the audience.

Experience is the proof that your organization has done this before or has completed similar tasks. When experience is not identical, relate parallel experience from similar subtasks.

Proof of performance is about results. When you completed the task, what was the benefit to the customer or impact on the customer's process?

Testimonials or *references* offer independent proof that the experience and performance cited are real. Testimonials carry emotionally persuasive impact in addition to the facts.

7

Use effective slides to support your message.

Effective slides should highlight key messages, not display every point. Think of slides as billboards, not text ads.

Slides should support your message rather than become the message. Presenters have problems when their slides serve too many additional purposes:

- Cue or prompt the speaker
- Support participants' note taking
- Review key points for audience members' subsequent use or study
- Substitute for written papers, guides, or manuals

Keep the following in mind when designing presentation graphics:

1. **Keep text simple.**

- Keep slides to one thought, concept, or idea.
- Use a sentence headline that states your key point on all but title slides. Left justify headline text.
- Limit lists to two-to-four items and six words per line.
- Use sentence case. Sentence case is the easiest to read, title case is harder to read, and ALL CAPS is the most difficult to read.
- Minimize bulleted lists because they do not show the links between items.
- Replace bulleted lists with graphical support for the key point stated in the title.
- Use one or two fonts or typefaces (at the most).
- Highlight with **bold**, *italics*, or color. Highlight key numbers. Avoid underlined text.

2. **Keep the graphics uncluttered.**

- Present information supporting your title assertion visually. Use images, graphics, or visual arrangements of text. Connect arrangements of text with lines or arrows.
- Show only key numbers when the actual number is important.
- Show only trend lines when the trend is your key point.

3. **Guide eyes to the main point.**

- Use larger type.
- Use an arrow.
- Use motion or (with caution) a video clip.
- Leave white space between visual elements, rather than white space for borders. When projected, white space on the border is less noticeable.
- Use *builds* with dense slides.

4. **Organize clearly:**

- Use an image on each title slide that orients the audience to your key message, objective, or subject.

See Color *and* Graphics, ***Proposal Guide.***

- Follow title slides with an introductory or mapping slide that previews direction. Use images on mapping slides that act as mnemonics for each distinct part of your presentation. Repeat these images on the initial slide for each part.
- End with a concluding slide that restates your initial assertion. Incorporate your opening image and summary support image on this concluding slide. If you move to questions or discussions, leave your concluding slide on the screen.

5. **Follow these additional suggestions:**

- Use a landscape style permitting larger print and longer, easier-to-read phrases.
- Use 28 point or larger type for titles and 18-24 point for body text, depending upon room size.
- Use simple sans-serif typefaces.
- Keep the grammatical structure of bullet points parallel, making content easier to understand and present.
- Proof carefully; do not rely exclusively on spell checking software.
- Use numbers in display lists when you may want to refer to a few specific items.
- Use phrases, not sentences.

Choose colors and templates carefully. Consider your corporate image, the audience, and your objective. Some audiences comment on the background or motion while missing the presenter's point.

Many decorative images in standard presentation templates actually detract from your message and reduce audience recall. Avoid dark backgrounds and reverse print when you need to observe audience reactions or present in bright rooms. Reverse print on dark backgrounds must be either larger or bolder.

8

Black the screen when presenting key points that are not supported by a slide. Focus the audience on the presenter, not the screen.

Deliver with confidence.

Confident delivery demands rehearsal. Professional comedians and actors rehearse extensively to develop a natural delivery.

Rehearsals enable you to test six critical aspects of your presentation:

Timing—Does it match the customers' expectations?

Intonation and Emphasis—Do you hit each point correctly?

Technology—Can you use all hardware, software, lights, and screens? Do the visuals project correctly and clearly for all viewers?

Confidence—Have you rehearsed to enable you to focus on your customers and to adjust to their reactions?

Audience Reaction—Does the test group get your message?

Questions and Answers—Are questions allowed during or after your presentation? Do you want to encourage questions? How will questions affect timing? In team presentations, who will respond? How do you plan to respond?

9

Establish the ground rules, then follow them.

Follow customers' ground rules or establish them collaboratively. Collaboration promotes acceptance.

In less formal situations, frequently check the customers' understanding and acceptance. Participation keeps the customer's attention.

Presentation experts differ on how and when to allow questions. No single approach is best in all situations. One approach is to ask the audience to hold questions for the end. With this approach, nervous presenters can stay on topic and on schedule. However, interactivity is lost, and the presentation can end dully when questions abruptly cease.

Another approach is to encourage questions during the presentation to involve customers, gauge reaction, and tailor content. With this approach, presenters must be skilled enough to stay on topic and on schedule. Allow interruptions if you have adequate presentation skills.

Retain enough time with either approach to summarize and close with power and enthusiasm.

Pricing to Win is a process for achieving the price to win by developing an offer that is competitive within the customer's value system. Essential process inputs include acquisition requirements, the customer's budget, competitors' likely bids, realistic costs to deliver the offered solution, and alternative solutions.

"The same general conditions that facilitate a company's ability to use other business development best practices contribute to that company's ability to build and sustain pricing to win and competitive assessment best practices."

Final Report: Benchmark Study on Implementing PTW/ CA Capability in a Company, Business Development Institute International, 31 March 2011.

Understanding pricing to win requires common definitions and perspectives on evolving trends in business development best practice. First, key definitions:

- **Price** is the amount of money expected, required, or given in payment for the solution.
- **Cost** is the cost to the seller to supply the solution. If the seller makes a profit, then the price exceeds the cost.
- **Price to compete** is your interim estimate of the customer's perception of a competitive range before final requirements are known. Use it to guide initial solution design.
- **Price to win** is the combination of price and capability yielding a probability of win that meets the seller's strategic objectives based on the requirements and evaluation process. Hence, price to win is not just a number. Rather it is a number linked to a set of capabilities that generate specific measurable benefits to the buyer.
- **Pricing to win** is the process for achieving or arriving at the price to win and is the focus of this topic section.

Pricing to win is the next major focus in the evolution of business development best practice. In markets involving complex sales, business development practices tend to evolve in this order:

- Professional sales techniques are implemented, first tactical, then strategic.
- Professional proposal planning and management processes are implemented.
- Formal capture planning and management processes are implemented.
- A formal pricing-to-win process is implemented.

Visionary managers initiate each wave. When competitors reduce the sector leader's competitive advantage by emulating the leader's processes, the leader initiates the next wave of improvements.

Pricing to Win

1. Integrate pricing to win as a fundamental aspect of your business development lifecycle.
2. Recognize basic customer buying types to anticipate their buying behaviors.
3. Determine the customer's addressable budget.
4. Consider the customer's expected price.
5. Estimate and refine the price to compete based upon competitors' bids and actual award prices on prior similar contracts.
6. Estimate and refine a price to win using an opportunity-based, bottom-up approach.
7. Compare likely bids and solutions using the winning price window (WPW).
8. Develop a strategy to achieve the price to win.
9. Incorporate customer evaluation processes into your pricing strategy.
10. Recognize the impacts of game changers, including political, economic, social, technological, legal, and environmental (PESTLE) factors or events.
11. Refine your solution based on changes in the competitive landscape.
12. Refine your strategies based on changes in your solution or competitive landscape.
13. Re-assess your pricing strategies post-award and update your pricing-to-win database.

Academic, B2B, and Government sector pricing-to-win language differs. Academics largely focus on consumer and mass markets, which are easier to analyze and model. Organizations pursuing major, one-off Government and B2B contracts, the focus of this topic section, use Government-focused terms because the leading pricing-to-win practitioners are in the Government-focused sector. Non-profits might have different definitions of profit, fee, price, cost, and cost-sharing, but the fundamentals apply.

From an academic perspective, pricing to win is a subset of strategic pricing, an active academic research topic in economics, purchasing, industrial marketing, and business development. Academic research focuses on the importance of internal and external pricing factors when pursuing transfer, cost-plus, parity, second market, complementary product, or low-cost pricing strategies. Internal factors relate to the selling organization. External factors relate to competitors, customers, and customers' buying environments (as in regulated markets).

Leading business development professionals view pricing to win as a strategic capability and competition-sensitive advantage. The most capable organizations have pricing-to-win departments, employ full-time practitioners, and often contract with independent consultants to cross-check their internal analyses.

Some organizations rely entirely on consultants, valuing their independent perspective and part-time cost. However, many others continue to rely on capture managers, account managers, program managers, cost volume managers, and their senior management team to arrive at an acceptable price to win on an *ad hoc* basis grounded in their experience.

Capture Guide pricing-to-win guidelines are applicable to a single major opportunity or groups of similar opportunities. Placed in context:

- **Strategic competitor analysis** focuses broadly on the capabilities, capacities, personalities, and market penetration strategies of your competitors.
- **Tactical competitive analysis** focuses on the same items in the context of a single opportunity.
- **Pricing to win** focuses on the trade-offs between this customer's requirements, budget, and values; your objectives, capabilities, solution, and costs; and competitors' likely objectives, capabilities, solution, costs, and strategies.

1 Integrate pricing to win as a fundamental aspect of your business development lifecycle.

See DECISION GATE REVIEWS; *and the entire* ***Business Development Lifecycle Guide.***

Few sellers quote a price without considering whether it is a potentially winning price. So pricing to win is an old concept under a new label, often executed in an *ad hoc* fashion based upon the seller's personal experience. Sellers' internal processes, techniques, and roles blur as managers attempt to distinguish pricing from costing, identify internal and external factors, separate facts from opinion, reduce bias, and assign roles. Similarly, independent pricing-to-win consultants use different terms and processes, tout different data sources as discriminators, and bring different experience with customers, markets, technologies, and competitive environments.

Embrace common processes and definitions as your first pricing-to-win integration step. Figure 1 depicts the Shipley Business Development Lifecycle by phase at the top, aligned with a table listing relevant pricing-to-win activities by phase and concluding decision gate. The activities listed in column two are notional, repeated, and adapted to each opportunity.

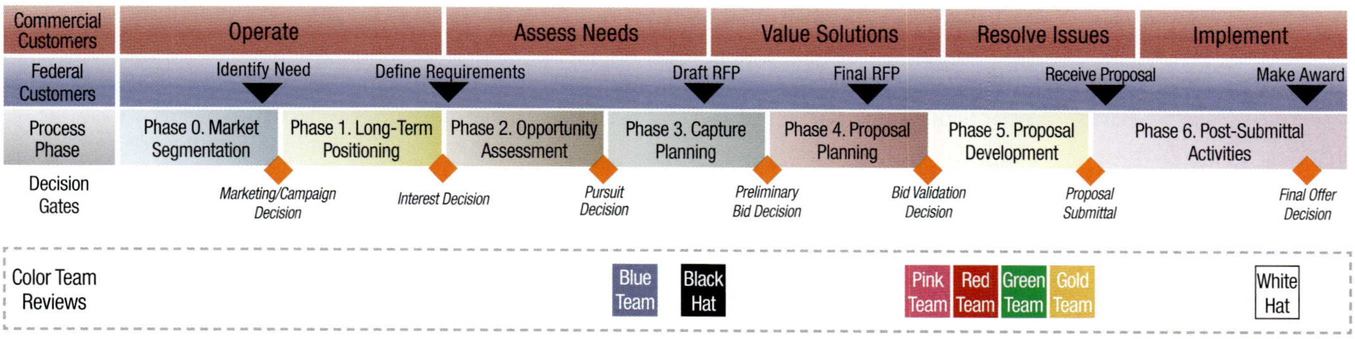

PHASE	PRICING-TO-WIN RELEVANT ACTIVITY	CONCLUDING DECISION GATE
0 Market Segmentation	• Develop strategic customer, competitor, and organizational pricing-to-win data (not specific to upcoming opportunity) • Establish pricing-to-win data storage and retrieval system	Marketing/Campaign Decision
1 Long-Term Positioning	• Update and validate strategic data • Forecast discriminators • Invest to develop discriminators • Identify preliminary opportunity-specific data	Interest Decision
2 Opportunity Assessment	• Initiate customer analysis • Identify probable competitors • Estimate award potential	Pursuit Decision
3 Capture Planning	• Input to Blue Team (capture plan review) • Input to Black Hat review (strategy and solution) • Identify *game changers* and review investment decisions • Value discriminators • Refine estimate of award value	Preliminary Bid Decision
4 Proposal Planning	• Update Black Hat review input (strategy and solution) • Obtain independent competitive assessment and cross-checks • Update Blue Team 2 (proposal plan review) input • Review *game changers* • Extend contract line items into a work breakdown structure; set design-to-cost targets or bogies (internal, subcontractors, vendors) • Document estimating guidelines, assumptions, and rationale • Review/refine/adjust pricing-to-win targets • Confirm inter-volume pricing-to-win implementation, strategy, solution alignment at Pink Team review • Set pricing assumptions regarding risk premiums, margins, negotiation strategy • Estimate price to win	Bid Validation Decision
5 Proposal Preparation	• Freeze solution and work breakdown structure • Confirm alignment of price to win throughout cost volume • Finalize risk premiums, margins, negotiation strategy • Refine price to win	Submit Proposal
6 Post Submittal Activities	• Revisit and update pricing-to-win analysis • Identify and confirm *game changers* • Refine value of discriminators • Set final proposal revision (FPR) parameters • Prepare negotiation plan • Update price to win	Contract Award

Figure 1. Integrate Pricing-to-Win Activities with Your Business Development Lifecycle. *Every phase of the business development lifecycle includes activities related to pricing to win. These activities are interdependent with solution development and refinement and capture strategy.*

2

Recognize basic customer buying types to anticipate their buying behaviors.

See VALUE PROPOSITION.

Recognize customer buying types as a simplification applicable to most markets. Often buying decisions are made by committees comprising individuals with different issues and concepts of value.

Understanding customers' buying types helps you zero in on a winning price. Consider three types of customers:

- **Budget-limited** customers cannot afford the capability they want but will spend all their available budget and usually be disappointed.
- **Capability-satisfied** customers buy only what they need at the lowest available price.
- **Best-value** customers trade price against capability. Educated ones understand the trade-offs between value and price. Naïve ones mistakenly believe they can purchase the desired capability at an unrealistically low price.

  Under U.S. Federal procurement regulations, best value has specific legal meanings in addition to the larger context of trading price against capability. Two types of best value selection processes can be used: trade-off and lowest price technically acceptable. Trade-offs allow higher prices or lower technical capabilities to be selected when an offer is judged to yield the best overall value. Extra capability can be rewarded. Conversely, the lowest price technically acceptable process mandates selection of the lowest-priced offer among those that are at least minimally compliant. In that case, no value is assigned to additional capability.

By understanding the type of customer you are dealing with, you can better identify and position your price to win. Keep in mind that price to win is a combination of price and capability.

If the customer perceives equal capabilities, a rational customer will select the solution with the lowest price. Hence, differentiate your offer if you want the customer to pay more for your superior solution. How much more you can charge depends upon the customer's perception of your added value and whether they have sufficient budget.

Given sufficiently long lead times, you might be able to persuade and help the budget–limited customer to obtain a larger budget; convince the capability-satisfied customer that either some portion of a competitor's extra capability is unnecessary or some aspect of your solution is essential, or conversely that they need more capability (adds value); or educate the naïve best-value customer. If not, then align your solution with the customer type or no-bid. Ignoring this reality might be the single greatest reason bidders lose.

3

Determine the customer's addressable budget.

In general, confident, experienced buyers are more comfortable disclosing and discussing their addressable budget. Less confident and experienced buyers might resist, believing buyers will automatically propose at the maximum. If so, emphasize your need to develop a realistic solution that they can afford.

Customers cannot typically spend all available funding on external purchases of goods or services. They reserve some portion to cover expenses associated with the purchase, and the remainder is the addressable budget.

Determine how much of the customer's budget is addressable, the amount likely to be available for a purchase, by identifying patterns from prior budgets. Customers typically deduct or reserve a portion of the budget for these types of items:

- Project management costs
- Risk reserves to cover potential cost increases, errors or omissions in the specifications, or changes in quantities
- Scope creep
- Agency or departmental overheads (sometimes required to support other programs)
- Fees for ancillary services, such as information technology, communications, engineering or technical support, quality assurance, test support, etc.
- Travel and temporary duty surcharges
- Buying agency or purchasing department surcharges

Determining the customer's budget and funding profile might be as easy as asking. As a rule, the earlier in the buying process, the less fixed the customer's budget. Bid requests might state the budget, especially on task orders.

Glean budget information from websites, public statements, and news releases. Determine if overall budgets have increased or decreased over prior years and whether this trend might affect this purchase. For example, one company bidding on a state services job resisted adapting its solution despite the governor's public announcement that all department budgets would be cut by 20 percent. Needless to say, it did not win.

Figure 2 is a relatively simple illustration of how the addressable budget might be estimated based on historic reserves and deductions. The percentages shown should not be extrapolated to other programs.

	BUDGET (millions)	PERCENT
Budgeted line-item	$250	100
Less:		
Project management overhead	$17.5	7
Risk reserve	$7.5	3
Contracting/purchase expenses	$7.5	3
Agency reserve	$7.5	3
Addressable budget	$210	84

Figure 2. Determining Maximum Addressable Budget. *Given the history that 16 percent of the budget has been reserved as shown and $250 million budgeted, the maximum addressable budget is $210 million.*

As the opportunity matures, repeatedly analyze the customer's addressable budget in greater detail. Refine your budget analysis by considering these questions:

- What is likely to happen with overall funding? What is the year-to-year trend? How might this trend affect this purchase?
- What is the typical *hold back* percentage? Is the amount a percentage of the total contract, a percentage of named components, a fixed charge per item, or a combination with a maximum charge?
- What is the price breakdown by probable or actual contract item?
- Will they seek or insert cost or revenue-sharing, bonding, seller financing, or mandatory set-aside requirements?
- Are small, minority, or disadvantaged business terms included?
- Will they make or consider multiple awards, dividing the available funds? If so, what are the probable maximum and minimum awards? Will the awards be for similar amounts or allocated according to past performance, capability, or price?
- What is the funding profile: timing, type, and source? When will funds be authorized and then available, and does the authority to spend end or extend into subsequent budget cycles?
- Do funding provisions restrict what can be purchased? For example, capital funds often cannot be used for operating and support costs.
- Does the source of funds, whether budgeted, borrowed, or generated by fees, restrict the use, amount, or predictability?
- Does the customer management team have incentives that influence the funding profile? For example, some outsourcing expenses are intentionally back-loaded to show greater savings in the initial years, either to improve management bonuses or in anticipation of improved out-year revenues.
- What is the contract type, and what are the associated allowable margins or reserves?
- What historical "cost adjustments" has this customer made when evaluating your proposals and competitors' proposals? Consider risk adjustments implied by past performance and those associated with the proposed technical and management solution.
- Is there an ante, a requirement for an item, service, or capability that will not be paid to be developed as part of the contract? An ante might comprise research and development funds, pre-engineering, testing, bonding, warranty, or transition and start-up expenses. While some government purchasing regulations limit such requirements, they are often encountered in commercial practice and may be found in a modified sense with government customers.
- What are the logistics and support implications? Often 60 percent of procurement funds are reserved for operations, spares, field support, depot support, operational integration, information technology, upgrades, and technology refreshes.

See COSTING.

4

Consider the customer's expected price.

Individual, business, and government buyers all have price expectations. Individuals might research typical prices, business buyers prepare expenditure requests, and government organizations typically follow regulated, defined processes.

Government regulations often require the buying organization to prepare should-cost analyses, independent cost estimates (ICE), or independent government estimates (IGE) before issuing bid requests. B2B organizations typically require an expenditure request that includes a detailed business case, schedule, project description, and cost plan for purchasing approval, even when funds are budgeted.

Customers employ multiple methods when preparing should-cost estimates:

- Comparing the total cost to the total cost of other, similar purchases
- Using detailed parametric or bottom-up estimating models
- Hiring a consultant to develop a should-cost estimate
- Relying on competitors' estimates or white papers
- Extracting an estimate from public sources
- Issuing a Request For Information (RFI)

The more complex the sale, the more likely customers will have prepared some type of cost estimate. Ask customers to share their estimates and/or estimating methods with you.

5

Estimate and refine the price to compete based upon competitors' bids and actual award prices on prior similar contracts.

This is a top-down approach based on both prior customer awards and competitors' bids relative to those awards. In general, this approach resembles a prospective buyer or seller in a consumer market who attempts to determine the market price of an item or service.

Early in the sales cycle, estimate and cross-check your estimate of the price to compete. Begin with the customer's should-cost analysis, if available. Examine customer buying trends, seeking evidence of how those expectations might evolve. Even during preliminary discussions, focus on solutions near the price to compete.

As the pursuit continues, repeatedly refine your price-to-compete estimate to establish a leading position with the customer. Consider previous contracts awarded to likely competitors compared to addressable budgets for those procurements. The awarded prices on those contracts are good preliminary indicators of where competitors positioned their offers relative to customer budgets. Use your findings to estimate where competitors might position their offers on the current procurement. While the most relevant contracts are those issued by the same customer, similar contracts awarded by other customers offer good insight.

Arrive at a price to compete after comparing your estimates from various sources. Develop your solution with that price to compete in mind.

No single method works consistently. Adapt your approach to exploit the best available data. Figure 3 illustrates a purchasing pattern based upon prior awards. Estimate the price to compete based on similar customer and competitor buying history.

	CONTRACT	WINNER	BUDGET	AWARD	YEAR	PORTION AVAILABLE
Purchase History	Alpha	Global	10	8	20X2	0.80
	Beta	AeroMax	20	16.4	20X3	0.82
	Delta	Beacon	5	3.8	20X4	0.76
	Gamma	Global	12	10	20X5	0.83
Next Purchase	Omega		16	13.1 – 13.4	20X6	0.82 - 0.84 (?)

Figure 3. Estimating the Price to Compete Based on Award History. *Given historic data on the Alpha, Beta, Delta, and Gamma contracts, two patterns seem evident: 1) The percentage of addressable budget seems to be increasing slightly over time, and 2) Smaller purchases appear to require a larger percentage reserve, assuming common items are being purchased. Therefore, the anticipated Omega contract was estimated at 0.82 to 0.84, implying a price to compete of 13.1 to 13.4. Most analysts would target towards the lower end, at about 13.*

6

Estimate a price to win using an opportunity-based, bottom-up approach.

Cross-check estimates from as many sources as possible. Compare the top-down results described in Guideline 5 with the bottom-up results described in Guideline 6. Employ different analysts, sources of data, analytical methods, and parameters. Verify the currency, accuracy, and assumptions implicit in analysts' data.

See COLOR TEAM REVIEWS.

Focus on your primary competitors. If you are competing in a crowded market, focus on types of competitors. Rely on your tactical competitive analysis to outline competitors' likely solutions, and then estimate how they will price each solution.

While the following steps appear relatively direct, pricing-to-win analysts find the process challenging, iterative, time-consuming, and frustratingly subjective. Analysts on complex systems bids report spending months developing and refining their analyses.

At a high level, estimate an opportunity-based, bottom-up price to win using the following process:

- Develop a work breakdown structure (WBS) for each competitor or type of competitor. To reduce the bias of the immediate architects of your probable system, enlist the assistance of uninvolved designers of similar systems who are familiar with competitors' system design and delivery approaches.
- Price competitors' systems using a bottom-up approach. Price WBS components based on their prior bids. Adjust prices to correct for changes in rates, methods, technology, sources, and other relevant factors.
- Sum WBS element prices, and then adjust the total using competitive intelligence regarding competitors' immediate business pressures and objectives. Consider current or anticipated backlogs, margin or profit expectations, strategic direction, and prior tactical responses to competitive pressures. Consider their relationship with the customer, incumbent or non-incumbent status, and even the personalities of key members of their management team. How committed are they to winning this bid?
- Consider the strengths and weaknesses of competitors' solutions. How might they respond by adapting their solutions and pricing? How might the customer value these changes?
- Assess your relative position by preparing a summary matrix depicting competitors' solutions and your solution.
- Select a price to win—a combination of price and capabilities—that provides your desired win probability. You might select a lower price at higher capability than you expect competitors to offer. But, business considerations might also drive you toward other postures. For example, you might deliberately offer a higher price with greater profit margin, depending on the customer's recognition of greater value in your solution, rather than blindly bidding the lowest possible price. Base your price to win on your understanding of how the customer will evaluate offers and select the winner.
- Retain your assumptions and analysis for subsequent iterations as you obtain new and improved intelligence.

Determining competitors' probable solutions, strategies, and pricing is often assigned in part or entirely to a Black Hat review team, depending upon the capability of the team and maturity of the organization's pricing-to-win process. Organizations with mature pricing-to-win capabilities will often independently analyze competitors' solutions and prices, providing input to the Black Hat review team. If so, the Black Hat review team cross-checks this input and focuses on probable capture strategies and gaming aspects. If pricing-to-win input is lacking or immature, the Black Hat review team attempts to fill the gap, but they often lack the time to develop new data or confirm explicit and implicit assumptions.

7

Compare likely bids and solutions using the winning price window (WPW).

The WPW in figure 4 depicts the customer's view of their options plotted in two dimensions, price and capability. The WPW is a conceptual tool, intended to help you assess alternatives and arrive at a price to win.

The boundaries are defined as follows:

- **Maximum budget** is the maximum amount the customer has budgeted.
- **Addressable budget** is the amount the customer has available for a purchase after deducting expenses associated with the purchase.
- **Minimum credible budget** is the amount below which the customer doubts the credibility of obtaining an acceptable solution.
- **Minimum acceptable capability** is the minimum capability acceptable to this customer.
- **Maximum justifiable capability** is the maximum capability that this customer can justify. While more capability might be possible and available, this customer does not perceive a practical use; it would be considered *gold plating*.

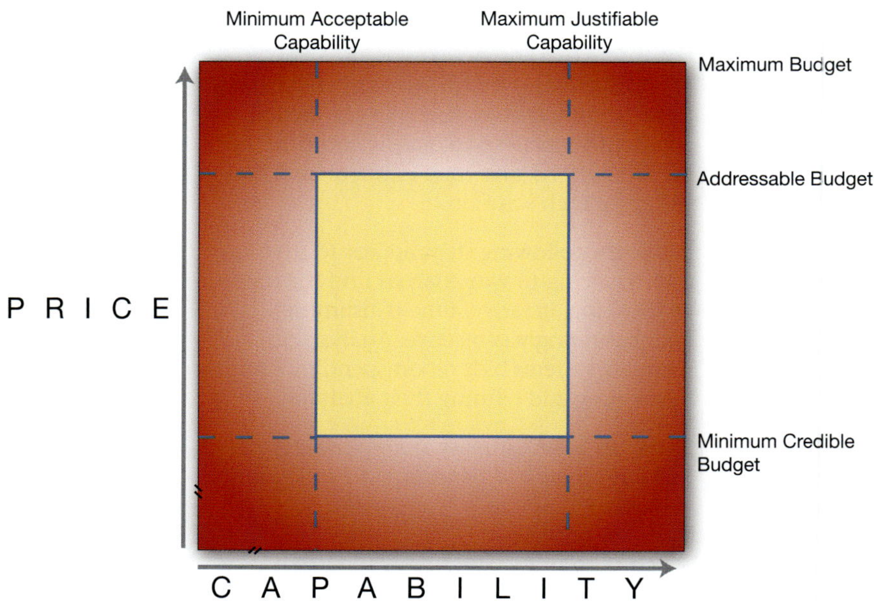

Figure 4. Winning Price Window. *Use the WPW to compare and contrast competitors' probable positions relative to yours. The absence of a scale reflects the relative nature of your assessment. For example, is your price higher or lower than competitors, and is it within the customer's budget parameters? Do not expect quantitative precision.*

Over time, the WPW becomes smaller, as shown in figure 5, as the customer better understands organizational needs, potential solutions, and relative values. Your pricing-to-win process objective is to iteratively and more accurately define the boundaries of the WPW, and then to favorably position your price to win versus competitors.

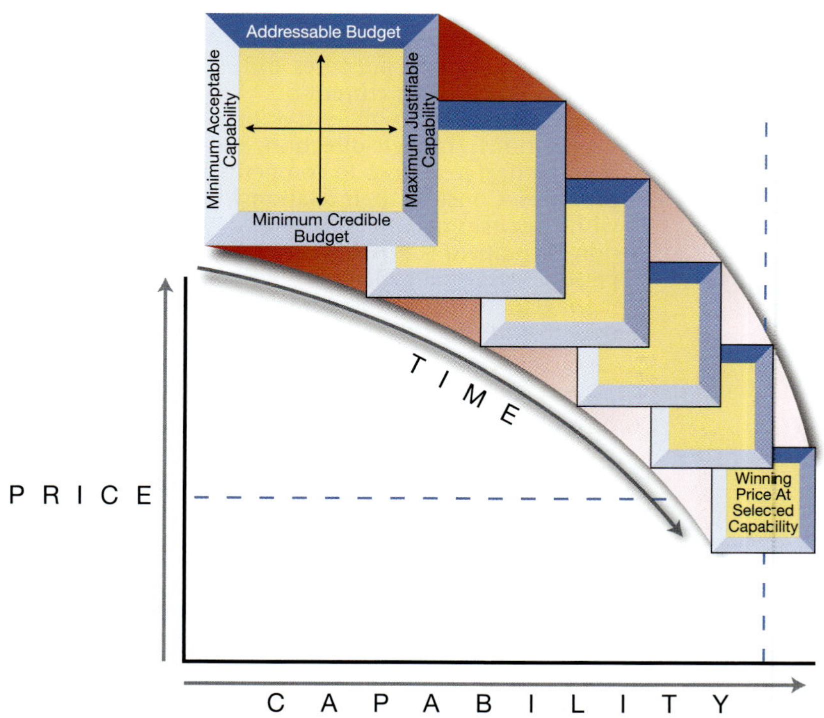

Figure 5. Narrowing the Winning Price Window. *The WPW contains the winning price. Conceptually, these price-capability boundaries narrow as the customer better understands organizational needs and the values offered by potential solutions. Your theoretical but rarely achieved goal is to identify the actual award price prior to submitting a bid.*

8

Develop a strategy to achieve the price to win.

Developing and implementing a strategy to achieve the price to win are primary capture team responsibilities.

Your price to win is a combination of your solution and price. Improve your position by analyzing the relative costs and benefits of existing and potential features of your solution. Add features that offer the greatest added value at minimum relative cost. Eliminate expensive features that offer relatively minimal benefit.

For many organizations, developing a strategy to achieve the price to win marks the transition between the work of pricing-to-win analysts and the capture team that develops, prices, and refines the solution and then works collaboratively with the customer, trying to influence the customer to prefer that solution. To minimize bias, many pricing-to-win analysts resist working on the solution, as they often must reassess the refined solution. Accurately assessing a solution that you helped develop is difficult.

Ask your capture team to refine the solution, considering the following alternatives:

- Lower costs by teaming and adjusting work shares
- Absorb development costs, adjust assumptions regarding risk, payback period, cost of capital, and development of prototypes or development models
- Supplement design costs using internal or external research and development funds
- Establish new cost centers (to reduce the cost of corporate overhead allocations)
- Modify assumptions about the placement of proposed personnel within pay grades (e. g., at the 25% vs. 50% or 75% levels)
- Adjust the span of control to reduce management positions
- Change *managers* to *task leads* so that they are presumed to contribute to productive work, not just manage
- Adopt processes/tools that enhance productivity
- Rework task estimates based upon requirements rather than historic costs (modify implicit assumptions)
- Develop creative warranty approaches
- Adjust margin
- Increase capability by adding valued features/discriminators
- Decrease capability within the WPW
- Decrease capability below the minimum limit by persuading the customer to alter their perception of needs and values
- Raise customer capability expectations by helping justify higher capabilities not available from competitors (creating discriminators)
- Maximize profit while still offering a lower price to win than competitors
- Consider noncompliant solutions or offers

9

Incorporate customer evaluation processes into your pricing strategy.

Extending the principle that the only relevant view is what the customer believes, the customer's method of valuing solutions is the only relevant approach.

Note: Examples in this section were developed to emphasize the importance of the customer's pricing evaluation process and not to suggest deceptive pricing tactics. However, ignoring the customer's price evaluation model is naïve.

Customers' evaluation processes can dramatically affect the relative competitiveness of your solution. Customers with a rigidly defined and disciplined evaluation process, most common in government markets, seek to equalize evaluations to minimize bias, whether real or perceived. As a result, the evaluation is often based on the prior contract rather than the probable need.

For example, a telecommunication services contract might specify a technology and quantity that was typical but will become obsolete. Suppose the past contract included a line item for 1,000 pagers. The contract price was $100 per month, for an extended line item annual cost of $1.2 million. Realizing few people continue to carry pagers, Bidder A assumes only 5 pagers will be ordered under the new contract, so the contract prices pagers at $5 per month, even though their internal cost will be $90 per month. The evaluated price, $5 each x 1,000 pagers x 12 months would be $60,000, a $1.14 million annual savings over the existing contract. But if the estimated quantity is correct, the cost to supply the pagers will be $90 each x 5 pagers x 12 months, or $5,400. Bidder A might then enrich the overall profit margin by quoting a higher margin on a different line item evaluated at lower-than-anticipated purchase quantities.

A similar tactic is applicable to labor categories and rates or tasks and prices that the customer will weigh heavily during evaluation but seldom purchase. Many indefinite delivery indefinite quantity (IDIQ) contracts are evaluated assuming a type and quantity of services, but the actual purchases will be under subsequent, individual task orders. Savvy bidders might attractively price their offering under the expected formula, knowing from historical information that the customer will purchase a different labor mix.

Within an individual task, a bidder might propose a working *task leader* rather than a *task manager*, knowing that the customer assumes that managers only manage, while a task leader performs productive work. Even if the rates for the task lead and task manager are identical, the evaluation process might presume more direct labor hours are required when a task manager is proposed.

10

Add game changers to the contingency portion of your capture plan, and then repeatedly review and update them.

Recognize the impacts of game changers, including political, economic, social, technological, legal, and environmental (PESTLE) factors or events.

A game changer is information that invalidates your implicit pricing-to-win assumptions. Confirm the existence of game changers by reviewing prior major losses, especially surprise losses. Did the award go to a little known or unidentified competitor, for an unexpectedly low price, or to a new or unknown technology? Were the contract terms, timing of key events, or involvement of unknown personnel a surprise? If so, you encountered game changers.

Game changers might originate from the customer, competitors, your organization, or external situational factors. Note that similar game changers affect both competitors and your organization. Figure 6 lists common game changers by origin.

Some external situational game changers involve trends, such as global warming or the growing scarcity of specific resources. At what point do trends become relevant and significant?

Other game changers are sudden and more difficult to forecast, such as war, earthquakes, tsunamis, or industrial accidents. While you might not be able to predict certain events, you might opt to propose contract terms and conditions to reduce your risk.

COMMON GAME CHANGERS		
Customer	***Competitors and Your Organization***	***PESTLE (Political, Economic, Social, Technological, Legal, and Environmental)***
• Budget change (size, funding category, timing) • Schedule change • Key personnel change • Revised priorities, objectives, direction • New requirements • Gain or loss of strategic importance	• Merger, acquisition, divestiture • Loss/change of key personnel • Major cost or schedule overruns on other contracts • Teaming shift • Financial pressures from markets, management, or creditors • Changes in strategic objectives, processes, or organization • Recent losses or wins, related or not	• Changes in government, elected, or regulatory officials; war or conflict • Changes in financial markets, cost and availability of resources • Shift in social conventions or mores • Shift in the capability, availability, or cost of new technologies • Changes in laws, regulations, or the interpretation of regulations • Changes in the environment (incremental climate change, industrial accident, abrupt climate event)

Figure 6. Potential Game Changers. *Game changers invalidate your pricing-to-win assumptions. Identify reasons customers, competitors, and your organization might not act as anticipated. Determine if and how significantly trends will affect this procurement. For example, will a growing emphasis on "green" initiatives really affect this customer's evaluation?*

11

A continuing business development challenge is minimizing bias in pricing-to-win activities while implementing the result in capture planning activities.

Refine your solution based on changes in the competitive landscape.

Attaining a price to win is iterative. Repeat the tactical activities listed under Guideline 8 when changes in competitive intelligence dictate. Given new information, changes in assumptions, or identification of game changers, repeatedly refine your solution.

Arguably, refining your solution is a capture team activity rather than pricing-to-win activity. Base solution refinements on the customer's perceptions rather than your own views of what you *know to be correct*.

If dealing with a budget-limited customer, ask:

- Have we identified and removed non-essential features that add cost but might appear to offer minimal commensurate value?
- Can we identify elements that could be made *optional* if the customer needs to further reduce acquisition cost?
- Can we restructure the offering to better meet the funding profile?

If dealing with a capability-satisfied customer, ask:

- Have we met the customer's minimum capability expectations?
- Have we included capabilities that could be eliminated to lower our price and yet remain competitive?
- Can we add or substitute features offering greater capability and value than our competitors?
- Can we convince the customer to raise expectations, making it harder for competitors to meet requirements?
- Have we reviewed competitors' likely offerings to identify new or overlooked approaches that we could incorporate into our solution at lower cost?

If dealing with an educated best value customer, ask:

- Have we maximized and prioritized the value-cost trade-offs for major solution features?
- What changes maximize value at the minimum cost?
- Have we confirmed and reinforced the customer's understanding of best value?

If dealing with a naïve best value customer, ask:

- Have we attempted to educate our naïve customer?
- Do we have sufficient access, time, and resources to educate them?
- While we might disagree with their assessment, can we modify our proposed solution at acceptable risk? If not, should we no-bid?

12 Refine your strategies based on changes in your solution or competitive landscape.

Strategies must be implemented to be effective.

Assuming that you have refined your solution per Guideline 11, focus on influencing the customer to prefer your solution. You must convince the customer that your refinements add value, offer improved capabilities, prices, or both.

Update your Integrated Solution Worksheet, figure 7, part of the capture plan template. If sufficiently early in the process, use it to collaborate with the customer, identifying and confirming the underlying issues and requirements. If the requirements are defined, use it to help refine the underlying issues, your solution, competitors' potential solutions, discriminators, gaps, strategies, and tactics.

Concentrate on the final two columns. Assign responsibility for each action item to a single, responsible person, whether they complete the action or direct the completion. Simply changing your solution without explaining how your changes benefit the customer is off-putting to the customer and often worsens your position.

The only aspect of capture strategy that improves your position with the customer is the tactical implementation. Internally focused aspects might be satisfying, but they do not improve your position.

ShipleyAssociates **Integrated Solution Worksheet**

Item No.	Customer Issues	Customer Requirements	Available Solution	Gap	Competitor Solution	Discriminators	Strategy	Action Required
1	System must be available.	8 hr. response time.	2 hr. response time	1 hr	3 hr. response time	Faster response but more expensive?	Emphasize no additional cost with cellular.	Show current response time. Show photo-service with cell phone.

Figure 7. Update Integrated Solution Worksheet. *Assuming this was completed in your capture plan, update it row by row. Focus primarily on the last two columns: Strategy and Action Required. Add columns or link each row to a specific implementation action plan. When time and resources are limited, prioritize and focus on key actions.*

13 Re-assess your pricing strategies after proposal submittal and update your competitive intelligence database.

After proposal submittal, re-evaluate your position with the customer. While the order will vary depending upon the customer and procurement, anticipate taking the following types of post-submittal actions:

- Respond to customer requests for clarifications, seek feedback, and anticipate revised requirements.
- Support past performance investigations and *gray beard* visits (visits by senior members of the buying team).
- Prepare for structured presentations and interchanges.
- Prepare and submit requested proposal revisions.
- Prepare a formal negotiation plan.
- Negotiate a final contract.

After proposal submittal, repeat your pricing-to-win process in a focused, abbreviated form:

- Revisit your competitive position and price to win in the WPW. Concentrate on the short list of remaining competitors.
- Reassess the positive and negative value gaps of your discriminators. Validate your quantitative value assessments.

- *Read between the lines* of customer statements. Are they subtly suggesting a preference or giving you hints about what may be necessary to close the deal?
- Have you detected any *game changers* on the part of the customer or competitors?
- Revisit your solution. Consider potential revisions within procurement parameters.
- Re-price revisions. Cross-check pricing assumptions.
- Update your strategy in writing. Then specify your tactics for each anticipated event.
- Prepare to concisely and clearly link, explain, and justify changes in your solution and pricing.

See VALUE PROPOSITION, ***Capture Guide***; and POST SUBMITTAL ACTIVITIES, ***Business Development Lifecycle Guide.***

When invited to negotiate a contract, prepare a negotiation plan. In some business negotiations, the negotiator loses sight of the goal, pushes too far, and loses the opportunity to achieve the initial goal. Successful negotiations are 80 percent preparation and 20 percent execution.

Identify your interests and those of your customer. Develop clear criteria to evaluate and measure options. Successful negotiators establish a zone of potential agreement, setting high and low outcome objectives. Consider the following facets:

- Quantify the value of the potential deal to you and the customer.
- Secure the support of your management and teammates on the parameters of an acceptable deal.
- Determine your bargaining range: opening position, target, and minimum acceptable.
- Estimate the customer's range: opening position, target, and maximum acceptable.
- Determine your leverage, a function of the quantified value of your discriminators. Base concessions on quantitative value assessments.
- Develop a preferred negotiation agenda, listing issues in decreasing order of importance, that you and possibly your customer will want to discuss. Propose and justify your agenda, but prepare to adapt to the customer's agenda.
- Identify potential ethical issues and how you might resolve them.
- Prepare for extended negotiations. Avoid making concessions due to time pressures by anticipating and minimizing the impacts to your team.
- Structure your negotiating team with clearly defined roles, much like an oral presentation or proposal.
- Take careful notes, clarify questions before answering, debrief immediately after every session, and then prepare for the next session.

Win or lose, document lessons learned and other findings in your competitive intelligence database. Begin preparing for your next opportunity, whether with this customer or other customers, this competitor or other competitors.

Process is defined as a systematic series of actions or steps directed toward a specific end. Organizations that follow the best business development practices win more business.

Organizations with effective business development processes gain the following benefits:

- Reduced costs
- Increased productivity
- Improved forecasting
- Increased management visibility and control

Defining, building, and sustaining an effective business development process require management focus and continuous effort. Barriers include corporate inertia, individual resistance to change, and constantly changing priorities that blur focus and erode commitment.

The impetus to reengineer an organization's business development process often stems from one of the following situations:

- Merged or reorganized organizations
- Changes in management
- Failure to meet sales or win-rate goals
- Staffing fluctuations
- Sale of the organization
- Analyst's concerns affecting stock price
- Maturing markets
- Loss of key customers or contracts

To develop a best-practice business development process, implement the following guidelines.

Process

1. Commit to a single, flexible, tailorable, scalable business development process based on industry best practices and championed at the executive level.
2. Align your business development process with your customers' buying cycles.
3. Define process phases broadly, delineated by clear decision gates with verifiable inputs and outputs.
4. Use document-based reviews at decision gates to control and add value to the process.
5. Adapt your process to individual opportunities by using flexible support tools.
6. Define business development roles, responsibilities, and levels of authority, including thresholds by type of opportunities.
7. Align your business development process with corporate policies, strategies, practices, and other processes.
8. Document your business development process to make it consistent and repeatable.
9. Train participants to give them the understanding and skills to follow the process.
10. Designate a process owner to collect metrics, foster continuous improvement, and maintain tools and infrastructure.

1

Commit to a single, flexible, tailorable, scalable business development process based on industry best practices and championed at the executive level.

The Business Development Capability Maturity Model (BD-CMM®) is an excellent guide to best practices. *See* **BD-CMM** , ***Capture Guide.***

Capability Maturity Model and CMM are registered in the U.S. Patent and Trademark Office by Carnegie Mellon University.

Organizations with a single process can conduct business more efficiently and effectively. Every opportunity falls within the single process—no exceptions. Individuals assigned to capture and proposal teams can immediately focus on the opportunity rather than determining or justifying what needs to be done.

A flexible process works for you, not against you, by including best practices based on the type of opportunity. Categorize two-to-four types of opportunities.

A tailorable process implies that phases, decision gates, and color team reviews are included based on the category of opportunity. Milestones might be mandatory, recommended, optional, or not applicable.

A scalable process can be adapted to the size, delivery deadline, and available resources. For example, a mandatory kickoff meeting might be shortened, conducted virtually, and include fewer participants. A color team review might be serial and virtual rather than a co-located, single event. You can determine industry best practice by regularly comparing your process to other organizations, by participating in industry forums and professional associations, and by engaging professionals that specialize in business development best practice reviews and business development process re-engineering.

A champion at the executive level will help your organization realize the benefits of committing to a single, flexible, tailorable, scalable business development process. Two examples illustrate how such a champion can influence the adoption of improved practices through both small and large actions:

> After sitting through 4 days of business development training, the managing director of a large organization was asked to approve an executive summary. He returned the executive summary with the following: *"You have attended the training. This is no longer acceptable."* Word of the incident spread quickly and everyone adopted the new standards and approach.

> An executive vice president of business development wanted to establish a single process with global standards for business development to improve business capture effectiveness. After actively participating in the development and documentation of a single business development process, he commissioned custom training for all process participants. He attended the entire first workshop with all of his direct reports.
>
> At the next 10 workshops, he personally introduced the workshop, reviewed participants' work, and concluded the workshop. All subsequent workshops were introduced and concluded by one of his direct reports. Within 3 years, this organization improved from second to first in global market share.

2 Align your business development process with your customers' buying cycles.

Customers care about their needs, not yours. Customers have different needs at different phases of the buying cycle. Design your process to address customers' needs as their needs change. The process outlined in figure 1 meets the single, flexible, and scalable criteria of Guideline 1.

The fixed milestones required for every opportunity establish the framework of a single process. Flexibility and scalability come from intelligently tailoring both the milestones and the steps between milestones. The top two bars in the figure depict customer buying phases and milestones. The bottom two bars show the alignment with selling phases and milestones.

See VALUE PROPOSITIONS.

Customers ***Operate*** before they think about buying. Needs are latent, yet products wear, personnel change, and needs evolve. During the Operate phase, smart sellers increase their understanding of customers' needs, position their organizations to meet them, and identify discrete business opportunities.

During the ***Assess Needs*** phase, customers' latent needs become explicit. Customers determine whether each need merits satisfying. Customers usually experience or recognize a compelling event that spurs them to seriously assess their needs. Help customers assess the pros and cons of satisfying each need. Value-added selling begins here, with customers and sellers collaborating to define requirements.

During the ***Value Solutions*** phase, customers initially identify potential solutions, then assess the relative value of those solutions to their organizations. Ideally, the customer and seller collaboratively quantify the added value to the customer's organization. The earlier you participate in this phase, the more open a customer is to your ideas.

During the ***Resolve Issues*** phase, customers tentatively select a solution and try to determine what could go wrong. Risk avoidance is paramount, so emphasize risk management and the value of the solution to the customer.

During the post-award ***Implement*** phase, customers are focused on attaining the anticipated benefits of the purchased solution. Reinforce the value delivered, and highlight the additional value of further enhancements. Begin positioning your next sale.

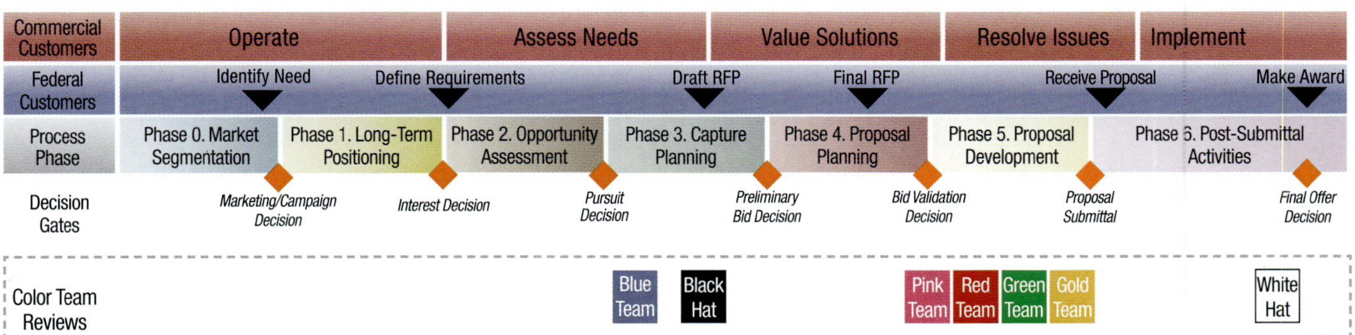

Figure 1. Seven-Phase Business Development Process. *The seven-phase business development process aligns with buying phases. Readily identifiable customer and selling milestones are shown. Customer milestones mark key customer decisions. Decision gates separate the selling phases. Color team reviews improve pursuits.*

3 Define process phases broadly, delineated by clear decision gates with verifiable inputs and outputs.

See Decision Gate Reviews and Color Team Reviews.

Define phases broadly to include the wide variety of opportunities your organization pursues. Narrow definitions encourage participants to work outside the process. The framework business development process introduced in figure 1 is expanded in figure 2.

Phases are separated by management decision gate reviews: qualify, pursuit, preliminary bid, bid validation, and submit. Clusters of potential activities are shown under each phase. Documents generated during those activities verify the output of phases and are input for subsequent phases.

This framework process is divided into seven phases. Phases 0 and 1 are iterative; Phases 2–6 are opportunity-specific.

- **Market Segmentation.** Management considers potential new market niches or customers to identify possible growth paths.
- **Long-Term Positioning.** Campaign plans are executed to establish your organization's presence and capabilities, aimed at identifying leads or opportunities.
- **Opportunity Assessment.** Newly identified opportunities are assessed to determine your organization's interest and whether they are winnable.
- **Capture Planning.** Individuals in customers' organizations are influenced to prefer your solution and organization.
- **Proposal Planning.** The proposal effort is planned while sales efforts continue.
- **Proposal Preparation.** The proposal is prepared, approved, and submitted.
- **Post-Submittal Activities.** Customers' questions are answered, leading to contract negotiation and award.

Defining clear, mandatory decision gates with verifiable inputs and outputs establishes a solid framework for all opportunities, large or small. Predefined quality checks at each gate minimize wasted effort and increase capture effectiveness. Each decision gate is described below:

- **Interest Decision.** Determine whether an identified opportunity fits your organization's goals, capabilities, and interests sufficiently to justify expending resources to gather more information, develop your relationship with the customer, and begin developing a solution.
- **Pursuit Decision.** Determine whether you have a realistic chance of influencing the customer to prefer your solution and your organization.
- **Preliminary Bid Decision.** Determine whether the opportunity and your success influencing the customer warrant allocating resources to begin planning the proposal and your solution before receiving the final bid request.
- **Bid Validation Decision.** Determine whether your capture activities have placed you in a position to win the job, justifying the expenditure of proposal resources, after considering any requirements changes, risks, and competitive conditions.
- **Proposal Submittal Decision.** Decide, before submitting your proposal, and after taking into account all risk factors, whether your organization is satisfied with all aspects of the proposed solution and price.
- **Final Offer Decision.** Decide whether to accept offered terms and conditions or submit proposal revised at customer's request.

4 Use document-based reviews at decision gates to control and add value to the process.

Documents are the only evidence that an intellectual task has been completed. Without documents, you cannot control and manage intellectual work. The quality of a business development review document reflects the quality of the work done to research, develop the lead, and collaborate with the customer. Each decision gate should incorporate standard documentation requirements, appropriately tailored for the type and size of the opportunity.

Manage to your standards. Do not omit reviews or compromise your standards. Figure 2 suggests documents for each decision gate. These may need to be adapted to reflect the requirements of your organization. The availability and quality of these documents at the gate are indicators of your readiness to advance to the next phase. Poor documentation should raise serious doubt about continuing to spend resources.

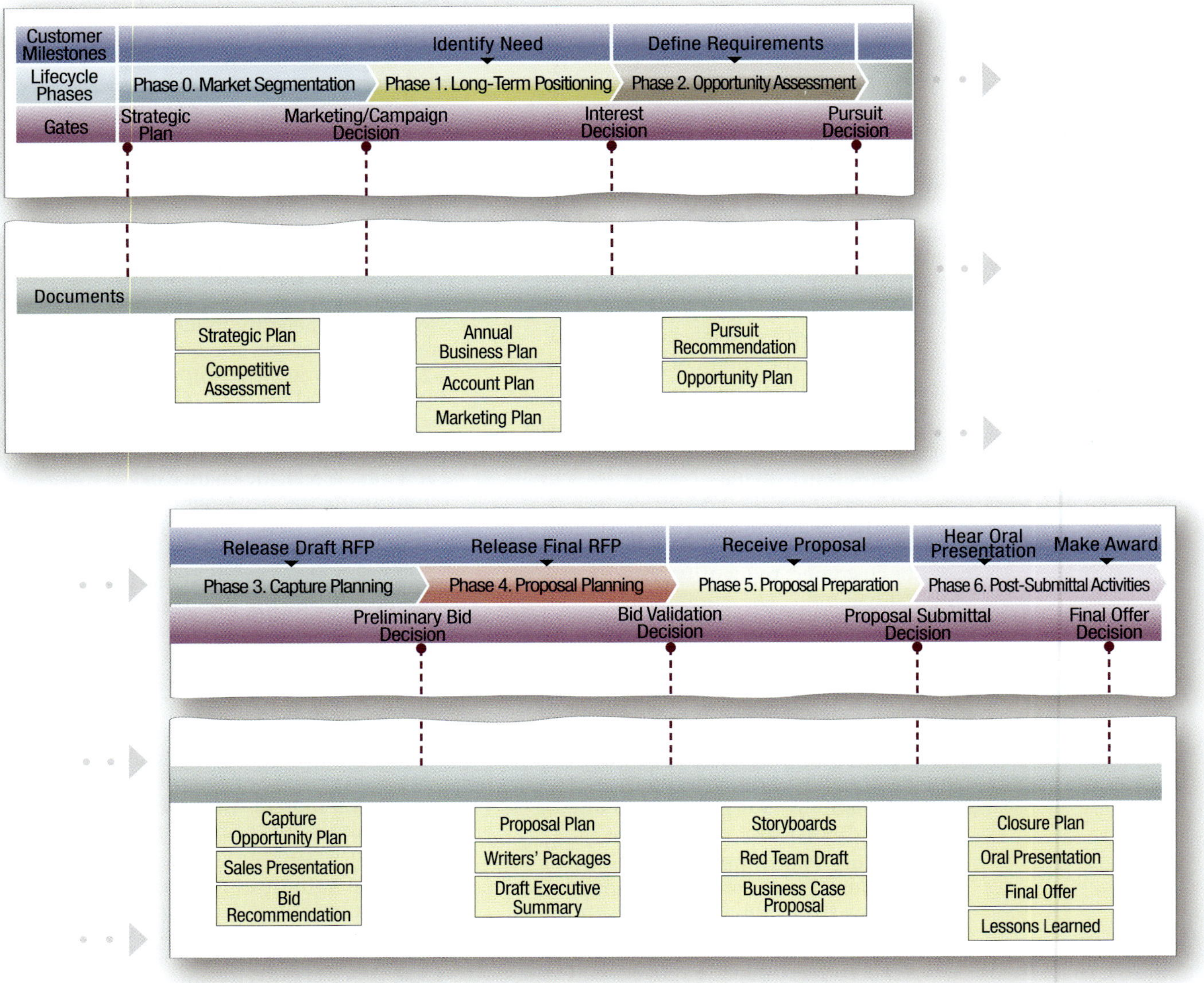

Figure 2. Sample Process Framework for New Business Capture. *This framework process is aligned with the customer's buying cycle. Management decision gates apply to major opportunities. Simpler circumstances might call for fewer gates, following guidelines of your process documentation. Representative documents are shown along the bottom of the chart. Add or subtract according to your needs.*

5 Adapt your process to individual opportunities by using flexible support tools.

No single process is right for every business organization and every opportunity. The one shown in figure 2 is widely useful but might not be right for your products, services, or market. The tasks completed during each phase may need to be adjusted based on the following considerations:

- Value of bid, both in absolute terms and in comparison to other business you have
- Knowledge of customer, especially relating to prior working relationships
- Time projected to be available during each phase of the business development cycle
- Similarity of new business to other work your organization has performed
- Knowledge of other competitors
- Expectations in the marketplace concerning sophistication of proposals and other aspects of business development process

Likewise, the information required to support the decision gates may be different. For example, in a commodity market, knowledge of competitors may not play a large role in deciding whether to bid; instead, information about price will be more significant in each phase.

In a repetitive service industry, you may have limited potential to influence the buyer's preferred solution. Instead, focus on identifying the best personnel resources for a job early in the process.

When business development staff circumvent your process, your process may no longer fit your circumstances. Processes can be changed but should not be modified without good reason.

See **Proposal Preparation Tools**, ***Proposal Guide.***

Regardless of the tasks that are right for your organization or the information needed for decision making, a consistent process will help you spend more of your business development resources pursuing better opportunities. You will typically submit fewer bids but will improve your win rate and total dollars won.

Do not let individual account managers or marketing personnel decide what should be accomplished at each phase. Decide what steps are important based on rational criteria, establish the guidelines for each decision, then follow your process.

High-level process definition provides structure, but you need flexible tools to respond to shifting market demands. Otherwise, the temptation to abandon your process—and give up its benefits—will be strong.

Tools need to support both knowledge and process management. Knowledge management includes boilerplate development, retrieval, and maintenance. It also supports collaborative solution development by giving access to previous work and products. Process management tools direct the user, save time, and improve effectiveness.

Potential tools come in many forms, from paper templates and forms to fully integrated web-based, electronic systems. To be broadly accepted, your process must do more than give direction—it must help users do their jobs effectively and efficiently. Tools that save time and improve effectiveness help users and promote acceptance and adherence to your process.

The best business development tools are adaptable to a broad range of opportunities and proposals. They help collect, organize, and analyze information so better decisions can be made. Ultimately, they help your organization prepare winning proposals.

Not all tools are created equal. Some tools speed the activity cycle, permitting a user to produce more proposals. But if the effectiveness of the proposal is unchanged, the cost of the tool may exceed the benefits. The best tools empower the user to be better organized, more customer-focused, and more responsive to the specific requirements of each business opportunity.

6 Define business development roles, responsibilities, and levels of authority, including thresholds by types of opportunities.

Roles are customary functions of a person in business development, such as capture manager, proposal manager, proposal specialist, writer, and estimator. A single person can fill multiple roles. In some organizations, a person in the account manager position might assume sales, proposal manager, proposal writer, estimator, and reviewer roles.

Responsibilities are tasks that people are accountable for, whether they complete the task themselves or assign the task to another. In business development, people in roles are assigned specific responsibilities. Traditionally, an individual in the proposal manager role is responsible for the preparation of the proposal document to a defined standard.

Levels of authority delimit the power of a person to command, direct, or decide. Levels of authority establish whether the person can make a decision and the limits of the decision. For example, the level of authority to make pursuit, bid, and bid submittal decisions usually varies with the size and risk of the opportunity.

In a similar way, authority to expend marketing funds on capture activities may be assigned based on familiarity with the customer. A departmental sales manager may receive opportunities with existing customers and markets, but a division manager may be assigned to handle new products or services with unfamiliar customers.

Business development processes are more flexible and scalable when roles, responsibilities, and levels of authority are clearly defined. Decisions are clearer, easier, and faster. Individuals know what actions are within their personal scope and when to seek involvement or approval elsewhere. Wasted efforts are reduced. Managers can keep projects on track by verifying that roles are assigned and responsibilities understood. They can steer the direction of the organization by adjusting roles and responsibilities to encourage changes in staff behavior.

7

Align your business development process with corporate policies, strategies, practices, and other processes.

Alignment is critical in all areas. A corporate policy of openness and honesty is incompatible with bait-and-switch sales tactics. A corporate strategy to be the technology leader is more compatible with a sales approach that emphasizes added value than one that stresses low price. For each opportunity, align your sales strategy, proposal strategy, boilerplate, and solution.

Align performance metrics, incentives, and proposal development processes:

- Share sales or capture team information with the proposal team.
- Streamline the proposal review process to support a short sales and proposal delivery schedule.
- Align capture, solution development, and project delivery processes to reduce transition risk.
- Balance reviewers' rewards for preventing risk with the potential cost of lost sales.

8

Document your process to make it consistent and repeatable.

Define all process elements before creating process flow diagrams and documenting the process. Definitions are linked, and changes will create a ripple effect. For example, adding a Proposal Management Plan review before RFP release for strategic bids will change the proposal manager's role and responsibilities, the process milestones and activities, and tailoring guidelines.

After process element definitions are final, document the process. Documentation can assume many forms. Because your process must guide and help users, ask yourself the following questions:

- Where and when will users refer to the documentation?
- Do users work in a central office or in remote locations?
- Will users always have laptops available when traveling?
- How will the form and format affect availability, acceptance, and repeated use?
- How easy will it be to update and keep users' copies current?

Many organizations develop small, compact process guides ranging from 3x5-inch to 5x7-inch bound formats. Increasingly, process managers document online and link the online process to user tools or job aids.

Ideally, the tool disguises much of the process. Much as you complete online order forms, well-designed tools are easy to use and require limited user training beyond concepts.

When working with teams, mix veterans and new contributors when possible. Mix just-in-time training and one-on-one coaching.

Most importantly, follow your process and use your tools. Contributors follow what you do more than what you say.

9

Train participants to give them the understanding and skills to follow the process.

Even users who understand and accept the process need the skills to execute and adapt it appropriately. The same applies to support tools. Users must be able to locate, acquire, and use tools properly.

An initial and ongoing investment in training is critical. To achieve maximum return, training must be process-specific rather than role-specific. Otherwise, people will not understand the reasons for their assigned tasks.

Business development process and tool training cannot consist of lectures and one-time demonstrations. Participants must practice the expected skills during the training and receive immediate feedback to improve their performance. Without practice, participants usually return to their pre-training approach.

10 Designate a process owner to collect metrics, foster continuous improvement, and maintain tools and infrastructure.

Processes erode quickly without an owner. Turnover, loss of learning, and even active resistance to process discipline reduce process effectiveness. Consider these all too common occurrences:

- A template with an outdated logo is used, creating an inconsistent brand image
- An electronic template incompatible with an upgraded operating system is abandoned, forcing business development staff back to inaccurate, inefficient, manual techniques
- Boilerplate graphics and text describing obsolete products and services prompt a customer to select another source
- Inadequate reviews lead to unacceptable risk or low profit margins
- Contract disputes arise because the bidder is not fully aware of the content of a proposal

Assigning an owner to implement, monitor, and improve the process keeps the benefits alive.

Metrics are a basis for continuous improvement—we manage what we measure. Using good metrics, you can monitor sales support costs, cycle times, and proposal quality. All are usually related to higher win rates.

Metrics help process owners understand which elements of their processes work well and which need to be changed. Accurate and credible metrics are the only valid way to justify requests for additional resources, to resist reductions in current resources, or to measure the value of enabling technologies and tools.

Consider the following questions when determining what metrics to collect:

- **How will you use this metric?** If you cannot anticipate its use, do not track it. For example, tracking turnaround time from different outside printing vendors could help you decide which printer has earned more of your business. The same statistic from an internal department that is giving good service is less useful.
- **Can the metric be collected with minimum impact to staff and clients?** Try to capture metrics as by-products of your normal process. For example, collect labor hours from time sheets. Determine page counts from printing records.
- **Does the potential value of the data exceed the cost of collection?** A relatively expensive program to obtain customers' feedback on wins and losses is often justified. Conversely, one process owner decided not to compute a cost per page even though it could be calculated from available data. Central expenses were minimal, proposal teams worked virtually from home offices, so travel costs were eliminated, and internal printing costs were annually allocated to business units on a revenue basis. Neither the process owner nor the responsible mangers could think of a use for the cost-per-page metric.
- **Does the metric broaden your potential understanding of a process that you own or can influence?** Keeping metrics on organizations or individuals outside your control and influence may only lead to conflict. If you have no control over your field sales force, why track data on account executives? Leave that to sales management.

Avoid tracking metrics that overlap unless you are trying to determine which metric is most representative. For example, overlapping metrics might be kept on desktop publishing (DTP). You could track pages per day of combined graphics and text, or separate measures of pages per day of text and graphics per day. The appropriate measure might depend on whether your DTP professional also does the graphics and whether the ratio of graphics per page is expected to change. Figure 3 lists potential business development process metrics.

COMMONLY COLLECTED BUSINESS DEVELOPMENT METRICS
Proposal Quality
Duration (start to finish)
Staff hours expended
Hours by resource
Win/Loss
Dollars Won/Lost
Number of copies
Page count
Number of graphics
Percent new vs. existing graphics
Number and value of opportunities added to pipeline
Number and value of opportunities pursued
Number and value of opportunities retired by customer
Capture budget vs. actual by opportunity and phase
Percent of budget spent pre-RFP

Figure 3. Potential Business Development Process and Proposal Metrics. *Business development and proposal process owners track many of the listed metrics, but never track all of them. Balance the number of metrics collected and the collection cost against the potential value of the metric.*

Sales Letters include any document sent to a customer that is designed to advance a potential sale. Effective sales letters are customer-focused, clear, concise, and well-organized.

See **Customer Focus** *and* **Organization**, ***Proposal Guide.***

See **Executive Summaries** *and* **Letter Proposals**, ***Proposal Guide.***

The purpose of each sales letter is to advance the sale to the next realistically achievable objective, clearly supported by the benefits to the customer. Writers of sales letters must be able to answer two questions:

1. What is my purpose in writing this letter?
2. What would I like the reader to agree to do next?

When sales letters fail, the writer often failed to answer the previous two questions. Clear and correct writing is an effective way to help customers understand you and accept your ideas. Poor writing causes confusion, potential distrust, and possible rejection of your ideas.

The process described for strategizing, organizing, drafting, and revising effective sales letters is similar to the approach recommended to prepare executive summaries and letter proposals. Both are specialized forms of sales letters.

Many types of sales letters are written during a typical sales cycle, as shown in figure 1. Note how the objective of each letter changes as the sale advances.

The most effective capture managers are sales professionals, like it or not. Hence, capture managers write, review, and approve sales letters to their customers.

Sales Letters

1. Follow the disciplined POWeR™ writing process to quickly and consistently write effective sales letters.
2. Use the Strategy Template to strategize your sales letters.
3. Follow the Four-Box organizational structure.
4. Draft quickly and uncritically, following your Four-Box Template.
5. Revise to add value, clarity, and brevity.

Five model sales letters are included in **Model Documents.**

This visual representation of the sales cycle follows the same business development process defined in **Process**, rules 2 and 3.

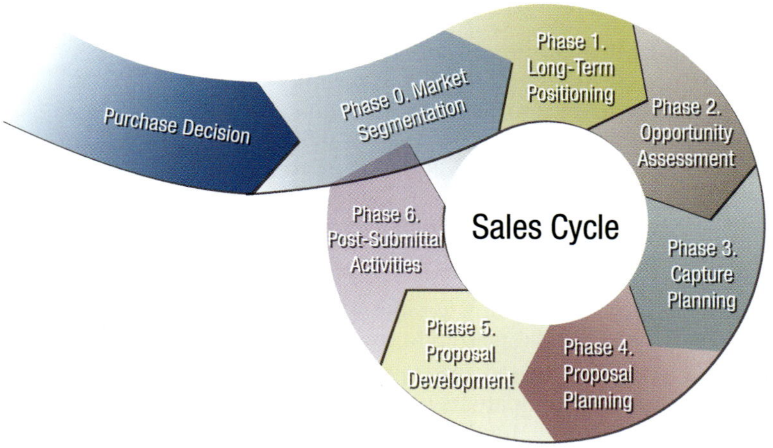

Figure 1. Effective Sales Letters Have Clear Objectives. *Sales professionals prepare a wide variety of letters. For each type of sales letter, a typical sales objective is suggested, specifically, what the seller would like the customer to agree to do next. Note how the objective of each sales letter changes as the sale advances.*

1 Follow the disciplined POWeR™ writing process to quickly and consistently write effective sales letters.

The best sales professionals plan to advance the sale with every client contact, including their sales letters. Sometimes writing a sales letter is easy; everything flows. Other times writers struggle and dislike the result. Resorting to tailoring previous sales letters is often expedient but ineffective because no two customers have identical needs.

The only way to quickly and consistently prepare effective sales letters is to follow a disciplined process, one that you both understand and have practiced. Following a consistent process helps you focus on your key messages within a consistent framework.

Avoid or at least minimize writer's block by following this five-step **POWeR**™ writing process:

POWeR

P *lanning*
O *rganizing*
W *riting*
e *xamining*
R *evising*

The acronym **POWeR** has four uppercase letters and a lower case *e*. The uppercase letters represent stages or steps that the writer controls. The lowercase *e* represents the examining stage where other people are asked to suggest improvements before the message is revised.

Follow these sequential steps when you prepare any kind of sales letter. Substeps in each phase are summarized in figure 2.

Planning
• Determine your objective (to do, know, and/or feel) • Analyze the prospective audience • Analyze message content • Select the optimal medium • Develop content
Organizing
• As instructed by the customer • Summarize, then support • Use Four-Box organizational approach • Determine what will be emphasized
Writing
• Draft • Use emphasis techniques
examining
• Cool the draft • Seek outside review (peers, managers, customer)
Revising
• Make your message clear • Make your message concise • Make your message correct

Figure 2. Improve Communication Effectiveness and Efficiency by Using the POWeR™ Writing Process. *This five-step process is the most effective and efficient way to develop written and oral messages. This approach is implicit within the business development processes and tools discussed in this Capture Guide.*

2

Use the Strategy Template to strategize your sales letters.

Purpose is best defined as *what the writer wants the reader to do and to know.*

Prepare your strategy by completing the Strategy Template shown in figure 3. Use the Strategy Template every time until you are thoroughly comfortable with this process.

Many sales documents fail because they are vague and unclear, accurately reflecting the fuzzy thinking and minimal planning of the author. Ask two questions to test the strategy of any sales document:

- What was the writer's purpose?
- What does the writer want the reader to agree to do next? *(action)*

The first question is broad. The second is focused. The purpose of most sales documents is to obtain action or to inform. Action is required to advance the sale, the preferred purpose. To inform is a relatively weak purpose.

An effective sales letter motivates the customer to the desired action because of the persuasive information in the letter.

What does the customer need to know that would persuade the customer to take that action? A customer-focused strategy is based on the assumption that people act in their own best interest. If you are looking for a Win-Win situation, then your customer's objectives and your objectives must align.

In complex sales, sales documents often have multiple readers, including the decision maker and others who influence the decision maker. List the various customers or readers, then list their issues. Whenever possible, develop issues collaboratively with customers.

The *Strategy Template* is most useful when developing a new document. Experienced and skilled writers can skip this template under two conditions:

1. You are revising an existing document.
2. You are confident your strategy is correct.

As your skills improve, go directly to the Four-Box Organizer found in Guideline 5.

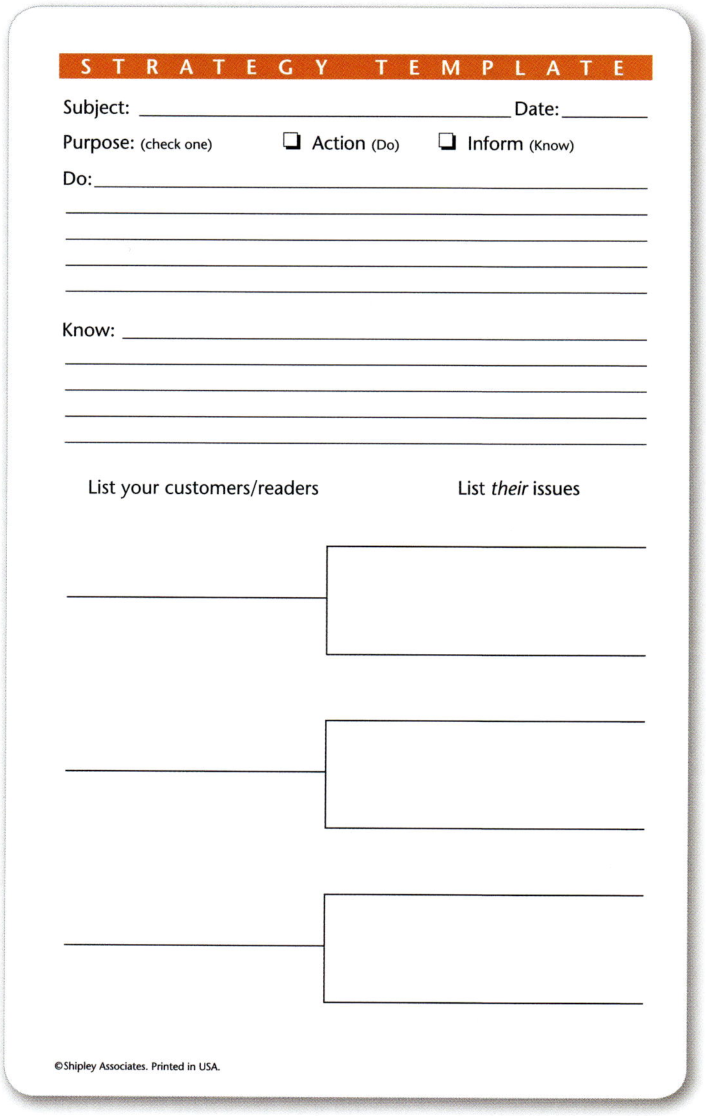
STRATEGY TEMPLATE

Subject: ____________________ Date: ________

Purpose: (check one) ❑ Action (Do) ❑ Inform (Know)

Do: ____________________

Know: ____________________

List your customers/readers | List *their* issues

©Shipley Associates. Printed in USA.

Figure 3. Use the Strategy Template to Develop Your Strategy. *Using the Strategy Template will help you develop a more persuasive strategy. Avoid two errors: (1) Dismissing the Strategy Template as too obvious, and (2) Filling it with empty jargon.*

3

Follow the Four-Box organizational structure.

Use the Four-Box Template shown in figure 4 to present your argument in a customer-focused, persuasive style. Use the annotations in the margin and within the template as a guide. Your ideas will evolve as you move from the Strategy Template to the Four-Box Template. Expect imperfection.

Draft an informative subject line. Summarize your most significant *Do/Know* statements. Try to include benefits and features. Make it as short as you can while still being fully informative. The ideal subject line length is about 6 to 12 words. Shorter is less likely to be informative; longer is more likely to reduce impact and readership.

See Choosing Correct Words, Customer Focus, *and* Lists, *Proposal Guide.*

Begin with a signal word to immediately announce the action desired and to signal the content to the reader. Typical signal words vary with your purpose:

ACTION PURPOSE	INFORMATION PURPOSE
DO: Proposal Recommendation Request Invitation	KNOW: Agenda Notice Announcement Response

Good example

Invitation to meet with Silicon Glen's Exec to discuss how outsourcing can reduce office support costs.

Signal Word — Summary of most significant *Do/Know* statements — **Benefits** *(Optional)*

In Box 1, use setups if needed to connect to a previous event. Most readers are initially trying to place your sales letter in context. Keep your setups short. Often a short phrase will suffice:

Good examples

As you requested in our January 15 meeting, . . .

In our September 15 phone conversation, you said coping with rapid change and reducing cost were driving your fiscal year planning by . . .

Then summarize the customer's overall need in a customer-focused manner. Customer ownership of the need must be explicit.

In Box 2, establish the customer's issues, tying them to the overall need and making ownership explicit. For emphasis, introduce issues in a display list. List them as the customer did or in decreasing order of importance to the customer.

In Box 3, link all of your information to one of the customer's issues. If you cannot forge the link, your information is irrelevant. Eliminate irrelevant or extraneous information. Address each client issue in the order introduced in Box 2.

In Box 4, restate your main ideas linked to the benefits to the customer. Indicate the action required, and directly state the next step. Be proactive. Avoid ending with stale jargon or clichés.

Figure 4. The Four-Box Template. *Use this template to convert your strategy from the Strategy Template into a customer-focused, clearly organized, and persuasive sales document. Follow the suggestions in the template. Use this template to organize every sales letter.*

4 Draft quickly and uncritically, following your Four-Box Template.

Most sales professionals find that after completing the *Strategy Template* and *Four-Box Template,* their letters practically write themselves.

Draft quickly, expecting imperfection. Writing is creative; revising is critical. If you try to do both at the same time, you will do neither well, and you will take much longer.

Frequently refer to the *Strategy Template* and *Four-Box Template* to stay focused.

5 Revise to add value, clarity, and brevity.

Revise in three stages to save time. Fix the major items before the minor items. View revision as an opportunity to improve your sales letter. This is a realistic goal if you have followed the first three steps. If not, you often feel the urge to start over.

Follow the three-step revision process outlined in figure 5.

Few of us can see our own mistakes. Always ask someone else to review your sales letters.

The *Peer Review Template,* shown in figure 6, is a tool designed to help peers and managers constructively review sales letters.

FIRST STAGE: BE CLEAR

Subject Line
- Begin with a *signal* word.
- State what the reader should *Do* or *Know*.
- Include *Benefit* (optional).

Objective
- State up front.
- Be specific and clear.

Setups
- Use if necessary.
- Keep short.

Customer Focus
- Name customer before yourself.
- State benefits before features.
- Make hot button ownership explicit.
- Tie hot buttons to your solution.

Content and Organization
- Summarize; then preview your content.
- Organize around customer's hot buttons.

Key Information Highlighted
- Use informative headings and subheadings.
- Use lists.
- Use white space for emphasis.
- Use **boldface**, underlining, *italics*, CAPITALS, color.
- Use clear graphics with action captions.

SECOND STAGE: BE CONCISE

Paragraphs
- Use six lines maximum.
- Use one major idea per paragraph.

Sentences (15-20 word maximum)
- Use active voice, *Who does what?*
- Use strong verbs.
- Cut false subjects: *it, there.*

Words
- Cut gobbledygook.
- Cut wordy phrases.
- Solve word problems.
- Cut the fat.

THIRD STAGE: BE CORRECT

Proofread Thoroughly
- Check grammar, punctuation, spelling, word choice, and number usage.

Know Where to Find the Rules
- Franklin Covey *Style Guide.*
- Current dictionary.
- Specialized references.

Figure 5. Revise in Three Stages. *In the first stage, address content. Make sure you present the right message about the customer's issues and offer real value. In the second stage, make your message as concise as possible. In the third stage, correct spelling, punctuation, and grammar. Careless errors suggest potential poor quality elsewhere.*

PEER REVIEW TEMPLATE

What was the writer's purpose?

What did the writer want the reader to agree to do/know next?

Would the requested action be the next realistically achievable step most likely to advance this sale? ❑ Yes ❑ No

If not, what do you recommend?

List the customer's/reader's hot buttons:
-
-
-
-

©Shipley Associates. Printed in USA.

Figure 6. Peer Review Template. *Managers and peers can improve their coaching of writers by: (1) Comparing the results of the Peer Review Template with the information found in the Strategy Template and the Four-Box Template and (2) Evaluating sales documents using only the Peer Review Template. If this template is difficult to complete, the document is unlikely to be successful.*

Strategy is a plan or method for achieving a goal. Strategy and tactics are often confused. In the purest sense, strategy is your pre-engagement position; tactics are the actions you take to implement your strategy, to convey it persuasively. Both are required to win.

The guidelines for strategy include preconditioning, targeting, analyzing, and then determining and packaging your solution.

Organizations that are most effective at winning business have aligned their strategies and processes throughout, including their approach to business development. Their business, market, capture, sales, and proposal strategies and tactics are aligned, coordinated, and consistent.

Misaligned strategies result in inconsistent, confusing, and off-putting customer messages. This dissonance prompts customers to doubt your message.

If the following example describes your organization, you can improve your business capture effectiveness:

> Account executives position their solution based on successful previous solutions. Individuals write proposals with little direction from sales, using extensive boilerplate due to limited response time and numerous requests to bid. When asked to make a finals presentation, senior executives deliver standard presentations.

In this example, messages to the customer are seller focused, and the content changes from message to message. As a result, customers doubt both your understanding of their needs and your commitment to satisfying their needs.

See **Process**.

Strategy

1. Distinguish strategy at different phases of the business development process.
2. Analyze your current position using standard, universally understood, integrated, and accepted tools.
3. Define and agree to use common terms and definitions.
4. Define a specific capture objective after your pursuit decision to better focus on that unique opportunity.
5. Identify economic buyers, users, and technical buyers; then list their issues.
6. Use a power rating to meld individual buyers' issues into a set of organizational issues.
7. Use an Integrated Solution Worksheet to arrive at a competitive solution that is aligned with the customer's issues and requirements.
8. Prepare a Bidder Comparison Chart (BCC).
9. Draft specific strategy statements that define both what you will do and how you will implement that strategy.
10. Select the best solution and approach, and develop a specific value proposition for each customer.
11. Create a price-to-win strategy to drive your solution.
12. Use trade-offs to validate your approach and ghost the competition.
13. Implement your action plan.

1 Distinguish strategy at different phases of the business development process.

Strategy might be the most misused word in business. "Strategy" might refer to a position, an action, the entire solution, an aspect of the solution, or a favorite catch phrase or slogan.

To craft and present an aligned message, all members of the selling team must agree to use a common process and common definitions:

- **Business strategy** is an organization's plan to achieve overall business objectives.
- **Market strategy** is an organization's plan to achieve specific market objectives, typically involving multiple sales.
- **Capture strategy** is the plan to win a specific, defined opportunity.
- **Sales strategy** should be identical to a capture strategy; i.e., opportunity specific, but sales strategy has been used so generically that the term was not used in the *Capture Guide* or *Proposal Guide*.
- **Proposal strategy** is a plan to write a persuasive, winning proposal. The proposal strategy is a subset of the capture strategy. The message is the same; only the tactical aspects of implementation differ.

Win strategy is often used to describe the over-arching actions required to win an opportunity. In reality, *capture strategy* and *win strategy* are identical, but some practitioners have opted to limit *capture strategy* to the specific positioning actions of the capture team.

In capture planning, you plan and take actions to convey information that persuades each customer to prefer, or at minimum, favorably regard your organization and solution. You might convey that information in white papers, presentations, meetings, site visits, demonstrations, and media buys or events. In a proposal, you should be conveying identical, aligned information in words, text, and graphics.

2 Analyze your current position using standard, universally understood, integrated, and accepted tools.

Strategy drives tactics. You always have a position in any sales situation, whether you understand it or not. Developing an effective strategy requires: (1) Determining your current position, and then (2) Improving it versus competitors' positions.

Using standard tools and templates to develop your strategy improves the quality of the strategy, saves time, and improves the quality of implementation. When strategy development is improvised, implementation is haphazard, uncoordinated, and inconsistent. Standard templates not only reduce development time, but the embedded discipline improves the quality of information developed and enhances understanding among capture team members.

Organizations that use common tools to develop strategy spend less time clarifying terms and process and have more time to focus on substance and implementation.

Integrate the tools used by sales, sales support, management, engineering, and product management. Integrated tools save time by reducing the time spent copying or reinventing information at subsequent process phases.

No single tool or suite of tools is ideal. Select tools that are useful and acceptable to most participants. If you are following a particular sales discipline, extend and augment accepted, useful, proven, and familiar elements.

Replacing your current tool suite with a new one invokes resistance because your action suggests that the prior suite was defective, and you are compelling users to relearn an entirely new system. Enhance, amend, and augment your standard tool set whenever possible.

3

Define and agree to use common terms and definitions.

To improve focus, we often consolidate numerous issues and motivators into three to five hot button issues. Lists of 20 or more items are rapidly forgotten.

Customers own issues; sellers own gaps. Concerns that the seller has about a solution or approach are called gaps, the difference between what the customer wants and what the seller can offer. The customer, not the seller, owns issues.

Effective communication requires common terms and definitions. Three of the most universally used and misunderstood terms relating to strategy are issues, motivators, and hot buttons or hot button issues. The relationship of these three terms is illustrated in figure 1. Issues are customer concerns and worry items that keep them awake at night.

Motivators are the objectives that the customer is trying to achieve:

- Improve profits.
- Increase sales.
- Reduce costs.
- Improve safety.
- Reduce risk.
- Improve quality.

Hot button issues are a consolidated set of issues and motivators, preferably three to five items. State hot button issues using the customer's words. Then align your solution or approach to the customer's hot buttons. For example, if a customer is concerned about improving service delivery quality, what aspects of your solution will help them address service delivery quality?

All motivators are issues, but not all issues are motivators. For example, training could be an example of a hot button that is an issue but not a motivator. Few customers are motivated to buy because they get to attend training. However, if users were poorly trained on a previous similar purchase, and problems ensued, then training could be a customer's hot button issue.

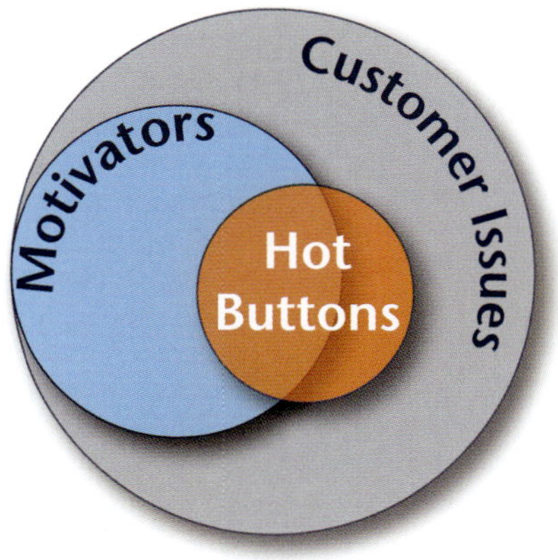

Figure 1. The Relationship Among Issues, Motivators, and Hot Buttons. *Hot buttons are mostly motivators but could also include a small number of issues that are not motivators.*

4

Define a specific capture objective after your pursuit decision to better focus on that unique opportunity.

Shortly after your pursuit decision, draft a brief, precise capture objective that meets the following criteria:

- **Specific**. States the products and services that the customer might purchase from your organization, the purchase entity/ location, and the person who will make the purchase decision, if known.
- **Measureable**. States the budget for the purchase.
- **Timed**. States the timing of the purchase.
- **Result**. States, quantitatively if possible, the benefits and process change the customer anticipates.

Poor Capture Objective

Capture $5 million worth of product and service revenue from Bank-4-U during fiscal year 20XX.

Better Capture Objective

Win 3-year contract extension to supply and support all copy and fax equipment at Bank-4-U's Reno headquarters. The $3.5 million contract renewal will be awarded on or before June 15, 20XX. Bank-4-U's total cost will remain flat, equaling the current annual cost for identical services.

You often pursue multiple purchases from the same organization. But if you find yourself trying to describe multiple buyers or purchase times, you are likely facing multiple opportunities that are better addressed individually. While you might employ common strategies and tactics, each opportunity is unique and is better addressed individually before you merge tactics.

5 Identify economic buyers, users, and technical buyers; then list their issues.

Roles may overlap. For example, the president of a small technical company might be both the economic and technical buyer.

Some sales professionals say that there is only one buyer, the individual empowered to make the final purchase decision. All other types of buyers, such as users or technical buyers, are called influencers.

Economic buyers are the individuals who give final approval to purchase. They sign the check and retain veto power. Economic buyers tend to be concerned about the trade-off between price and performance. They focus on bottom line impact. While many people may offer input and recommendations, only economic buyers can give final approval.

Users are the people who judge the potential impact on their job performance. Their personal success is impacted by the sale, so their concerns are often emotional and subjective. Users' issues are reliability, support, ease of operation, maintenance, safety, potential impact on morale, and potential impact on their personal success. Because they use or supervise the use of your product or service, they can ruin a sale.

Technical buyers are gatekeepers. They cannot give final approval, but they can give a final "No." Technical buyers often determine the short list. They tend to focus on the features of a product or service as measured against objective specifications established to screen offers.

Technical buyers may not be technical in the scientific sense. Purchasing agents, lawyers, contracts people, and licensing or regulatory authorities are technical buyers. Because technical buyers are primarily focused on how well you meet their screening tests, the better you understand their criteria, the better your chances of getting their recommendations.

Another way to examine buyers is according to their source of power. Power could be economic, control (typically users), or technical. Or power could be by level of management, such as executive management, middle management, and operations.

After identifying all the different types of buyers, list the issues of each individual buyer. The most important issues of the entire organization are usually associated with a majority of the buyers.

6 Use a power rating to meld individual buyers' issues into a set of organizational issues.

Capture plan templates vary. Rather than incorporating the Integrated Solution Worksheet (ISW) as a single, large table, some practitioners opt to divide it into a series of tables. If so, make sure that the tables are linked, and common data is transferred to subsequent tables.

See Capture Planning *and* Executive Summary.

Additional uses for the Integrated Solution Worksheet and Bidder Comparison Chart are discussed in Capture Planning, Executive Summary, and Teaming.

One-on-one selling affords the opportunity to address individuals' issues. However, this is not possible when you are preparing a proposal that will be evaluated by multiple buyers. Combine individuals' issues into a set of organizational issues that can be addressed in a single proposal or presentation.

Use the power rating to determine the relative importance of the group's issues. The power rating is the product of the power of the individual buyer, the decision maker, and influencers, times the relative importance of that issue to each individual.

Use the template shown in figure 2 to produce a combined, weighted list of issues from the individual buyers' issues.

Positioning the Opportunity

1. Identify Decision Makers, Influencers, and Their Issues

Complete the following:

Date: ____________ Account Executive: ____________

Prospect Organization: ____________ Division: ____________

Opportunity: (Briefly describe the opportunity and need)

Role	Name	Position	Power (1–5)	Issue	Importance (1–5)	Power Rating (Power x Importance)
Decision Maker						
Influencer						
Influencer						
Influencer						
Influencer						

©1992, 2003 Shipley Associates. Printed in USA. 1

NAME	POSITION	POWER	ISSUE	IMPORT-ANCE	POWER RATING
Ms. Bankhead		10	Look and feel	10	100
			Reliability	6	60
			Price	3	30
Mr. Douglas		2	Price	5	10

ISSUE	TOTAL POWER RATING	CUSTOMER'S WEIGHT
Look and feel	100	50
Reliability	60	30
Price	40	20
		100%

Figure 2. Power Rating Calculation Shows Organizational Issues. *Allocate a rating from 1-10 for the 'Power' that each individual buyer has in the buying decision (1 = least influence; 10 = most influence). Then list the issues that concern each buyer and allocate an 'Importance' rating from 1-10 for each of these issues—the rating reflecting how important each issue is to that particular buyer. Then multiply the 'Power' by the 'Importance' to give a 'Power Rating' for each issue, then group the issues together across multiple buyers and total their Power Ratings. Finally, choose the top 6-8 organizational issues and scale their scores so that they total 100.*

7 Use an Integrated Solution Worksheet to arrive at a competitive solution that is aligned with the customer's issues and requirements.

The Integrated Solution Worksheet (ISW) is a powerful analysis tool throughout the capture process. The ISW is first developed as part of the capture plan. The ISW is shown in figure 3.

Use the ISW to collaborate with the customer early in the process to define the issues and influence requirements. The first seller to do this is established as the preferred provider.

If the customer already has a solution in mind, the ISW helps define the underlying issues driving the customer's requirements. Analyze your competitive position, then work to favorably influence the requirements. Aim to become the customer's preferred provider.

Next, extend your analysis to outline your solution, identify gaps, outline competitors' likely solutions, and identify discriminators. Then define the strategies and actions required to better position your solution with the customer, as discussed in Guideline 9.

ShipleyAssociates **Integrated Solution Worksheet**

Item No.	Customer Issues	Customer Requirements	Available Solution	Gap	Competitor Solution	Discriminators	Strategy	Action Required
1	System must be available.	8 hr. response time.	2 hr. response time	1 hr.	3 hr. response time	Faster response but more expensive?	Emphasize no additional cost with cellular.	Show current response time. Show photo-service with cell phone.

Figure 3. Integrated Solution Worksheet. *Begin by filling the issues column when you are early in the process. If the customer has identified Requirements, fill the requirements column. Then complete each row, linking each item in the row.*

8

Note: Figures 3 and 4 show alternative approaches to a Bidder Comparison Chart. The figure 3 approach is best suited to smaller, short-response opportunities where the primary focus is on three to five hot button issues. The figure 4 approach is best suited to larger, more complex opportunities where you might identify numerous hot button issues.

Prepare a Bidder Comparison Chart (BCC).

While the ISW is focused on stated requirements, solution development, and your competitive position against customer requirements, the BCC is focused on issues, both stated and unstated, and developing strategies and tactics to improve your competitive position.

Use the BCC, shown in figure 4, to analyze how the customer's current perception of your solution and organization compares to various competitors'. Use it repeatedly throughout the capture process to measure the effectiveness of your positioning.

The BCC, like the ISW, is potentially an excellent collaborative tool for the seller and the customer.

ISSUES	WEIGHT	US (SCORE)	COMPANY A	COMPANY B
Specific Experience	30	25	20	15
Low Price	20	5	10	15
Familiarity with Manager Named	20	15	10	10
Ability to Meet Schedule	30	25	21	15
TOTAL SCORE	100	70	61	55

Figure 4. Bidder Comparison Chart. *First list the customer's issues, then the relative weight of each issue as perceived by the customer. Establish the relative weight of each issue in one of three ways: (1) Use the customer's evaluation criteria, (2) Assign a weight, forcing the total score to equal 100, (3) Assign an arbitrary weight (such as 1-5). Then assign a score (perhaps 1-10). The overall relative weight is the product of the arbitrary weight and the assigned score. Complete each row horizontally, indicating your estimate of the customer's perception of each competitor's ability to satisfy that issue. Compare the products of the weight times the score. The absolute value of the numbers assigned is not important. Only the comparative value matters.*

Place the BCC in context. Data flows from both your account plan and initial capture analysis. As shown in figure 5, input data based upon customer issues and requirements, relevant strengths and weaknesses of your organization and solution, and relevant strengths and weaknesses of your competitors' solutions and organizations. The output analysis drives your strategies, customer messages, and theme statements.

For definitions, discussions, and examples of features, advantages, benefits, discriminators, and theme statements, please go to those sections in the *Proposal Guide*.

Figure 5. Customer Issues and Requirements Drive Strategy. *Draft at least one strategy statement (per Guideline 9) for every issue listed in the Bidder Comparison Chart. Note that this variant of the Chart is geared to larger, more complex opportunities.*

9

Draft specific strategy statements that define both what you will do and how you will implement that strategy.

Strategy statements are key capture plan elements. Collaboratively develop, review, and share capture strategy statements across the capture team. Extend and embellish each capture strategy statement as you prepare the series of action plans for the capture plan. Note that a single strategy statement might be supported and implemented in multiple action plans.

See **Theme Statements,** ***Proposal Guide.***

Strategy can be implemented in four fundamental ways:.

1. Emphasize your strengths.
2. Mitigate your weaknesses.
3. Highlight your competitors' weaknesses.
4. Downplay your competitors' strengths.

Effective strategy statements incorporate both strategic and tactical aspects. The strategic aspect establishes your position. The tactical aspect defines how you will implement the strategy and action steps. Use the template in figure 5 to develop effective strategy statements. Think of the tactical aspect as, "how you will do it."

Strategy statements and theme statements are often confused. Strategy statements focus on what you plan to do to influence the customer. Strategy statements are internal, never seen by customers. Theme statements are words that you plan to say, orally or in writing, to influence the customer.

Strategy statements apply at the capture, proposal, and proposal section levels. Capture strategy statements are global and apply to all aspects of the sales cycle.

As the owner of the capture strategy, the capture manager must ensure that the proposal strategy is aligned with the capture strategy. If not, you confuse the customer.

Asking your proposal manager or proposal developers to develop a proposal strategy in the absence of a guiding capture strategy is foolish, inefficient, and reduces your win probability. Review your capture strategy with the proposal manager, and then ask the proposal manager to draft proposal strategy statements. After reviewing, improving, and approving the set of proposal strategy statements, ask the proposal manager to draft a series of supportive theme statements. One best practice is to develop a theme tree as a series of cascading theme statements that open major proposal sections.

See **Storyboards and Mockups,** ***Proposal Guide.***

The capture manager should prepare a series of capture strategy statements similar to the following example, which is an extension of the fourth item in figure 3, the *ability to meet schedule.*

CAPTURE STRATEGY EXAMPLE	
What:	• We will emphasize our ability to complete the design-build of a distribution center on time.
By:	• Taking the customer on a plant tour of the XYZ distribution center in Orlando, FL. • Citing three other distribution centers completed on schedule during the past 5 years. • Providing contact names, phone numbers, and quotes verifying our on-time completion of three similar projects.

Given each capture strategy statement, the proposal manager then prepares supportive, aligned proposal strategy statements. The capture manager should review and approve proposal strategy statements, which are distributed to proposal writers/developers at the proposal kickoff meeting.

ALIGNED PROPOSAL STRATEGY EXAMPLE	
What:	• We will emphasize our ability to complete the design-build of a distribution center on time.
By:	• Including in our proposal, photos of the XYZ distribution center in Orlando, FL. • Citing three other distribution centers (in a table) in our proposal, all listing the center, place, owner, promised completion date, and actual completion date. • Listing in our proposal, the contact names, phone numbers, and quotes verifying our on-time completion of three similar projects.

Section strategy statements (typically included in proposal storyboards) are more limited in scope but similar to proposal strategy statements in form, content, and implementation.

Strategy statements are planning statements. Proposal strategy statements cite what a writer will do when preparing a proposal section. These statements are not actual text or graphics that will appear in the proposal. Customers never see strategy statements. Customers only see or hear theme statements, one possible result of the strategy statement.

A well-written proposal strategy statement enables the reader to visualize how the strategy will appear on the page. For example:

- *Describe* or *Discuss* implies text.
- *Show* implies a graphic.
- *Include* implies a sketch, drawing, photo, table, flow chart, or graph.
- *Cite* or *Quote* implies text set off or emphasized by different formatting or white space.

If you cannot visualize the page, ask the proposal manager or writer to refine the proposal strategy statement. Often proposal strategy statements and potential theme statements are prepared and distributed to section writers, but then the writers do not use these statements.

Increase theme statement use in the proposal by taking these actions:

- Assign each theme statement to one or more proposal sections.
- Challenge writers to use the theme statement as drafted or to improve it, usually by making it more specific.
- Confirm that the theme statement was used, improved, or not used because it was not accurate.

Strengths and weakness of you and competitors are based on customer perceptions, not your perceptions.

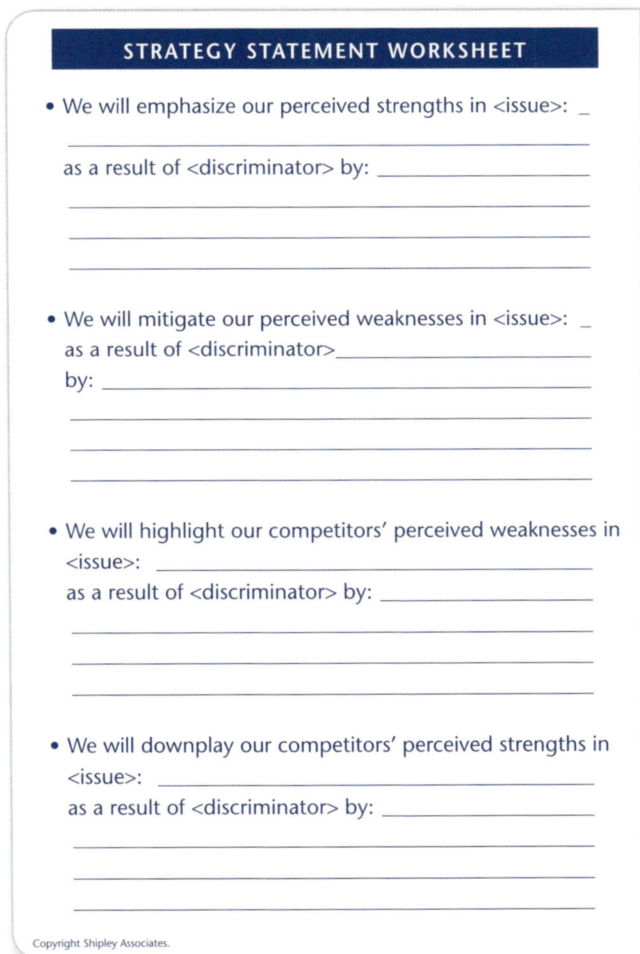
STRATEGY STATEMENT WORKSHEET

- We will emphasize our perceived strengths in <issue>: __________
  as a result of <discriminator> by: __________
- We will mitigate our perceived weaknesses in <issue>: __________
  as a result of <discriminator>__________
  by: __________
- We will highlight our competitors' perceived weaknesses in <issue>: __________
  as a result of <discriminator> by: __________
- We will downplay our competitors' perceived strengths in <issue>: __________
  as a result of <discriminator> by: __________

Copyright Shipley Associates.

Figure 6. Strategy Statement Template. *Using either the Integrated Solution Worksheet (figure 2) or the Bidder Comparison Chart (figure 3), identify your relative position versus each of your competitors. Then draft at least one strategy statement for each issue or requirement. Treat the "How" portion as possibilities, implementing those that you can support with facts or resources. Distribute capture strategy statements to the capture team, and distribute proposal strategy statements to the proposal team at kickoff.*

10 Select the best solution and approach, and develop a specific value proposition for each customer.

See **Value Propositions.**

Total added value is the sum of the benefits minus the purchase and implementation cost.

After targeting an opportunity and analyzing your position, freezing your solution may seem obvious. Even so, too many sellers either delay selecting a solution, continue to modify their solution, or carry too many solutions, alternates, or options through the sales cycle. The result hurts in several ways:

- Members of the selling team present generic, vague, and unconvincing solutions to the customer in both presentations and proposals.
- Product and service specialists are compelled to prepare multiple solutions, so the quality of each solution and presentation declines.
- Customers are confused by the options, made uncomfortable with the seller's vacillation, and are generally not persuaded to select your solution.

Value propositions are a fundamental aspect of how your solution is packaged and presented to the customer. The relatively judgmental and softer concept of best value is cited as an evaluation factor in many government and commercial bid requirements. Rather than being forced to adhere to specific and potentially incomplete quantitative criteria, best value reserves room for judgment.

Value propositions are a disciplined and quantitative way to present your solution and are used by some organizations in B2B selling environments. Sales professionals' presentations and proposals typically link solution features to customer benefits. Fundamentally, a value proposition is the summation of the benefits of your solution less the purchase and implementation costs:

> Value proposition = Benefits of seller's solution – (Purchase + Implementation Cost)

Having determined your solution, prepare value propositions for each type of buyer: economic buyer, users, and technical buyers. Value propositions flow directly from the sales objective, but the better ones are detailed, specific, and quantified.

Value propositions establish the value basis for the business relationship. They describe how your solution will improve the customer's business and how the improvement will be measured. Tailor value proposition(s) to each type of buying influence.

Comprehensive value propositions include the following elements:

- Quantified business improvement
- Timing
- Solution
- Investment Cost
- Payback
- Results measurement and tracking

Develop value propositions collaboratively with the customer. Collaboration increases the probability that the customer's organization will accept your quantitative analysis.

Ideally, authorized representatives of the customer and seller organizations sign the written value proposition and mutually agree to proceed without competitive proposals. Customer signatures are unlikely unless they help develop the value proposition.

This sample value proposition targets the economic buyer:

> Global Corporation will realize a $3,500,000 reduction in information technology support costs over the next 5 years, commencing May 1, 20XX, by contracting with Computer Heroes, at a cost of $2,000,000 per year. Global Corporation will be paid $500,000 for all of Global's IT assets, and Computer Heroes will provide all IT support. Global Corporation will enjoy a 30 percent annual reduction in IT costs, assuming the agreed prices and the same services currently required continue to be delivered. All costs will be posted and viewable on-line and documented in monthly invoices.

The over-arching value proposition is typically stated in the executive summary. If you state a quantified value proposition in the executive summary, consider organizing the executive summary around components of your value proposition. Essentially, the quantified component values sum to the total value.

Place supporting value propositions targeting the economic buyer, technical buyer, users, and contract managers in the relevant volume summary or major section summary.

11 Create a price-to-win strategy to drive your solution.

Historically, costing and pricing have been approached as separate, confidential, or proprietary issues. Numerous conflicts are implicit:

- Sales and marketing seek the lowest possible price.
- Technical people seek a technically *safe* price, knowing that technology is uncertain and requirements *creep*.
- Program managers seek a price that they can deliver, knowing some task will be omitted or underscoped.
- Pricers seek a price based on known prior costs.
- Management seeks a strong profit margin, low risk, and low investment.
- Customers seek a low, but realistic, price that is within their budget.

And, of course, we all know that our competitors routinely *buy* the business by quoting at negative margins or misunderstanding the real scope of the requirement.

A conceptual view of acceptable price ranges to customers, competitors, and your organization is shown in figure 6 as the acceptable price-to-win window. The winning price is acceptable to the customer, acceptable to your organization, and less or unacceptable to competitors. You arrive at the price-to-win iteratively as you develop increasingly better data about the customer's perceptions, your cost and profit parameters, and the cost and profit parameters of competitors.

Both you and your competitor would like the customer to exclude the other party. However, customers seek to maximize competition, so the price-to-win window is their preferred option.

Analyze each competitor's acceptable price range by considering their prior pricing strategies. Organizations tend to repeat prior pricing strategies, especially strategies used on winning competitions. An organization's approach to pricing is usually more relevant than the actual quoted price for a product or service.

Figure 6. Conceptual View of Price to Win. *Arriving at the price-to-win is a process of iteratively reducing the upper and lower limits of what is acceptable to customers, yourself, and competitors. Add a circular price range for each competitor.*

See **Pricing to Win.**

With streamlined acquisitions and best-value procurements, customers vacillate between seeking a collaborative, integrated approach and insisting that bidders keep the technical/management solution entirely separate from the costing and pricing.

Embed cost and price-to-win considerations throughout your business development process, on par with solution development:

- Help the customer triangulate cost/price through should-cost models, cost as an independent variable (CAIV), and grass roots estimating.
- Maintain a consistent approach to costing and pricing across the program, beginning with an integrated set of assumptions to be used as the basis for estimates. Share these assumptions and subsequent changes across your team, including teaming partners when they impact their costs.

Price-to-win is a strategic management issue, not just a pricing issue. The winning price is not the sum of your estimated costs plus acceptable profit. If your cost plus acceptable profit exceeds your estimated price-to-win, you need to change your solution or not bid.

12 Use trade-offs to validate your approach and ghost the competition.

Trade-offs show you have considered alternatives and selected the best solution for the customer. Instead of selecting the first item available or your usual approach, discussing trade-offs demonstrates that you considered the customer's needs, risks, and budget, and offered a solution that offers best value at acceptable risk.

Ghosting is simply offering a trade-off when one of the alternatives that you rejected is offered by the competition. You ghost the competition when you raise the specter of competitors' potential weaknesses.

The primary way to downplay competitors' strengths and highlight their weaknesses is through ghosting. Never mention competitors by name. Instead, reject their approaches.

One of the advantages of ghosting is that you do not have to fully justify your position. You only create doubt, as shown in the following examples:

We first thought a full design-build approach would be ideal, as it could shorten the time to completion by 3 months. However, with the lack of reliable data on the stability of the soil at the site and the potential for hazardous materials, we have proposed a full site characterization and analysis prior to design. Our conservative approach reduces the risk of construction interruptions and potentially more costly site remediation.

Figure 7 offers some additional ghosting approaches. Use ghosting judiciously. Overuse can annoy the customer.

COMPETITOR'S WEAKNESS	YOU STRESS
Safety problems	Cite your strong safety record. Offer industry averages for comparison.
Labor unrest	Emphasize the importance of reliable workforce. Note that avoiding the cost of a strike justifies higher hourly wages.
High design cost	Emphasize low overheads and specific industry focus.
Poor reliability	Stress redundant design costs less than lost revenues from poor availability.
Extended downtime	Emphasize your local service center and built-in diagnostics.
Cost overruns	Cite the extra care taken in estimating, material selection, and purchasing.

Figure 7. Use Ghosting to Validate Your Approach. *Plan your ghosts carefully at the capture and proposal manager levels. Determine what ghosts will be introduced and where they will be raised during capture and inserted in your proposal. Trade-off analyses are appropriate in every capture presentation and proposal section where realistic alternatives are available.*

13 Implement your action plan.

A limited strategy that is implemented is superior to an excellent, unimplemented strategy. Like other planning tasks, maintain a balance between strategy development and implementation.

Action is required to persuade the customer to select your solution. Figure 8 lists some of the reasons strategies are not implemented and suggests improved approaches.

WHY STRATEGIES ARE NOT IMPLEMENTED	IMPROVED APPROACHES
Capture actions are not assigned to a single, responsible individual.	Assign one person with resources and completion dates.
No consequence for failure to complete.	Establish regular capture plan reviews.
Strategy regarded as confidential.	Communicate to all team members.
Strategy developed late.	Develop and review the capture strategy after the pursuit decision. Extend the capture strategy to a proposal strategy and distribute at proposal kickoff.
Proposal strategy not evident in drafts.	Use storyboards to flow strategy into sections. Always review drafts with the approved storyboards present.
Writers include unsupported claims.	Insist that all claims must be substantiated.

Figure 8. Improve Strategy Implementation. *Follow these recommendations to better implement your strategy throughout the sales cycle. Balance the time spent planning versus implementing.*

Teaming is a strategy where two organizations agree to jointly pursue an opportunity to improve their chances of winning. In a broad sense, teaming can range from informal prime-subcontractor relationships to the creation of a new joint-venture organization.

Capture managers pursue teaming arrangements from different perspectives. The most common reason to team is if the resulting competitive advantage justifies the additional management burden and potential loss of work share.

Organizations pursue teaming arrangements for a number of other reasons:

- Eliminate a competitor.
- Lock up a subcontractor.
- Obtain access to a particular market.
- Meet customer work share requirements.
- Attempt to win more favorable terms from a partner.
- Obtain information about a competitor through the teaming partner.
- Share the financial risk and development cost.
- Obtain access to new processes, methods, facilities, or business confidential information.

The General Motors-Toyota Tumi joint venture auto assembly operation in California was an example of joint venture teaming to obtain access to new markets, distribution networks, processes, methods, facilities, and confidential business information.

Teaming

1. Make teaming decisions early in the capture process.
2. Develop selection criteria and then use the Bidder Comparison Chart (BCC) to analyze potential teaming combinations.
3. Negotiate a common vision as the basis for teaming and agree to a written teaming agreement.
4. Establish a management structure with clear lines of authority.
5. Consult with customers and consider their roles in team formation.
6. Define each teaming partner's work share in advance in a Work Breakdown Structure (WBS).
7. Separate decisions about work share and team management.
8. Address teaming issues, responsibilities, and authorities promptly before they destroy the team.

1 Make teaming decisions early in the capture process.

The primary reason to make an early teaming decision is the same reason professional sports teams seek the highest possible draft position for new players — you get the best selection. Make early teaming decisions for the following reasons:

- The most advantageous partners are still available.
- The best talent is still available.
- You need a signed agreement to collaborate freely. Teaming discussions take time, involving senior management, attorneys, and formal contracts.
- Funding is easier to obtain early, before funds are committed to other uses.
- Positioning your team with the customer takes acceptance time. The more time you have, the greater the opportunity to influence the customer to accept and prefer your team.
- Teaming partners help you prepare and implement the strategy.

2 Develop selection criteria and then use the Bidder Comparison Chart to analyze potential teaming combinations.

Develop selection criteria based upon customer requirements and issues, not just counterbalancing strengths and weaknesses of the teaming organizations.

For example, a customer would like to fund development of a fuel-efficient vehicle that achieves 200 miles per gallon. Company A is a world leader in diesel and gasoline engine design and manufacture. Company B designs and builds the most efficient electric motors. Company C designs and builds efficient storage batteries. While the strengths and weaknesses of A, B, and C are complementary, the customer's hot button issue might be how to rapidly and cost effectively integrate all three technologies.

Identify probable selection criteria, including technical, management, past performance, cost, timing, funding, regulatory, social, political, business type, ownership, and legal. Consider hidden or unspoken issues as well as stated requirements. Identify issues that might be driving stated requirements.

Use the Bidder Comparison Chart (BCC) to objectively analyze the strength of various teaming combinations from the customer's perspective. As illustrated in figure 1, primary customer issues and requirements are listed in the left column. All requirements are assumed equal with a maximum possible score of "5." List potential teaming combinations, then rate the teams on each factor from the customer's perspective.

In figure 1, the competition is for a research contract to test the feasibility of using composites in bridge components. Both Fiberdyne and Sterling are similar research organizations with no clear edge over the other bidders. RH is primarily a fiber and resin materials producer, while FF is primarily a manufacturer of large, composite components. American Bridge (AB), as a bridge builder, seems to be in a hopeless situation, but it has strengths where all others are weak. The best combinations seem to be AB with F or S. From AB's view, F or S might be preferable to others because this is primarily a research contract.

The Integrated Solution Worksheet (ISW) can also be used to analyze different solutions with different teaming partners. Use both tools to make your teaming analysis more objective and to easily identify strengths, weaknesses, and gaps in your offering.

PROGRAM REQUIREMENTS	FIBERDYNE (F)	STERLING (S)	RH	FF	AMERICAN BRIDGE (AB)	CONSULTING ENGINEERS (CES)	AB & F OR S	AB & RH	AB & FF	AB & CES
Evaluate economic feasibility	2	2	3	2	5	5	5	5	5	5
Evaluate technical feasibility	4	4	4	3	3	4	4	4	4	4
Evaluate materials	5	5	4	3	1	3	5	4	3	3
Analyze design impact	5	2	3	2	4	3	5	4	3	3
Survey relevant applications of components	5	5	4	3	1	3	5	4	3	3
Evaluate production methods	4	4	4	5	3	2	4	4	5	3
Develop component designs	4	4	4	5	3	2	4	4	5	3
Prepare final report	4	4	4	5	3	3	4	4	5	3
Publish findings	3	3	3	2	4	3	4	4	4	4
Present at industry forums	3	3	3	2	2	4	3	3	2	4
Total	36	36	36	33	30	35	42	40	41	38

Figure 1. Use Bidder Comparison Matrix to Analyze Teaming Combinations. *This tool lets you compare the relative strengths and weaknesses of individual bidders and various teaming combinations.*

3 Negotiate a common vision as the basis for teaming and agree to a written teaming agreement.

In the best teaming relationships, team members share a common vision, strategy, and values. An organization driven to be the low cost producer is likely to conflict with an organization focused on customer service or technical leadership. An organization with a collaborative management team will conflict with one headed by a CEO with a single-minded approach.

Contrasting visions, approaches, or management values breed conflict, which should prompt you to reexamine the merits of this teaming combination. Team members should recognize the need for each member and respect each member's role and contribution.

See Virtual Team Management, *Proposal Guide.*

Teaming arrangements need to be negotiated, written, and signed as early as possible in the capture phase. In one major competition, the lawyers representing joint-venture partners were still arguing about the joint venture agreement at the time of the final Red Team. The strained relationships between the partners, reluctance to share information, and poor coordination were clear to the Red Team and detectable in the proposal.

When negotiating a teaming agreement, resolve the prime, subcontractor, and vendor issues discussed in Guideline 4, the positional issues in Guideline 5, the work share issues discussed in Guidelines 6 and 7, and the intellectual property, cost, and other legal issues discussed in Guideline 8. If left unresolved, these issues can subsequently destroy the team, your ability to form another team, and your credibility with the customer.

Schedule team-building activities promptly after forming your team to improve cooperation and reduce risk. Team building activities are relatively easy with a small capture team, but they are often skipped as unnecessary or frivolous. Team building activities are essential when integrating multi-organizational capture and proposal teams. Cohesive teams built during capture and proposal development reduce your transition risk into program execution.

Team-building activities apply to co-located and virtual teams, and they need not be expensive. Similar principles apply to both types of teams and are not repeated in this topic section.

4 Establish a management structure with clear lines of authority.

Shared team management does not work. Some teams rotate management responsibilities on longer-term contracts, but customers are often uncomfortable with potential lapses when management rotates. The best teams see themselves as distinct strategic business units where the primary loyalty of individuals on the team is to the team rather than the parent organization.

Your teaming relationship should be more robust than an arms-length subcontract. Teaming requires greater cooperation and trust than a typical subcontractor or vendor relationship.

Establish clear lines of authority, especially when individuals from different parent organizations are co-located. Customers want to know which individuals have what level of authority so they know who can resolve potential problems and how quickly problems can be resolved. Convince the customer that you have a well-defined and understood mitigation process in place.

A former four-star general on the Red Team for a joint venture made the following comment:

> *In all my years as a source selection authority, we never made a single award to a joint venture. It wasn't that we had anything against joint ventures. The proposal simply wasn't clear about precisely who was in charge of what activities, and what were their preapproved levels of authority.*

Apply that observation to any type of teaming arrangement, from joint ventures to project teams within the same organization:

- Insert management organization charts in the proposal.
- Name key managers and key positions, if possible.
- Indicate team members' responsibilities, level of authority by type of decision, preapproved spending limits, and whether they have hiring/firing authority over their own employees and employees of teaming partners.

5

Consult with customers and consider their roles in team formation.

Customers have a stake in teaming combinations, preferred partners, and team contractual arrangements. Review potential teaming combinations and arrangements with the customer, if possible. Whether encouraged by the customer or not, justify why you have teamed, describe the role of each partner, and explain the unique reason that partner was selected.

Customers often review your teaming selection criteria as part of their evaluation and source selection process. For example, customers dislike teammates whose primary motivation is to reliably secure a share of the work without competition.

Occasionally, organizations feel compelled to team, either by the customer, their management, or conditions in their market. Forced teaming arrangements increase risk if the partners dislike or prefer to not work together. Consider whether forced teaming is worth the increased risk.

6

Define each teaming partner's work share in advance in a Work Breakdown Structure (WBS).

Even at the proposal stage, teams seldom jell until the work share is defined in a written WBS. Two things can happen if the work share is not defined; both are risky:

- Tasks are omitted because, "Someone else has those tasks." Omitted tasks are not described or priced, increasing financial and performance risk and decreasing your chances of winning.
- Tasks are included in multiple places, increasing the cost and making you less competitive. Citing different approaches to the same task suggests that you cannot work well as a team.

Appoint a subgroup to develop the WBS, comprising individuals representing every partner. Frequently, work shares must match the funding percentages of the purchasing organizations, specific work locations, and specific subcontractors selected. Typical examples are multinational procurements and export sales that include coproduction or offset requirements.

7

Separate decisions about work share and team management.

The organization with the largest work share does not have to be the prime management partner. Select the management partner with the best ability to manage the contract or the partner that the customer prefers. Consider the following example:

In this teaming arrangement, Partner A, with 80 percent of the work share, was to be the prime or managing partner to produce training simulators. Partner A was recognized by the customer for excellence in research and development (R&D). They had developed this training simulator, but they had no record of successfully managing a large production contract. Worse yet, Partner A typically delivered R&D contracts late and frequently overran costs.

Partner B, with only 20 percent of the work share, had an excellent record of production contract management experience. Nearly half of the 90-day bid preparation period passed before Partner A would agree to let Partner B become the managing partner.

8

Address teaming issues, responsibilities, and authorities promptly before they destroy the team.

While legal arrangements differ in joint-venture, prime-subcontractor, and vendor relationships, most section B guidelines apply universally.

Address capture planning; your proposal preparation process, management approach, and cost allocation; program or solution development costs; allocation of financial risk; intellectual property and licensing; contractual terms and conditions; and legal implications.

Validate your capture strategy with your teaming partners. Assign capture tasks to your partners. Involve them in your positioning and intelligence gathering efforts. Customers doubt repeated claims that you are a team when they often interact with a single organization.

Include teaming partners in key activities:

- Facilitating and contributing to review teams
- Making joint presentations to customers

- Validating your capture and proposal strategy
- Identifying relevant past performance examples
- Drafting proposal sections
- Participating in finals presentations or oral proposal presentations

See VIRTUAL TEAM MANAGEMENT, *Proposal Guide.*

Capture positioning and proposal preparation activities comprise a mini-project that leads to the major project. Both must have clear management structures with clear lines of authority. Seek a common process, management structure, and approach to covering capture and proposal preparation costs.

Co-locating the proposal team is ideal, but often not feasible. Virtual teaming is increasingly required to reduce costs and incorporate input from individuals who are committed to prior tasks or intermittently available.

Few individuals have common visions of what is meant by a virtual team. Managers of virtual teams must deal with four issues, listed in order of importance:

- **Process.** When the process and terms used differ, individuals cannot communicate clearly. Worse, they often do not know it. Teams with a common process and capable proposal manager will prepare a superior proposal in half the time.
- **Culture.** Teams in different time zones create obvious challenges. However, organizational culture variations are often more challenging than national culture variations. Do not underestimate the problems from different organizational cultures and the impact on hardware, software, and process. Individuals who know one platform, one software package, and one process will resist change to the bitter end.
- **Software.** Different operating systems, programs, releases or versions of programs, fonts, print drivers, networks, gateways, and communication protocols usually mean that the teaming partner's input seldom arrives as you thought it would.
- **Hardware.** Contributors often work on different platforms with different capabilities, support needs, and networking characteristics.

Too much of the current focus in virtual proposals is around hardware and software issues. The most difficult and lingering issues involve process and cultural differences.

No organization wants to lose its intellectual property (IP) and establish a competitor. Establish what must be disclosed for efficient contract performance. Licensing under a royalty arrangement is one alternative. Resolve IP issues with your attorney.

Value Propositions establish the value basis for the business relationship. They describe how the seller's solution will improve the customer's business and how that improvement will be measured.

Value propositions are opportunity and customer specific and are developed collaboratively with the customer over the course of the sale.

Value propositions go beyond traditional theme statements by incorporating as many as possible of the following elements:

- Quantifies the anticipated business improvement
- Specifies the timing of the benefits
- Specifies the timing of the costs
- States the payback period
- Specifies how the results will be measured and tracked

Because executives, users, and technical buyers have different issues and values, prepare a different value proposition for each type of buyer. For each distinct opportunity, state the total added value of all value propositions in a single summary value proposition.

Value Propositions

1. Establish a single sales objective as the first step in developing a value proposition.
2. Exploit value propositions as a collaborative selling tool.
3. Use a template to develop value propositions.
4. Develop unique value propositions for each type of buyer.
5. Organize your executive summary around your value propositions.
6. Address common obstacles to using value propositions.

1 Establish a single sales objective as the first step in developing a value proposition.

Shortly after your pursuit decision, draft a brief, precise sales objective that meets the following criteria:

- **Specific**—States what products and services are to be purchased and who will purchase them.
- **Measurable**—Tells how much is to be purchased.
- **Timed**—Cites when the purchase will be made.
- **Result**—States, quantitatively if possible, the result or process change the prospect anticipates.

Sample sales objective

Our sales objective is to persuade Global Corporation to outsource information technology (IT) support, currently costing them $2,850,000 annually. Global is seeking an annual cost reduction of 30 percent, commencing May 1, 20XX, and would like the provider to purchase the existing IT assets.

Like most initial sales objectives, not all criteria are met. The purchasing organization is named but not the purchasing individual. Current costs are named, but not the cost of the seller's solution or the cost of the customer's assets. Drafting a sales objective is a good way to determine what additional information you need.

Sellers often pursue multiple purchases from the same organization. If you find yourself using *and* to describe multiple buyers and multiple purchase times, you might be facing multiple opportunities that are better addressed by multiple sales objectives.

2

Exploit value propositions as a collaborative selling tool.

The objective of collaborating with the prospect to develop a value proposition is to convince the customer to award the contract without competitive proposals. The customer must be convinced that the opportunity cost of delaying exceeds the potential savings from competing the contract.

Collaboration between the customer and the seller offers the following potential advantages:

- Both gain a clearer understanding of the customer's objectives and potential benefits.
- Both better understand the actions required of each party, which reduces risk.
- The customer becomes the seller's advocate in the customer's organization.

Value propositions flow directly from the sales objective. The best value propositions are specific. Ideally, authorized representatives of both the customer's and the seller's organizations sign the formal value proposition, and they mutually agree to proceed without competitive proposals.

3

Use a template to develop value propositions.

Templates help sellers draft better value propositions in less time. When a template is not used, the result is often vague, qualitative, and hard to measure.

Value propositions should include the following elements:

- Quantified business improvement
- Timing
- Solution
- Investment cost
- Payback
- Results measurement and tracking

A template for drafting value propositions is shown in figure 1.

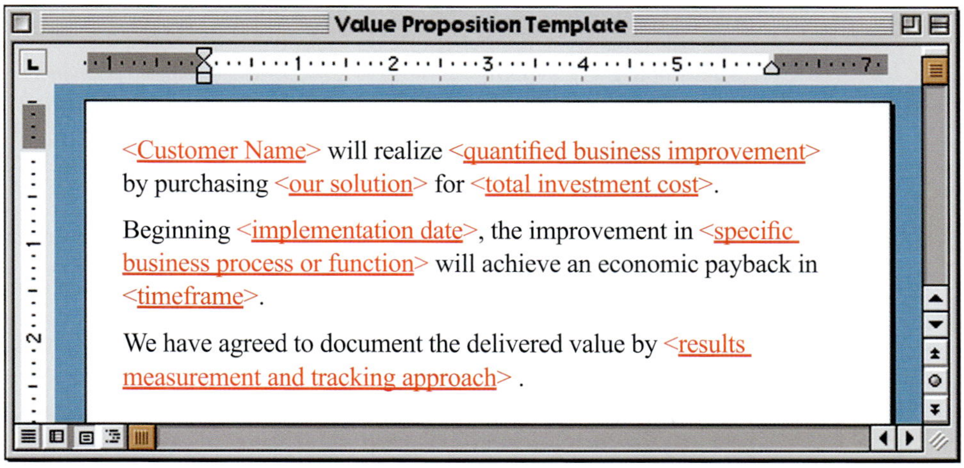

Figure 1. Use a Template to Develop Value Propositions. *The better value propositions are developed with the customer and contain the elements listed. Value propositions sound stronger if the benefits are placed at the beginning.*

4

Develop unique value propositions for each type of buyer.

Three broad types of buyers are the economic buyer, the users, and the technical buyers.

The **Economic buyers** give final approval to purchase. They sign the check and retain veto power. Economic buyers tend to be concerned about the trade-off between price and performance. They focus on bottom line impact. While many people may offer input and recommendations, only the economic buyer can give final approval.

The **users** are the people who judge the potential impact on their job performance. Their personal success is impacted by the sale, so their concerns are often emotional and subjective. Users' issues are reliability, support, ease of operation, maintenance, safety,

While value propositions targeted at individual buyers may overlap, the summary value proposition targeting the economic buyer incorporates all benefits and costs.

potential impact on morale, and potential impact on their personal success. Because they use or supervise the use of your product or service, they can ruin a good sale.

The **technical buyers** are gatekeepers. They cannot give final approval, but they can give a final *No*. Technical buyers often determine the short list. They tend to focus on the features of a product or service against objective specifications established to screen offers.

Technical buyers may not be technical in the scientific sense. Purchasing agents, lawyers, contracts people, and licensing or regulatory authorities are technical buyers. Because technical buyers are primarily focused on how well you meet their screening tests, the better you understand their criteria, the better your chances of getting their recommendations.

Another way to examine buyers is according to their source of power. Power could be economic, users (control), or technical (knowledge). Alternatively, power could be indicated by level of management, such as executive management, middle management, or operations.

Tailor value proposition(s) to each type of buying influence. The following three value propositions target each type of buyer and are extensions of the earlier example of a single sales objective under Guideline 1:

Value Proposition for the economic buyer

Global Corporation will realize a $3,750,000 reduction in information technology support costs over the next 5 years, commencing May 1, 20XX, by contracting with Computer Heroes, Ltd., at a cost of $2,000,000 per year. Global Corporation will be paid $500,000 for all of Global's IT assets, and Computer Heroes will provide all IT support. Global Corporation will enjoy a 30 percent annual reduction in IT costs, assuming the agreed prices and the same levels of services currently required continue to be required and delivered. All costs will be available to you online and documented in monthly invoices.

Value Proposition for user

Commencing May 1, 20XX, the department allocations for IT support for the current types and levels of service will be reduced an average of 30 percent. Outdated legacy systems will be transitioned to lower cost, current, commercial off-the-shelf hardware and software. Departmental managers will be free to focus on core management tasks without the distractions of IT issues. All costs will be available and verifiable on-line and documented in monthly invoices tied to Global work order numbers. With Computer Heroes assuming responsibility for all hardware and software (paying Global $500,000 for the current assets), department managers will no longer have to submit and defend IT capital requests.

Value Proposition for technical buyer (IT professionals)

Commencing May 1, 20XX, IT professionals will have extensive and varied opportunities for personal growth and advancement within their profession. Computer Heroes will offer positions to all IT employees and will maintain current pay levels for those positions. As an industry leader, all positions will be reviewed and adjusted to industry standards. Opportunities for training and advancement will be offered to all employees on an equal basis through our Intranet website, our employee newsletter, regular all-hands e-mails, and job site postings.

Value Proposition for technical buyer (contracts)

Commencing May 1, 20XX, all IT support, both employees and assets, will be seamlessly transitioned to Computer Heroes, saving Global Corporation $750,000 per year over current costs. All cost savings will be calculated on the basis of providing identical levels of service and can be verified on-line by comparing monthly, itemized invoices.

5 Organize your executive summary around your value propositions.

See Executive Summary.

If developing value propositions is an integral part of your business development process, organize your executive summary around your value propositions.

Begin the executive summary by stating the summary value proposition that targets the economic buyer, the sole person who can sign the check. Follow the summary value proposition with the underlying value propositions. Then present all aspects of your solution against one of the underlying value propositions, substantiating how your approach delivers the value claimed. Conclude by showing how the underlying value propositions add up to the opening summary value proposition.

Use the Four-Box organizational structure discussed in the Executive Summary section and summarized in figure 2. For organizational purposes, treat each underlying or subvalue proposition as a hot button.

Some aspects of value cannot be quantified. Sometimes, individuals in either customers' or sellers' organizations cannot agree on the quantitative added value.

Always state the intangible or nonquantified values of your proposed solution. If the quantified added values of competitors' solutions are close to yours, the intangible added values could win the contract. State your quantitative added value before your qualitative added value.

See Executive Summaries *and* Sales Letters.

BOX 1—Present the summary value proposition prepared for the economic buyer. State the collaborative basis for this value proposition, indicating ownership by both the customer and the seller.

BOX 2—Present two to five subvalue propositions in a bulleted list. The total should equal the total value cited in Box 1.

BOX 3—Present each subvalue proposition in the order introduced. All proposed products and services must be aligned with one of the subvalue propositions. By the completion of Box 3, all aspects of your offer should be covered. Expand or contract the space devoted to each subvalue proposition according to its relative importance to the customer.

BOX 4—Summarize the total value and total cost, previously cited in Box 1. Close by previewing the next logical step in the sales process, usually how your proposal is organized. If immediate negotiations are possible, suggest a time to begin.

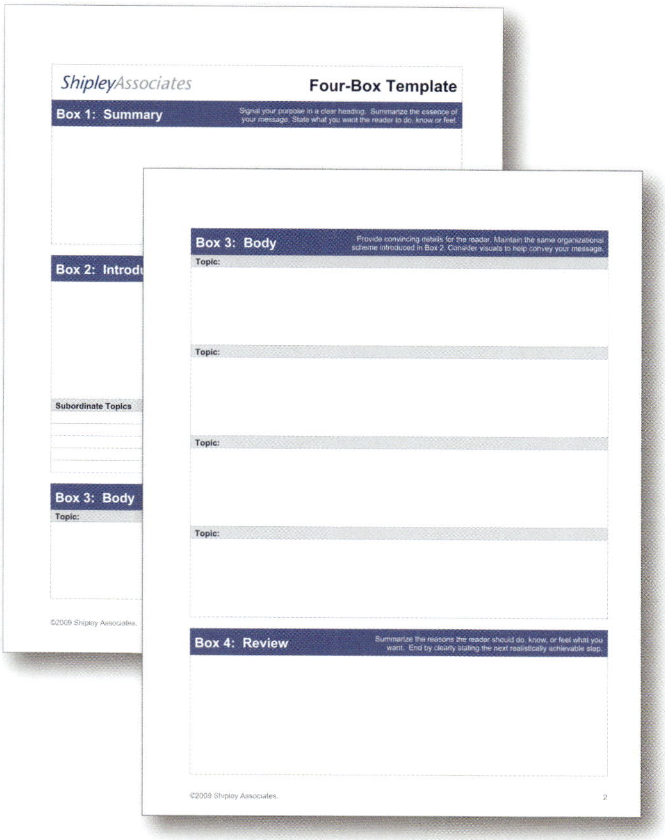

Figure 2. Organize Your Executive Summary Around Your Value Proposition. *Open with your summary value proposition to the economic buyer. Regard each major subvalue proposition as a hot button. Then align all major aspects of your offer against one of the subvalue propositions. Close with a short summary of your total value proposition, and preview how your proposal is organized.*

6 Address common obstacles to using value propositions.

Using *theme statements* is a common practice in proposals in all markets. A best practice is to quantify the benefits in the theme statement, then substantiate the claim in the proposal shortly after the theme statement.

See Theme Statements, ***Proposal Guide.***

Individuals working in regulated government markets where contacts between the seller and the customer are limited or prohibited can still benefit from developing value propositions. A quantified value proposition based on reasonable assumptions will be more persuasive than a vague, qualitative claim to offer best value.

Most organizations have difficulty with value propositions. Figure 3 below lists some of the common problems and suggests potential solutions.

The deep understanding of the customer's business required to develop a value proposition can favorably discriminate your organization. With government purchasers adopting commercial acquisition practices, value propositions might give you an edge.

REASONS VALUE PROPOSITIONS MISUSED	POTENTIAL SOLUTIONS
Legal or contracts people refuse to allow any specific statements to limit potential liability.	Carefully state all assumptions and conditions.
Few people understand value propositions as a disciplined concept	Train all participants in the process.
Short sales cycles limit customer-seller collaboration.	Develop *generic* value propositions.
Excessive targeting of multiple opportunities limits customer-seller collaboration.	Improve Pursuit and Bid/No Bid milestone discipline.
Seller-developed value propositions are summarily rejected by customers.	Find a friendly collaborator, sell on a basis other than *best value,* or no bid.
Customers' distrust of the seller or purchasing restrictions limit or bar collaboration with sellers.	Develop greater trust, or sell on a basis other than *best value.*

Figure 3. Overcoming Obstacles. *Common obstacles to effective use of value propositions can be overcome by taking a larger business perspective.*

Model Documents Table of Contents

Model Documents

Model Documents illustrate best practices and alternative approaches to capture planning tools and job aids. The Model Documents Table of Contents (preceding page) lists capture planning-related documents in the *Capture Guide* and the *Proposal Guide*. None of the models are intended to be used *as is*. Use them to improve your understanding of capture planning principles and as a baseline to develop your own documents and tools.

Using Model Documents

Model documents follow the guidelines discussed in this *Capture Guide* and the *Proposal Guide* as closely as possible.

Some documents illustrate potential formats; others were altered to disguise the original seller or customer. Some have been shortened or displayed in a reduced, thumbnail form to make this *Capture Guide* more compact.

The following suggestions will help you use these models to improve your approach to capture planning.

1. Rely on the overall organization to illustrate concepts rather than exact details. Adapt the format, content, and medium to your organization and selling environment.
2. The exact terms and phrases will vary by market and selling environment. Select words that are acceptable and known, and then define terms explicitly for users.
3. Read the notes and adaptation recommendations carefully. Guidelines are not rules, so use sound judgment when tailoring these documents and models.
4. Collect your own models from colleagues, through professional organizations, via industry conferences, and web sources.
5. Refine documents and templates regardless of the source. A best practice is to repeatedly amend and adapt your own documents to make them clearer, easier to use, and more applicable to the immediate opportunity. Consistent with this best practice, we repeatedly amend and improve our models, tools, guidelines, workshop materials, and templates, so the versions shown here might differ from prior or subsequent versions.

Capture plans evolve as new information is gathered and circumstances evolve. Adapt the medium and format, whether text, presentation, collaborative web site, or on-line database. Suggested modifications to the model presentation format shown in this section apply equally to other media.

This presentation model capture plan template is consistent with the one used in Shipley's *Capturing Federal Business* training workshop. The brief presentation format is designed to illustrate key briefing elements, but it is not intended to be comprehensive or used without adaptation.

The specific elements of this model template are starting points to develop a standard plan that meets your organization's needs and typical business opportunities. Augment or delete content and slides for each briefing element. Adapt the document style if your management prefers to see evidence of detailed reasoning and analysis.

The slides on the following pages are aligned with key briefing elements. Review the instructions, tips for completing each element, and potential adaptations for each of five basic selling environments:

NG	Selling to national governments.
RG	Selling to regional governments.
B2B	Selling business to business.
Primes	Selling to primes as a 1st or 2nd tier subcontractor.
TO	Selling task orders under master contracts.

The gate review symbols and conventions shown on this page suggest when each type of content might be added, improved, and updated over the life of a capture plan. Tailor these suggestions to match needs and processes of your organization.

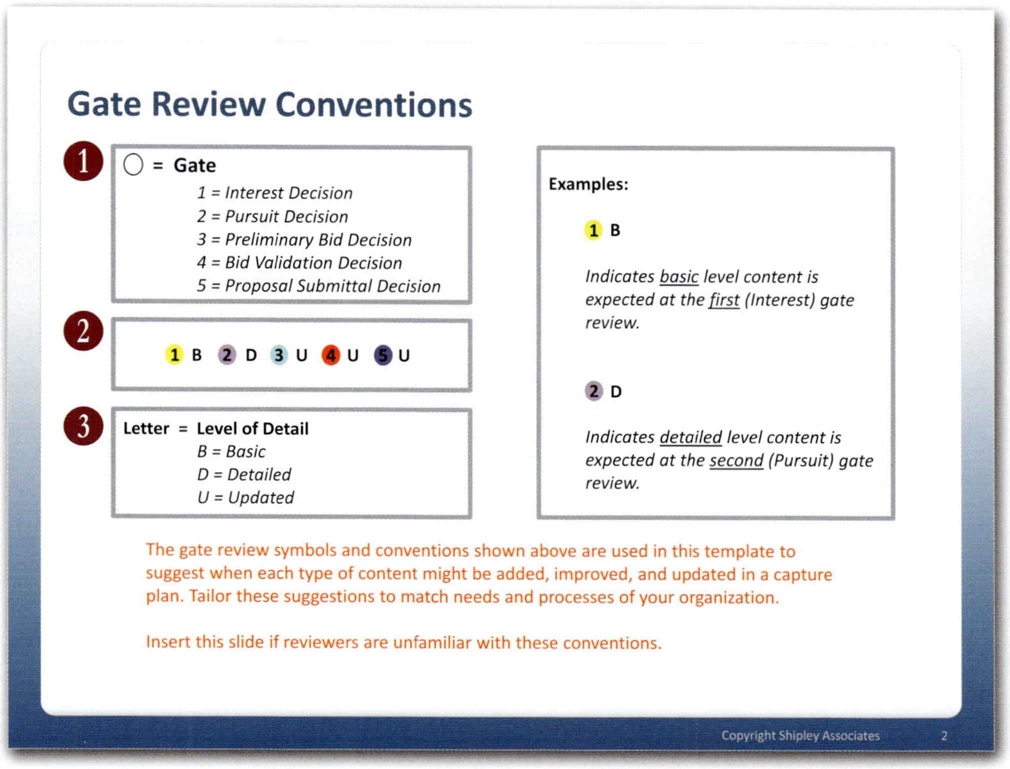

❶ The numbered circles indicate the decision gate review at which particular content is usually first introduced. The numbers correspond to the decision gates listed below but should be adapted to your organization's decision gate milestones:

1 = Interest Decision

2 = Pursuit Decision

3 = Preliminary Bid Decision

4 = Bid Validation Decision

5 = Proposal Submittal Decision

❷ Colors indicate the phase leading to that decision gate review.

❸ The letter next to the decision milestone number indicates the relative level of content detail for each review:

B = Basic

D = Detailed

U = Updated

Capture Plan Template

1-Presentation Model (with tailoring annotations)

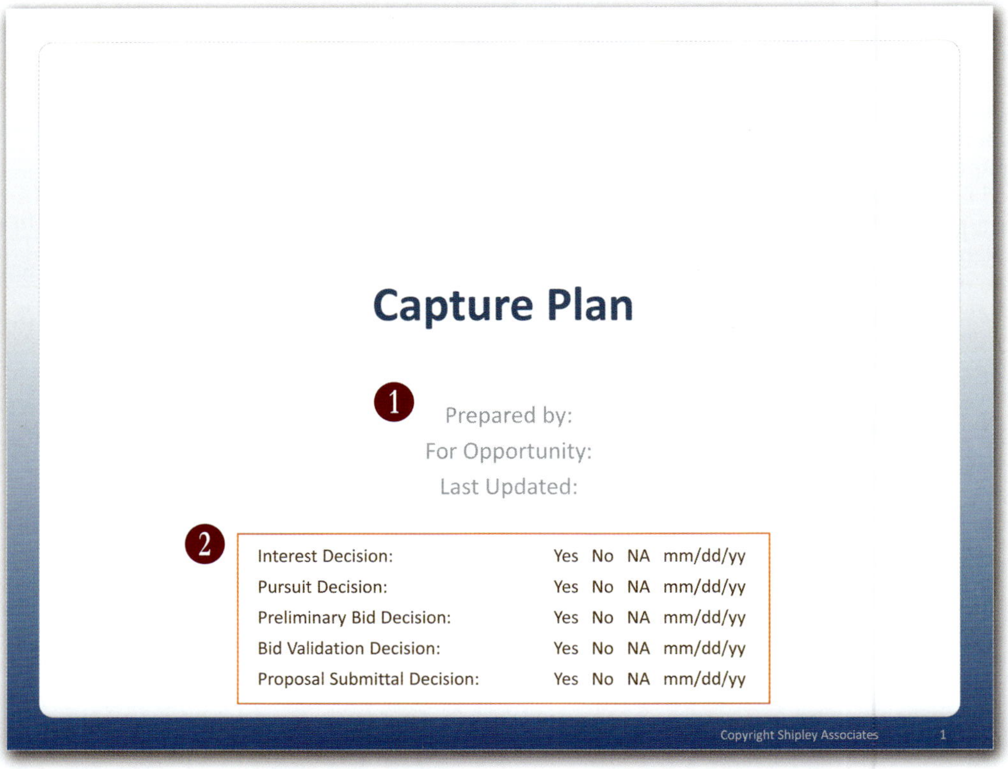

❶ Identify opportunity

- List preparer.
- Update frequently.
- Consider a system that highlights changes for those familiar with prior versions.

❷ Gate decisions

- Record gate decisions on the title page, including dates milestones were passed.

Summarize key program elements. Adapt the level of detail to the medium. If presented as a slide, use the *Notes* feature to add detail for individuals who cannot attend the briefing. Adapt or transfer information from the account plan, if available.

Create the capture plan executive summary after the rest of the plan is as complete as possible. Then update it frequently, at minimum, before each gate and color review. Repeat, support, and expand on executive summary items in the capture plan.

Note: Do not confuse the capture plan executive summary, shown here, with the proposal executive summary.

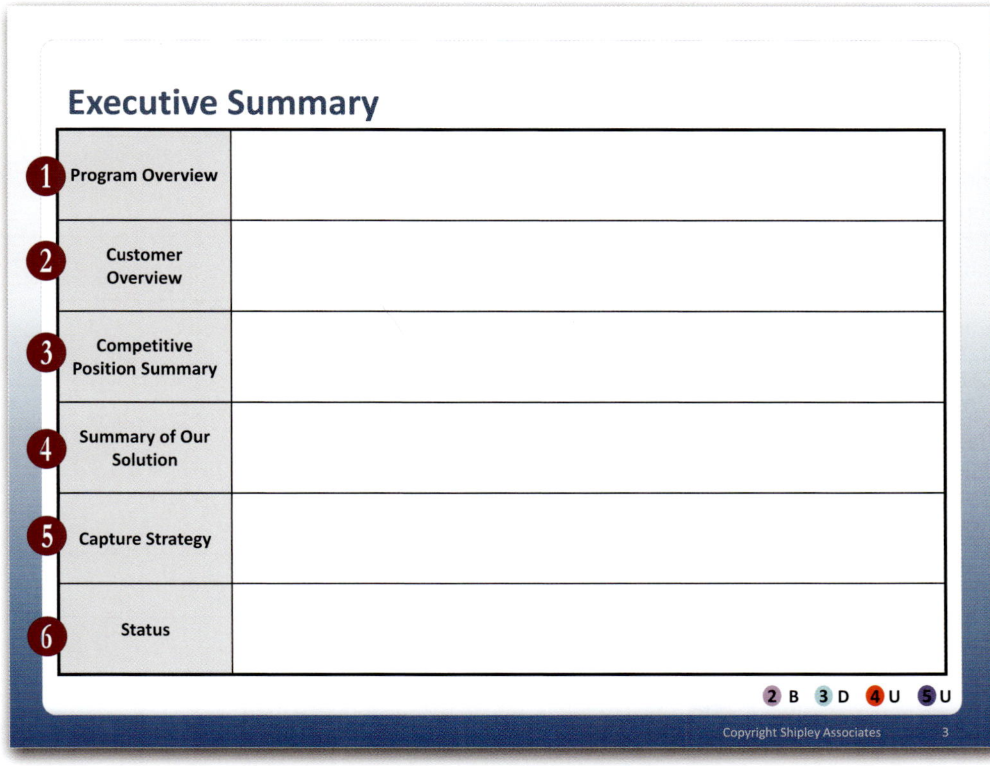

1 Program Overview

- Summarize the services and products sought. Note the estimated contract value and duration.

2 Customer Overview

- Summarize key customer information.

3 Competitive Position Summary

- List and rank competitors from the customer's perspective.
- List incumbent(s) and teaming combinations, as applicable.
- Link rankings to the Bidder Comparison Chart.

4 Summary of Your Solution

- Outline major solution elements.
- Indicate the potential or actual team, as appropriate.

5 Capture Strategy

- List 3-5 over-arching approaches planned to position your organization and solution as the preferred option.

6 Status

- Summarize current capture efforts.
- Highlight near-term critical tasks, milestones, and required decisions.
- Update frequently.

Selling Environment Adaptations	
NG	Adapt to internal organizational standards. Some managers will insist on having additional summary information for large, complex opportunities. If so, overview the opportunity, then add slides or pages with more information. Remember this is only an executive summary, and the plan includes more information on every topic. Do not pack too much information onto dense, unreadable presentation slides. Consider adding detailed information in slide *Notes*.
RG	Same as for NGs
B2B	Keep it succinct. Resist adding information. Management focus declines as the length increases. Further, commercial opportunities often proceed at a pace that places a premium on action rather than lengthy analysis.
Primes	In Customer Overview, list the end customer, the prime, and intervening subcontractors, as applicable. If the prime is targeting end customers beyond this procurement, list potential end customers.
TO	Focus on the individual organization, division or department, and buyer. Naming a large organization is not that helpful.

Capture Plan Template

1-Presentation Model (with tailoring annotations)

Describe what the customer wants to buy. Consider the Buying Cycle depicted in the top line of figure 2, **Color Team Reviews.** The customer's concept of the desired solution evolves over the buying cycle. A primary capture goal is to collaboratively shape the solution with the customer. The earlier in the buying cycle, the greater your opportunity to influence the preferred solution.

See **Customer-Focused Capture Skills and Tactics.**

EXTERNAL ANALYSIS

Opportunity Description

Elements	Description
1 Customer	
2 Program Summary	
3 Key Requirements	
4 Deliverables	
5 Budget and Fiscal-Year Funding Profile	
6 Schedule	
7 Type of Contract	
8 Other: (Specify)	

1 B 2 D 3 U 4 U 5 U

1. Customer
   - List the buying organization. Be specific, citing the agency, branch, division, or department. Cite the parent organization, if applicable.

2. Program Summary
   - Summarize what is wanted, the customer's envisioned services and/or products.
   - Cite the customer's vision and desired outcome: What problem is being solved, pain alleviated, or need satisfied?
   - Cite program objectives, if available.

3. Key Requirements
   - List requirements by category:
     - Technical
     - Management
     - Key personnel
     - Past performance
     - Cost/price, terms, warranties
     - Security
   - Add or delete categories as appropriate.

4. Deliverables
   - Services
   - Products
   - Data

5. Budget and Fiscal Year Funding Profile
   - Amount
   - Sources (who pays or has the budget)
   - Types of funds
   - Timing of funding

6. Schedule
   - List known buying milestone dates:
     - Industry day
     - Bidders' conference
     - Site visits
     - Draft and final solicitation release
     - Question deadline
     - Proposal submittal
     - Oral presentations
     - Contract award
     - Project initiation
   - Highlight near-term dates and update frequently.

7 Type of Contract

- List the type of contract.
- Note if a single or multiple award(s).
- Provide actual or estimated total contract value.
- Specify contract value by time period.
- Identify length of contract and renewal options.

8 Other

- Cite special provisions (data rights ownership, warranties, performance warranties, bonding, insurance).
- Organizational conflict of interest.
- Small, minority, or disadvantaged business requirements.

Selling Environment Adaptations	
NG	Modifications and additions could be extensive for large, complex opportunities. Cite where additional data is available for review rather than inserting all data in the opportunity description. Remember the capture plan is a plan, not an encyclopedia. Maintain your knowledge base separately.
RG	Adapt plan elements to be consistent with your typical business opportunities. Maintain summary-level information, and reference detailed support documents.
B2B	The type of funding will seldom be an issue. Focus on the funding source and availability. B2B customers often seek information for a subsequent purchase or for negotiation leverage with a preferred source.
Primes	List the end customer, the prime, and intervening subcontractors, as applicable. If the prime is targeting end customers beyond this procurement, note those as well. Be realistic about the potential of the opportunity, as customers often hint at multiple purchases in order to obtain volume pricing and better terms.
TO	Do not rehash your original efforts to win the master contract, which may be with a separate organization entirely. Focus instead on the specific task and buying division or department.

Capture Plan Template

1-Presentation Model (with tailoring annotations)

Extend the customer profile from the account plan, when available. Add detail as you collaborate with the customer, vendors, and anyone who knows or offers information about the customer.

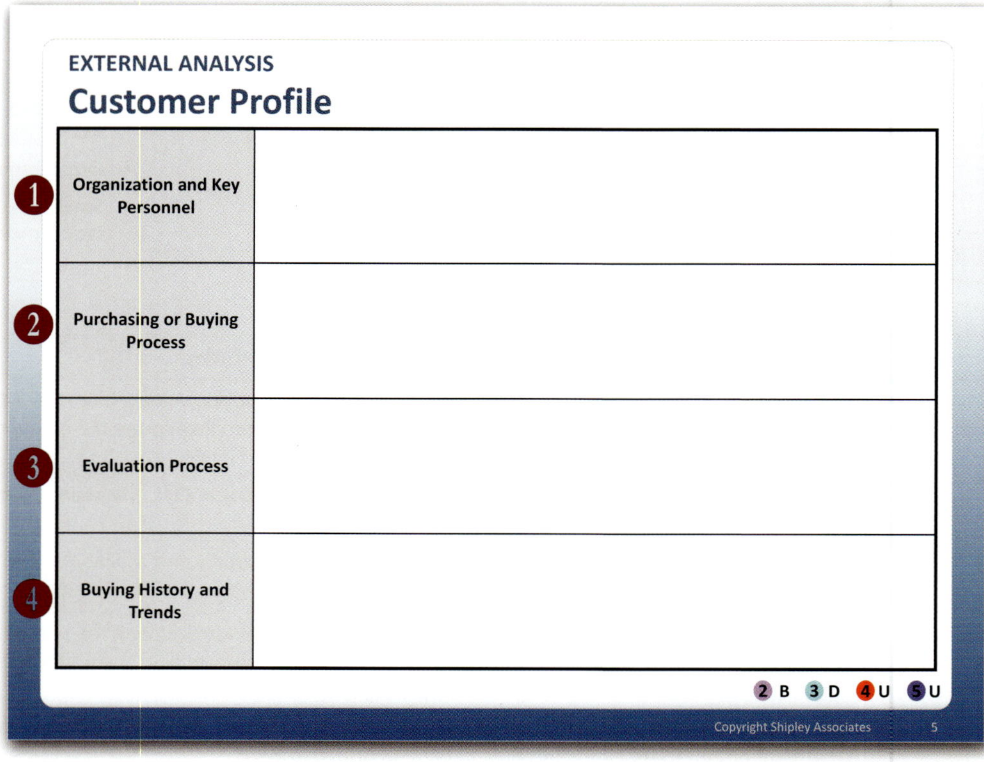

❶ Organization and Key Personnel

- Describe the organization. Insert or reference organization charts. Good general sources are often available on customers' websites.
- Ask customers to describe their internal structure, especially the immediate buying and user organizations.
- List key personnel.
- Classify personnel as decision makers, influencers, gatekeepers, or potential coaches.

❷ Purchasing or Buying Process

- Outline the customer's buying process and how it is managed.
- Note the current position in the buying process.

❸ Evaluation Process

- Describe or diagram evaluation steps.
- Link dates to the steps.
- Name and describe probable evaluators.
- List potential evaluation criteria.

❹ Buying History and Trends

- List similar purchases made by this organization or individuals who might influence the purchase decision.

List key parameters of those purchases: program name, location, value, common elements, winners, losing bidders, publicly and privately stated reasons for the selection, and outcomes (performance, schedule, quality, and cost compliance).

Selling Environment Adaptations	
NG	Do not assume all national government processes are similar. Stated processes might not be actual processes. Look for hidden influencers. Consider cultural norms, adding cultural elements to customer profiles.
RG	As with NGs, expect different processes and deviations from stated processes.
B2B	Purchasing and evaluation discipline ranges from undefined to highly defined and strictly followed. Reflect customary practices of the customer. B2B buyers are free to deviate from stated processes, so determine if such deviations are common practice. Historic buying trends, a significant installed base, and preferences for key individuals who now work for a competitor are strong no-bid indicators.
Primes	While the immediate customer's approach is paramount, consider which of the related customers might influence the evaluation and buying decision. Is the purchasing process open to audit or likely to be reviewed by the end or prime customer?
TO	Focus on the individual organization, division, department, and buyer. Naming a large organization is not that helpful.

Hot button issues comprise key customer motivators and concerns or worry items. Record the exact words that you hear repeatedly in conversations or see repeatedly in documents. Substituting terms that you are more comfortable with borders on arrogance or suggests that you are not listening. Guard against citing generally agreed industry lore that is outdated, generic, or not linked to this customer.

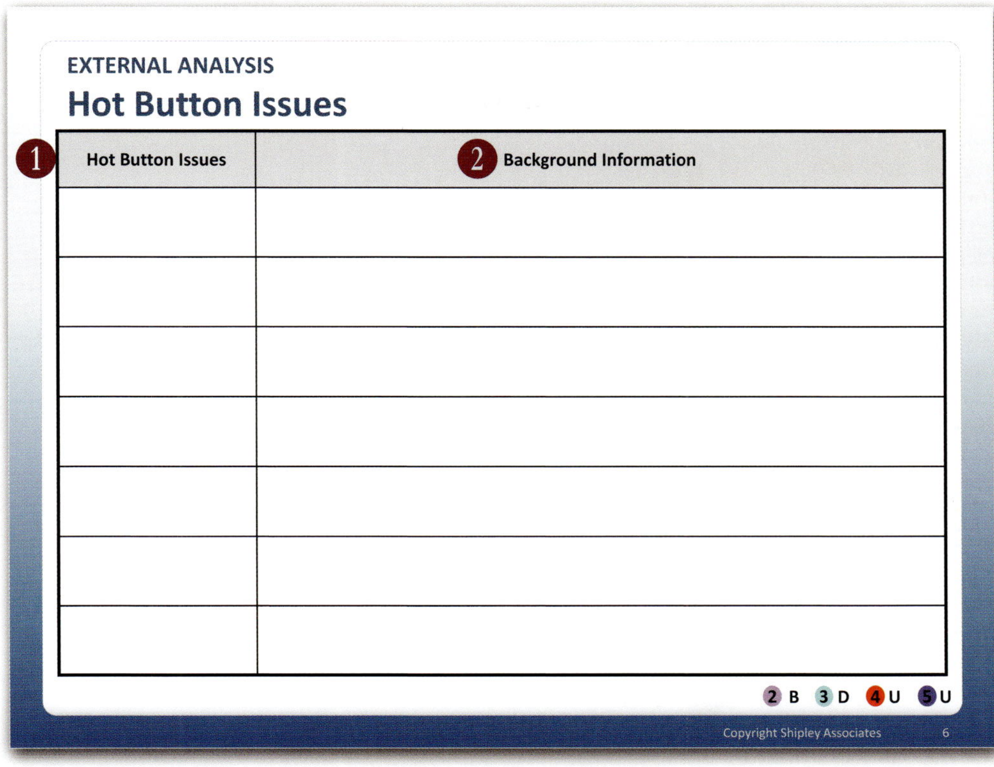

1. Hot Button Issues
   - List the most critical issues that will influence the buying decision.

2. Background
   - Cite the desired future state. Why is this an issue?
   - What are the consequences or costs of the current state?

Selling Environment Adaptations	
NG	Analyze complex opportunities from three perspectives: 1. Evaluation criteria, often stated in generic terms. 2. Four to ten primary hot button issues, which offer a good summary of needs that are easier to address. 3. A limited number of critical requirements. In complex procurements, you might identify tens to hundreds of requirements. While each requirement must eventually be addressed, tracking that many can be confusing and time consuming, prompting you to treat unequal requirements equally.
RG	NG adaptations often apply to large regional and international opportunities, and the B2B adaptations apply to smaller opportunities.
B2B	Limit hot button issues to less than 10, and ideally 3-5. Meld stated hot button issues with evaluation criteria, and address them in the executive summary. When hot button issues exceed 6, group them and address the groups.
Primes	List the hot button issues of the end customer, the prime, and intervening subcontractors. Then prepare a combined list, according customers with the most power in the purchasing decision the most weight. Address excluded issues within the framework of the combined hot button issues list.
TO	Focus on the immediate issues of the individual organization, division or department, and buyer. Create *pull* by noting how the immediate issues support the overarching vision, motivators, and issues of the organization above the immediate buyer.

Your competitors' past marketing strategies and approaches are often the best indicators of how they will approach a new opportunity. Predicting what they will do in a particular case is almost impossible unless you have an ongoing and effective competitive intelligence process. Maintain a knowledge base about your competitors' past activities to mine for insights on new capture efforts.

EXTERNAL ANALYSIS

Competitor Intelligence – Competitor A

1 Market Approach and Position	
2 Products and/or Services	
3 Historical Pricing Patterns	
4 Business Development	
5 Customer Relationship	
6 Relevant Experience	
7 Past Performance	

3 B 4 D 5 U

Copyright Shipley Associates 7

Complete competitor intelligence templates for each competitor. Duplicate capture plan pages if the number of competitors exceeds those in your template

1 Market Approach and Position

- Indicate focus by job size, customer, and geography.
- Indicate position as leader, follower, new entrant, specialty provider, etc.
- Indicate commitment to the market, importance of this opportunity to future success, and linked or ongoing related work. What is the impact of a loss or no-bid?
- Note how aggressively and flexibly they have pursued similar opportunities.

2 Products and/or Services

- List which services/products are likely to be offered and the source.
- List required adaptations to make them compliant.
- Note if subcontractors or teaming partners are required or probable.

3 Historical Pricing Patterns

- Note if they tend to offer high or low prices.
- Note if they prefer or avoid specific contract vehicles, such as fixed price, cost-plus, performance-based, etc.

4 Business Development

- List typical marketing messages, themes, positioning, and claimed differentiators.
- Note who is involved by name; note the number, type, and experience of management and support staff.
- Note the relative power of management versus individual field sales or account managers.
- If they contract for site representation, note the role, influence, and effectiveness of this site representative versus direct employees.
- Note if they rely on individual or team selling.
- Note if they team and how they integrate teaming partners in selling, strategy development, solution development, and program management. List preferred teaming partners by name or type.

5 Customer Relationship

- Does this customer know the organization, division, and management team well? Is it a positive, neutral, or negative perception?
- List personal links or history among individuals in the competitor and customer organization. Have they worked for common organizations or on common projects? Are they linked through professional organizations or common interests?

6 Relevant Experience

- List relevant experience. Relevance might be via common issues, services, people, or products.

7 Past Performance

- Link past performance to prior relevant experience examples, if available. Note how they performed on similar work. Quantitative performance data is difficult to obtain, so cite the source. The most credible performance data to this customer will be about jobs performed for this customer.
- Cite generally accepted industry data for perspective or when actual performance data is not available.

Selling Environment Adaptations	
NG	The above guidelines apply to the NG sector.
RG	Scale the level of detail to the size of the opportunity. While publicly available data might be limited, customers are often more willing to share information than you might expect. Inquire. You might be surprised what you discover.
B2B	The smaller the opportunity, the more likely the decision will hinge on personal relationships. Emphasize identifying personal relationships, as they often explain purchasing history in this sector. Decision makers in the B2B sector have considerable discretion to value long-term ownership costs and supplier relationships over minor pricing differences.
Primes	Compatible and familiar support infrastructures are often critical. Learning a new system, training staff, or adapting to new procedures can be costly and risky. Consider possible competition from within the prime's organization. Primes often own a competitive source and use vendor bids to obtain more competitive internal quotes. Alternatively, does the prime have existing contracts that could be extended or expanded at less direct or administrative cost?
TO	Limit competitor analysis to task orders under this master contract. Focus short term—on recent months, not recent years. Further limit your analysis to competitors who are preferred or acceptable. Focus on your competitors' capacity, capability, and availability of key personnel within the delivery window. Task orders often have short time frames, so consider designing-to-cost rather than requirements. Customers seldom have the time to seek additional funds.

Capture Plan Template

1-Presentation Model (with tailoring annotations)

Evaluate each potential competitor based on what the customer is likely to know or believe, not just what you think is true. Customer perceptions are paramount, even when wrong.

Complete competitor intelligence templates for each competitor.

EXTERNAL ANALYSIS

Competitor Intelligence – Competitor A

	1 Strengths	2 Weaknesses
Customer Perceptions	▪ ▪ ▪ ▪ ▪	▪ ▪ ▪ ▪ ▪

3 Customer Issues	4 Available Solution	5 Discriminator	6 Gap

3 B 4 D 5 U

Copyright Shipley Associates 8

1 Strengths

- List known strengths relevant to this opportunity.
- List customer-perceived strengths, even if not real.

2 Weaknesses

- List known weaknesses relevant to this opportunity.
- List customer-perceived weaknesses, even if not real.

3 Customer Issues

- Use the hot button issues listed on the *Customer Issues and Hot Buttons* page.
- Use the same hot button list for all competitors.

4 Available Solution

- List the probable solution available from this competitor to satisfy each hot button.

5 Discriminator

- List potential discriminator(s). Discriminators are features that: (1) Differ from at least one of the features of competitors' solutions, and (2) Are linked to this customer issue.

6 Gap

- List the difference between the requirement and available solution.
- Gaps can be positive or negative. Note that both positive and negative gaps usually have compensating consequences. For example, a solution that does not meet the capability requirement (negative gap) might cost less (positive gap).

Selling Environment Adaptations	
NG	Consider adding a Requirements column. While complex, some practitioners prefer to go directly to the *Integrated Solution Worksheet.*
RG	Scale the granularity and number of issues to the size of the opportunity. If the opportunity warrants pursuit, then this particular page and the inherent analysis are vital.
B2B	When time is short, eliminate Strengths and Weaknesses. Focus on the bottom portion of the page because commercial purchases often play out too rapidly for you to significantly influence customer perceptions.
Primes	Assuming you have prepared a short list of issues, apply the above B2B advice.
TO	As with the B2B and Primes advice, focus on the bottom portion of the page and the task(s) being bid. Emphasize the issues of the key decision maker and influencers, melded with the evaluation criteria.

Apply the same approach to analyze your position as applied to analyzing your competitors. Guard against bias by seeking input from customer coaches, former employees, industry veterans, and people from your organization.

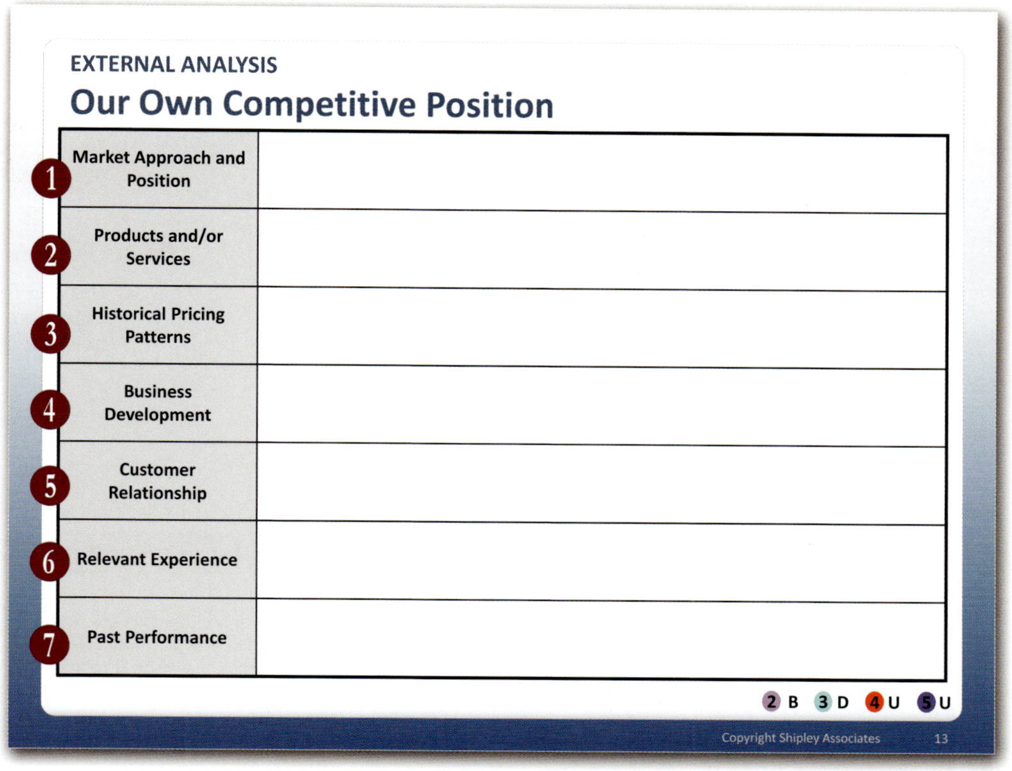

1 Market Approach and Position

- Indicate your focus by job size, customer, and geography.
- Indicate your position as leader, follower, new entrant, specialty provider, etc.
- Indicate your commitment, importance of this job to your success, and linked or ongoing potential. What is the impact of a loss or no-bid?
- Note how aggressively and flexibly you have pursued similar opportunities.

2 Products and/or Services

- List services, products, and the source that comprise your base offering.
- List adaptations needed to make them compliant.
- Note if subcontractors or teaming partners are required or probable.

3 Historical Pricing Patterns

- Note if your prices are perceived to be high or low. Is that perception accurate?
- Note if you prefer or avoid specific contract vehicles, such as fixed price, cost-plus, performance-based, etc.

4 Business Development

- List your typical marketing messages, themes, positions, and claimed differentiators.
- Note who is involved by name. Note the number, type, and experience of management and support staff.
- Note the relative power of management versus individual field sales or account managers.
- If you use contract site representatives, note the role and influence of the site representatives versus direct employees.
- Note if you rely on individual or team selling.
- If you team, note how you plan to integrate teaming partners in selling, strategy development, solution development, and program management. List preferred teaming partners by name or type.

❺ Customer Relationship

- Does this customer know your organization, division, and management team well? Is the perception positive, neutral, or negative?
- List any personal links or history among individuals in your organization and the customer organization. Have these individuals worked for common organizations or on common projects? Are they linked through professional organizations or common interests?

❻ Relevant Experience

- List relevant experience. Relevance might be via common issues, services, people, or products.

❼ Past Performance

- Link past performance to prior relevant experience examples, if available. Note how you performed on similar work.

Selling Environment Adaptations	
NG	The above guidelines apply to the NG sector.
RG	Scale the level of detail to the size of the opportunity.
B2B	The smaller the opportunity, the more likely the decision will hinge on personal relationships. Emphasize identifying personal relationships, as they often explain purchasing history in this sector. Decision makers in the B2B sector have more discretion to value long-term ownership costs over minor pricing differences. The common wisdom is: *Friends buy from friends.*
Primes	Compatible, familiar, support infrastructures are often critical. Learning a new system, training staff, or adapting to new procedures can be costly and risky. Consider possible competition from within the prime's organization. Primes often own a competitive source, and use vendor bids to obtain more competitive internal quotes. Alternatively, does the prime have existing contracts that could be extended or expanded at less direct or administrative cost?
TO	Limit analysis to task orders you have had under this master contract. Focus short term, on recent months, not recent years. Focus on your capacity, capability, and availability of key personnel within the delivery window. Task orders often have short time frames, so consider designing to cost rather than requirements. Customers seldom have the time to seek additional funds.

Base evaluation of your competitive position on customer perceptions rather than internal assumptions or beliefs. When selling, the customer's perceptions are paramount, even if the customer is wrong.

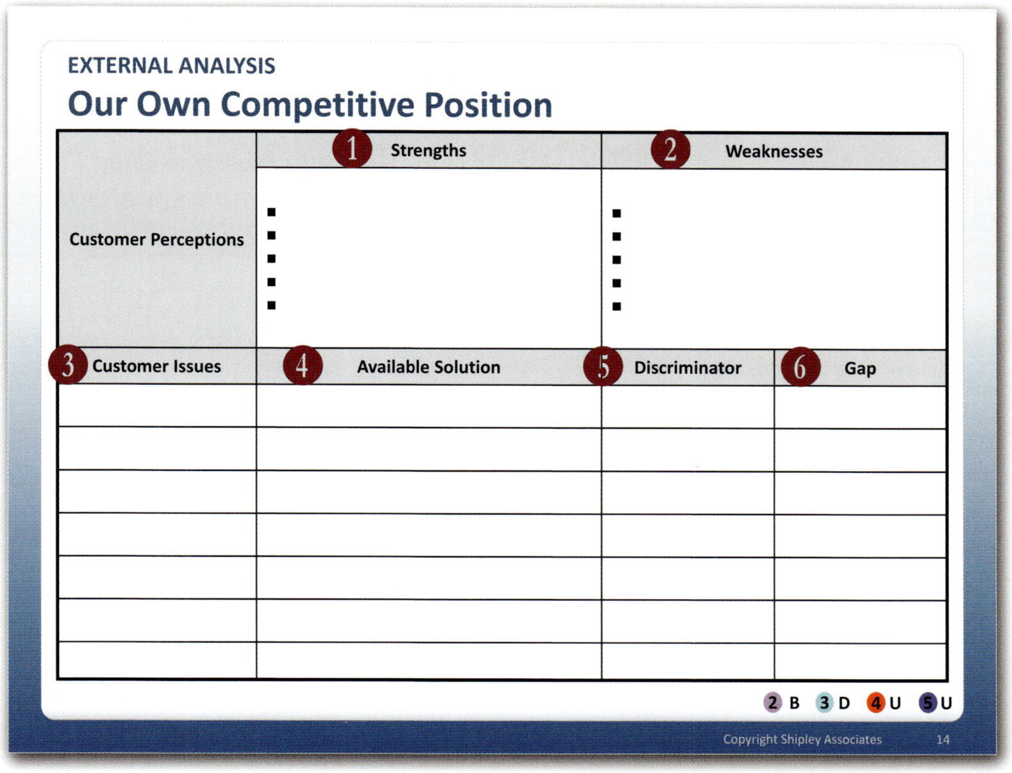

1 Strengths

- List your real strengths relevant to this opportunity.
- List customer-perceived strengths, even if not real.

2 Weaknesses

- List your known weaknesses relevant to this opportunity.
- List customer-perceived weaknesses, even if not real.

3 Customer Issues

- Use the same list as was used when analyzing competitors.

4 Available Solution

- List your probable solution for each hot button issue.

5 Discriminator

- List potential discriminator(s). Discriminators are features that: (1) Differ from at least one of the competitor's solutions, and (2) Are linked to this customer issue.

6 Gap

- List the difference between the requirement and your available solution.
- Gaps can be positive or negative. Positive and negative gaps usually have compensating consequences.

Selling Environment Adaptations	
NG	Consider adding a *Requirements* column. While complex, some practitioners prefer to go directly to the *Integrated Solution Worksheet*.
RG	Scale the granularity and number of issues to the size of the opportunity. If the opportunity warrants pursuit, then this particular page and the inherent analysis are vital.
B2B	When time is short, eliminate Strengths and Weaknesses. Focus on the bottom portion of the page.
Primes	Assuming you have prepared a short list of issues, apply the above B2B advice.
TO	As with the B2B and Primes sector advice, focus on the bottom portion of the page and the task(s) being bid. Emphasize the issues of the key decision maker and influencers, melded with the evaluation criteria.

Complete a Bidder Comparison Chart based on the prior competitive analysis. Complete this comparison for every opportunity, regardless of size.

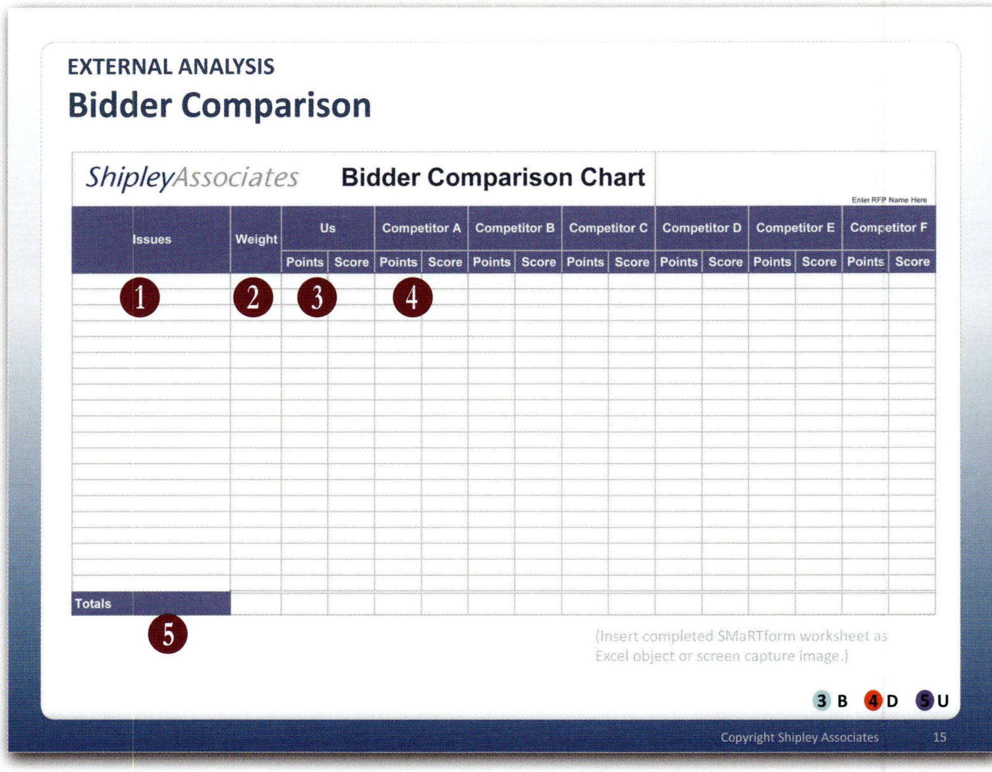

1 Issues

- Use the same list of issues from prior competitive analysis.
- Update your analysis regularly.
- List all issues before moving to subsequent columns.

2 Weight

- Establish weights based on customer-perceived relative importance.
- Consider the following weighting scheme: 1 = needed; 2 = important; 3 = most important. Other scales are acceptable if you have the knowledge to satisfactorily differentiate importance of issues to the customer.

3 Points

- Rank your organization and each competitor on a consistent scale.
- Various weights are acceptable, such as the evaluation criteria weights when available.
- Here is a potential scale to rank your position and competitors' positions:
  - 1–2 = Problem area. Must be improved. Grounds for elimination.
  - 3–4 = Needs improvement. Cause for concern. Negative trend.
  - 5–6 = Average. Adequate. O.K. if customer is seeking marginally compliant solution.
  - 7–8 = Better than average. Strong performance.
  - 9–10 = Substantially exceeds requirements or expectations.

4 Score

- Multiply the weight by the points for the issue score.

5 Totals

- Total the columns.
- Compare the relative totals. Do they make sense? If not, are you missing an issue? Is the issue weighting too high or too low?
- Avoid changing weights and rankings to get the desired result.
- Review with a knowledgeable, independent authority, if possible.

Selling Environment Adaptations	
NG	No adaptations are needed. Assign weights aligned with the evaluation criteria, forcing the total to 100. Then allocate available points.
RG	Adopt the B2B approach for smaller opportunities. Consider the NG advice for larger ones.
B2B	When time is short, go straight to the Bidder Comparison Chart and eliminate the prior competitive analysis. Limit the issues list.
Primes	If you've prepared a short list of issues, then the B2B advice applies.
TO	Due to the rapid response nature of task bids, adopt the abbreviated B2B approach.

Capture Plan Template

1-Presentation Model (with tailoring annotations)

This page summarizes your ongoing price-to-win analysis. The overall approach is to bound the winning price into a successively narrower range.

See PRICING TO WIN.

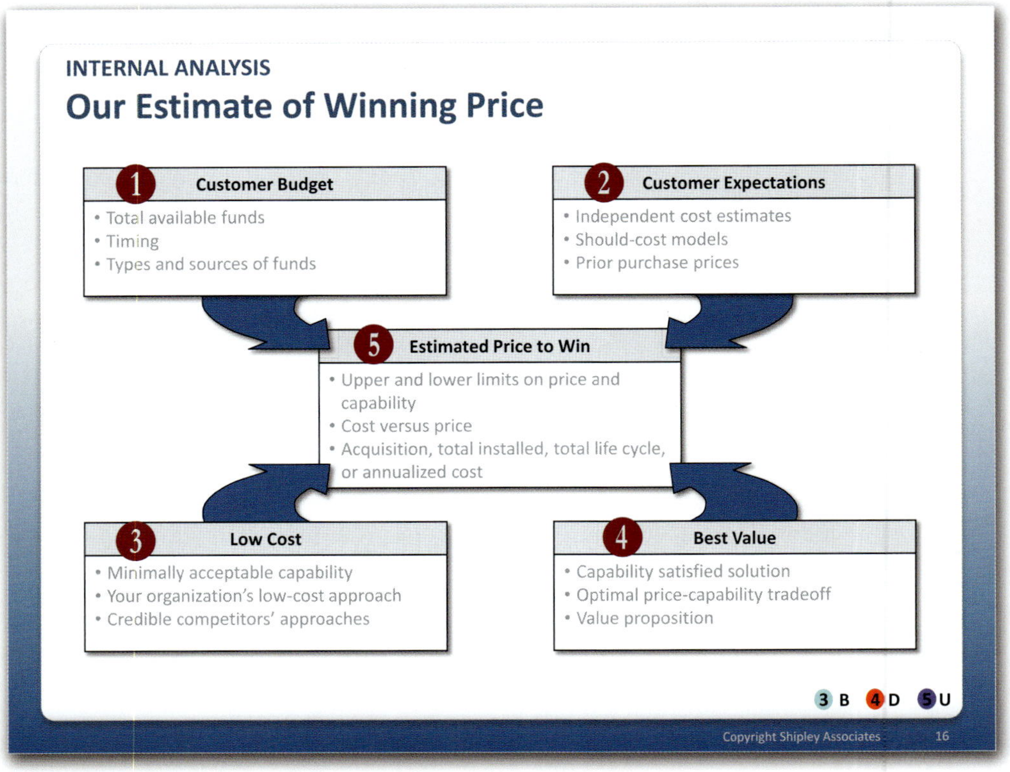

❶ Customer Budget

- Summarize the customer's available budget for the purchase, not total budget for the project. The purchase budget excludes acquisition and internal implementation costs.
- Consider budget timing and cash flow.
- Note the type and source of funds, when relevant (capital investment, operational, budgeted, requested in future budgets).

❷ Customer Expectations

- Consider independent cost estimates by the customer or consultants.
- Apply should-cost or parametric pricing models.
- Determine prior purchase prices by this customer for similar products or services.

❸ Low Cost

- Identify and price the minimally acceptable capability.
- Determine the lowest cost approach for your organization.
- Consider how competitors could achieve lower prices.

❹ Best Value

- Conduct a price-capability trade-off to estimate the customer's willingness to pay more for additional capability. A customer will sometimes pay a margin above a minimum-capability solution's price, but usually no more than 10–15 percent.
- Create a value proposition tailored to the customer's needs. Include a quantified business benefit, timing, and costs of the benefits, a calculated payback period, and methods for measuring results.

❺ Estimated Price to Win

- Identify and price the capability-satisfied solution.
- List the customer's probable upper and lower price limits at desired, specified, acceptable, and minimum capability levels. What price is too low to be credible or too high to be affordable?
- Note whether the customer has the flexibility to accept solutions below the specified capability.
- Does the customer care about your perceived margins and underlying cost, or only total price?
- Does the price-to-win need to consider costs/prices in special ways to satisfy the customer, such as total installed, lifecycle, or annualized costs/prices?

Selling Environment Adaptations	
NG	National government price-to-win considerations can probably be summarized in this simple form. Analysis will be complex. Expect to add additional information and tables or spreadsheets.
RG	Adaptations might be simplifications of the NG process. Underlying costs tend to be easier to analyze due to the more commercial nature of the services and products involved. Regional governments often fund acquisitions from future generated revenues. For example, a reservations system to use public facilities might be paid for by a portion of user fees. Here, net revenues, guaranteed minimum revenue streams, and risk sharing might be more important than acquisition price.
B2B	Ideally, a seller can collaborate with the customer to estimate the costs of alternative solutions. B2B customers are more likely to quantitatively value the benefits of solutions. As with some RG acquisitions, B2B buyers are more likely to consider discounted future revenue streams as important as acquisition costs.
Primes	Pricing targets are often well-defined in this sector. If primes are competing to win, or have already won, they have assumed a price. Once the prime wins, they often pressure subcontractors to cut their prices to improve the prime's margins.
TO	Many task orders have defined pricing, terms, and warranties or guarantees established in the master contract. Typical pricing variables include labor category, labor quantity, and perhaps quality/capability level. Adapt the summary blocks to reflect relevant parameters.

Capture Plan Template

1-Presentation Model (with tailoring annotations)

Extend the Bidder Comparison Chart (BCC) into the Integrated Solution Worksheet (ISW) to outline the parameters of your technical and management solution. Then define the strategy and tactics needed to position your solution as the preferred solution. The BCC and ISW are the two most important analysis tools in the capture plan.

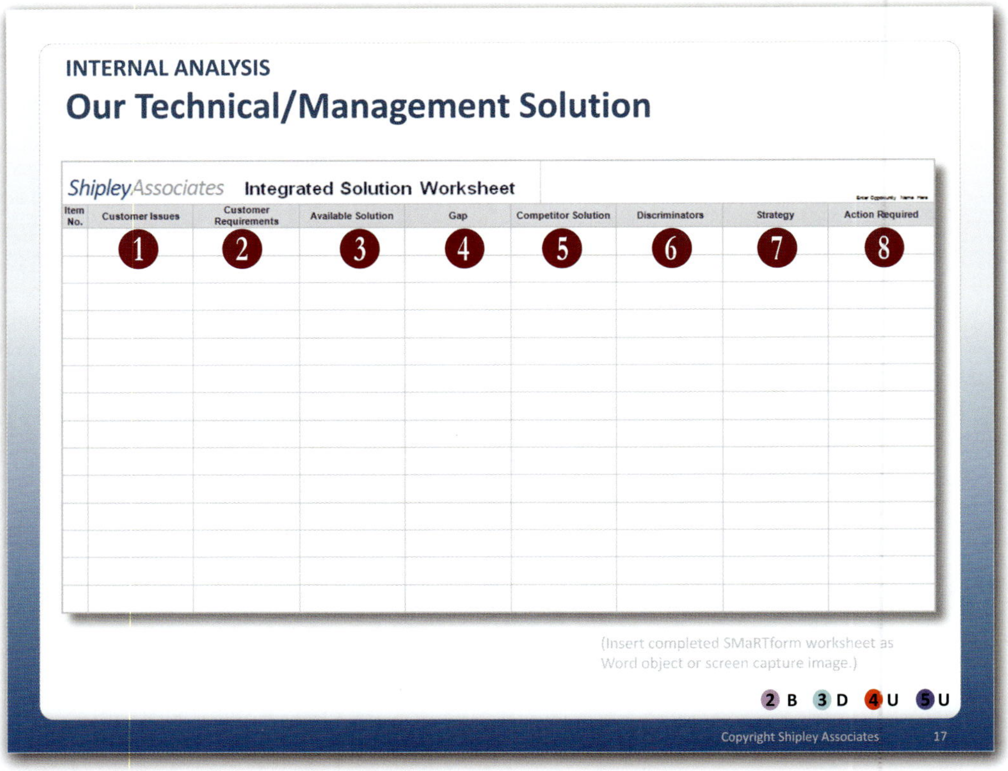

❶ Customer Issues

- Transfer the issues listed on the BCC.

❷ Customer Requirements

- List known or probable requirements linked to customer issues.
- If you see issues without corresponding requirements, consider what might be required.
- If you see requirements without corresponding issues, consider:
  - Have you missed potential issues?
  - Have you erroneously persuaded yourself that something you hope to sell is needed or wanted by this customer? Do you have a solution in search of a customer?

❸ Available Solution

- List what you have available now.
- Update as you develop or refine your solution as requirements evolve.

❹ Gap

- Note the difference between what is required and your available solution, whether positive or negative. This gap becomes a potential discriminator.

❺ Competitor Solution

- List the best competitor's probable solution to each requirement.

❻ Discriminators

- List features of your solution that differ from the features of one or more of the competitors' solutions.
- The more important the issue and the greater the difference, the more important the discriminator.

❼ Strategy

- List the potential positions that you might take to:
  - Emphasize your strengths.
  - Mitigate your weaknesses.
  - Neutralize competitors' strengths.
  - Highlight competitors' weaknesses.

8 Action Required

- List potential tactical actions that help persuade the customer to accept your strategy or position.
- Because space is limited, expand these actions later when preparing detailed strategy implementation action plans.
- Listing a potential tactic does not commit you to take the action. Implement only those actions that will have the greatest impact within the parameters of your resources, schedule, and the rules of the competition.

Selling Environment Adaptations	
NG	The primary adaptations in this selling environment are to expand the strategy and tactics into detailed action plans.
RG	Action plans are often more limited due to more limited resources, but you have greater freedom to implement creative actions.
B2B	Actions are seldom limited by the rules of engagement. Instead, gaining the support of potential capture team members and guiding their actions might prove more challenging.
Primes	Issues and requirements are usually narrowly defined, so your strategy and tactical options are limited. Persuading the prime to add you to the collaborative solution team is often the most effective option.
TO	Short-response task orders offer limited time for positioning and tactical action. Focus on understanding the underlying task issues, clarifying the requirements, and then repeatedly linking features of your solution to those issues. Repeatedly demonstrating your understanding of the underlying issues is often the primary discriminator.

Specify the composition of your team. Defined broadly, the team might comprise multiple divisions or departments of the same organization, a joint-venture arrangement, or a prime, subcontractors, and various vendors. Some teams include elements of the customer's organization on an ongoing basis or in transition, as in an outsourcing arrangement where the winner takes over an existing function, personnel, and facilities.

INTERNAL ANALYSIS

Teaming and Subcontracting

1 Partner	2 Role and Work Share	3 Rationale

3 B 4 D 5 U

Copyright Shipley Associates 18

Note: Work share negotiations are sensitive, often delayed, and frequently lead to conflicts and pricing errors (both over- and under-pricing). Primes seldom want agreed work shares, while subcontractors seek written contractual commitments.

1 Partner

- List the organization and point of contact.

2 Role and Work Share

- List their role and agreed work share, if any.

3 Rationale

- Indicate why each teaming partner was selected from the prime's perspective. Possible rationales include:
  - Solicitation requirement.
  - Gap in your solution (technical, price, support advantage).
  - Meeting small, minority, or disadvantaged business contracting goals.
  - Unique technical or management skills.
  - Positive position with the customer.
  - Currently on incumbent's team.
  - Recommended or requested by the customer.
  - Eliminate them from competitors' teams.
- Conversely, indicate why the teaming partners either selected or agreed to team with the prime. Use these justifications to position your team as the preferred team.

Selling Environment Adaptations	
NG	No adaptation required. Major partners should play a major role in the capture effort. Customers sense when they encounter a team in name only.
RG	Include if the subcontractor plays a major, discriminating role.
B2B	Teaming is not as common in B2B selling as it is in government selling. Do not overlook partners and major subcontractors' discriminators, such as just-in-time delivery, surge capability, and access to key technologies.
Primes	Seek exclusivity and a defined minimum work share as a reward. Demonstrate competence by collaboratively contributing to the capture, solution development, and proposal preparation activities.
TO	If teams are involved in task orders, clarify each organization's and individual's roles. Role and task omissions increase risk. Role and task overlaps increase cost estimates, making you less competitive.

Strategy statements in a capture plan comprise two elements:

1. Your desired position: your goal, how you want to be perceived by the customer.
2. The tactical actions that you will take to improve your position with the customer.

When fully defined in action plans, the tactical actions specify who takes the actions and when they will be taken.

Later, when you begin planning your proposal, you will convert capture strategy statements into proposal strategy statements. The goals will be the same, but the tactical implementation will be about things written or displayed in a verbal presentation; thus, persuading the customer to accept your position. *See* Strategy.

The first two strategy-development pages are specific to your strengths and weaknesses. The second two reflect competitors' strengths and weaknesses. Often they overlap, as emphasizing your strength often simultaneously highlights a competitor's weakness.

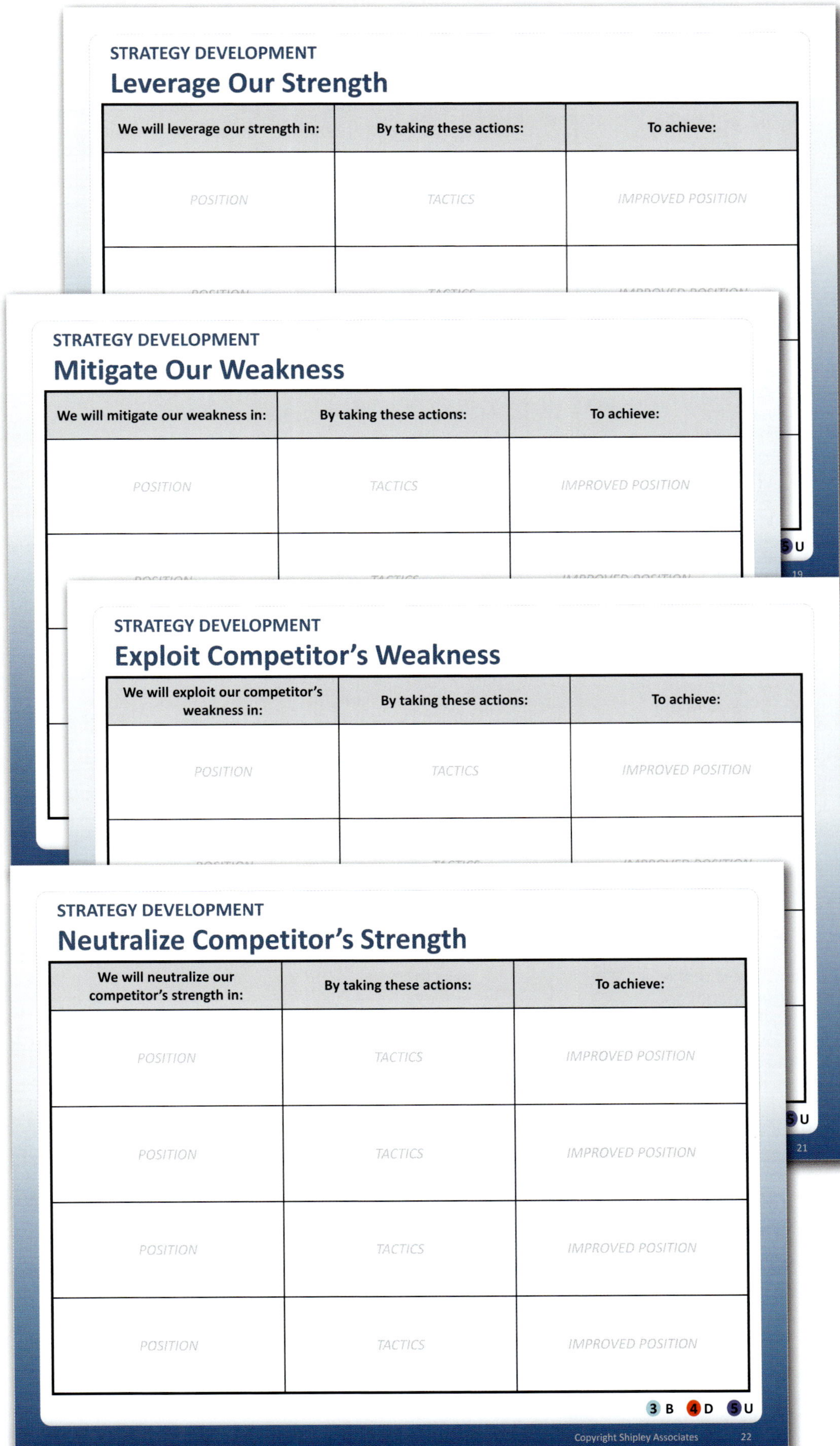

Capture Plan Template

1-Presentation Model (with tailoring annotations)

The analysis and planning process documented in a capture plan is useless until action is taken. Assigning positioning actions, assessing outcomes, and then adapting subsequent tasks based upon results are the essential role of the capture manager.

One key difference between typical roles of a capture manager and sales professional is that a capture manager coordinates the positioning activities of a large capture team, often including senior management personnel. Most sales professionals focus primarily on individual selling tasks, with less emphasis on managing others to participate in the positioning or selling.

Action plans specify activities to be performed, objectives to be met, assigned personnel, deadlines, locations, costs, and status. Contingencies should be anticipated, and risks must be characterized and mitigated. Adjust the format and content of action plans to circumstances of the opportunity and task management practices of the organization. Use existing scheduling and task management tools to manage capture activities, which are really just important organizational projects.

The sample action plans shown include representative entries. The level of detail shown is usually adequate for management review. Capture team members usually need more detailed information to successfully meet task objectives.

ACTION PLANS

Customer Contact Plan

Contact Objective	Who	When	Where	Cost	Status/ Comments
Initial capability briefing to customer's chief engineer	*M. Johnson*	*April 1, 20XX*	*DOT Test Laboratory*	*$1,800 Travel*	*Delayed till May 15*

ACTION PLANS

Intelligence Collection Plan

Intelligence Objective	Who	Need Date	How	Cost	Status/ Comments
Determine funding level for next FY budget	*DC Staff*	*March 15, 20XX*	*Talk to congr. staff*	*None (OH)*	*On track*

ACTION PLANS

Our Contingency Plan

Event	Probability	Impact	Response	Status/ Comments
Preferred vendor will not team	*Low*	*Medium*	*Manufacture parts in-house*	*Pilot production completed*

ACTION PLANS

Solution Development Plan (if required)

Solution Element	Who	Need Date	Cost	Status/ Comments
Demonstrate 1GB/sec autonomous data transfer rate	*Dept. H1610*	*Sept. 15, 20XX*	*$75K (IR&D)*	*Auto-synch may delay*

3 B 4 D 5 U

Copyright Shipley Associates 26

Include attachments appropriate to your organization. These items might be physically attached or shown as electronic links to a secure website. If you prefer, incorporate them into the body of the capture plan. The list shown in the sample is illustrative but not exhaustive. In general, the largest opportunities will require the most additional information.

EXECUTION AND MONITORING

Capture Plan Attachments

- Capture team organization chart
- Schedule (if needed to augment action plans)
  - Kickoff meeting
  - Management reviews
  - Key milestones from action plans
- Budget (in required corporate format)
- Decision gate review template
- Business and win potential
- Resource plan
- Capture briefing template
- Draft executive summary of proposal

 28

The same capture plan information shown in presentation form in Model Document 1 can be maintained using a web-based collaboration tool, such as SharePoint. Common information from the Executive Summary slide is shown to illustrate the concept.

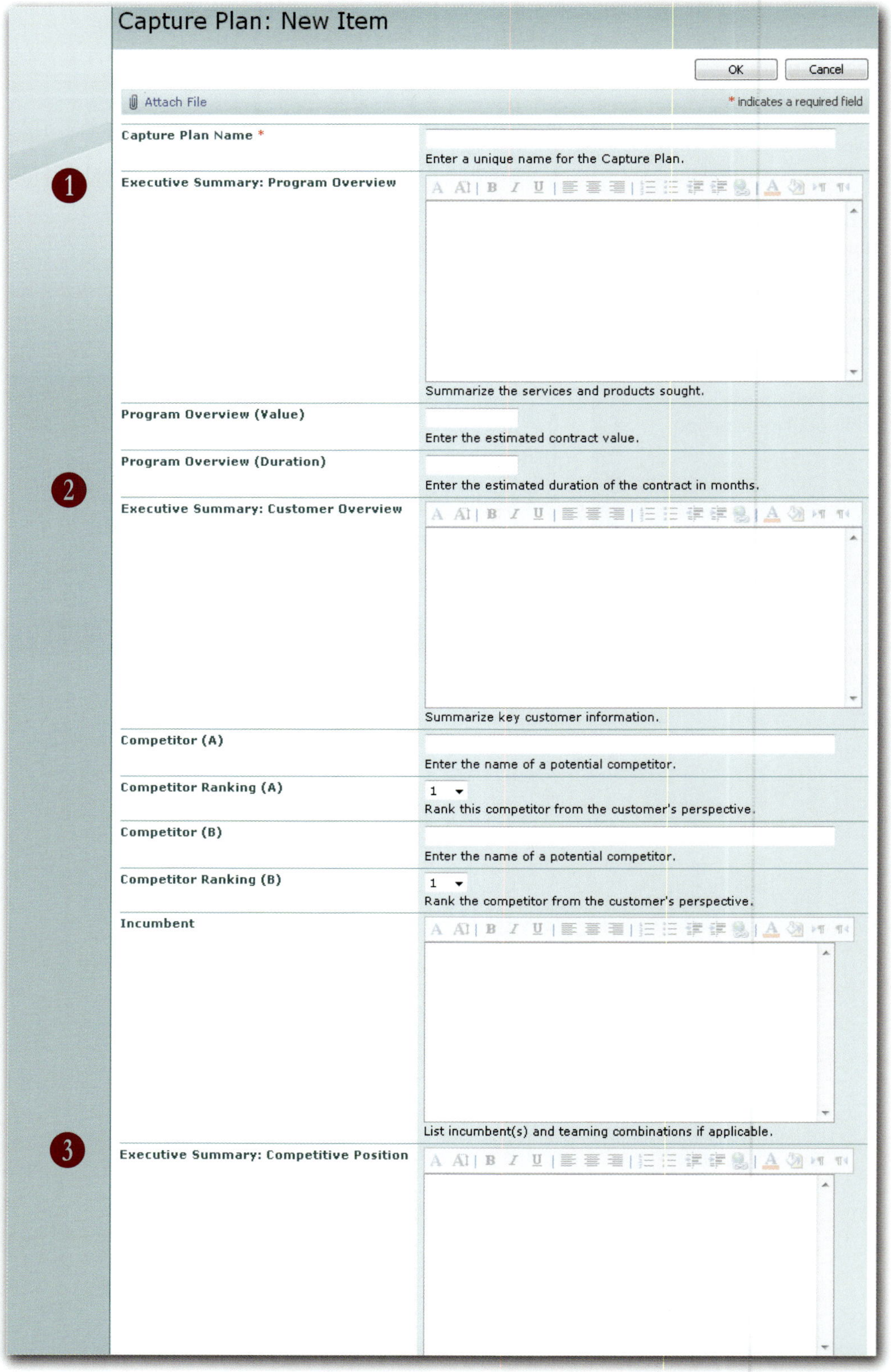

Capture Plan: New Item

OK Cancel

Attach File * indicates a required field

Capture Plan Name *
Enter a unique name for the Capture Plan.

Executive Summary: Program Overview
Summarize the services and products sought.

Program Overview (Value)
Enter the estimated contract value.

Program Overview (Duration)
Enter the estimated duration of the contract in months.

Executive Summary: Customer Overview
Summarize key customer information.

Competitor (A)
Enter the name of a potential competitor.

Competitor Ranking (A)
1
Rank this competitor from the customer's perspective.

Competitor (B)
Enter the name of a potential competitor.

Competitor Ranking (B)
1
Rank the competitor from the customer's perspective.

Incumbent
List incumbent(s) and teaming combinations if applicable.

Executive Summary: Competitive Position

1 Program Overview

- Summarize the services and products sought. Note the estimated contract value and duration.

2 Customer Overview

- Summarize key customer information.

3 Competitive Position Summary

- List and rank competitors from the customer's perspective.
- List incumbent(s) and teaming combinations, as applicable.
- Link rankings to the Bidder Comparison Chart.

Continued

❹ Summary of Your Solution

- Outline major solution elements.
- Indicate the potential or actual team, as appropriate.

❺ Capture Strategy

- List 3–5 overarching approaches planned to position your organization and solution as the preferred option.

❻ Status

- Summarize current capture efforts.
- Highlight near-term critical tasks, milestones, and required decisions.
- Update frequently.

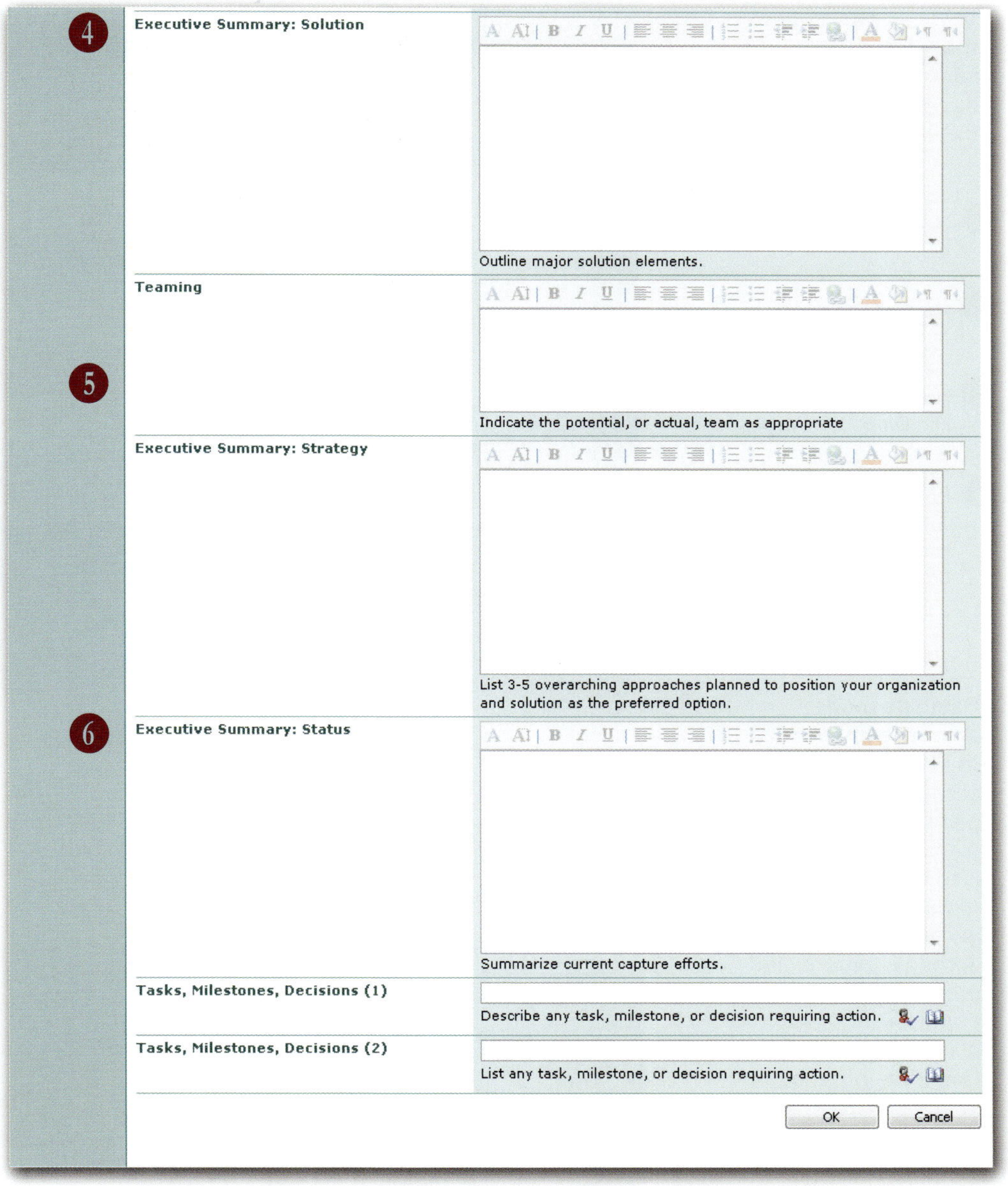

Capture Plan Template

3-Database Model (with web access)

These screen captures show common information sharing but do not illustrate the entire tool.

1. Hot button entered.
2. Hot button defined.
3. Hot button "Drag and Drop."
4. Hot button associated with individual in the customer organization.

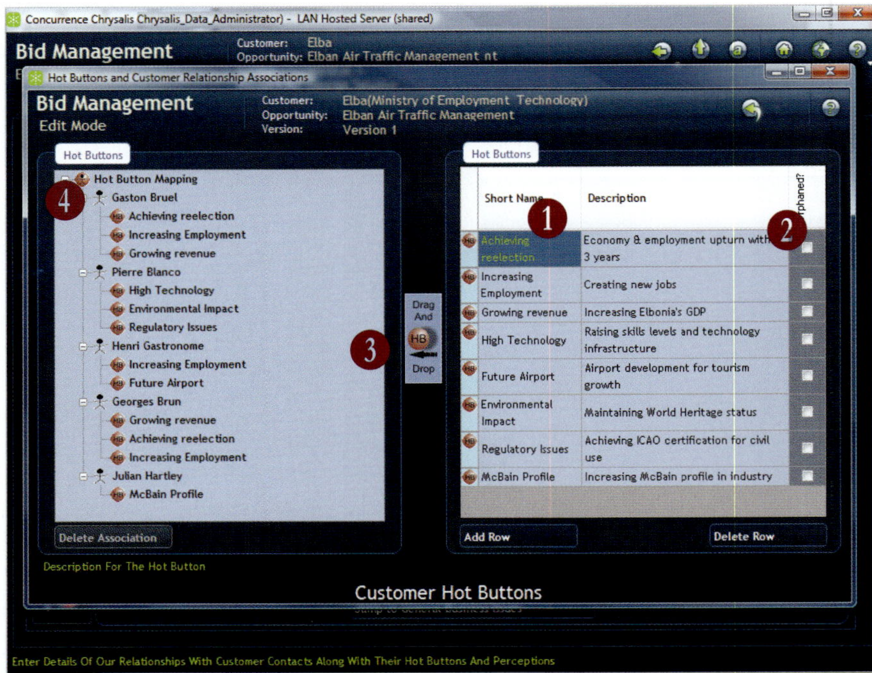

Database models automate information sharing among account plans, capture plans, and proposal plans. The objective is to reduce the time required and errors introduced when account, capture, and proposal managers populate subsequent plans from prior plans. Common information in one plan is instantly updated and shared in linked plans.

1. Account contacts selected as relevant to bid plan for an individual opportunity.
2. Information related to that contact is automatically transferred without re-entry.
3. Account profiles, account contacts, competitors, and competitor contacts can be selected, if relevant, and transferred into the bid plan.

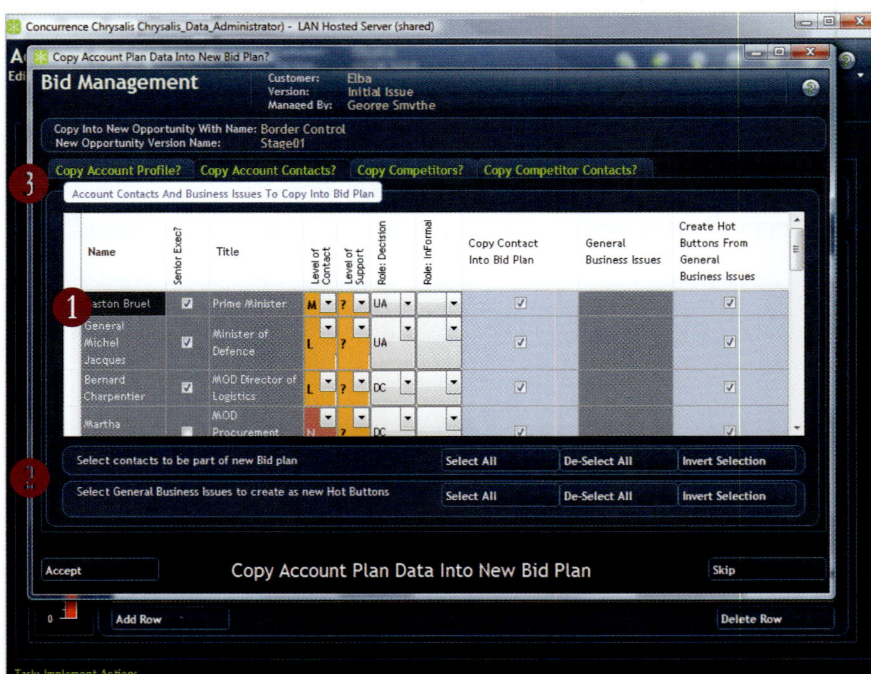

Written account plans can be populated, viewed, and printed. This excerpt shows the account plan customer contact and associated hot button data entered in the prior screen.

Summary Account Plan: Elba
Account Plan Version Initial Issue

concurrence CHRYSALIS

Account People

Summary:
Our contacts and our relationship with them

Key:
Level of Contact: N=None, L=Low, M=Medium, H=High
Level of Support: N=None, L=Low, M=Medium, H=High, ?=Unsure, X=Adversary
Formal Role: UA=Ultimate Authority, FI=Financial, LE=Legal, OP=Operations, AP=Administrative, TK=Technical, ?=Unsure, S=Sponsor, PS=Power Sponsor.

Key People In The Account, Their General Business Issues & Our Relationships

Name	Senior Exec?	Title	Level of Contact	Level of Support	Role: Decision	Role: Informal	General Business Issues	Influenced By	Team Member Assigned
Gaston Bruel	✔	Prime Minister	N	?	UA		Employment Maintaining Power Achieving re-election Past budget limitations Growing revenue Balance of Trade		
General Michel Jacques	✔	Minister of Defence	L	?	UA		Army bias Counter Terrorism MOD budget Equipment Obsolescence Capability Procurement	Bernard Charpentier, Brigadier Francois Galeon	Tony Birch
Bernard Charpentier	✔	MOD Director of Logistics	L	?	DC		Equipment obsolescence Past	Martha Hilbrand	Barry Boss

Report Generated by *Concurrence Chrysalis* 23/05/2010
Commercial-In-Confidence
Page 12

Written bid- or opportunity-specific capture plans can also be populated, viewed, and printed. This excerpt shows the transfer of relevant customer contact and associated hot button data from the account plan to the bid plan.

Opportunity:	Elban Air Traffic Management
Plan Version	Version 1
For Account:	Elba

concurrence CHRYSALIS

Customer People

Summary:
Our contacts and our relationship with them—relevant to this opportunity

Key:
Level of Contact: N=None, L=Low, M=Medium, H=High
Level of Support: N=None, L=Low, M=Medium, H=High, ?=Unsure, X=Adversary
Formal Role: UA=Ultimate Authority, FI=Financial, LE=Legal, OP=Operations, AP=Administrative, TK=Technical, ?=Unsure, S=Sponsor, PS=Power Sponsor.

Key People In The Account, and Our Relationships

Name	Senior Exec?	Title	Level of Contact	Level of Support	Role: Decision	Role: Informal	Perceived Strengths	Perceived Weaknesses	Hot Buttons
Gaston Bruel	✔	Prime Minister	N	?	UA				Achieving re-election Increasing Employment Growing revenue Environmental Impact
Pierre Blanco	✔	Minister of Employment & Technology	L	?	UA				Achieving re-election Increasing Employment Growing Revenue High Technology Regulatory Issues
Henri Gastronome	✔	Chairman EATS	N	M	DC				Increasing Employment Future Airport
Georges	✔	Minister of Defense	N	M	?				Achieving re-election

Report Generated by *Concurrence Chrysalis* 23/05/2010
Commercial-In-Confidence
Page 9

Capture Plan Template

4-Capture Template: Mid-Size Organization

This text-based template could also be used for presentations. The organization was a mid-sized organization engaged in international, non-government business.

ShipleyAssociates

CAPTURE PLAN

PROJECT SUMMARY			
Program Name Scope Customer Contract Type Start Date End Date		Financial Summary	
		Sources FY Breakdown Restrictions	

INTERNAL CONTACTS			
Role	Person Assigned	Telephone	Email
Primary Client Contact Project Leader/Manager Technical Specialist Financial Analyst Other			

TIMING AND MILESTONE DUE DATES					
	Planned	Actual		Planned	Actual
Pursuit Decision Strategy Review RFP Release Bid Validation Proposal Kickoff			Proposal Review Proposal Approval Proposal Submittal Proposal Presentation Contract Award		

© Shipley Associates. All Rights Reserved. Used by Permission

Page 1 of 8

ShipleyAssociates

CAPTURE PLAN

CUSTOMER INFORMATION		
Hot Buttons	•	
Major Concerns	•	
Other Relevant Issues	•	
Key Dates and/or Milestones	•	
Decision Process	•	
Role	Name	Special Considerations
Decision Maker Decision Maker Program Manager Contracting Officer Other		

© Shipley Associates. All Rights Reserved. Used by Permission

Page 2 of 8

ShipleyAssociates

CAPTURE PLAN

REQUIREMENTS ASSESSMENT	
Technical Issues	•
Management Issues	•
Cost/Price Issues	•
Personnel Issues	•
Contractual or Other Business Issues	•

ShipleyAssociates

CAPTURE PLAN

PROGRAM ASSESSMENT	
Customer Relationship	•
Strategic Fit / Relevance to Core Business	•
Technical Risks	•
Management and Business Risks	•
Other Factors Affecting Decision to Proceed	•

ShipleyAssociates

CAPTURE PLAN

COMPETITIVE ASSESSMENT, PART A			
	US	[Name Competitor A]	[Name Competitor A]
Probable Approach	•	•	•
Discrimina-tors	•	•	•
Strengths	•	•	•
Weaknesses	•	•	•

Page 5 of 8

ShipleyAssociates

CAPTURE PLAN

COMPETITIVE ASSESSMENT, PART B				
	Customer Hot Buttons and Buying Criteria	US	[Competitor]	[Competitor]
Hot Buttons				
Technical				
Manage-ment				
Cost / Price				
Other				

Page 6 of 8

ShipleyAssociates

CAPTURE PLAN

STRATEGY PLAN	
Technical Strategy	•
Management Strategy	•
Cost/Price Strategy	•
Other Strategy	•

Strategy Action Item	Person Assigned	Due Date

ShipleyAssociates

CAPTURE PLAN

CLIENT DEVELOPMENT PLAN			
Contact/Objective	Person(s) Assigned	Date	Targeted Outcome(s)

SOLUTION DEVELOPMENT PLAN			
Contact/Objective	Person(s) Assigned	Date	Targeted Outcome(s)

Capture Plan/Proposal Management Plan Template

5-Capture & Proposal Planner for B2B Organizations

This model template combines typical capture planning activities on its pages 1-3, with proposal planning and writing activities on pages 4-9. Content developed in one section is used in subsequent sections.

This template was built for B2B organizations that prepare proposals on 5- to 10-day schedules, using relatively small proposal teams of one to five individuals.

The capture portion is focused on the first three pages; the remainder is designed to align capture planning information with the proposal. This template is used in Shipley's *Winning Proposal Strategies* workshop.

1. Identify Decision Makers, Influencers, and Their Issues

Complete the following:

Date: ________ Account Executive: ________
Prospect: ________ Division: ________
Organization: ________

Opportunity: (Briefly describe the opportunity and need)

Role	Name	Position	Power	Issue	Importance	Power Rating
Decision Maker						
Influencer						
Influencer						
Influencer						
Influencer						

1 ShipleyAssociates

2. Build a Bidder Comparison Matrix

a. List the key client issues from the prior template in column 1. Consolidate common issues.

b. Assume you have identified 100 percent of the client's issues. In column 2, assign a weight to each **as you think the client would**. All weights must total 100.

c. In column 3, jot down the rating the clients would give you today out of the total available points. If 20 points were available, how many would you be given?

d. Add a column for each additional competitor. If you have numerous competitors, consider grouping them into types, then rate the group.

e. Total the columns. Do the numbers make sense? Where are your assumptions weak? Revise until you are satisfied.

f. In the last column, note the positive or negative discriminator that is the primary reason for the competitor's rating.

Bidder Comparison Matrix

Issues (a)	Client's Weight (b)	Us (c)	Competitor A (d)	Discriminator (f)
Total	**100**			

2 ShipleyAssociates

3. Draft Sales Strategy Statements

Effective proposal strategy statements indicate what you will do and how you will implement it in your proposal. Draft a sales strategy statement for each issue in the Bidder Comparison Matrix. Incorporate the discriminator associated with each issue in your strategy statement.

#	Issue	Strategy Statement	
		What We will	By • • •
#	Issue	Strategy Statement	
		What We will	By • • •
#	Issue	Strategy Statement	
		What We will	By • • •
#	Issue	Strategy Statement	
		What We will	By • • •
#	Issue	Strategy Statement	
		What We will	By • • •

3 ShipleyAssociates

Planning the Proposal

1. Allocate Your Time

While small proposals prepared by a single person usually do not require a detailed schedule, you do need to allocate your time efficiently. Considering the guidelines shown, set the date and hour for each milestone.

Planning	Preparing	Amending
10 to 25%	55 to 75%	10 to 20%

Date & Time — Date & Time — Date & Time — Date & Time

2. Define Your Baseline Solution

3. Define Your Price-to-Win

Note your best estimate. Include price breakdowns if applicable.

4 ShipleyAssociates

Capture Plan/Proposal Management Plan Template

5-Capture & Proposal Planner for B2B Organizations

Planning the Proposal

4. Develop a Proposal Outline, then the Requirements Checklist *(Exercise)*

#	Section Title	Compliance Requirement

5 ShipleyAssociates

Planning the Proposal

5. Extend Sales Strategy into Proposal Strategy

Effective proposal strategy statements indicate what you will say or do in your proposal to support your sales strategy. Paste your sales strategy statements into the first two columns and then list what you will do in your proposal to support that strategy. Allocate each strategy statement to every applicable section, noting the section number in the last column. Add duplicate pages if necessary.

#	Issue	Sales Strategy Statement		Proposal Strategy Statements	Proposal Section #
		What	By	By	

6 ShipleyAssociates

Planning the Proposal

6. Design Your Proposal—Develop a Style Sheet

Select a style that will appeal to your client and that can be produced with your current systems. Consider the different styles offered below.

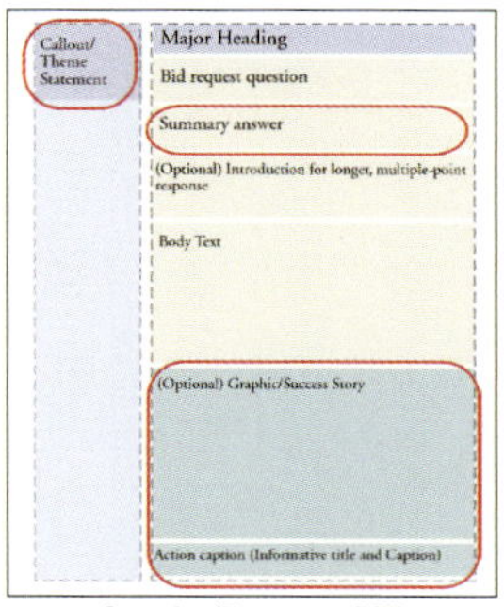

Question/Response RFP

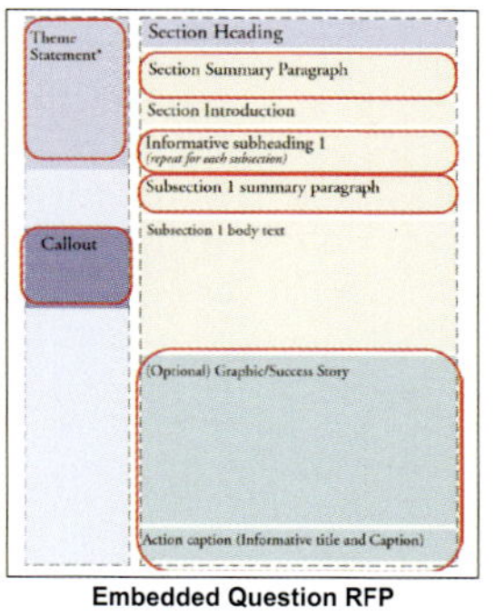

Embedded Question RFP

7 ShipleyAssociates

Writing the Proposal

Implement Your Proposal Strategy

Implement your proposal strategy in headings, themes, visuals, captions, and summaries.

Headings. Use the exact heading suggested by your client in the bid request. If no heading is suggested, draft **informative headings**, similar to a newspaper headline. Draft the headings for your section. (See "Headings," *Proposal Guide*, pp. 63-66.)

Themes. Themes succinctly express the point you want the reader to remember. The best themes **link features and benefits** in a single, short sentence. Long themes usually make better section summaries. Draft a theme statement for your proposal section. (See "Theme Statements," *Proposal Guide*, pp. 209-214.)

Visuals and Action Captions. Every visual should have an action caption that clearly makes a point without forcing the reader to read proposal text. We **recommend two-part captions**. Part 1, the **informative title**, identifies the visual and interests the reader in the caption. Part 2, the action caption, expresses the point(s) you want the reader to understand. Like themes, good action captions link features and benefits. Unlike themes, good action captions can comprise several sentences. Draft a two-part caption. (See "Captions," *Proposal Guide*, pp. 1-5.)

Informative Title: __________

Action Caption: __________

8 ShipleyAssociates

Writing the Proposal

Implement Your Proposal Strategy (continued)

Section Summaries. Draft a one or two-paragraph section summary for each major section. (See workbook, p. Prepare-11.)

Section Introductions. Draft a short introduction, preview, or roadmap for each major section. Introductions list the topics to be covered in order. (See workbook, p. Prepare-11.)

What's Next?

Congratulations! You have completed the hardest part of writing a proposal. We suggest you keep the following steps in mind as you complete your proposal:

1. Review your draft and then ask one of your peers to review it. Use the following checklist. Ask them to suggest ways that you can improve your proposal, then revise as needed.
2. Red Team the proposal when possible. Red Team members should be familiar with the client and the client's requirements. Consider using the *Proposal Assessment Worksheet*.
3. Incorporate valid Red Team recommendations. Complete a final detailed edit. Print, package appropriately, and submit. Present your proposal personally when possible.

9 ShipleyAssociates

1 Attention line targets a group of individuals.

2 The informative subject heading begins with a benefit to entice the reader.

See Features, Advantages, and Benefits; Headings; Organization, *and* Theme Statements, ***Proposal Guide.***

3 Opens with a potential issue or pain to gain interest, then states the benefit the seller hopes to deliver. Identifies the writer and requests a defined but limited meeting.

See Sales Letters.

4 Indicates the writer's basis for the customer's issues without being arrogant.

See Customer Focus, ***Proposal Guide.***

5 Bullet lists of potential benefits for emphasis while previewing the organization of the rest of the letter.

See Lists *and* Organization, ***Proposal Guide.***

6 Headings precisely reflect the previewed topics and are bold for increased emphasis.

See Lists *and* Organization, ***Proposal Guide.***

7 Summarizes the opening issue and requests the meeting.

See Organization, ***Proposal Guide,*** *and* Sales Letters.

8 Vividly describes the requested meeting and links it to the benefits.

See Sales Letters.

9 Marketing research suggests 95 out of 100 people read a *P.S.* first. The *P.S.* is read when other parts are skipped. Proactively states the next step in the same, precise tone used to visualize the requested meeting.

CPAs-R-Us   1040 A Street, Centerville UT 84010   801.333.7000
www.cpas-r-us.com

8 May 15, 20XX

1 Attention: Executive Committee (Joe Best, Walt Rosen, Kevin Davidson)

ACME Corporation
P. O. Box 30
Fort Worth, TX 76137

2 **Subject: Save Taxes with Tailored Solutions from CPAs-R-Us**

3 Organizations and individuals often pay unnecessary taxes. As one of the owners of CPAs-R-Us, I am writing to you to determine who is the most appropriate person in ACME to meet with me for 45 minutes on January 11 or 12 when I am in Fort Worth. By tailoring your tax planning, both ACME and your executives can gain the most favorable tax posture and ensure that you pay only the tax required by law.

4 If your organization is like many others that we advise, you could significantly reduce the annual tax bill of both your organization and senior executives with tax planning assistance from CPAs-R-Us:

5
- Save taxes through proper planning
- Enhance executive income with individually tailored tax planning
- Save time and cost with tailored international, national, and local tax solutions

Save taxes through proper planning

You can minimize international, federal and local taxes on business transactions with CPAs-R-Us's continuous tax planning. You get regular advice for maximizing credit (research activity and other areas), anticipating problems, and planning for opportunities rather than just reacting to past events.

As you expand, you'll need the timely, efficient tax planning we can give you as a result of our size and extensive practical experience with a large clientele.

6 **Enhance executive income with individually tailored tax planning**

Your executives can enhance their income and benefits with a tailored program to help them build capital through income tax savings, while Acme benefits from favorable funding arrangements and improved executive retention.

Save time and cost with tailored international, national, and local tax solutions

You'll benefit from our frequent contact with national and district IRS offices as we obtain early answers to tax questions and rulings on tax aspects of proposed transactions. You'll avoid tax controversy and cut time and costs because of our expertise in resolving tax disputes efficiently and informally.

7 If you feel you might be spending more on taxes than required, we should meet. I won't waste your time, we won't discuss the tax code, and you will not be subjected to "sales tactics."

8 What you will experience is a direct, concise presentation that may open up new opportunities for ACME and ACME executives to minimize cost, improve cash flow, and enhance your executive's personal income.

Sincerely,

G.R. Eyeshade

G.R. Eyeshade, CPA
800-333-3333

9 P.S. I will personally follow up this letter with a phone call on Friday, January 5, between 3:00 and 5:00 p.m. Please let your executive assistant know your answer so I may schedule the meeting when I call if appropriate.

Sales prospecting letters are usually designed to persuade the customer to agree to hear more or take minor action. The more action requested of the customer, the less likely the letter will be successful. Effective sales letters must persuade without offending. The *pitch* must be positive, informative, sincere, factual, and credible. This letter opens and closes with the pitch. The features of the seller's offer in the middle are emphasized by boldface headings.

Sales Letters

7-Follow-up to a Phone Call

1 The informative subject line begins with a signal word, *Invitation*, that signals the writer's objective, then states *what* and *why*. The *why* is an anticipated benefit to the customer.

2 Capitalizing only the first word in a title is an acceptable and increasingly common practice. Select a style and use it consistently in the same document.

See Headings, ***Proposal Guide.***

3 The short setup refers to and summarizes a previous conversation.

See Sales Letters.

4 The customer's issues are stated and ownership is explicit.

See Customer Focus, ***Proposal Guide.***

5 Both subheadings mirror the issues in the introduction.

See Sales Letters.

6 Note how most paragraphs begin by referring to the customer, improving the overall customer focus of the letter. Benefits are stated before features.

See Customer Focus *and* Features, Advantages, and Benefits, ***Proposal Guide.***

7 The seller proactively sets a follow-up time, justifies the timing as being in the best interest of the customer, and restates potential benefits.

February 16, 20XX

Tom Tidy
Vice President, Administration
Silicon Glen Manufacturing
75 Research Park Drive
San Jose, CA 95321

1 2 **Subject: Invitation to meet with Silicon Glen's Executive Committee to discuss how outsourcing can reduce office support costs**

Dear Tom:

3 In our February 15 phone conversation, you said coping with rapid change and reducing costs were driving your FY20XX planning and were vital to Silicon Glen's survival. You said that if cost reductions of up to 30 percent were possible, you would set up a meeting with Silicon Glen's Executive Committee.

4 You indicated two issues concerned all Silicon Glen executives:

- Accelerating new product development
- Driving down costs at Silicon Glen

Accelerating new product development

Executives are frequently distracted by routine support issues. When the agreed office services are provided by Office Imaging (OI), executives can focus on product development. 6

5 Your executives can monitor the status of any support task on-line using our ISO 9000 certified Customer Care® management software. An on-site manager uses the same package to select and manage all outside vendors as required. You can also use the latest, most cost-effective imaging products, a big help to time-constrained managers and designers.

Driving down costs at Silicon Glen

Silicon Glen's office support costs will decline or OI will not offer a contract. We will collaborate with you on a detailed cost analysis with the results committed contractually.

Your cost reduction is partially based on OI's greater buying power on equipment and supplies. We further reduce your cost by sharing the site management load with other current contracts in your immediate area.

6 Shipping costs of your extensive training and support manuals can be cut by 80 percent because we can print and ship locally, including your international locations.

While not yet discussed, most of our new clients are concerned about the future of transferred employees. Actually, OI can offer real advancement opportunities in their career fields that are often not available in highly technical organizations like Silicon Glen.

7 Due to the urgency of your planning cycle, I will call you next Monday to confirm the date and time of our meeting to further discuss how OI can help you accelerate product development while reducing costs. You may call me at 800-555-5555 if I can answer any questions.

Sincerely,

Sarah R Williamson

Sarah R. Williamson

Office Imaging
1000 Hollister Parkway
San Andreas, CA 94301
415.322.0001
www.officeimaging.com

1 The signal word is really two words. The heading includes both a feature and a benefit.

See **Features, Advantages, and Benefits** *and* **Sales Letters, *Proposal Guide*.**

2 The short setup refers to the prior meeting and restates the customer's request. The paragraph summarizes the customer's needs and establishes perspective.

See **Sales Letters.**

3 The customer's goals are stated and ownership is explicit.

See **Customer Focus, *Proposal Guide*.**

4 Subheadings mirror the stated goals from the prior introduction.

See **Sales Letters.**

5 Details are subordinate to the goals in the paragraphs. Benefits continue to be emphasized and tied to features of the seller's offer.

See **Organization, *Proposal Guide*** *and* **Sales Letters.**

6 The writer's goal is to gain the customer's agreement on how the proposed consulting services will be evaluated. The *recommended approach* of the subject line is detailed in an attached evaluation plan.

7 The next step is to review and ideally agree to accept the plan to evaluate the effectiveness of and scope of services proposed.

ShipleyAssociates | 532 North 900 West • Kaysville, Utah 84037 • 888.772.WINS (9467) • www.shipleywins.com

November 15, 20XX

Ann Archer
Marketing Director
Global Aerospace
Goddard Street
St. Louis, MO

1 **Subject: Recommended Approach to Evaluate How Proposal Assistance Can Increase Global's Sales**

Dear Ann:

2 In our November 14 meeting, you and Jane Smith asked me to outline how Global Aerospace could benefit from proposal consulting assistance during the next 12 to 18 months. Given the 46 proposals Global is currently preparing, the 26 additional opportunities qualified, and your lack of additional trained employees available, a prompt decision is critical.

3 **You cited three goals for the next 12 to 18 months:**

- Maximize backlog during the current market upturn
- Improve your business capture effectiveness ratio
- Use existing resources most effectively

Maximize backlog during the current market upturn

You can increase your win rate and total backlog capture by carefully applying our professional assistance to all bids, based on our 82 percent win rate. With all of Global's available resources assigned to 46 bid teams, pursuing many of the 26 additional qualified opportunities without assistance will likely reduce your win rate and possible total sales revenue.

4 **Improve your business capture effectiveness ratio**

By reducing or eliminating the rework in proposal preparation, we can document that total preparation costs are reduced 30 to 50 percent. And proposal quality improves, contributing to a higher win rate. While outside consulting is more expensive on a daily basis, Global avoids the cost and distraction of recruiting, training, and layoffs. 5

Use existing resources most effectively

Global's experts can contribute to more bids more efficiently with efficient proposal management and support from Shipley Associates. You employ only the experts you need, when you need them.

6 I am confident that by following the attached evaluation plan, we can both evaluate and scope what type of proposal consulting assistance would best help Global Aerospace capture the most business cost effectively.

7 I will call you next Monday after you and Jane Smith have had a chance to look it over. Please call me at 888-772-9467 if you have any questions in the meantime.

Sincerely,

Paula Dunn

Paula Dunn
Account Manager

Attachment

Many professional sales methodologies recommend the approach used in this sales letter. The seller's aim is to gain control of or at least influence the evaluation process without being manipulative. If the customer feels manipulated, the sale is lost. Customers will accept this approach only if it seems to be in their best interests.

1 The subject line immediately signals that this is a personal invitation. The desired action is in the subject line.

See Headings, ***Proposal Guide.***

2 The invitation is repeated in the first sentence. The setup is placed at the end of the sentence, tied to the customer's issues. A setup needs to be short and early but does not have to be placed at the beginning of the first sentence.

See Organization, ***Proposal Guide*** *and* Sales Letters.

3 The issues are explicitly owned by the prospect.

See Customer Focus, ***Proposal Guide.***

4 The subtitles mirror the customer's issues and are introduced as run-in headings. The boldface type adds less emphasis than headings on a separate line.

See Page and Document Design, ***Proposal Guide.***

5 All of the seller's supporting details are placed against the relevant issue. Each supporting paragraph names the customer first, increasing the degree of customer focus.

See Customer Focus, ***Proposal Guide.***

6 The opening sentence summarizes the seller's request. The second sentence states the next step the customer can expect from the selling organization and leaves a phone number if the customer wants to call earlier.

See Sales Letters.

Chemical Partners
20001 West Huntsville Highway
P.O. Drawer 304
Huntsville, TX 77336-0304
409/762-3000
www.chempartners.com

March 20, 20XX

Mr. James Bond
Laboratory Manager
Secret Clinical Laboratories
Hidden Boulevard
Thinville, CA 00700

1 Subject: Your invitation to observe a demonstration of our Triglyceride Separation Center (TSC)

Dear James:

2 Attend a demonstration of our Triglyceride Separation Center (TSC) to see how this system will address the concerns and needs that you expressed in our meeting last week.

You expressed a need for:

3
- Quicker turnaround on test results
- Greater automation to handle the increased work load
- Minimal rebaselining after system change

4 **Quicker turnaround on test results.** You will experience quicker turnaround on test results because the TSC has an extended curve range of 500 mg/ml. The extended curve range reduces the number of dilutions required, and thus shortens the reporting time on test results.

> *Since implementing the TSC system, we have increased throughput by 15 percent, reduced labor costs 20 percent due to increased automation, and cut downtime for rebaselining by 23 percent . . .*
>
> —Ms. Nancy Rosedauge, CEO, LabTech, Ltd.

Greater automation to handle the increased work load. Your lab can enjoy a totally automated procedure with 24 results in 45 minutes, using this TSC system. 5

Minimal rebaselining after system change. As you will see in the enclosed comparative study, converting your system to the TSC will require only minimal rebaselining. The study shows excellent agreement between your Polyglobal One-Step assay and our TSC, although the TSC produces slightly lower values.

6 You could see a demonstration at the local Triglyceride Center in Thinville. Jane, our local representative, will call to schedule a demonstration for you. If you have additional questions, please consult the enclosed product overview and call us at 800-700-0007.

Best regards,

Ima Starr

Ima Starr
Chemical Partners, Inc.

cc: S. M. Body

❶ The informative subject line begins with the signal word labeling the letter as a *request*. A feature is linked to two benefits.

See Features, Advantages, and Benefits *and* Headings, *Proposal Guide.*

❷ The request begins with the benefit to the customer, the only reason for the customer to agree to the request. The setup, a reference to the customer's RFP, is delayed until after the benefit. Every request in every sentence is linked to a benefit.

See Features, Advantages, and Benefits, *Proposal Guide.*

❸ This sentence introduces the structure of the letter.

See Organization and Page and Document Design, *Proposal Guide.*

❹ Each request for modification begins with the customer benefit, then states the current RFP language. Then the change is justified in detail from the customer's perspective.

See Features, Advantages, and Benefits *and* Organization, *Proposal Guide.*

❺ The seller has made the change easy for the customer by including complete text for the change.

❻ Labels in the left margin make the letter easy to follow. The clear page design enables the reader to more easily focus on the content.

See Page and Document Design, *Proposal Guide.*

IT Partners, Inc.
1000 Derby Road
Chicago, IL 50501
312.333.3000

January 15, 20XX

Art A. Quire
Purchasing Manager
Big Corporation
Winston Street
San Diego, CA

❶ **Subject: Request to modify Big Corporation's IT outsourcing RFP to reduce cost and enhance flexibility**

Dear Art:

❷ To better meet Big Corporation's IT outsourcing objectives of reduced cost and enhanced flexibility, we recommend two changes in your RFP dated December 15, 20XX. Our recommended changes will help Big Corporation meet its objectives while obtaining more competitive bids. To ensure our proposal is fully compliant and responsive, a prompt decision is critical.

❸ For each recommended modification, we have quoted your RFP, explained our reasoning, and offered a draft RFP text replacement. We request two modifications.

❹

1. To reduce your cost and improve flexibility, eliminate the 10-year firm fixed price provision.

Current provision:	*All bidders must quote firm fixed prices for each and every year of the 10-year contract.*
Comments:	The uncertainty of inflation in out-years will force all bidders to increase prices to cover inflation risk. Any increase or decrease in the type or level of services required will limit Big Corporation's flexibility to adjust. You could be locked into old technologies and unable to quickly respond to your customers.
❺ Recommended change:	*All bidders must quote firm, fixed prices on each task, with the annual cost being the simple sum of the cost of all tasks. All required tasks and task pricing will be reviewed annually.*

2. To improve flexibility by easing the restriction on any change in "key positions."

❻

Current provision:	*All bidders must name all persons proposed for all key positions, and no substitutions are permitted.*
Comments:	As written, the provision could be interpreted to apply from the proposal stage through the entire 10-year term of the contract. Big Corporation's requirements likely will change, requiring different skills in key positions. Individuals also may change jobs or even choose to retire. Allowing changes with your approval will permit both organizations to employ the best person available to meet the current need.
Recommended change:	*All bidders must name all persons proposed for all key positions. Substitutions are permitted only after review and approval by Big Corporation's designated contract administrator.*

7 The summary restates the benefit and the requested action.

See ORGANIZATION, *Proposal Guide.*

8 The seller proactively offers to follow up and leaves a contact number.

See SALES LETTERS.

9 The attached electronic file reduces the effort required for the customer to make the requested changes.

Big Corporation IT RFP
January 15, 20XX
Page 2

7 I hope you agree that the two RFP changes recommended will help Big Corporation reduce cost and improve flexibility. We look forward to receiving an addendum to your RFP so that we can prepare a fully compliant and responsive proposal.

8 I will call you on Tuesday to clarify any details, or you can reach me at 801-333-3000.

Sincerely,

Daniel Miller

Daniel Miller

9 Proposal Manager

Attachment: 1 PC computer disc with electronic file in MSWord® adn text-only formats

1 Capture plans, like any document written for senior management, should have an executive summary of one page or less.

See Capture Planning, Executive Summary.

2 This bullet list summarizes the executive summary.

See Lists *and* Organization, *Proposal Guide.*

3 This short setup and summary provide the necessary context and summarize the immediate opportunity.

See Organization, *Proposal Guide.*

4 The numbered list previews how the capture plan is organized. The numbers and titles are identical to the subsection titles to eliminate confusion.

See Lists *and* Organization, *Proposal Guide.*

5 Notes the need for reviews and updates.

See Capture Planning *and* Process.

6 Establishes the market need for those unfamiliar with the market.

7 Previews the organization and purpose of a seven-page section.

See Organization, *Proposal Guide.*

Fiberdyne Capture Plan **DOT Bridge Composites Research**

1 Executive Summary

2
- ***$200 million annual market***
- ***Entry controlled by FHWA***
- ***Available now: $1–$3 million applications research and demonstration contract.***
- ***Probable teaming partner required***
- ***Commit resources early***

3 Fiberdyne has the opportunity to position itself to capture a significant portion of a potential $200 million market. The Department of Transportation (DOT) is sponsoring the initial applications demonstrations to prove the viability of using fiber reinforced composites in bridge construction and renovation.

We have prepared this capture plan to efficiently focus Fiberdyne's limited marketing resources on capturing the DOT's initial $2 million demonstration program. Our capture plan consists of four major sections:

4
- 1.0 External Analysis
- 2.0 Internal Analysis
- 3.0 Capture Strategy
- 4.0 Implementation and Control

5 We look forward to the planned monthly senior management reviews and will update this plan to include both management suggestions and new information.

1.0 External Analysis

6 The poor condition of bridges in the U.S. and internationally and the fierce competition for funding has encouraged industry experts to explore the use of innovative methods and improved materials. The Department of Transportation's (DOT) Federal Highway Administration (FHWA) establishes the specifications that must be met to receive Federal funding. Fiberdyne materials must be reviewed, tested, and approved by FHWA officials to be accepted in bridge building applications.

7 Our external analysis examines the customer, the situation, key program requirements, and probable competitors. Our purpose is to identify potential opportunities for Fiberdyne materials and threats to acceptance of our materials in bridge building applications.

1

8 Uses informative headings where headings are not dictated. Most organizations have an established, required organization for capture plans.

See Capture Planning.

9 Subtitles within sections are placed in the left margin to permit readers to immediately understand how the section is organized and to skip to any section of immediate interest.

See Page and Document Design, *Proposal Guide.*

10 The immediate customer is established within the context of the large customer organization.

11 Only the key people are listed. The diagram instantly shows their organizational relationships, while the action caption indicates their assignment.

See Action Captions *and* Graphics, *Proposal Guide.*

12 This is a two-part action caption with a heading and full-sentence caption. Note that the graphic is introduced in the prior text.

See Action Captions, *Proposal Guide.*

13 The funding is established and might increase. Note the sources of information are identified.

See Capture Planning.

14 The anticipated role of specific individuals in the evaluation permits the seller to focus on individuals' issues and perceptions.

See Capture Planning *and* Persuasion.

Fiberdyne Capture Plan | **DOT Bridge Composites Research**

8 **1.1 The Customer: FHWA guidelines drive bridge building and repair specifications**

9 ***Organization and Key People***

10 Within the DOT, the "road guys" are in the FHWA. The FHWA sets standards for road and bridge construction and repair. While states do all of the contracting for work, the Feds kick in various percentages of funding for projects that meet FHWA specifications. The FHWA regularly investigates new materials and methods that will use the Federal funds more efficiently.

11 The Research Division of the FHWA headed by Assistant Undersecretary of Transportation, Dr. Brown, is charged with new materials research and testing. The key members of Dr. Brown's organization are sketched in figure 1.

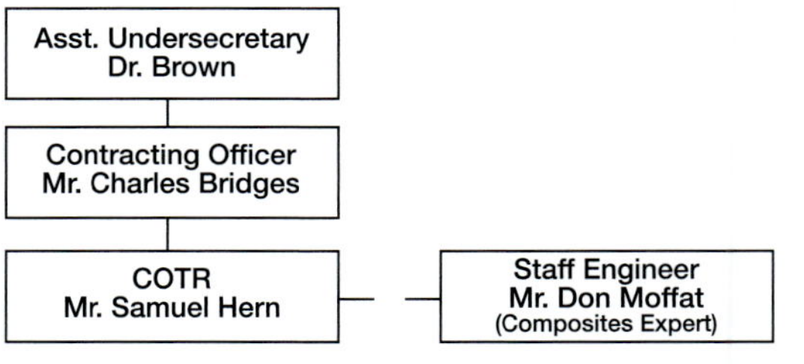

12 Figure 1. FWWA Research Division Structure. *These FHWA employees have been assigned to the proposed project to research high-performance bridge materials.*

Acquisition Process

13 Mr. Charles Bridges, the PCO, said that the research budget is set, but internal competition for the funds within the DOT continues. He expects a minimum of $1 million and a maximum of $3 million to be budgeted, depending on the extent of the demonstration. Mr. Samuel Hern, the COTR, is reluctant and primarily concerned about something going wrong on his watch. Dr. Brown, a strong supporter of developing improved materials, will push the project through the DOT funding cycle. Mr. Don Moffat, a relatively new FHWA staff engineer, has been our best source of information. To date no company seems to have the inside track.

Evaluation Process

14 We expect Bridges, Hern, and Moffat will be evaluators. Dr. Brown will probably not evaluate formally, but will be involved as much as his schedule permits. We expect at least three more people to be added to the evaluation team. As long as the total contract stays below $3 million, the PCO is likely to evaluate the cost proposals.

Dotted lines indicate material eliminated for brevity.

2

15 A disciplined effort was made to analyze the key individuals, understand their motivations, and suggest potential marketing actions.

16 A bulleted list was used for added emphasis. Note how the list is named immediately prior to the list.

We have identified several experiences of key FHWA people in figure 2 and linked those experiences with potential Fiberdyne marketing actions.

15

Type of Experience	Customer Result	Goal	Potential Marketing Action	Reasoning
Don Moffat has unique expertise with composites in bridges.	Led to current job at FHWA. Employed and promoted.	Build his technical credibility in FHWA.	Keep Moffat informed. Share technical information. Learn more about his Golden Gate Bridge experience. Dr. Hats to participate in sales call.	Primary influencer, likely evaluator, build familiarity with our proprietary fibers.
Sam Hern has seen careers tarnished by risky projects.	Avoids new technology whenever possible. Minimizes risk.	Emphasize proven materials and low risk approach.	Emphasize bridge application experience, management, scheduling approach. Stay practical, simplify technology. Keep composites techies away.	Build comfort, acceptance. Wary of new technology.
Charles Bridges is a contracting pro.	Promoted by following the rules.	Build idea that FDyn follows the rules.	Indicate FDyn interest. Obtain permission to discuss with FHWA employees.	Build familiarity, acceptance.
Dr. Brown developed reputation as an innovator.	Rapid advancement.	Innovation to draw attention w/low risk.	Presentation by Dr. Hats (technical) and FDyn CEO (management). Introduce project manager.	Build acceptance of FDyn's tech. and management competence.

Figure 2. FHWA Experience. *Key FHWA employee experiences are listed along with potential marketing actions.*

Issues and Hot Buttons

We have identified the following customer issues and hot buttons:

16

- Low risk
- Advanced materials, especially with composites
- Dual-use technology
- Bridge building experience and expertise
- Respected image as a leader and trend-setter with consulting engineers, constructors, suppliers, Federal officials, and academia
- Ability to contribute some portion of the project costs, not to exceed matching the Federal contribution
- Proven ability to manage costs and meet schedules

See **Lists.**

(17) The informative heading both creates interest and focuses on the buying officials.

(18) The bulleted list quickly establishes market context.

(19) The customer history focuses on the decision maker, not the entire organization.

(20) The source of the requirements establishes the customers' ownership. All items in the list are parallel in structure.

Fiberdyne Capture Plan | **DOT Bridge Composites Research**

Environmental Factors

(17) **1.2 Situation: FHWA officials are interested in proving the viability of improved materials.**

Some facts about the U.S. bridge building market:

(18)
- $30 billion is spent on public highway construction annually.
- $6 billion is spent on bridges—70 percent is for new construction, 20 percent is for alterations and reconstruction, and 10 percent is for maintenance and repair.

Even though many bridges are off-system, Federal approval of Fiberdyne's proprietary materials will be required before many others accept them. Our successful entry of a potentially $100 million domestic market and subsequent international market requires FHWA sponsored applications testing. The opportunity to obtain partial Federal funding for the applications testing is attractive.

⋮

Customer History

(19) Dr. Brown has a history of identifying innovative opportunities, pushing them through, being recognized, and then getting promoted. His primary motivation seems to be to make the project a success, and he appears willing to maintain an accessible approach.

Dr. Brown is aware of the rival Corps of Engineers program and would like to beat them.

1.3 Program Requirements

While a statement of work and RFP have not been written, we have identified several requirements in our conversations with FHWA personnel. We are not certain which ones will actually be included:

Key Requirements

(20)
- Evaluate the economic and technical feasibility of using composite materials in bridge building applications.
- Test and evaluate various types of advanced composite materials.
- Analyze the impact of composites on design parameters.
- Survey current relevant applications of composites.
- Investigate applications to cables and structural members.
- Evaluate production methods.

4

See Customer Focus, Headings, *and* Lists, ***Proposal Guide.***

21 Sellers in concentrated markets can identify specific competitors. The breadth of competitors led the writer to analyze competitors by type. Much competitor analysis can be lifted from business, market, and sales plans.

See Capture Planning, Process, *and* Strategy.

22 The graphic is introduced in the prior text.

See Action Captions, ***Proposal Guide.***

23 This is a bidder comparison matrix, comparing potential bidders or types of bidders against the customer's requirements.

See Strategy.

24 All types of graphics should have action captions to help the reader interpret the graphic as the writer intended. Placement is consistently below the graphic when space permits.

See Action Captions *and* Page and Document Design, ***Proposal Guide.***

Fiberdyne Capture Plan | **DOT Bridge Composites Research**

- Develop designs for representative components, then construct and test the components.
- Prepare a detailed final report and publish it in an appropriate industry journal.
- Present and discuss results at appropriate industry forums.

1.4 Competitor Analysis

Numerous potential competitors exist and are classified by type:

Five Types of Competitors 21

- Research companies like ourselves, interested in royalties
- Raw material producers, producing fiber and resin
- Converters, who manufacture composite products
- Bridge builders
- Consulting engineers

We have examined the typical factors that could affect the FHWA's buying decision against each type of competitor in figure 3.

Note: Figure 3 not included for brevity.

⋮

Competitive Comparison of Program Requirements 22

We next examined the program requirements identified in section 1.3, slightly rearranged and consolidated. The result is shown in figure 4.

FHWA Program Requirements	Fiberdyne	Research Companies (Sterling)	Material Producers (R. Horning)	Converter (Franklin Fiberglas)	Bridge Builder (American Bridge)	Consulting Engineers
⋮	⋮	⋮	⋮	⋮	⋮	⋮
Present results at industry forums	3	3	3	2	4	4
Total	41	40	41	31	29	37

Figure 4. Analysis of Competitive Factors. *Program requirements currently identified are ranked on a 1-(lowest) to 5-scale (highest). The results change significantly as the comparison becomes more specific, but the strengths and weaknesses are similar.*

25 Anticipating the probable competitive strategy of competitors is the purpose of a Black Hat team.

Fiberdyne Capture Plan **DOT Bridge Composites Research**

Competitive Strategy

We next examined the competitive strategies typically used by our competitors. The result is shown in figure 5.

25

Typical Approach or Competitive Strategy	Research Companies (Sterling)	Material Producers (R. Horning)	Converter (Franklin Fiberglas)	Bridge Builder (American Bridge)	Consulting Engineers
1. Type of Markets	Royalties, contract R&D	Large production contracts	Large components in large quantities	Builds bridges	Sells services at a fixed rate
2. Leader/follower	Fiber development leader	Production methods leader	Leader in new product application	Construction leader	Follower
3. Commitment to FHWA opptnty.	Establish own fibers	Positioning for volume sales	Positioning for product sales	Seeking discriminators: Comp. experience and mfg adv.	Positioning for design edge
4. Flexibility	Good	Limited	Limited	Limited	Limited
5. Pricing	High on own fibers	Invests in new markets	Invests in new markets	Aggressive	High
6. Probable sales approach	Emphasize R&D aspects, composites expertise	Will hire experts and/or team	Will hire experts and/or team	Emphasize bridge construction expertise, composites experience, and fabrication facility	Cite "big names" and use "little names"

Figure 5. Analysis of Competitive Strategies. *The probable competitive strategies of the different competitors are shown here. This matrix will be updated as more is learned.*

See Process, *and* Strategy.

26 The second major section opens with a summary and introduction.

See Organization, *Proposal Guide.*

27 The informative heading states the most important point, much like a theme statement in a proposal.

See Headings *and* Theme Statements, *Proposal Guide.*

28 Specific requirements are compared to specific capabilities rather than general strengths and weaknesses. Potential actions that require management support are clearly identified.

Fiberdyne Capture Plan | **DOT Bridge Composites Research**

2.0 Internal Analysis

26 The focus of our internal analysis is to develop a winning solution. We clearly want to emphasize our strengths. We must also identify our weaknesses, the gap between the FHWA's needs, competitors' approaches, and our current capability.

We have used gap analysis to develop a competitive solution.

Our internal analysis will also look at our financial resources, pricing, and potential risks.

Determine Solution

27 2.1 Fiberdyne Solutions: Fiberdyne Must Be Seen as the Obvious Choice to Demonstrate the Viability of Composite Materials.

We analyzed the gaps between the requirements and our currently available solution in figure 6.

28

FHWA Program Requirements	Available Solution	Gap	Action Required
Evaluate economic feasibility	None internal	Must know bridge building economics	Hire consultant or team
Evaluate technical feasibility	Dr. Hats and his staff	None	Emphasize unique capability of Dr. Hats
Evaluate materials	Dr. Hats and his staff	None	Emphasize broad look, beyond Fiberdyne's materials
Analyze design impact	None internal	Need bridge designer	Subcontract
⋮	⋮	⋮	⋮
Present results at industry forums	Dr. Hats and staff	None	List recent industry forum presentations

Figure 6. Gap Analysis. *Major program gaps can be closed by subcontracting or teaming.*

7

(29) An informative heading was added to highlight the overriding point of the section.

(30) Subheadings in the left margin permit readers with waning interest to get the main point of each paragraph without reading the paragraph.

(31) The stated assumptions and apparent agreement from several methods of analysis increase the credibility of the estimate.

See PERSUASION.

(32) Placing the proposal budget in the context of the potential net contribution margin offers a basis for comparison.

See PRESENTING COST AND PRICING DATA, *Proposal Guide.*

(33) The informative heading summarizes the greatest risk.

(34) All risk is limited to a high-level treatment of strengths, weaknesses, opportunities, and threats.

See RISK MANAGEMENT, *Proposal Guide.*

Fiberdyne Capture Plan | **DOT Bridge Composites Research**

(29) **2.2 Financial Resources and Pricing: Fiberdyne Must Be Seen as the Company Offering the Best Value for Their Expenditure**

(30) Fiberdyne lacks the financial resources offered by other, much larger companies. A Rowens Horning or Franklin Fiberglas . . .

⋮

Team to Reduce Costs — We should team with a larger company that will have or can hire the bridge building expertise that we lack. If we choose to go alone, hiring the appropriate consultants in bridge building would be costly.

Overheads Covered — For the project, all facilities and personnel can be charged at our full overhead rate, but our profit margins will have to be acceptably small, probably under 5 percent.

(31) ***Conservative Capture Budget of $60,000*** — Assuming the contract is written at $2 million, Fiberdyne normally budgets 1.5 percent of sales to capture business, or $30,000. Our normal win rate is 25 percent, but if we . . .

⋮

(32) Considering the annual net contribution margin potential of $1.75 million, budgeting $60,000 to win the business seems quite conservative . . .

⋮

(33) **2.3 Risk Analysis: Fiberdyne's greatest risk is missing the opportunity to position our proprietary fibers in the bridge building market**

Strengths — (34) Our strengths include Dr. Hats' reputation, testing capabilities, leading edge fiber development record, and familiarity with . . .

⋮

Weaknesses — Our weaknesses include limited experience with bridges and bridge design, limited record with the DOT, reputation for poor . . .

⋮

Opportunities — The greatest opportunity is to obtain FHWA endorsement . . .

⋮

Threats — We have identified several threats:

- FHWA could require a waiver of royalties on proprietary fibers
- Component failure of a bridge component could cause . . .

8

35 Like earlier sections, it opens with a summary and introduction.

See ORGANIZATION, ***Proposal Guide.***

3.0 Capture Strategy

35 Our capture strategy sets specific objectives that we must accomplish to win. The Integrated Solution Worksheet uses the customer's stated requirements to develop implied issues, our baseline solution, our discriminators and gaps and suggests potential strategies and actions. Readers with limited time may go directly to the bulleted lists of potential strategies at the end of section 3.1. Our approach to achieving the objectives is detailed in a series of action plans:

3.2 Intelligence Collection Plan

3.3 Call Plan

3.4 White Papers

3.5 Advertising and Promotion Plan

3.6 IR&D and Trade Studies

3.7 Contingency Plan

All action steps are not included, pending management review. Actions will be reviewed monthly.

Overall Capture Strategy Objective

3.1 Fiberdyne Strategy: We must establish in the eyes of six key FHWA employees that Fiberdyne is the most capable, qualified, and unbiased organization to demonstrate the viability of composite materials for bridge building applications

The large Integrated Customer Solution Worksheet in figure 7 should be read row by row horizontally. We will reexamine this worksheet monthly to track progress towards positioning Fiberdyne as the organization preferred by the FHWA. The trackability of items within the worksheet helps ensure that no key requirements, potential solutions, and strategies are lost.

36 When time is limited, complete this worksheet and omit other portions of the capture plan. Maintain the horizontal relationship between items.

See Capture Planning.

Fiberdyne Capture Plan **DOT Bridge Composites Research**

36

# (1)	Customer Issue (2)	Program/Product Requirement (3)	Available Solution (4)
1	Reduce bridge maintenance costs	Evaluate economic feasibility	None internal
2	Will it work?	Evaluate technical feasibility	Dr. Hats and his staff
3	Are proven materials available?	Evaluate materials	None internally
4	Will bridge designers accept composites?	Analyze design impact	Dr. Hats' staff
5	Risky? Fund "dual-use" technology	Survey relevant applications of composites	Dr. Hats and his staff
6	Are uniform quality materiels available in sufficient quantity?	Evaluate production methods	Dr. Hats and his staff
7	Testing must be reliable and realistic	Develop component designs	Design engineering group
8	Bridge designers and builders must accept results	Prepare final report	Dr. Hats' staff
9	Findings must be seen widely	Publish findings	Dr. Hats and his staff
10	Must obtain industry acceptance	Present results at industry forums	Dr. Hats and his staff

Figure 7. Integrated Customer Solution Worksheet. *Read this worksheet horizontally. Potential strategies and actions are summarized in the bulleted lists on the following pages.*

Fiberdyne Capture Plan **DOT Bridge Composites Research**

Discriminators (5)	Gap (6)	Strategy (7)	Action Required (8)
Negative—lack bridge building expertise	Must know bridge building economics	Hire consultant or team	Identify partner Negotiate contract
Dr. Hats Golden Gate cables Corps of Engineers in MT	None	Emphasize unique capability of Dr. Hats	Introduce to customer Submit past professional papers
Dr. Hats and staff	None	Emphasize broad look, beyond Fiberdyne's materials	Collect client comments Cite fibers we have evaluated and recommended that were developed by others
Negative—need a bridge designer	Need bridge designer	Subcontract	Identify subcontractor
Recognized composites expertise; developed many of leading applications	None	Emphasize previous similar experience	Try to arrange site visits Include samples List materials and tasks completed
Experience in all areas of contract manufacturing; have survey experience	None	Emphasize employees with similar experience	Invite customer for plant tour and reception with staff
In-house test capability and facilities, especially for large components	None	Feature extensive component design experience	Show examples on tour Put photos in proposal
None perceived—we are unknown	Perceived gap	Emphasize recent training	Include current samples
Extensive associations with technical journals	None	Emphasize publications expertise	List all staff publications
Extensive presentation experience	None	List recent industry presentations	Include copies of forum programs in our presentations & proposals

11

37 All strategy elements are elaborations from the final two columns of the Integrated Customer Solution worksheet.

See Capture Planning *and* Strategy.

Fiberdyne Capture Plan — **DOT Bridge Composites Research**

Emphasize Strengths

37 We must emphasize the following strengths:

- Stress our fiber and composite superiority
- Stress our prestigious principal investigator, Dr. Manny Hats
- Stress our depth of experience by emphasizing the Golden Gate Bridge cables and the Corps of Engineers project in Montana
- Emphasize our ability to connect materials expertise, component production, and applications
- Emphasize our in-place laboratory and ability to test full-scale components
- Emphasize how we have successfully pioneered composites in other markets like aerospace

Mitigate Weaknesses

- Mitigate our weaknesses in cost control by implementing a new inventory control system and training our people
- Mitigate past weaknesses in project definition by developing a clear, comprehensive WBS and SOW that the FHWA can use
- Mitigate lack of bridge design expertise by teaming with the Brooklyn Bridge Company
- Mitigate our scheduling weaknesses by purchasing, implementing, and demonstrating an integrated project management system

Highlight Competitors' Weaknesses

- Highlight difference between typical fiber composite applications and high-strength applications of composites
- Stress that the typical high-volume production methods cause voids, incomplete fiber wetting, and fiber damage; all lead to long-term failure
- Stress the unique R&D nature of the project
- Stress the limited availability of seasoned high-strength composites experts, such as Dr. Hats
- Point out the critical lessons learned at Windy Canyon, Montana
- Stress the difficulty in finding quality, full-scale test apparatus, justifying why Fiberdyne had to develop our own

12

38 An informative heading summarizes the most important point in each action plan.

See Headings, *Proposal Guide.*

39 All actions plan tasks require the same elements: objective, action, person assigned, timing, and measure to assess completion.

Fiberdyne Capture Plan | **DOT Bridge Composites Research**

Neutralize Competitor's Strengths

- Stress our solid team management approach
- Emphasize our team's ability to fully cost share as planned
- Emphasize Brooklyn Bridge's bridge design group and their leadership in the applications of new materials
- Deemphasize the importance of high-volume production expertise to a demonstration project
- Stress our prestigious principal investigator, Dr. Manny Hats, will manage the engineering; Mr. Adams of BB will manage the project

Objective

38 **3.2 Fiberdyne Intelligence Collection Plan: Our primary need is to learn more about our FHWA customer.**

Supporting Actions

39 Learn the FHWA history with similar purchasing decisions.

Schedule meetings with Dr. Brown, Charles Bridges, Sam Hern, and Don Moffat. Ask them.

Who:	Y.A. Title
When:	Within 30 da.
Measure:	Update plan and report during next plan review

⋮

Objective

3.3 Fiberdyne Call Plan: Our primary need is to establish our capabilities with key FHWA officials and influence the RFP.

Supporting Actions

Establish Fiberdyne as the industry leader with the FHWA.

Invite Dr. Brown and his staff to Fiberdyne to review our latest research and tour our laboratory facilities.

Who:	Y.A. Title
When:	Within 60 da.
Measure:	Update plan and report during next plan review

⋮

13

Fiberdyne Capture Plan — DOT Bridge Composites Research

⋮

Objective

Supporting Actions

3.4 Fiberdyne White Papers: Our focus is to be first to stake our claim to industry leadership in applying composites to bridges.

Establish our composites expertise in bridge building applications and counter the view that we do not understand bridges.

Combine our economic analysis of bridge building with our Golden Gate and Montana experience in a single white paper.

Who: Dr. Hats will supervise preparation

Y.A. Title will circulate it among key FHWA people.

When: Within 60 da.

Measure: Review draft as soon as it is complete

⋮

Objective

3.5 Advertising and Promotion: Our focus is to be first to stake our claim to industry leadership in applying composites to bridges.

Supporting Actions

Advertising has little application because our target audience is small. Limited promotion activities could be helpful.

Support and participate in the FHWA's semiannual industry forum. Offer to discuss applying high-strength composites to support cables and large structural components. Display samples from the Golden Gate and Montana projects.

Objective

Secure FHWA approval to join the program.

Supporting Actions

Who: Y.A. Title

When: Within 30 da.

Measure: Report in next update meeting

Prepare presentation.

Who: Dr. Hats

When: After approved by FHWA and 30 da. before the program.

Measure: Update plan and report during next plan review

14

40 Only major risks are included in the capture plan rather than every identifiable risk.

See CAPTURE PLANNING.

3.6 IR&D and Trade Studies: Our projected image of industry leadership in applying composites to bridges must be based on accurate facts.

Objective The FHWA project is partially a trade study. Fiberdyne's credibility will be enhanced if we appear to have an early start.

Supporting Actions Quickly survey public domain information and our files on competitive materials and products. Summarize the findings for internal use. Whether and how the information is used outside Fiberdyne will depend on our findings.

Who: N.O. Norganic

When: Within 15 da.

Measure: Report in next update meeting

3.7 Contingency Plan

Four threats were identified as part of our internal analysis. Each risk and our recommended risk management approach are summarized below.

40

Major Risk	Priority	Management Approach
FHWA requires bidders to waive royalties	1	Stress that the fiber offering best value should be used. Royalties must be justified economically. If not acceptable, we will have to risk taking exception, waiving the royalty, or not bidding.
Teaming could lead to loss of our proprietary advantages	2	Negotiate acceptable teaming agreement. Our partner is not a composites company.
Tests of our fibers by others could be biased	3	Win. Establish fair testing guidelines with the FHWA and get them written into the RFP.
A bridge component could fail during testing	4	Our company liability insurance will cover potential financial losses. The greater impact is on our long-term market success. Yet the risk is no different than our other types of business. Our normal design review processes are adequate. We will also ask our teaming partner to review and approve all designs.

41 All contributors need to know that senior management has approved the plan.

See Capture Planning.

42 Near term events are identified.

43 The roles of key managers of the capture plan are identified as well as the review process. Obsolete or outdated plans offer little value and prompt participants to lose interest.

See Capture Planning.

4.0 Implementation and Control

41 The draft of this capture plan was reviewed, revised, and approved by a team of Fiberdyne managers:

M.R. Big - CEO
B.L. Suit - V.P. Finance
I.M. Slick - Sr. V.P. Marketing
K.E. Blunt - V.P. Manufacturing and Engineering

42 A kick-off meeting for the capture team participants is scheduled for mm/dd/yy.

The purpose of the kick-off meeting is to reinforce top management support and to assign tasks.

Each participant will receive the portion of the plan that defines their tasks.

43 The capture team manager is Y.A. Title. If the opportunity proceeds as expected to the proposal state, A.B. Clark will be the proposal manager. The capture team will meet weekly. The capture manager will review progress monthly as a regular agenda item in the monthly management meeting. All capture plans are reviewed in greater detail as part of our quarterly marketing review.

The schedule of tasks follows. The schedule is maintained on scheduling software and will be updated weekly.

All implementation questions should be addressed to Y.A. Title, Capture Manager.

1. Begin with your top points that everyone should accept and remember. Assume a key person might leave after the first slide.

See Oral Proposals *and* Organization, *Proposal Guide.*

2. Preview the organization of your presentation to help managers focus on content rather than trying to discern how your presentation is organized.

1

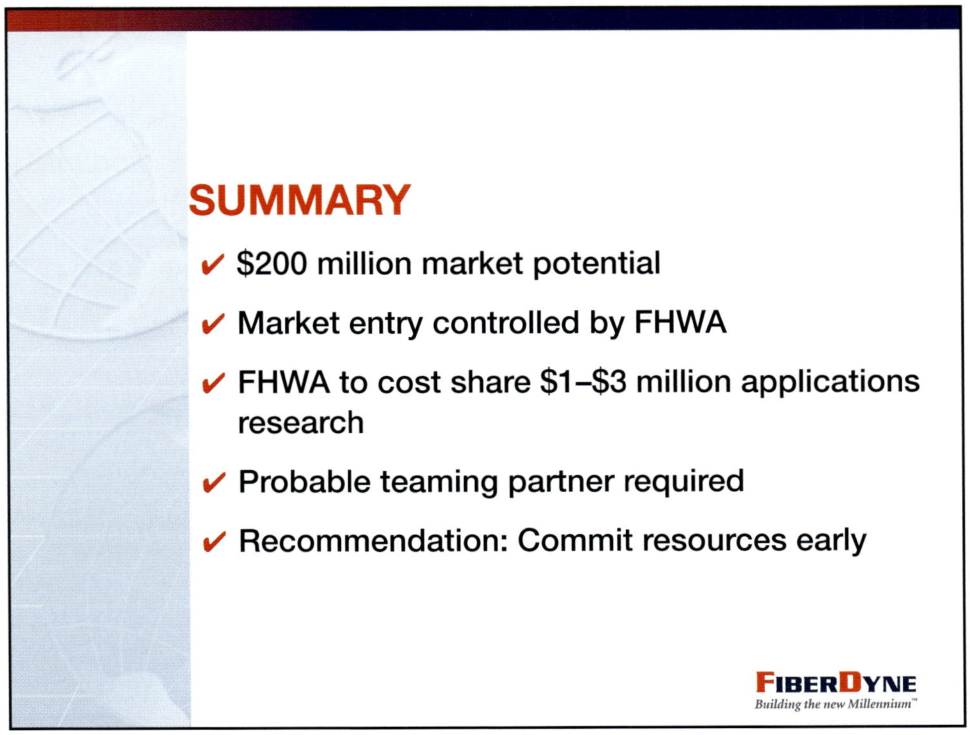

2

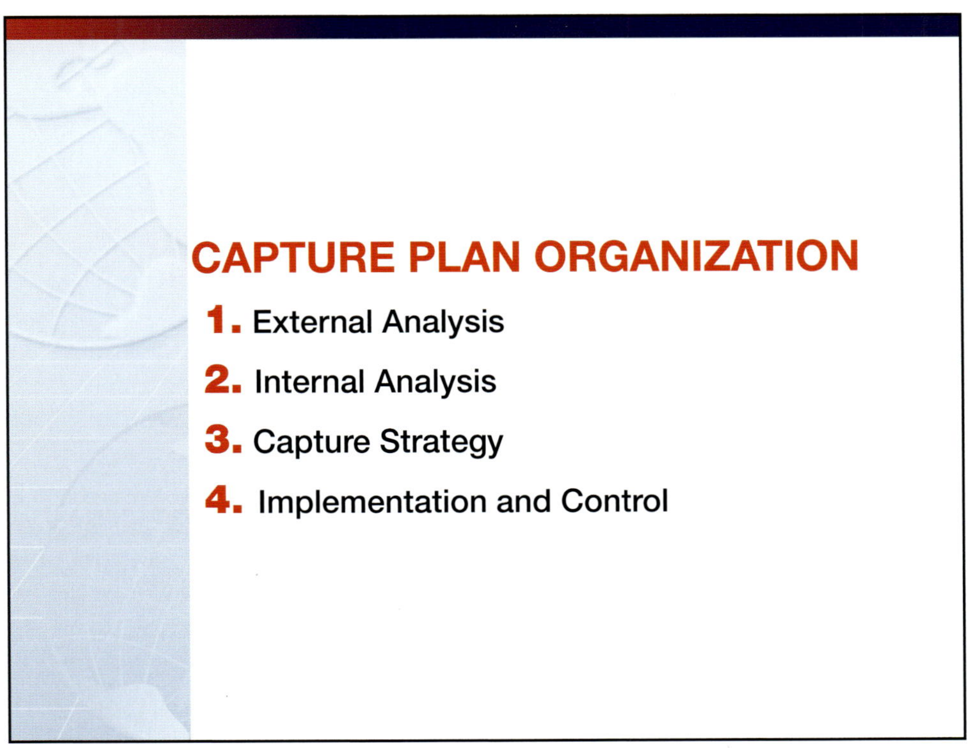

3 The heading indicates the section of the capture plan.

4 The same graphic as in the written plan shows organizational relationships. The graphic has been adjusted for the presentation. The presenter covers the information from the text and action caption.

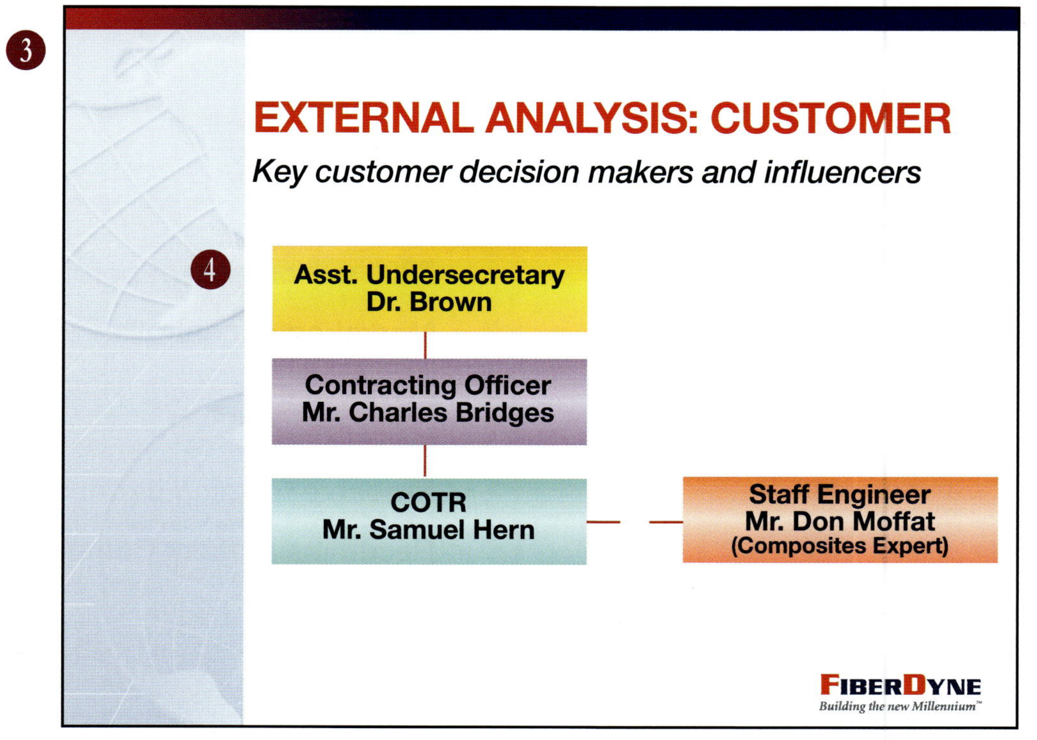

Index

A

B

C

This page is intentionally blank

This page is intentionally blank